CW00749702

MILE BY MILE

Rail Mileages of Britain and Ireland

Edited by
DAVID MAXEY

INTRODUCTION

THE following notes on the use of this book refer wholly to the British Rail sections and, in part, to the Metropolitan and Ireland sections. Notes specific to the latter appear on the appropriate pages.

The **Route Tables** have been compiled from B.R. Sectional Appendices of 1983-85, with 1986 amendments. They are presented regionally and are laid out to reflect the public timetable of October, 1986. The timetable numbers are shown on each passenger route table and in cross-reference to other pages.

The major trunk routes are presented as KEY PLANS (see list on p.3 and show cross-references to secondary, cross-country and branch lines at the point of their divergence. Similarly, the route tables for these lines give reference to other diverging lines, and so on. Having located the page which shows their "home" station, readers will be able to trace journeys to any destination by all available routes. Provision has also been made in this system for tracing the path of enthusiasts' railtours over non-standard routes.

The tables are laid out left to right as follows:

M.P. column — shows lineside milepost mileages; where these are the same as the route mileage (e.g. 0m. 00c. onwards), only the first and last M.P. figures are given. Changes are shown in the same column under the heading *C.M.M.* (change of milepost mileage). Reference to this column will enable readers to follow their progress during a journey, even when travelling an unfamiliar route.

M C column — gives distances in miles and chains for the route (80 chains = 1 mile). Where there is a regular alternative route (e.g. London — West of England), two miles and chains columns are given.

Locations column — shows passenger stations in bold type (unadvertised stations in non-bold). Junctions, level crossings, tunnels and other features are indented in non-bold.

The right-hand sides of the pages are a mixture of route cross-references and minor route tables/branches. Arrowheads indicate references to diverging lines (normally non-passenger lines in bold) with a timetable number where appropriate, and the page number on which the route table can be found. The minor routes are presented in the same way as those on the left of the pages, with mileposts/changes and miles and chains in two columns.

The Tables are mostly presented in the "down" direction, except where convenience of layout dictates otherwise. For the sake of clarity (and, not least, to avoid insulting readers' intelligence), the distance columns are not repeated backwards!

Private Railways are shown on the same page as the nearest B.R. station, with physical connections where applicable.

A number of lines shown (both passenger and non-passenger) are now closed or even lifted, although most were open when work on this project began! As many were traversed by railtours shortly before closure, they have been retained so that readers can back-track if desired.

New developments — Proposed stations have included wherever possible, as well as current sch such as the Windsor Link and the Rotherham divergen an appropriate time (probably 6-9 months hence), it is h to produce an **amendments listing** so that readers may subsequent changes and keep their copies up-to-da stamped, self-addressed envelope sent to the Publish the address below will ensure that readers receive a co this listing as soon as it becomes available.

While every care has been taken to ensure accuracy, the Editor and Publishers will be pleased to hear from ers who find obvious errors in the text and who can discrepancies in distances.

ACKNOWLEDGEMENTS

THE original idea for this book belongs to Phil Weaver painstakingly compiled the basic information. It has m been my task to up-date his work and present it in a which, it is hoped, readers will find convenient to use.

Although there is insufficient space to name them all vidually, I offer my thanks to the countless enthusiasts B.R. staff!) who have contributed information.

I am also indebted to Roger Bagnall, Operating Superi dent, Tyne & Wear Metro, John Reed, London Reg Transport, Bob Bayman, Operations Manager, Dock Light Railway, Mr J.K. Wright, Strathclyde P.T.E., Do Maolalai, Córas Iompair Éireann, Brian McConnell, Nor Ireland Railways, and to the officers of the private rail for their invaluable help and enthusiasm.

David Maxey,
Guildford, Surrey
January, 1987

Zero Mileposts

DURING research on this project, there has been much discussion the accuracy of zero mileposts, particularly at London termini. Or the Paddington error is acknowledged in B.R. records (see note p.8 but there is reason to doubt the 0m. 00c. figures quoted for other Lo don stations and for termini elsewhere on the network. It is genera believed that the original railway companies established zero at t boundary of land ownership rather than at buffer stops, a situati further confused by subsequent re-building and re-modelling.

Waterloo is a good example. Although B.R. records show zero for bo routes, it is generally agreed that the buffer stops are 0m. 06c. Zero thought to be at a point beyond the present cab road where t former through line joined the S.E.C.R. line at Waterloo East. Fort nately, none of this makes the slightest difference when travelling b ween intermediate stations on these routes!

Further research into this dilemma is taking place and the results, any, will be reported in future editions.

ISBN 0 906025 44 3

Published by
Peter Watts Publishing Limited
Stag House, Gydynap Lane, Inchbrook, Woodchest
Glos. GL5 5EZ

CONTENTS

LIST OF KEY PLANS

SECTION I - EASTERN REGION

(a) East Anglia

LIVERPOOL STREET - NORWICH (B.R. Table 11)

KEY PLAN

M. P.	M	C	Location	Connection
0 00	0	00	**Liverpool Street**	*Cambridge/Kings Lynn (22) - p.10* *Enfield (20) - p.11* *Chingford (20A) - p.11* *Hertford East (21) - p.11* *Camden Road (58) - p.12*
	1	10	**Bethnal Green**	
	1	18	Bethnal Green East Jcn.	
	2	69	Bow Jcn.	***Gas Factory Jcn. - p.13***
	3	50	Carpenters Road Sth, Jcn.	***Stratford Area - p.5***
	3	70	Stratford Central Jcn. West	***Stratford Area - p.5***
	3	75	Stratford Central Jcn. East	***Stratford Area - p.5***
	4	03	**Stratford**	
	4	39	**Maryland**	
	5	21	**Forest Gate**	
	5	63	Forest Gate Jcn.	*Woodgrange Park Jcn. - p.12*
	6	19	**Manor Park**	
	7	28	**Ilford**	
	8	14	Ilford Car Sheds	
	8	45	**Seven Kings**	
	9	23	**Goodmayes**	
	9	79	**Chadwell Heath**	
	12	30	**Romford**	Romford - Upminster (B.R. Table 4)
	12	39	Romford Jcn.	
	13	41	**Gidea Park**	
	14	76	**Harold Wood**	
	18	16	**Brentwood**	
	20	16	**Shenfield**	*Southend (5) - p.6*
	20	22	Shenfield Jcn.	
	23	50	**Ingatestone**	
	29	65	**Chelmsford**	
	35	74	**Hatfield Peverel**	
	38	48	**Witham**	*Braintree (11) - p.6*
	38	53	Witham Jcn.	
	42	21	**Kelvedon**	
	46	49	**Marks Tey**	*Sudbury (10) - p.6*
	51	52	**Colchester**	*Clacton (11) - p.6*
	51	65	Colchester Jcn.	
	56	04	Ardleigh LC	
	59	35	**Manningtree**	
	59	43	Manningtree South Jcn.	*Harwich (12) - p.7*
	59	69	Manningtree North Jcn.	*Harwich (12) - p.7*
	67	46	Halifax Jcn. GF	0 00 Halifax Jcn. GF 0 77 Griffin Wharf FLT
68 59	68	59	**Ipswich**	*Cambridge/Ely (15) - p.7* *Felixstowe (13) - p.7* *Lowestoft (14) - p.7*

ROMFORD - UPMINSTER (B.R. Table 4)

M	C	Location
0	00	**Romford**
0	09	Romford Jcn.
1	73	**Emerson Park**
3	36	**Upminster** (see p.13)

IVERPOOL STREET - NORWICH (B.R. Table 11) Cont.

M. P.	M C		
0 00	0 00	**Liverpool Street**	
8 59	68 59	**Ipswich**	
	68 72	Ipswich Goods Jcn.	
	69 42	East Suffolk Jcn.	
	70 53	Sproughton	
	73 46	Claydon LC	
	75 17	Baylham LC	
	77 11	**Needham Market**	
	80 54	**Stowmarket**	→ *Cambridge/Ely (15) - p.7*
	82 79	Haughley Jcn.	
	91 35	Mellis LC	
	95 04	**Diss**	
	97 42	Burston LC	
	100 60	Tivetshall Jcn. LC	
	109 53	Swainsthorpe LC	
2 67	112 67	Trowse Upper Jcn.	
M.M.			
3 00	133 68	Trowse Lower Jcn.	
3 43	114 31	Swing Bridge Jcn. * see note	
3 56	114 44	Thorpe Jcn.	
4 09	114 77	**Norwich**	→ *Yarmouth/Lowestoft (16) - p.8* *Sheringham (17) - p.8* *Ely/Peterborough (18) - p.8/9*

M C	
0 00	Trowse Upper Jcn.
1 22	Victoria Park NCB

M C	
0 00	Thorpe Jcn.
0 16	Norwich Goods Yard

he **Wensum Curve** (Swing Bridge Jcn. to Wensum Jcn. - **25 chains**) reopened briefly for through trains to Lowestoft (see p.8) during Summer 1986. When the orwich electrification is completed, the curve is expected to be re-instated permanently, but with a different alignment.

tratford Area

M C	
0 00	**Stratford**
0 13	Stratford Central Jcn. West
0 38	Carpenters Road North Jcn.
0 42	Channelsea South Jcn.
0 43	Channelsea North Jcn.
0 56	Lea Jcn. (see p.12)

M C	
0 00	Carpenters Rd. Sth. Jcn.
0 26	Carpenters Rd. Nth. Jcn.

M C	
0 00	Temple Mills East Jcn.*
0 44	High Meads Jcn.
0 58	Lea Jcn.

M. P.	M C	
3 68	0 00	**Stratford Low Level** (see p.12)
3 33	0 35	Channelsea South Jcn.
.M.M.		
0 00	0 36	Channelsea North Jcn.
0 15	0 51	High Meads Jcn.
.M.M.		
4 45	1 15	Temple Mills East Jcn.*
6 08	2 58	Temple Mills West
6 25	2 75	Lea Bridge
7 13	3 63	Copper Mill North Jcn. (see p.10)

M C	
0 00	**Stratford**
0 42	Temple Mills East Jcn.*

ormerly Loughton Branch Jcn. Sth.

LIVERPOOL STREET - SOUTHEND VICTORIA (B.R. Table 5)
WICKFORD - SOUTHMINSTER (B.R. Table 7)

M. P.	M C	Station
0 00	0 00	Liverpool Street
	4 03	Stratford
	12 30	Romford
	20 16	Shenfield
	20 22	Shenfield Jcn.
	21 32	Mountnessing Jcn.
	24 28	Billericay
	29 00	Wickford
	29 13	Wickford Jcn.
	33 09	Rayleigh
	36 10	Hockley
	38 54	Rochford
	40 67	Prittlewell
41 39	41 39	Southend Victoria

Liverpool Street to Shenfield: see p.4 for intermediates

[Southend Central (1) - p.13]

M C	Station
29 00	Wickford
29 13	Wickford Jcn.
31 40	Battlesbridge
34 51	Woodham Ferrers
37 27	Fambridge
40 27	Althorne
43 24	Burnham-on-Crouch
45 42	Southminster

WITHAM - BRAINTREE (B.R. Table 9)

M. P.	M C	Station
24 15	0 00	Witham
21 10	3 05	White Notley
19 75	4 20	Cressing
17 76	6 19	Braintree

MARKS TEY - SUDBURY (B.R. Table 10)

M. P.	M C	Station
46 63	0 00	Marks Tey
50 18	3 35	Chappell & Wakes Colne
53 45	6 62	Bures
58 38	11 55	Sudbury

LIVERPOOL STREET - CLACTON & WALTON-ON-NAZE (B.R. Table 11)

M. P.	M C	Station
0 00	0 00	Liverpool Street
	29 65	Chelmsford
	38 48	Witham
	51 52	Colchester
	51 65	Colchester Jcn.
	53 14	East Gate Jcn.
	53 38	Hythe Jcn.
	53 48	Hythe
	56 04	Wivenhoe
	57 63	Alresford
	60 66	Great Bentley
	62 76	Weeley
	65 08	Thorpe-le-Soken
	65 15	Thorpe-le-Soken Jcn.
	68 04	Burrs Road LC
69 56	69 56	Clacton

Liverpool Street to Colchester: see p.4 for intermediates

M C	Station
53 14	East Gate Jcn.
53 30	Colne Jcn.
53 76	St. Botolphs

M C	Station
0 00	St. Botolphs
0 46	Colne Jcn.
0 68	Hythe Jcn.

M C	Station
65 15	Thorpe-le-Soken Jcn.
67 52	Kirby Cross
68 66	Frinton on Sea
70 10	Walton-on-Naze

MANNINGTREE - HARWICH (B.R. Table 12)

M.P.	M C	
59 35	0 00	**Manningtree** (see p.4)
59 43	0 08	Manningtree South Jcn.
59 67	0 32	Manningtree East Jcn.
61 11	1 56	**Mistley**
65 03	5 48	**Wrabness**
68 11	8 56	Parkeston Goods Jcn.
68 73	9 38	**Parkeston Quay**
70 19	10 64	**Dovercourt**
70 61	11 26	**Harwich Town**

M C	
0 24	Manningtree North Jcn.
0 00	Manningtree East Jcn.

PSWICH - LOWESTOFT (B.R. Table 14)

M.P.	M C	
68 59	0 00	**Ipswich** (see p.4)
69 42	0 63	East Suffolk Jcn.
72 20	3 41	**Westerfield**
72 25	3 46	Westerfield Jcn.
75 79	7 20	Bealings LC
78 78	10 19	**Woodbridge**
80 28	11 49	**Melton**
84 43	15 64	**Wickham Market**
87 15	18 36	Beversham LC
91 08	22 29	**Saxmundham**
91 40	22 61	Saxmundham GF
95 35	26 56	**Darsham**
00 53	31 74	**Halesworth**
04 45	35 66	**Brampton**
09 13	40 34	**Beccles**
15 42	46 63	**Oulton Broad South**
16 27	47 48	Oulton Broad North Jcn.
C.M.M.		
23 41	48 72	**Lowestoft** → *Norwich (16) - p.8*

M C	
0 00	Saxmundham GF
4 39	Sizewell LC

IPSWICH - FELIXSTOWE (B.R. Table 13)

M.P.	M C	
72 25	3 46	Westerfield Jcn.
74 67	6 08	**Derby Road**
80 00	11 21	Levington No. 6 LC
82 67	14 08	**Trimley**
83 57	14 78	Felixstowe Beach Jcn.
84 35	15 56	**Felixstowe Town**

M.P.	M C	
83 57	0 00	Felixstowe Beach Jcn.
84 59	1 02	Felixstowe Beach LC

PSWICH - CAMBRIDGE & ELY (B.R. Table 15)

M.P.	M C	
68 59	0 00	**Ipswich** → *Liverpool Street (11) - p.4*
77 11	8 32	**Needham Market**
80 54	11 75	**Stowmarket**
82 79	14 20	Haughley Jcn.
C.M.M.		
37 11	17 61	**Elmswell**
32 52	22 20	**Thurston**
28 44	26 28	**Bury St. Edmunds**
18 69	36 03	**Kennett**
16 04	38 68	Chippenham Jcn.
13 61	41 11	**Newmarket**
10 54	44 18	**Dullingham**
7 65	47 07	Six Mile Bottom LC
4 36	50 36	Fulbourn LC
0 23	54 49	Coldham Lane Jcn.
C.M.M.		
55 52	55 48	**Cambridge** → *Liverpool St./Kings Lynn (22) - p.10*

	M C	
C.M.M.	38 68	Chippenham Jcn.
7 61	42 58	Soham
12 33	50 30	Ely Dock Jcn.
C.M.M.		
70 30	50 61	**Ely** ↓ *Norwich/Peterborough (18) - p.9*

NORWICH - LOWESTOFT & YARMOUTH (B.R. Table 16)

M. P.	M C		
0 00	0 00	**Norwich**	→ *Liverpool Street (11) - p.5*
	0 32	Thorpe Jcn.	
	0 54	Wensum Jcn. (see note - p.5)	
	1 71	Whitlingham Jcn.	→ *Cromer (17) - See Below*
	4 66	**Brundall Gardens**	
	5 63	**Brundall**	
	5 71	Brundall Jcn.	→ see branch below
	7 65	**Buckenham**	
	10 04	**Cantley**	
	12 14	**Reedham**	
	12 29	Reedham Jcn.	→ see branch below
	13 06	Reedham Swing Bridge	
	16 15	**Haddiscoe**	
	17 60	Somerleyton Swing Bridge	
	18 00	**Somerleyton**	
	22 05	**Oulton Broad North**	
	22 17	Oulton Broad North Jcn.	→ *Ipswich (14) - p.7*
23 41	23 41	**Lowestoft**	

M C	
5 71	Brundall Jcn.
7 78	**Lingwood**
10 33	**Acle**
18 29	**Yarmouth**

M C	
12 29	Reedham Jcn.
15 71	**Berney Arms**
20 46	**Yarmouth**

NORWICH - CROMER & SHERINGHAM (B.R. Table 17)

M. P.	M C	
0 00	0 00	**Norwich**
	0 32	Thorpe Jcn.
	0 54	Wensum Jcn.
	1 71	Whitlingham Jcn.
	5 71	**Salhouse**
	8 61	**Wroxham**
	13 09	**Worstead**
	15 75	**North Walsham**
19 62	19 62	**Gunton**
C.M.M.		
11 55	23 75	**Roughton Road**
C.M.M.		
46 27	26 31	Cromer Jcn.
46 42	26 46	**Cromer**
		(REV.)
46 42	0 00	**Cromer**
46 27	0 15	Cromer Jcn.
44 39	2 03	**West Runton**
42 61	3 61	**Sheringham**

North Norfolk Railway

M C	
0 00	**Sheringham**
2 66	**Weybourne**
3 00	**Kelling Heath**
5 20	**Holt**

Wells & Walsingham Railway

M C	
0 00	**Wells next the Sea**
1 10	**Warham Halt**
1 70	**Wighton Halt**
4 00	**Walsingham**

NORWICH - ELY, MARCH & PETERBOROUGH (B.R. Table 18)

M. P.	M C	Location	Connection
124 09	**0 00**	**Norwich**	→ *Liverpool Street (11) - p.5*
123 56	**0 33**	Thorpe Jcn.	
123 00	**1 09**	Trowse Lower Jcn.	
117 73	**6 16**	Hethersett LC	
113 72	**10 17**	**Wymondham**	
113 70	**10 19**	Wymondham South Jcn.	*C.M.M. 0 00*
111 27	**12 62**	**Spooner Row**	
104 39	**19 50**	**Eccles Road**	
101 38	**22 51**	**Harling Road**	
93 50	**30 39**	**Thetford**	
86 32	**37 57**	**Brandon**	
82 44	**41 45**	**Lakenheath**	
77 25	**46 64**	**Shippea Hill**	
71 72	**52 17**	Ely North Jcn. (N)	*M. P. 71 72*
71 65	**52 24**	Ely North Jcn. (S)	*M. P. 71 65*
70 30	**53 59**	**Ely** (see p.10) (REV.)	

C.M.M.	M C	Location
0 00	**0 00**	Wymondham South Jcn.
	3 53	Kimberley Park LC
	6 75	Thuxton LC
	10 75	Yaxham Road LC
	11 33	Dereham
	13 61	Hoe LC
15 61	**15 61**	North Elmham LC

M. P.	M C	Location
71 72	**52 17**	Ely North Jcn. (N)
71 65	**52 24**	Ely North Jcn. (S)
		(via West curve)
72 63	**53 22**	Ely West Jcn.

M. P.	M C	Location
70 30	**0 00**	**Ely**
71 65	**1 35**	Ely North Jcn. (S)
71 72	**1 42**	Ely North Jcn. (N)
		(via East curve)
72 39	**2 09**	Ely West Jcn.

M. P.	M C	Location	Connection
72 39	**0 00**	Ely West Jcn.	*72 63*
75 78	**3 39**	Third Drove LC	
80 13	**7 54**	**Manea**	
82 00	**9 41**	Stonea LC	
85 67	**13 28**	March East Jcn.	*M. P. 85 67*
85 76	**13 37**	**March**	
86 17	**13 58**	March West Jcn.	**0 00** March West Jcn.
90 03	**17 44**	Three Horse Shoes No. 1 LC	
94 61	**22 22**	**Whittlesea**	
97 16	**24 57**	Funthams Lane LC	
100 66	**28 27**	Crescent Jcn.	
C.M.M. 76 29	**28 31**	**Peterborough**	→ *Spalding/Lincoln (19) - p.16*; *ECML (South) KEY PLAN - p.14*; *Leicester/Birmingham (18) - p.46*

M. P. / C.M.M.	M C	Location
M. P. 85 67	**0 00**	March East Jcn.
C.M.M. 86 18	**0 24**	Whitemoor Jcn.
89 21	**3 27**	Coldham LC
92 26	**6 32**	Wisbech Bypass LC
93 60	**7 66**	Wisbech Goods Yard

M C	Location
0 13	Whitemoor Jcn.
0 00	March West Jcn.

M C	Location	M. P.
0 00	**Peterborough** (see p.14)	*47 00*
0 04	Crescent Jcn.	*46 67*
1 27	Fletton Jcn. GF	*45 42*
3 07	**Orton Mere**	

Nene Valley Railway

M. P.	M C	Location
47 00		Buffer stop
46 67	**0 00**	**Peterborough** (N.V.R.)
45 42	**1 25**	**Orton Mere**
44 43	**2 24**	**Ferry Meadows**
40 60	**6 07**	**Wansford**
39 44	**7 23**	**Yarwell Mill**
39 14		End of line

LIVERPOOL STREET - CAMBRIDGE - KINGS LYNN (B.R. Table 22)

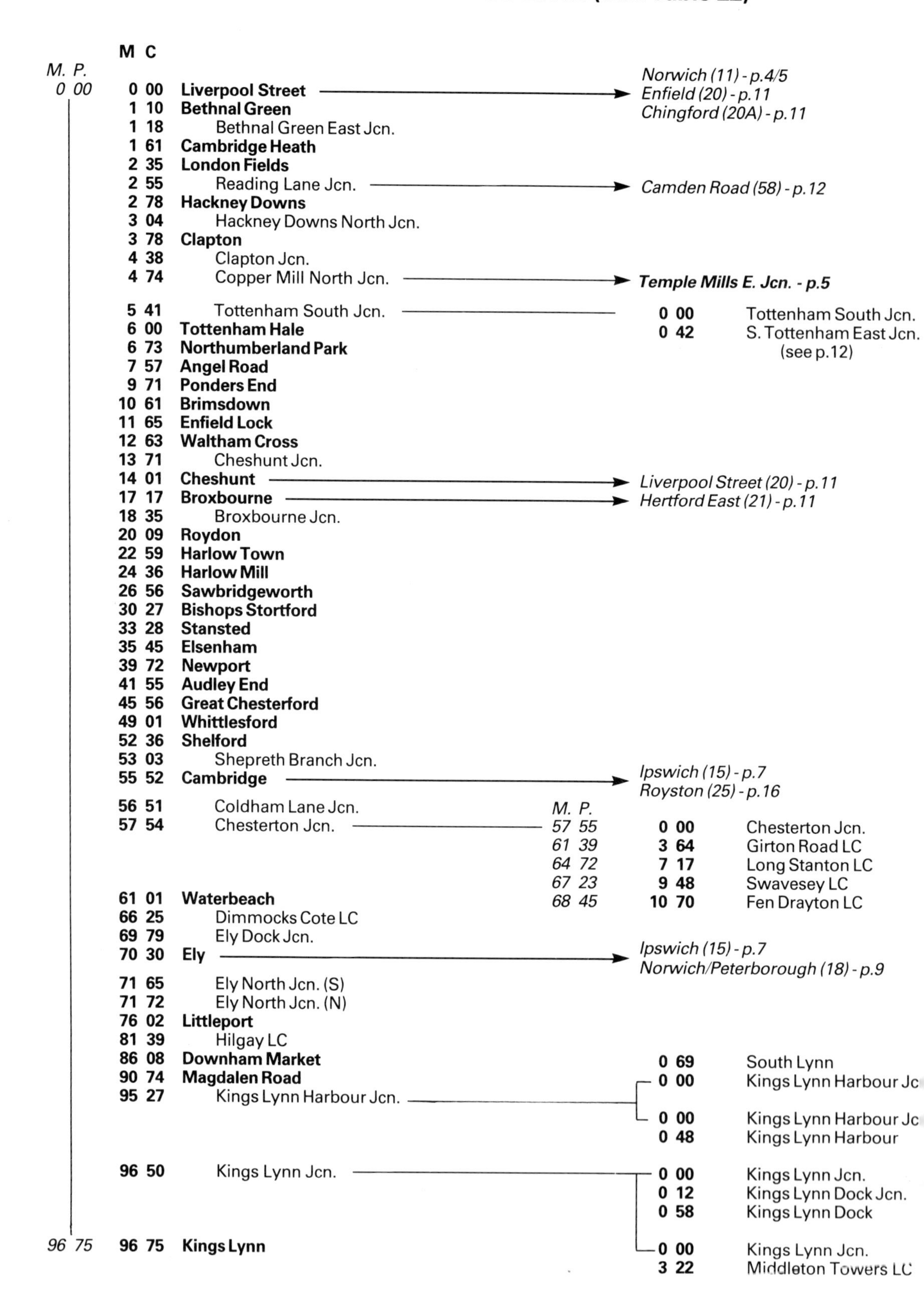

M. P.	M C	Location	Connections
0 00	0 00	**Liverpool Street**	*Norwich (11) - p.4/5* *Enfield (20) - p.11* *Chingford (20A) - p.11*
	1 10	**Bethnal Green**	
	1 18	Bethnal Green East Jcn.	
	1 61	**Cambridge Heath**	
	2 35	**London Fields**	
	2 55	Reading Lane Jcn.	*Camden Road (58) - p.12*
	2 78	**Hackney Downs**	
	3 04	Hackney Downs North Jcn.	
	3 78	**Clapton**	
	4 38	Clapton Jcn.	
	4 74	Copper Mill North Jcn.	***Temple Mills E. Jcn. - p.5***
	5 41	Tottenham South Jcn.	0 00 Tottenham South Jcn. 0 42 S. Tottenham East Jcn. (see p.12)
	6 00	**Tottenham Hale**	
	6 73	**Northumberland Park**	
	7 57	**Angel Road**	
	9 71	**Ponders End**	
	10 61	**Brimsdown**	
	11 65	**Enfield Lock**	
	12 63	**Waltham Cross**	
	13 71	Cheshunt Jcn.	
	14 01	**Cheshunt**	*Liverpool Street (20) - p.11*
	17 17	**Broxbourne**	*Hertford East (21) - p.11*
	18 35	Broxbourne Jcn.	
	20 09	**Roydon**	
	22 59	**Harlow Town**	
	24 36	**Harlow Mill**	
	26 56	**Sawbridgeworth**	
	30 27	**Bishops Stortford**	
	33 28	**Stansted**	
	35 45	**Elsenham**	
	39 72	**Newport**	
	41 55	**Audley End**	
	45 56	**Great Chesterford**	
	49 01	**Whittlesford**	
	52 36	**Shelford**	
	53 03	Shepreth Branch Jcn.	
	55 52	**Cambridge**	*Ipswich (15) - p.7* *Royston (25) - p.16*
	56 51	Coldham Lane Jcn.	
	57 54	Chesterton Jcn.	(branch below)
	61 01	**Waterbeach**	
	66 25	Dimmocks Cote LC	
	69 79	Ely Dock Jcn.	
	70 30	**Ely**	*Ipswich (15) - p.7* *Norwich/Peterborough (18) - p.9*
	71 65	Ely North Jcn. (S)	
	71 72	Ely North Jcn. (N)	
	76 02	**Littleport**	
	81 39	Hilgay LC	
	86 08	**Downham Market**	
	90 74	**Magdalen Road**	
	95 27	Kings Lynn Harbour Jcn.	(branches below)
	96 50	Kings Lynn Jcn.	(branches below)
96 75	96 75	**Kings Lynn**	

Chesterton Jcn. branch:

M. P.	M C	Location
57 55	0 00	Chesterton Jcn.
61 39	3 64	Girton Road LC
64 72	7 17	Long Stanton LC
67 23	9 48	Swavesey LC
68 45	10 70	Fen Drayton LC

Kings Lynn Harbour Jcn. branches:

M C	Location
0 69	South Lynn
0 00	Kings Lynn Harbour Jc
0 00	Kings Lynn Harbour Jc
0 48	Kings Lynn Harbour

Kings Lynn Jcn. branches:

M C	Location
0 00	Kings Lynn Jcn.
0 12	Kings Lynn Dock Jcn.
0 58	Kings Lynn Dock
0 00	Kings Lynn Jcn.
3 22	Middleton Towers LC

'VERPOOL STREET - ENFIELD TOWN & CHESHUNT (B.R. Table 20)

M. P.	M C			M. P.	M C	
0 00	**0 00**	**Liverpool Street**				
	1 10	**Bethnal Green**				
	1 18	Bethnal Green East Jcn.				
	1 61	**Cambridge Heath**				
	2 35	**London Fields**				
	2 55	Reading Lane Jcn.	→ *Camden Road (58) - p.12*			
	2 78	**Hackney Downs**				
	3 04	Hackney Downs North Jcn.				*Barking (2) - p.12* ↑
	3 64	**Rectory Road**				
	4 16	**Stoke Newington**				
	5 03	**Stamford Hill**			**0 13**	S. Tottenham West Jcn.
	5 42	Seven Sisters Jcn.	—		**0 00**	Seven Sisters Jcn.
	5 48	**Seven Sisters**				
	6 28	**Bruce Grove**				
	7 11	**White Hart Lane**				
	7 75	**Silver Street**				
	8 45	**Lower Edmonton**		*M. P.*		
	9 20	Bury Street Jcn.	—	*9 20*	**9 20**	Bury Street Jcn.
	10 32	**Southbury**			**9 69**	**Bush Hill Park**
	12 16	**Turkey Street**		*10 55*	**10 55**	**Enfield Town**
	13 45	**Theobalds Grove**				
14 28	**14 28**	Cheshunt Jcn.				
.M.M.						
14 01	**14 38**	**Cheshunt**	→ Cambridge (22) - p.10			

IVERPOOL STREET - CHINGFORD (B.R. Table 20A)

M. P.	M C	
0 00	**0 00**	**Liverpool Street** (see above)
	2 78	**Hackney Downs**
	3 04	Hackney Downs North Jcn.
	3 78	**Clapton**
	4 38	Clapton Jcn.
	5 55	**St. James Street**
	6 16	**Walthamstow Central**
	7 07	**Wood Street**
	8 52	**Highams Park**
10 33	**10 33**	**Chingford**

BROXBOURNE - HERTFORD EAST (B.R. Table 21)

M. P.	M C	
17 17	**0 00**	**Broxbourne** (see p.10)
18 35	**1 18**	Broxbourne Jcn.
18 71	**1 54**	**Rye House**
20 25	**3 08**	**St. Margarets**
22 18	**5 01**	**Ware**
24 19	**7 02**	**Hertford East**

[Hertford North (24/25) - p.15/16]

Navarino Road Jcn. Since the closure of Broad Street station, the Graham Road curve, connecting the North London Line with the Cambridge slow lines, has allowed weekday peak-hour services from Watford Junction to divert into Liverpool Street. Because of its short radius and maximum 1 in 32 gradient, the curve is restricted to EMU operation only (see p.12). *(David Maxey).*

CAMDEN ROAD (LMR) - LIVERPOOL STREET & NORTH WOOLWICH (B.R. Table 5

M. P.	M C	Location	Connection
			→ *Watford Jcn. (58/59) - p.53*
5 01	**0 00**	**Camden Road**	→ *Richmond (58) - p.53*
4 64	**0 17**	Camden Road East Jcn.	→ ***Freight Terminal Jcn. - p.14***
3 74	**1 07**	**Caledonian Road & Barnsbury**	
3 36	**1 45**	**Highbury & Islington**	
3 11	**1 70**	Canonbury Jcn.	→ ***Finsbury Park - p.14***
2 70	**2 11**	**Canonbury**	
2 21	**2 60**	Dalston Western Jcn.	→ *[Broad Street - p.52]*
		LMR/ER Boundary	
2 11	**2 70**	**Dalston Kingsland**	
C.M.M.			
1 11	**3 36**	Navarino Road Jcn.	— (see below)
1 32	**3 57**	**Hackney Central**	
2 01	**4 26**	**Homerton**	
2 68	**5 13**	**Hackney Wick**	
3 19	**5 44**	Lea Jcn.	→ ***High Meads Jcn. - p.5***
3 32	**5 57**	Channelsea North Jcn.	
3 33	**5 58**	Channelsea South Jcn.	→ ***Carpenters Road North Jcn. - p.5***
3 68	**6 13**	**Stratford Low Level**	
4 19	**6 44**	Stratford Market	
4 70	**7 15**	**West Ham**	
5 06	**7 31**	Abbey Mills Jcn.	
5 57	**8 02**	**Canning Town**	
6 72	**9 17**	**Custom House**	
7 79	**10 24**	**Silvertown**	
8 60	**11 05**	**North Woolwich**	

C.M.M.	M C	Location
2 79	**3 36**	Navarino Road Jcn.
2 55	**3 60**	Reading Lane Jcn.
2 35	**4 00**	**London Fields**
1 61	**4 54**	**Cambridge Heath**
1 18	**5 17**	Bethnal Green East Jcn.
1 10	**5 25**	**Bethnal Green**
0 00	**6 35**	**Liverpool Street** (pp.4/10)

GOSPEL OAK (LMR) - BARKING (B.R. Table 2)

M. P.	M C	Location	Connection
0 00		Gospel Oak Jcn.	→ *Richmond/Camden Road (58) - p.53*
C.M.M.	**0 00**	**Gospel Oak**	
2 42	**0 55**	Junction Road Jcn.	**0 00** Junction Road Jcn.; **0 57** Carlton Road Jcn. (see p.44)
3 00	**1 13**	**Upper Holloway**	
3 28	**1 41**	***LMR/ER Boundary***	
3 65	**1 78**	**Crouch Hill**	
4 15	**2 28**	Harringay Park Jcn.	**0 00** Harringay Park Jcn.; **0 22** Harringay West Jcn. (see p.14)
4 61	**2 74**	**Harringay Stadium**	
5 65	**3 78**	South Tottenham West Jcn.	→ ***Seven Sisters Jcn. - p.11***
5 69	**4 02**	**South Tottenham**	
5 73	**4 06**	South Tottenham East Jcn.	→ ***Tottenham South Jcn. - p.10***
7 21	**5 34**	**Blackhorse Road**	
8 11	**6 24**	**Walthamstow Queens Road**	
9 22	**7 35**	**Leyton Midland Road**	
10 00	**8 13**	**Leytonstone High Road**	
11 15	**9 28**	**Wanstead Park**	**0 31** Forest Gate Jcn. (p.4)
11 79	**10 12**	Woodgrange Park Jcn.	**0 00** Woodgrange Park Jcn.
12 09	**10 22**	**Woodgrange Park**	
13 12	**11 25**	Barking Station Jcn.	
13 14	**11 27**	Barking Tilbury Line Jcn. West	
C.M.M.			
7 42	**11 64**	**Barking**	→ *Southend/Shoebury (1) - p.13*

FENCHURCH STREET - SHOEBURYNESS via Basildon (B.R. Table 1)

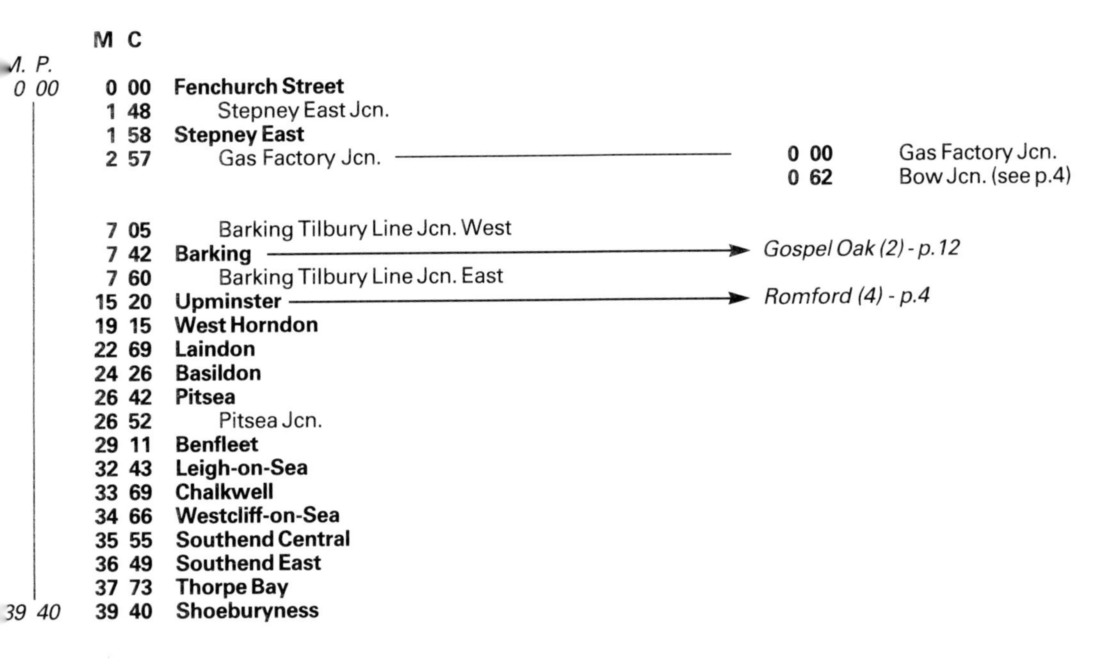

M. P.	M C			M C	
0 00	0 00	**Fenchurch Street**			
	1 48	Stepney East Jcn.			
	1 58	**Stepney East**			
	2 57	Gas Factory Jcn.	——	0 00	Gas Factory Jcn.
				0 62	Bow Jcn. (see p.4)
	7 05	Barking Tilbury Line Jcn. West			
	7 42	**Barking**	——►		*Gospel Oak (2) - p.12*
	7 60	Barking Tilbury Line Jcn. East			
	15 20	**Upminster**	——►		*Romford (4) - p.4*
	19 15	**West Horndon**			
	22 69	**Laindon**			
	24 26	**Basildon**			
	26 42	**Pitsea**			
	26 52	Pitsea Jcn.			
	29 11	**Benfleet**			
	32 43	**Leigh-on-Sea**			
	33 69	**Chalkwell**			
	34 66	**Westcliff-on-Sea**			
	35 55	**Southend Central**			
	36 49	**Southend East**			
	37 73	**Thorpe Bay**			
39 40	39 40	**Shoeburyness**			

FENCHURCH STREET - TILBURY TOWN & SOUTHEND CENTRAL (B.R. Table 1)
UPMINSTER - TILBURY RIVERSIDE

M. P.	M C		
0 00	0 00	**Fenchurch Street**	
	1 58	**Stepney East**	
	7 42	**Barking**	
	7 60	Barking Tilbury Line Jcn. E.	
	9 07	Ripple Lane	
	10 49	**Dagenham Dock**	
	12 54	**Rainham**	
	16 02	**Purfleet**	
	18 74	West Thurrock Jcn.	
	19 70	**Grays**	
	21 48	**Tilbury Town**	
	22 06	Tilbury W. Jcn.	
	22 30	Tilbury E. Jcn.	—— Tilbury E. Jcn.
	25 07	**East Tilbury**	
	26 41	Thames Haven Jcn.	—— Thames Haven Jcn.
27 17	27 17	**Stanford-le-Hope**	
C.M.M.	32 37	**Pitsea**	
26 52	32 43	Pitsea Jcn.	
29 11	35 02	**Benfleet**	
32 43	38 34	**Leigh-on-Sea**	
33 69	39 60	**Chalkwell**	
34 66	40 57	**Westcliff-on-Sea**	
35 55	41 46	**Southend Central**	*[Southend Victoria (5) - p.6]*

M. P.	M C	
0 00	0 00	**Upminster**
C.M.M.	3 11	**Ockenden**
18 74	6 53	West Thurrock Jcn.
19 70	7 49	**Grays**
21 48	9 27	**Tilbury Town**
22 06	9 65	Tilbury W. Jcn.
22 30	10 09	Tilbury S. Jcn.
22 45	10 24	**Tilbury Riverside**
		(REV.)
	0 00	**Tilbury Riverside**
	0 15	Tilbury S. Jcn.
	0 40	Tilbury E. Jcn.

M. P.	M C	
26 41	0 00	Thames Haven Jcn.
28 46	2 05	Shell No. 1 GF
29 04	2 43	Hydrocracker LC
30 44	4 03	Thames Haven Terminus GF

SECTION I - EASTERN REGION

(b) East Coast Main Line (South)

KINGS CROSS - DONCASTER (B.R. Table 26)

KEY PLAN

M. P. / From Moorgate M C	M C	Location	Key Plan
0 00	**0 00**	**Kings Cross**	
	0 64	Freight Terminal Jcn.	**0 34** Camden Road E. Jcn. (p
			0 00 Freight Terminal Jcn.
	1 12	Copenhagen Tunnel (North)	
3 41	**2 41**	**Finsbury Park**	**1 22** Canonbury Jcn. (p.12)
			0 00 **Finsbury Park**
4 29	**3 29**	Harringay West Jcn.	***Harringay Park Jcn. - p.12***
4 32	**3 32**	**Harringay**	
5 04	**4 04**	**Hornsey**	
5 68	**4 68**	Wood Green Jcn. (Down)	*Hertford N. Hitchin (24/25) - p15/16*
5 78	**4 78**	**Alexandra Palace**	
6 07	**5 07**	Wood Green Jcn. (Up)	
7 35	**6 35**	**New Southgate**	
9 30	**8 30**	**Oakleigh Park**	
10 12	**9 12**	**New Barnet**	
11 46	**10 46**	**Hadley Wood**	
13 57	**12 57**	**Potters Bar**	
15 37	**14 37**	**Brookmans Park**	
16 45	**15 45**	**Welham Green**	
18 54	**17 54**	**Hatfield**	
21 25	**20 25**	**Welwyn Garden City**	
	22 00	**Welwyn North**	
	25 03	**Knebworth**	
	26 45	Langley Jcn. (Up)	
M. P.	**26 61**	Langley Jcn. (Down)	
27 45	**27 45**	**Stevenage**	
	31 74	**Hitchin**	*Royston/Cambridge (25) - p.16*
	32 11	Cambridge Jcn.	
	41 13	**Biggleswade**	
	44 10	**Sandy**	
	51 58	**St. Neots**	
	58 70	**Huntingdon**	
	68 28	Connington North LC	
	70 02	Holme Lode LC	
	75 02	Fletton Jcn.	***Nene Valley Railway - p.9***
	76 25	Crescent Jcn.	
	76 29	**Peterborough**	*Ely/Norwich (18) - p.9* *Spalding/Lincoln (19) - p.16* *Leicester/Birmingham (18) - p.46*
	79 34	Werrington Jcn.	
	81 56	Helpston Jcn.	
	82 38	Maxey LC (no relation)	
	84 64	Tallington LC	
	87 08	Greatford LC	
	92 22	Little Bytham	
	99 61	Stoke Summit	
	105 05	Grantham South Jcn.	
105 38	**105 38**	**Grantham**	

KINGS CROSS - DONCASTER (B.R. Table 26) Cont.

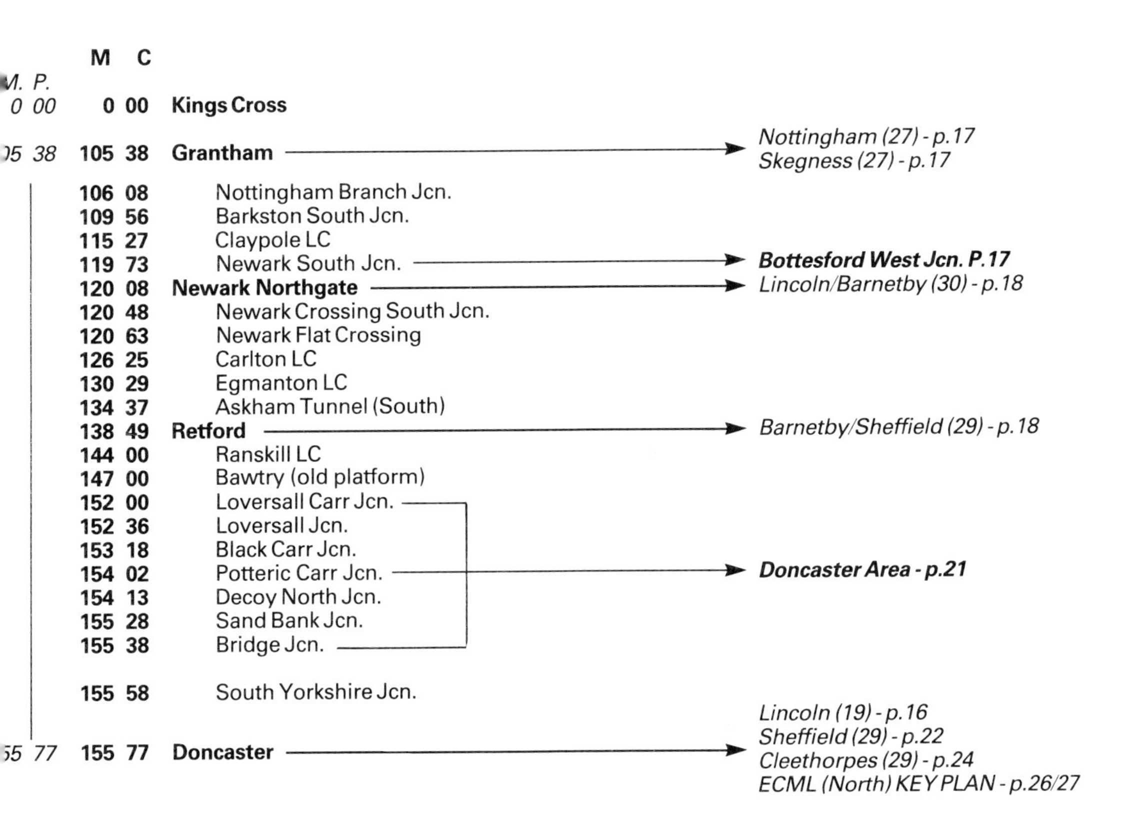

M. P.	M C	Location	Connections
0 00	0 00	**Kings Cross**	
05 38	105 38	**Grantham**	*Nottingham (27) - p.17* *Skegness (27) - p.17*
	106 08	Nottingham Branch Jcn.	
	109 56	Barkston South Jcn.	
	115 27	Claypole LC	
	119 73	Newark South Jcn.	***Bottesford West Jcn. P.17***
	120 08	**Newark Northgate**	*Lincoln/Barnetby (30) - p.18*
	120 48	Newark Crossing South Jcn.	
	120 63	Newark Flat Crossing	
	126 25	Carlton LC	
	130 29	Egmanton LC	
	134 37	Askham Tunnel (South)	
	138 49	**Retford**	*Barnetby/Sheffield (29) - p.18*
	144 00	Ranskill LC	
	147 00	Bawtry (old platform)	
	152 00	Loversall Carr Jcn.	
	152 36	Loversall Jcn.	
	153 18	Black Carr Jcn.	
	154 02	Potteric Carr Jcn.	***Doncaster Area - p.21*** (Loversall Carr Jcn. to Bridge Jcn.)
	154 13	Decoy North Jcn.	
	155 28	Sand Bank Jcn.	
	155 38	Bridge Jcn.	
	155 58	South Yorkshire Jcn.	
55 77	155 77	**Doncaster**	*Lincoln (19) - p.16* *Sheffield (29) - p.22* *Cleethorpes (29) - p.24* *ECML (North) KEY PLAN - p.26/27*

MOORGATE - HERTFORD NORTH (B.R. Table 24)

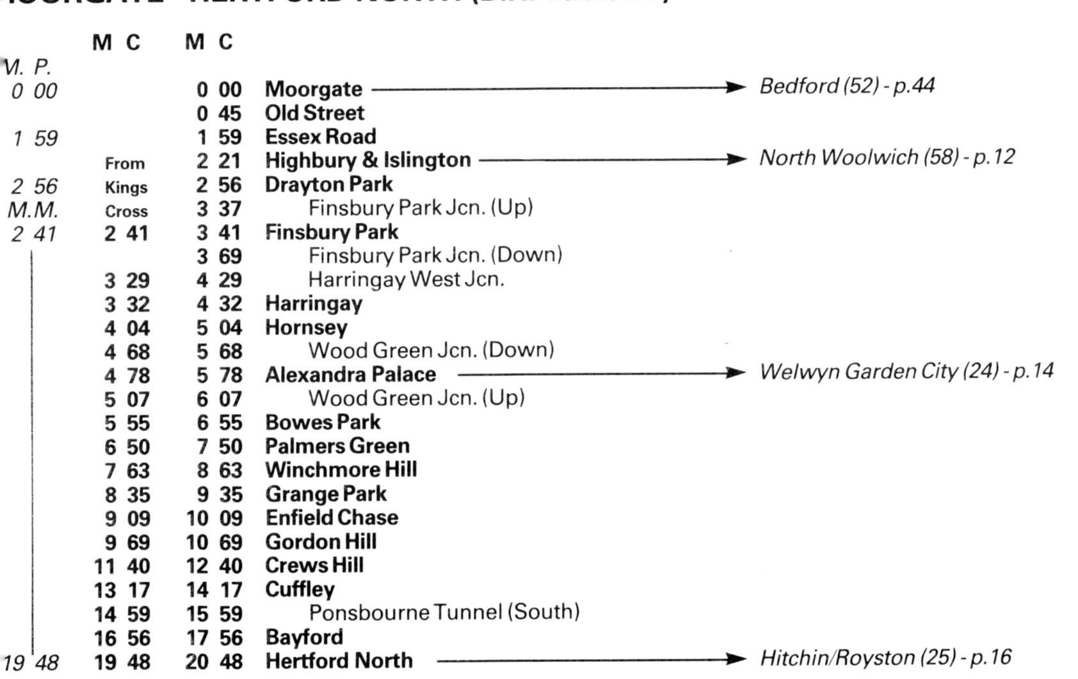

M. P.	M C (From Kings Cross M.M.)	M C	Location	Connections
0 00		0 00	**Moorgate**	*Bedford (52) - p.44*
		0 45	**Old Street**	
1 59		1 59	**Essex Road**	
		2 21	**Highbury & Islington**	*North Woolwich (58) - p.12*
2 56		2 56	**Drayton Park**	
M.M.		3 37	Finsbury Park Jcn. (Up)	
2 41	2 41	3 41	**Finsbury Park**	
		3 69	Finsbury Park Jcn. (Down)	
	3 29	4 29	Harringay West Jcn.	
	3 32	4 32	**Harringay**	
	4 04	5 04	**Hornsey**	
	4 68	5 68	Wood Green Jcn. (Down)	
	4 78	5 78	**Alexandra Palace**	*Welwyn Garden City (24) - p.14*
	5 07	6 07	Wood Green Jcn. (Up)	
	5 55	6 55	**Bowes Park**	
	6 50	7 50	**Palmers Green**	
	7 63	8 63	**Winchmore Hill**	
	8 35	9 35	**Grange Park**	
	9 09	10 09	**Enfield Chase**	
	9 69	10 69	**Gordon Hill**	
	11 40	12 40	**Crews Hill**	
	13 17	14 17	**Cuffley**	
	14 59	15 59	Ponsbourne Tunnel (South)	
	16 56	17 56	**Bayford**	
19 48	19 48	20 48	**Hertford North**	*Hitchin/Royston (25) - p.16*

[Hertford East (21) - p.11]

KINGS CROSS - ROYSTON - CAMBRIDGE/HERTFORD NORTH - ROYSTON (B.R. Table 25)

M. P.	M C	Location	Connection
0 00	0 00	**Kings Cross**	
	2 41	**Finsbury Park**	
	12 57	**Potters Bar**	
	17 54	**Hatfield**	
	20 25	**Welwyn Garden City**	
	22 00	**Welwyn North**	
	25 03	**Knebworth**	
	26 45	Langley Jcn. (Up)	
	26 61	Langley Jcn. (Down)	
	27 45	**Stevenage**	
	31 74	**Hitchin**	
	32 11	Cambridge Jcn.	
	34 50	**Letchworth**	
	36 47	**Baldock**	
	41 00	**Ashwell & Morden**	
	44 72	**Royston**	
	47 75	**Meldreth**	
	49 67	**Shepreth**	
50 77	50 77	**Foxton**	
C.M.M.			
53 03	55 26	Shepreth Branch Jcn.	
55 52	57 75	**Cambridge**	→ *Ipswich (15) - p.7*; *Liverpool St./Ely (22) - p.10*

Kings Cross/Moorgate (24) - p.15 ↑

M. P.	M C	Location
19 48	0 00	**Hertford North**
23 72	4 24	**Watton-at-Stone**
C.M.M.		
26 45	8 33	Langley Jcn. (Up)
26 61	8 48	Langley Jcn. (Down)
27 45	9 32	**Stevenage**
31 74	13 61	**Hitchin**
32 11	13 78	Cambridge Jcn.
34 50	16 37	**Letchworth**
36 47	18 34	**Baldock**
41 00	22 67	**Ashwell & Morden**
44 72	26 59	**Royston**

PETERBOROUGH - SPALDING - LINCOLN - DONCASTER (B.R. Table 19)

M. P.	M C	Location	Connection
76 29	0 00	**Peterborough**	*Ely/Norwich (18) - p.9*; *Leicester/Birmingham (18) - p.46*
79 34	3 05	Werrington Jcn.	
84 38	8 09	Stowgate LC	
90 02	13 53	Lucks Road LC	
C.M.M.			
44 26	16 48	**Spalding**	
49 26	21 48	Gosberton LC	
55 25	27 47	Blotoft Siding LC	
62 13	34 35	Sleaford South Jcn.	via avoiding line: 34 35 Sleaford South Jcn.
C.M.M.			
121 21	34 78	Sleaford East Jcn.	
120 53	35 46	**Sleaford** (see p.17)	
120 33	35 66	Sleaford West Jcn.	
C.M.M.			
63 48	37 74	Sleaford North Jcn.	35 70 Sleaford North Jcn. (2m. 04c. shorter)
65 65	40 11	**Ruskington**	
73 03	47 29	**Metheringham**	
76 70	51 16	Potterhanworth	
82 41	56 67	**Lincoln Central**	→ *Barnetby/Newark (30) - p.17/18*
83 29	57 55	West Holmes Jcn.	
84 13	58 39	Pyewipe Jcn.	→ ***Boultham Jcn. - p.18***
88 51	62 77	**Saxilby**	
90 04	64 30	Sykes Jcn.	0 00 Sykes Jcn.; 2 76 Torksey
98 09	72 35	**Gainsborough Lea Road**	
98 56	73 02	Trent East Jcn.	
98 69	73 15	Trent West Jcn.	→ *Retford/Barnetby (29) - p.18*
105 58	80 04	Haxey LC	
112 08	86 34	Finningley	
115 72	90 18	Bessacarr Jcn.	Up line only (7 chains shorter): 1 47 Bessacarr Jcn.; 0 75 Black Carr Jcn.
116 20	90 46	Flyover East Jcn.	
116 46	90 72	Flyover West Jcn.	
116 71	91 17	Decoy South Jcn.	0 11 Potteric Carr Jcn.
C.M.M.			
154 13	91 72	Decoy North Jcn.	0 00 Decoy North Jcn.
155 38	93 17	Bridge Jcn. (see p.21)	
155 77	93 56	**Doncaster**	→ *ECML (South) KEY PLAN - p.15*; *ECML (North) KEY PLAN - p.26*

SKEGNESS - GRANTHAM (B.R. Table 27)

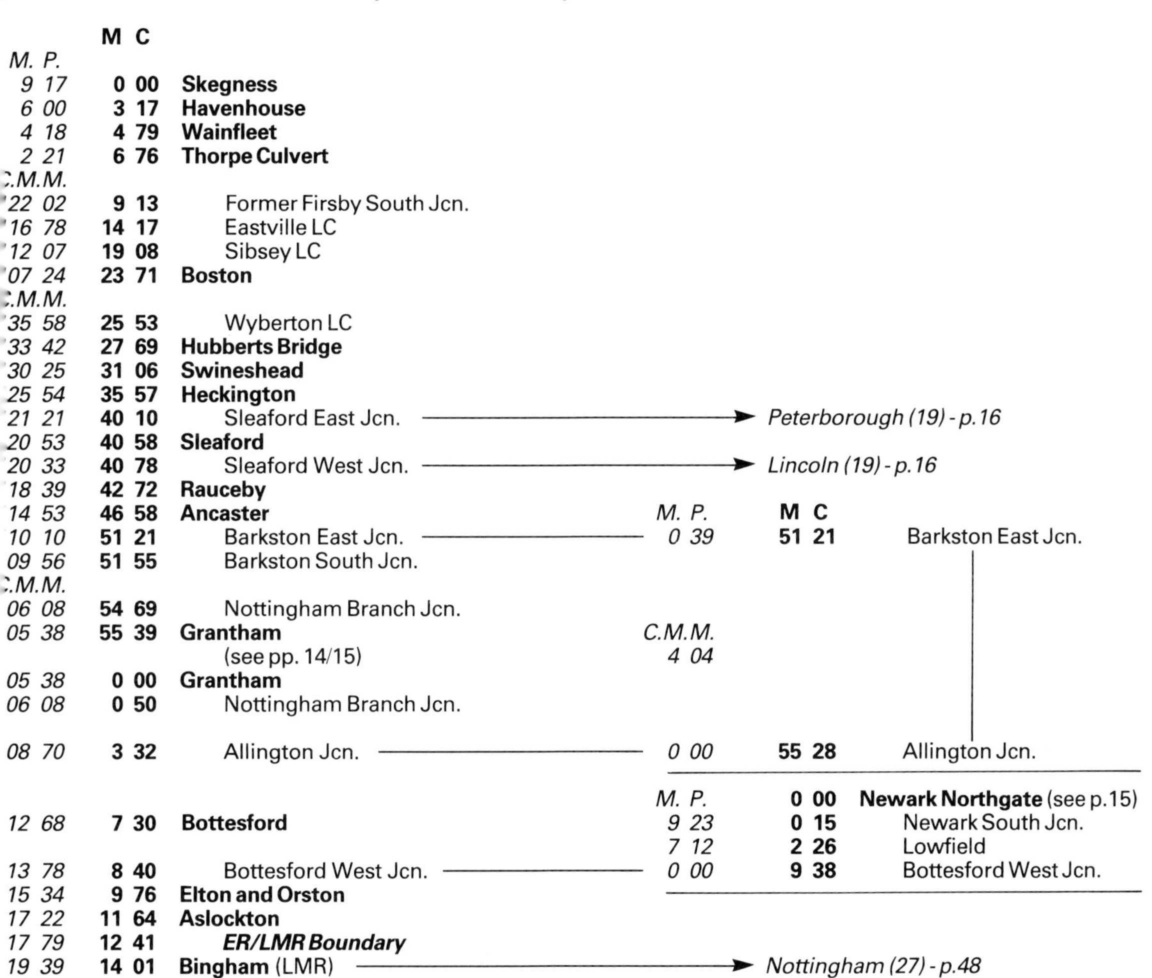

M.P.	M C	Location	M.P.	M C	Connection / Branch
	M C				
M. P.					
9 17	**0 00**	**Skegness**			
6 00	**3 17**	**Havenhouse**			
4 18	**4 79**	**Wainfleet**			
2 21	**6 76**	**Thorpe Culvert**			
C.M.M.					
22 02	**9 13**	Former Firsby South Jcn.			
16 78	**14 17**	Eastville LC			
12 07	**19 08**	Sibsey LC			
07 24	**23 71**	**Boston**			
C.M.M.					
35 58	**25 53**	Wyberton LC			
33 42	**27 69**	**Hubberts Bridge**			
30 25	**31 06**	**Swineshead**			
25 54	**35 57**	**Heckington**			
21 21	**40 10**	Sleaford East Jcn.			→ *Peterborough (19) - p.16*
20 53	**40 58**	**Sleaford**			
20 33	**40 78**	Sleaford West Jcn.			→ *Lincoln (19) - p.16*
18 39	**42 72**	**Rauceby**			
14 53	**46 58**	**Ancaster**	*M. P.*	**M C**	
10 10	**51 21**	Barkston East Jcn.	*0 39*	**51 21**	Barkston East Jcn.
09 56	**51 55**	Barkston South Jcn.			
C.M.M.					
06 08	**54 69**	Nottingham Branch Jcn.			
05 38	**55 39**	**Grantham**	*C.M.M.*		
		(see pp. 14/15)	*4 04*		
05 38	**0 00**	**Grantham**			
06 08	**0 50**	Nottingham Branch Jcn.			
08 70	**3 32**	Allington Jcn.	*0 00*	**55 28**	Allington Jcn.
			M. P.	**0 00**	**Newark Northgate** (see p.15)
12 68	**7 30**	**Bottesford**	*9 23*	**0 15**	Newark South Jcn.
			7 12	**2 26**	Lowfield
13 78	**8 40**	Bottesford West Jcn.	*0 00*	**9 38**	Bottesford West Jcn.
15 34	**9 76**	**Elton and Orston**			
17 22	**11 64**	**Aslockton**			
17 79	**12 41**	***ER/LMR Boundary***			
19 39	**14 01**	**Bingham** (LMR)			→ *Nottingham (27) - p.48*

BARNETBY - LINCOLN - NEWARK (B.R. Table 30)

M.P.	M C	Location	Connection
	M C		
M. P.			
94 56	**0 00**	**Barnetby**	→ *Doncaster/Cleethorpes (29) - p.24* *Retford/Sheffield (29) - p.18*
C.M.M.			
12 55	**0 44**	Wrawby Jcn.	
16 17	**4 06**	Howsham LC	
19 34	**7 23**	Moortown LC	
23 69	**11 58**	Claxby & Usselby LC	
26 54	**14 43**	**Market Rasen**	
30 53	**18 42**	Wickenby LC	
35 35	**23 14**	Langworth LC	
41 26	**29 15**	Pelham Street LC	
C.M.M.			
32 41	**29 27**	**Lincoln Central**	→ *Spalding/Doncaster (19) - p.16*

(continued on page 18)

BARNETBY - LINCOLN - NEWARK (B.R. Table 30)

	M C				
	0 00	**Barnetby** (see previous page)			
M. P.					
82 41	**29 27**	**Lincoln Central**			
C.M.M.					
32 70	**30 15**	West Holmes Jcn.		**0 65**	Pyewipe Jcn. (see p.16
32 40	**30 45**	Boultham Jcn. ———		**0 00**	Boultham Jcn.
29 49	**33 36**	**Hykeham**			
24 67	**38 18**	**Swinderby**			
22 13	**40 72**	**Collingham**			
C.M.M.			*M. P.*		
0 11	**45 11**	Newark Crossing E. Jcn. ———	*17 74*	**45 11**	Newark Crossing E. Jc
			17 69	**45 16**	Newark Flat Crossing
			16 78	**46 07**	**Newark Castle**
			16 32	**46 53**	***ER/LMR Boundary***
C.M.M.					↓
120 48	**45 22**	Newark Crossing S. Jcn.			
120 08	**45 62**	**Newark Northgate** (see p.15)			*Nottingham (30) - p.48*

BARNETBY - RETFORD - SHEFFIELD (B.R. Table 29)

M. P.	M C				
94 56	**0 00**	**Barnetby** ——→			*Doncaster/Cleethorpes (29) - p.24*
94 12	**0 44**	Wrawby Jcn.			
91 01	**3 55**	**Brigg**			
87 06	**7 50**	Ermine Street LC			
84 65	**9 71**	**Kirton Lindsey**			
80 23	**14 33**	Bonsall Lane LC			
74 42	**20 14**	**Gainsborough Central**			
73 24	**21 32**	Trent East Jcn.			
73 12	**21 44**	Trent West Jcn. ——→			*Lincoln/Doncaster (19) - p.16*
68 32	**26 24**	Clarborough Jcn. ———		**0 00**	Clarborough Jcn.
				3 47	Cottam Power Station
			M. P.		
64 32	**30 24**	**Retford** (Low Level)	*138 49*	**0 00**	**Retford** (see p.15)
63 46	**31 10**	Thrumpton W. Jcn. (Down)	*C.M.M.*		
63 29	**31 27**	Thrumpton W. Jcn. (Up)			
63 28	**31 28**	Thrumpton Crossing Jcn. ———	*63 28*	**1 01**	Thrumpton Crossing
58 54	**36 02**	Manton Wood			
56 58	**37 78**	**Worksop**			
55 62	**38 74**	Shireoaks East Jcn.			
55 00	**39 56**	Shireoaks West Jcn. ——→			***Shirebrook - p.20***
54 56	**40 00**	**Shireoaks** ——→			***Doncaster - p.20***
53 59	**40 77**	Brancliffe East Jcn.			
51 53	**43 03**	**Kiveton Park**			
50 34	**44 22**	**Kiveton Bridge**			
48 12	**46 44**	Brookhouse Colliery			
46 56	**48 00**	Woodhouse Jcn. ——→			***Chesterfield - p.19***
46 18	**48 38**	**Woodhouse**			
43 23	**51 33**	**Darnall**			
43 03	**51 53**	Darnall West Jcn. ——→			***Tinsley - p.23***
			M. P.		
42 29	**52 27**	Woodburn Jcn. ———	*42 29*	**0 00**	Woodburn Jcn.
			38 36	**3 73**	Wadsley Bridge
			33 35	**8 74**	Deepcar
C.M.M.					
158 77	**53 24**	Nunnery Main Line Jcn.			
					Doncaster (29) - p.22
					Leeds/York (34) - p.29/33
158 40	**53 61**	**Sheffield** ——→			*St. Pancras (53) - p.45*
					Manchester (29) - p.72

NORTH NOTTS./SOUTH DERBYSHIRE COALFIELD

1. Chesterfield - Woodhouse

M. P.	M C		
46 20	0 00	**Chesterfield** →	*St. Pancras/Sheffield (53) - p.45*
46 59	0 39	Tapton Jcn.	
46 76	2 56	Barrow Hill South Jcn.	
49 46	3 26	Barrow Hill North Jcn. →	***High Marnham - See Below***
50 64	4 44	Foxlow Jcn.	
51 58	5 38	Renishaw Park	
.M.M.			
48 06	9 28	Beighton Jcn. →	***Tinsley - p.23***
47 42	9 72	Beighton Stn. Jcn. LC	
46 52	10 62	Woodhouse Jcn.	
46 18	11 16	**Woodhouse** →	*Sheffield (29) - p.18* +4m 18c.

2. Barrow Hill - Shirebrook - High Marnham

M. P.	M C		M. P.	M C	
49 53	0 00	Barrow Hill North Jcn.		0 00	Foxlow Jcn.
50 56	1 03	Hall Lane Jcn.		0 61	Hall Lane Jcn.
51 04	1 31	Arkwright Colliery Jcn.	53 06	0 00	Arkwright Colliery Jcn.
			56 24	3 18	Arkwright Colliery
52 20	2 47	Seymour Jcn.	7 61	0 00	Seymour Jcn.
			7 05	0 56	Markham Colliery Jcn.
			5 23	2 38	Bolsover
.M.M.					
54 15	5 33	Oxcroft Jcn. GF		0 00	Oxcroft Jcn. GF
				1 00	Oxcroft Opencast
49 37	10 11	Elmton & Creswell Jcn. →	***Shireoaks - p.20***		
47 71	11 57	Norwood Crossing			
.M.M.					
9 72	13 66	Shirebrook East Jcn.			
10 60	14 54	Warsop Jcn.		0 00	Warsop Jcn.
				0 45	Shirebrook Jcn.
13 20	17 14	Welbeck Colliery Jcn.		0 00	Welbeck Colliery Jcn.
				2 62	Welbeck Colliery
15 15	19 09	Clipstone West Jcn. →	***Clipstone S. Jcn. - p.20***		
15 40	19 34	Clipstone East Jcn.			
17 21	21 15	Thoresby Colliery Jcn.		0 00	Thoresby Colliery Jcn.
				1 18	Thoresby Colliery
19 33	23 27	Ollerton Colliery			
20 15	24 09	Boughton Jcn.		0 00	Boughton Jcn.
				4 22	Bevercotes Colliery
23 52	27 46	Tuxford			
27 48	31 42	High Marnham			

NORTH NOTTS/SOUTH DERBYSHIRE COALFIELD

3. Clipstone Jcns. — Mansfield, Rufford, Blidworth & Bilsthorpe

M. P.	M C		M. P.	M C	
11 04	**0 00**	Clipstone West Jcn.	*11 09*	**0 00**	Clipstone East Jcn.
10 66	**0 18**	Clipstone South Jcn. ——	*10 66*	**0 23**	Clipstone South Jcn.
9 76	**1 08**	Mansfield Concentration Sidings			
C.M.M.					
0 00	**1 62**	Rufford Jcn. ——		**0 00**	Rufford Jcn.
				0 48	Clipstone Colliery
			M. P.		
			9 22	**0 00**	Rufford Jcn.
			6 32	**2 70**	Mansfield Colliery
0 24	**2 06**	Rufford Colliery Jcn. ——		**0 00**	Rufford Colliery Jcn.
				2 19	Rufford Colliery
			M. P.		
1 08	**2 70**	Bilsthorpe Colliery Jcn. ——	*1 08*	**0 00**	Bilsthorpe Colliery Jcn.
			4 11	**3 03**	Blidworth Colliery
4 39	**6 21**	Bilsthorpe Colliery			

4. Worksop — Shirebrook — Pye Bridge Jcn.

Retford/Sheffield - p.18

M. P.	M C		M. P.	M C	
56 58	**0 00**	**Worksop**	*54 56*	**0 00**	**Shireoaks**
55 62	**0 76**	Shireoaks East Jcn.	*55 00*	**0 24**	Shireoaks West Jcn.
C.M.M.			*C.M.M.*		
153 71	**1 35**	Woodend Jcn. ——	*153 71*	**0 69**	Woodend Jcn.
152 31	**2 75**	Steetley Colliery Sidings			
149 37	**5 69**	Elmton & Creswell Jcn. →			***Barrow Hill - p.19***
145 62	**9 44**	Shirebrook East Jcn.			
145 14	**10 12**	Shirebrook Jcn. →			***Warsop Jcn. - p.19***
144 19	**11 07**	***ER/LMR Boundary***			
141 50	**13 56**	Sherwood Colliery Sidings South			
				0 66	Metal Box Siding
138 79	**16 27**	Kirkby Summit Jcn. ——		**0 00**	Kirkby Summit Jcn.
135 46	**19 60**	Pinxton LC			
134 76	**20 30**	Sleight's East LC			
133 61	**21 45**	Pye Bridge Jcn. →			***Toton/Nottingham - p.47***

SHIREOAKS - DONCASTER (South Yorkshire Joint Line)

M. P.	M C		M. P.	M C	
54 56	**0 00**	**Shireoaks** →			***Retford/Sheffield (29) - p.18***
C.M.M.					
0 00	**0 77**	Brancliffe East Jcn.			
3 17	**4 14**	Dinnington Colliery Jcn.			
3 40	**4 37**	Laughton East Jcn. ——	*3 40*	**0 00**	Laughton East Jcn.
			6 15	**2 55**	Thurcroft Sidings
9 31	**10 28**	Maltby Colliery			
11 20	**12 17**	Firbeck Jcn. ——	*11 20*	**0 00**	Firbeck Jcn.
			14 21	**3 01**	Harworth Colliery
15 17	**16 14**	St. Catherines Jcn. →			***Doncaster Area - p.21***

ONCASTER AREA

M. P.	M C		Connection
	0 00	**Shireoaks**	
'5 17	16 14	St. Catherines Jcn.	see St. Catherines Jcn. branches below
'5 55	16 52	Low Ellers Curve Jcn.	see Low Ellers Curve Jcn. branch below
'7 69	18 66	Markham Sidings	
?0 49	21 46	Kirk Sandall Jcn.	→ *Cleethorpes (29) - p.24*

M. P.	M C	
71 60	**16 14**	St. Catherines Jcn.
68 65	**19 09**	Yorkshire Main Colliery

M. P.	M C	
15 17	**16 14**	St. Catherines Jcn.
15 71	**16 68**	Decoy South Jcn.
C.M.M.		
154 13	**17 38**	Decoy North Jcn. ECML

M. P.	M C	
15 55	**16 52**	Low Ellers Curve Jcn.
C.M.M.		
154 01	**17 53**	Potteric Carr Jcn. ECML

M. P.	M C		Connection
;2 00	0 00	Loversall Carr Jcn. ECML	Loversall Carr Jcn. **0 00** – Rossington Colliery **2 76**

M. P.	M C		Connection
;2 12	0 12	Rossington Colliery Jcn.	
;3 19	1 19	Flyover West Jcn.	→ *Lincoln (19) - p.16*
M.M.			
'6 71	1 44	Decoy South Jcn.	
M.M.			
;4 13	2 19	Decoy North Jcn. ECML	

M. P.	M C		Connection
;2 36	0 00	Loversall Jcn. ECML	
;2 79	0 43	Flyover East Jcn.	→ *Lincoln (19) - p.16*
M.M.			
'6 46	0 69	Flyover West Jcn.	
'6 71	1 14	Decoy South Jcn.	
M.M.			
;4 13	1 69	Decoy North Jcn.	→ *ECML KEY PLAN - p.15*

M. P.	M C		Connection
;5 38	0 00	Bridge Jcn.	
M.M.			
?2 35	0 19	St. James Jcn.	→ *Sheffield (29) - p.22*
	0 00	Hextorpe Jcn.	→ *Sheffield (29) - p.22*
	3 24	Bentley Jcn.	→ *Cleethorpes (29) - p.24*

Newcastle East Jcn. The classic view taken from the castle keep as 55022 *'Royal Scots Grey'* heads for Berwick and Edinburgh in July, 1977. The lines on the extreme left cross the High Level Bridge before diverging towards Gateshead or Sunderland (see p.27/41/42). *(John Augustson)*

Sheff - Doncaster 18m 29ch
Via old route (prior 87!)

DONCASTER - SHEFFIELD (B.R. Table 29)

M.P.	M C	Location	Connection
155 77	0 00	**Doncaster**	*ECML (South) KEY PLAN - p.14/15* *ECML (North) KEY PLAN - p.26/27*
C.M.M.			
22 58	0 19	South Yorkshire Jcn.	
22 35	0 42	St. James Jcn.	→ ***Bridge Jcn. - p.21***
20 76	2 01	Hexthorpe Jcn.	→ ***Bentley Jcn. - p.21***
18 60	4 17	Cadeby	
18 13	4 64	**Conisbrough**	
15 71	7 06	**Mexborough**	
C.M.M.			
10 17	7 13	Mexborough East Jcn.	→ ***Barnsley - See Below***
7 73	9 37	Thrybergh Jcn.	(see branch below)
C.M.M.			
164 48	10 30	Aldwarke North Jcn.	→ ***Tinsley - p.23*** + 3m 15c
164 43	10 35	Aldwarke South Jcn.	
162 24	12 54	Masborough Station Jcn.	
162 00	12 78	**Rotherham**	**Rotherham Central Station - see note p.33**
		Holmes Jcn.	
C.M.M.			
161 52	15 23	Wincobank Station Jcn.	→ *Barnsley (34) - p.29*
161 27	15 48	**Brightside**	
161 06	15 69	Brightside Jcn.	→ ***Tinsley - p.23***
159 34	17 41	**Attercliffe**	
158 77	17 78	Nunnery Main Line Jcn.	
158 40	18 35	**Sheffield**	→ *Retford (29) - p.18* *Leeds (34) - p.29* *York (34) - p.33* *Manchester (29) - p.72* *St. Pancras (53) - p.45*

Thrybergh Jcn. branch:

C.M.M.	M C	Location
13 13	0 00	Thrybergh Jcn.
11 08	2 05	Silverwood Jcn.
10 39	2 54	End of Branch

Mexborough - Barnsley

M.P.	M C	Location	Connection
15 71	0 00	**Mexborough**	
15 64	0 07	Mexborough East Jcn.	
14 07	1 64	Wath Central Jcn.	(see branch below)
12 14	3 57	Elsecar Jcn. LC	(see branch below)
10 16	5 55	Mitchells Main LC	(see branch below)
7 47	8 24	Quarry Jcn.	
6 54	9 17	**Barnsley**	→ *Sheffield/Leeds (34) - p.29* *Huddersfield (34) - p.29*

Wath Central Jcn. branch:

M.P.	M C	Location
0 06	0 00	Wath Central Jcn.
0 22	0 16	Manvers Colliery LC
0 73	0 67	Dearne Jcn. ↓ *York (34) - p.33*

Elsecar Jcn. branch:

M.P.	M C	Location
12 79	0 00	Wath Yard Sidings
12 14	0 65	Elsecar Jcn. LC
C.M.M.		
0 70	1 55	Cortonwood Loop GF

Mitchells Main LC branch:

M C	Location
0 00	Mitchells Main LC
1 55	Dovecliffe LC

Sheff-Leeds Via Nun/Treeton/TI 41m75ch

TINSLEY AREA

1. Woodburn/Darnall West - Aldwarke Jcns.

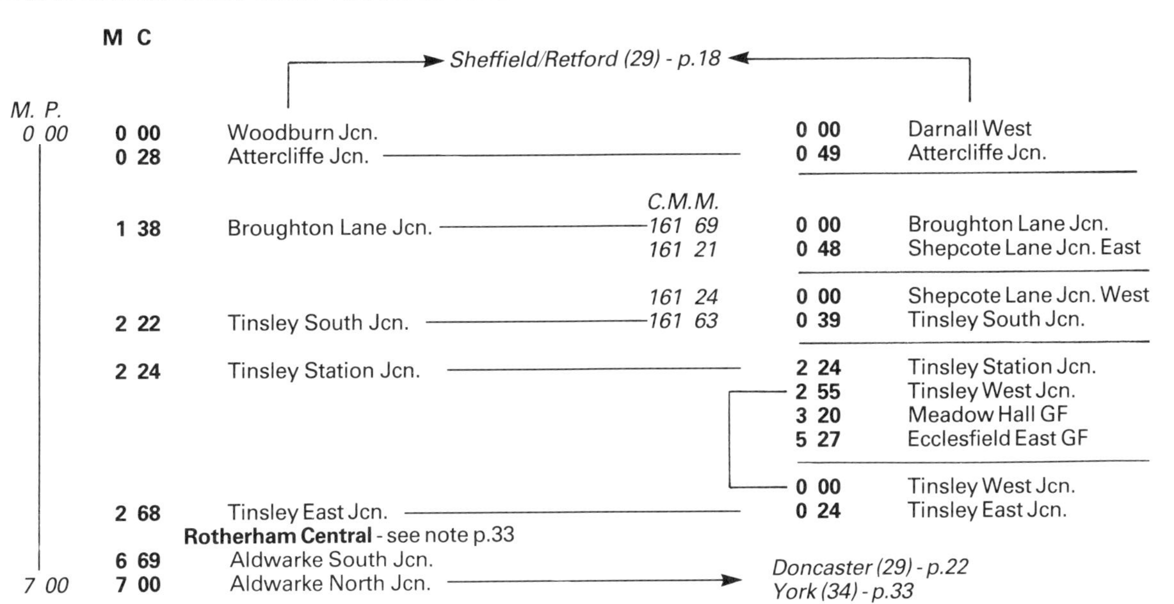

M C
Sheffield/Retford (29) - p.18
M. P.
0 00 0 00 Woodburn Jcn.
0 28 Attercliffe Jcn.
0 00 Darnall West
0 49 Attercliffe Jcn.
C.M.M.
1 38 Broughton Lane Jcn. 161 69
161 21
0 00 Broughton Lane Jcn.
0 48 Shepcote Lane Jcn. East
161 24
2 22 Tinsley South Jcn. 161 63
0 00 Shepcote Lane Jcn. West
0 39 Tinsley South Jcn.
2 24 Tinsley Station Jcn.
2 24 Tinsley Station Jcn.
2 55 Tinsley West Jcn.
3 20 Meadow Hall GF
5 27 Ecclesfield East GF
0 00 Tinsley West Jcn.
2 68 Tinsley East Jcn.
0 24 Tinsley East Jcn.
Rotherham Central - see note p.33
6 69 Aldwarke South Jcn.
7 00 7 00 Aldwarke North Jcn.
Doncaster (29) - p.22
York (34) - p.33

2. Brightside - Treeton Jcns.

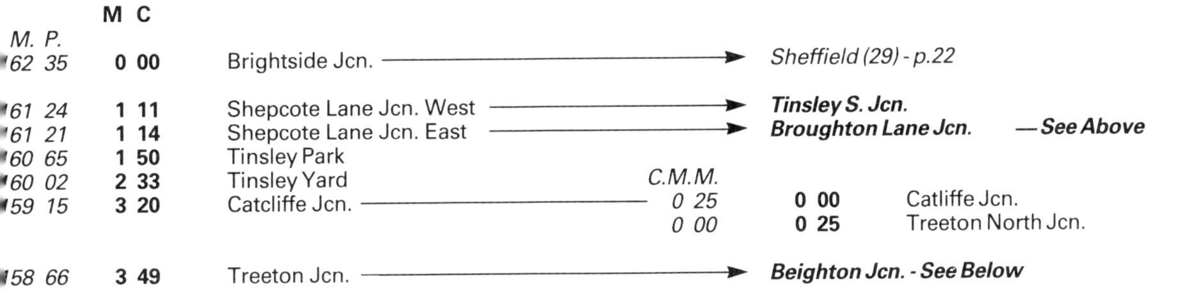

M C
M. P.
162 35 0 00 Brightside Jcn.
Sheffield (29) - p.22
161 24 1 11 Shepcote Lane Jcn. West
Tinsley S. Jcn.
161 21 1 14 Shepcote Lane Jcn. East
Broughton Lane Jcn. — See Above
160 65 1 50 Tinsley Park
160 02 2 33 Tinsley Yard
C.M.M.
159 15 3 20 Catcliffe Jcn. 0 25
0 00
0 00 Catliffe Jcn.
0 25 Treeton North Jcn.
158 66 3 49 Treeton Jcn.
Beighton Jcn. - See Below

3. Beighton - Masborough Station Jcn

M. P.	M C		
155 48	0 00	Beighton Jcn.	**Chesterfield - p.19**
158 65	3 17	Treeton Jcn.	**Catcliffe Jcn. - See Above**
159 19	3 51	Treeton North Jcn.	
160 61	5 13	Masborough Sorting Sidings South Jcn.	
162 00	6 32	**Rotherham**	*Doncaster (29) - p.22*
162 24	6 56	Masborough Station Jcn.	*York (34) - p.33*

DONCASTER - CLEETHORPES (B.R. Table 29)

M. P.	M C	Location		Connection
155 77	0 00	**Doncaster**	→	*ECML (South) KEY PLAN - p.14/15* *ECML (North) KEY PLAN - p.26/27*
C.M.M.				
0 03	0 29	Marshgate Jcn.		
1 04	1 30	Bentley Jcn.	→	***Hexthorpe Jcn. - p.21***
3 24	3 50	Kirk Sandall Jcn.	→	***St. Catherines Jcn. - p.21***
6 27	6 53	Stainforth Jcn.	→	***Adwick Jcn. - p.27***
6 40	6 66	**Stainforth & Hatfield**		
8 08	8 34	Thorne Jcn.		
9 41	9 67	**Thorne South**		
13 02	13 28	Medge Hall LC		
15 43	15 69	**Crowle**		
19 21	19 47	**Althorpe**		
20 22	20 48	Gunhouse Jcn.		
22 54	23 00	**Scunthorpe**		
23 15	23 41	Scunthorpe West Jcn.		
23 51	23 77	Trent Jcn.		
24 10	24 36	North Lincoln Jcn.		
25 34	25 60	Foreign Ore Branch Jcn.		
26 59	27 05	Appleby LC		
31 33	31 59	**Elsham**		
C.M.M.				
94 12	33 60	Wrawby Jcn.	→	*Retford/Sheffield (29) - p.17* *Lincoln/Newark (30) - p.18*
94 56	34 24	**Barnetby**		
99 33	39 01	**Brocklesby**		
99 39	39 07	Brocklesby Jcn.		
100 48	40 16	Habrough Jcn.		
101 13	40 61	**Habrough**	→	*Barton (29) - See Below*
104 72	44 40	**Stallingborough**		
105 75	45 43	**Healing**		
107 19	46 67	**Great Coates**		
107 69	47 37	Marsh Jcn. West		
108 08	47 56	Marsh Jcn. East	→	***Immingham - p.25***
109 20	48 68	**Grimsby Town**		
110 12	49 60	**Grimsby Docks**		
110 79	50 47	**New Clee**		
112 37	52 05	**Cleethorpes**		

Thorne Jcn. branch:

C.M.M.	M C	Location
7 69	8 34	Thorne Jcn.
C.M.M.		
14 02	9 76	**Thorne North**
10 00	13 78	Creykes LC
6 46	17 32	**Goole** (see p.34/35)

Scunthorpe West Jcn. branch:

M C	Location
0 00	Scunthorpe West Jcn.
0 28	Dawes Lane Jcn.
1 42	Crosby Mines
2 03	Normanby Park

Trent Jcn. branch:

M C	Location
0 00	Trent Jcn.
0 35	Dawes Lane Jcn.

Brocklesby Jcn. branch:

M. P.	M C	Location
99 39	0 00	Brocklesby Jcn.
100 31	0 72	Ulceby South Jcn.

HABROUGH - BARTON ON HUMBER (B.R. Table 29)

M. P.	M C	Location		Connection
101 13	0 00	**Habrough**		
C.M.M.				
0 39	0 45	Habrough Jcn.		
C.M.M.				
100 31	1 51	Ulceby South Jcn.	→	***Brocklesby Jcn. - See Above***
100 36	1 56	**Ulceby**		
100 44	1 64	Ulceby North Jcn.	→	***Immingham - p.25***
103 04	4 24	**Thornton Abbey**		
104 51	5 71	**Goxhill**		
106 52	7 72	**New Holland**		
108 05	9 25	**Barrow Haven**		
110 19	11 39	**Barton-on-Humber**		

Ulceby North Jcn. - Immingham - Marsh Jcns.

M. P.	M C	
100 44	**0 00**	Ulceby North Jcn.
104 05	**3 41**	Humber Road Jcn.
106 34	**5 70**	Immingham East Jcn.
C.M.M.		
1 25	**7 31**	Marsh Lane LC
3 36	**9 42**	Woad Lane LC
4 33	**10 39**	***BR/BTDB Boundary***
C.M.M.		
108 73	**11 05**	West Marsh Jcn.
108 44	**11 34**	***BTDB/BR Boundary***
108 34	**11 44**	Great Coates No. 1
108 05	**11 73**	Marsh Jcn. North
107 69	**12 09**	Marsh Jcn. West

M. P.	M C	
104 05	**3 41**	Humber Road Jcn.
104 76	**4 32**	Immingham W. Jcn. West
C.M.M.		
0 00	**4 46**	Humber Road LC
2 70	**7 36**	Killingholme (End of Branch)

M. P.	M C	
106 34	**5 70**	Immingham East Jcn.
106 75	**6 31**	Immingham Eastern Jetty

M C	
0 00	Marsh Jcn. North
0 14	Marsh Jcn. East

Barnetby (29) — *p.24* — *Cleethorpes (29)*

York Yard North. 40181 & D200 with the 'Tees-Tyne Boggard' charter on 27th October, 1984. The nose of the leading loco is level with milepost 1 on the East Coast Main Line (*extreme left*). To the far right, a collection of new Class 455/7 units for the Southern Region stands outside the B.R.E.L. Works (see p. 26/33). *(Steve Turner).*

SECTION I - EASTERN REGION

(c) East Coast Main Line (North)

DONCASTER - BERWICK UPON TWEED (B.R. Table 26)

KEY PLAN

M. P.	M C	Location	Connection
0 00	**0 00**	**Kings Cross**	
155 77	**155 77**	**Doncaster** →	*ECML (South) KEY PLAN - p.15* *Leeds (26/33) - p.28*
	156 26	Marshgate Jcn.	
	160 16	Shaftholme Jcn. →	***Knottingley - p.27***
	160 48	Joan Croft Jcn. →	***Applehurst Jcn. - p.27***
	164 14	Fenwick LC	
	169 16	Temple Hirst Jcn. →	*Selby (26) - p.36*
	174 10	Hambleton South Jcn. →	***Hambleton West Jcn. - p.27***
	174 75	Hambleton North Jcn. →	***Hambleton East Jcn. - p.27***
	182 79	Colton Jcn. →	*Sheffield (34) - p.33* *Leeds (34) - p.36*
	183 65	Colton North Jcn.	
	186 67	Dringhouses Jcn.	
188 08	**188 08**	Holgate Jcn. →	***York Yards - p.33***
C.M.M.			
0 00	**188 40**	**York** →	*Harrogate/Leeds (35) - p.32* *Scarborough (39) - p.37*
0 20	**188 60**	Clifton →	***York Yards - p.33***
1 51	**190 11**	Skelton Jcn.	
3 11	**191 51**	Skelton Bridge	
9 40	**198 00**	Tollerton	
15 28	**203 68**	Pilmoor	
22 16	**210 56**	**Thirsk**	
28 71	**217 31**	Longlands Jcn. →	***Boroughbridge Road Jcn. - p.38***
29 76	**218 36**	**Northallerton** →	***Eaglescliffe - p.38***
30 09	**218 49**	High Jcn.	
30 63	**219 23**	Castle Hills Jcn. →	***Redmire - p.38***
38 72	**227 32**	Eryholme	
43 61	**232 21**	Darlington South Jcn.	*Bishop Auckland (41) - p.38*
44 10	**232 50**	**Darlington** →	***Eastgate - p.39***
44 36	**232 76**	Darlington North Jcn.	*Middlesbrough/Saltburn (41) - p.39*
44 58	**233 18**	Parkgate Jcn.	
49 36	**237 76**	Aycliffe	
56 17	**244 57**	Ferryhill South Jcn. →	***Norton Jcns. - p.41***
57 50	**246 10**	Kelloe Bank Foot Jcn. →	***Kelloe Bank Foot - p.41***
58 73	**247 33**	Tursdale Jcn. →	***Pelaw - p.41***
60 21	**248 61**	Hett Mill LC	
66 13	**254 53**	**Durham**	
71 72	**260 32**	**Chester-le-Street**	
75 62	**264 22**	Tyne Yard	
77 37	**265 77**	Low Fell Jcn. →	***Norwood Jcn. - p.42***
79 42	**268 02**	King Edward Bridge South Jcn.	
79 57	**268 17**	King Edward Bridge North Jcn. →	***Newcastle Central Area - p.42***
80 05	**268 45**	Newcastle West Jcn. →	***Newburn - p.42***
80 16	**268 56**	**Newcastle**	

DONCASTER - BERWICK UPON TWEED (B.R. Table 26) cont.

C.M.M	M C		
	0 00	**Kings Cross**	
	155 77	**Doncaster**	Via HLB = +34ch.
	188 40	**York**	
0 00	**268 56**	**Newcastle** →	*Hartlepool (43) - p.41* *Carlisle (48) - p.42*
0 14	**268 70**	Newcastle East Jcn. →	***Newcastle Central Area - p.42***
0 46	**269 22**	**Manors**	
1 25	**270 01**	Riverside Jcn. →	***Carville - p.42***
1 74	**270 50**	Heaton South Jcn.	
2 48	**271 24**	Heaton North Jcn.	
4 24	**273 00**	Benton North Jcn. →	***Blyth/Lynemouth*** - *p.43* ***Callerton*** VIA B/TYNE +3m 09c
9 74	**278 50**	**Cramlington**	
13 74	**282 50**	Stannington LC	
16 50	**285 26**	**Morpeth** →	***Bedlington - p.43***
17 26	**286 02**	Morpeth North Jcn.	
18 44	**287 20**	**Pegswood**	
20 63	**289 39**	Butterwell Jcn. →	***Butterwell Colliery North - p.43***
23 20	**291 76**	**Widdrington**	
25 49	**294 25**	Chevington LC	
28 43	**297 19**	**Acklington**	
31 67	**300 43**	Warkworth LC	
34 69	**303 45**	**Alnmouth**	
39 34	**308 10**	Little Mill LC	
43 00	**311 56**	Christon Bank LC	
45 78	**314 54**	**Chathill**	
49 17	**317 73**	Lucker LC	
52 48	**321 24**	Crag Mill LC	
55 31	**324 07**	Fenham Low Moor LC	
58 52	**327 28**	Beal LC	
63 46	**332 22**	Scremerston LC	
67 00	**335 56**	**Berwick-upon-Tweed** →	*Edinburgh (26) - p.136*
69 67	**338 43**	***ER/ScR Boundary***	

M. P.	M C		*C.M.M.*	M C	
56 70	**0 00**	Stainforth Jcn. (see p.24)			
53 46	**3 24**	Thorpe Marsh CEGB			
53 27	**3 43**	Applehurst Jcn. —	*0 49*	**3 43**	Applehurst Jcn.
			0 00	**4 12**	Joan Croft Jcn. ECML
50 59	**6 11**	Skellow Jcn. —	*160 59*	**6 11**	Skellow Jcn.
			160 09	**6 61**	Carcroft Jcn. ↓
M.M.					
50 65	**7 00**	Adwick Jcn. →			*Leeds/Doncaster (26) - p.28*

	M C			M C	
68 75	**0 00**	Shaftholme Jcn. ECML			
66 26	**2 49**	Askern		**0 32**	Askern Colliery
65 12	**3 63**	Norton LC —		**0 00**	Norton LC
62 14	**6 61**	Post Office Lane LC			
58 66	**10 09**	Knottingley South Jcn. —		**0 00**	Knottingley South Jcn.
				0 20	Knottingley East Jcn. ↓
M.M.					
2 71	**10 55**	Knottingley West Jcn. →			*Leeds/Goole (28) - p.35*
2 27	**11 19**	Ferrybridge North Jcn. →			*York (34) - p.33*

	M C			M C	
74 10	**0 00**	Hambleton South Jcn. ECML	*4 00*	**0 00**	Hambleton North Jcn.
75 33	**1 23**	Hambleton West Jcn. ↓	*3 34*	**0 46**	Hambleton East Jcn. ↓
		Leeds (39) —	*p.36*	—	*Selby/Hull (39)*

DONCASTER - LEEDS (B.R. Tables 26 & 33)

M P.	M C	Location	*M. P.*	Connections
155 77	0 00	**Doncaster** →		*ECML (South) KEY PLAN - p.15* *ECML (North) KEY PLAN - p.26*
156 28	0 31	Marshgate Jcn.		
158 40	2 43	Castle Hills South Jcn. —		0 00 Castle Hills South Jcn. 0 16 Castle Hills West Jcn. 1 41 Brodsworth Colliery
				0 24 Castle Hills West Jcn.
158 67	2 70	Castle Hills North Jcn. —		0 00 Castle Hills North Jcn.
160 09	4 12	Carcroft Jcn. →		***Skellow Jcn. - p.27***
160 65	4 68	Adwick Jcn.		
164 48	8 51	**South Elmsall**		0 52 Moorthorpe Jcn. (p..33)
165 74	9 77	South Kirkby Jcn. —		0 00 South Kirkby Jcn.
169 15	13 18	**Fitzwilliam**		
171 73	15 76	Hare Park Jcn. —	*171 73*	0 00 Hare Park Jcn.
			173 22	1 29 Crofton West Jcn. (p.34)
175 38	19 41	Wakefield Westgate South Jcn.		
175 65	19 68	**Wakefield Westgate** →		*Wakefield/Kirkgate (33) - p.30*
180 61	24 64	Ardsley Tunnel (South)		
184 22	28 25	Gelderd Road Jcn. →		***Wortley Jcns. - See Below***
C.M.M.		VIA WORTLEY JCNS		
20 70	29 47	Leeds West Jcn. 29.50		
20 47	29 70	**Leeds** → 29.73		*Sheffield (34) - p.29* *Huddersfield (39) - p.31* *Ilkley (36) - p.32* *Skipton (36) - p.32* *Harrogate/York (35) - p.32* *Goole (28) - p.35* *York/Hull (39) - p.36*

SHEFF - LEEDS, VIADUCT 38M 60CH
GELDERD 38M 63CH.

LEEDS — BRADFORD INTERCHANGE (B.R. Table 40)

M. P.	M C	Location	*M. P.*	Connections
20 47	0 00	**Leeds**		
C.M.M.				
0 00	0 23	Leeds West Jcn.		
0 05	0 28	Leeds North Jcn.		
C.M.M.				
42 23	0 48	Whitehall Jcn. →		***Engine Shed Jcn. - p.29***
C.M.M.				
185 04	0 66	Holbeck East Jcn.		
C.M.M.				
0 02	0 69	Holbeck West Jcn. —	*185 01*	0 00 Holbeck West Jcn.
			184 39	0 42 Wortley South Jcn.
			184 22	0 59 Gelderd Road Jcn.
				(see above)
			184 22	0 54 Gelderd Road Jcn.
			184 39	0 37 Wortley South Jcn.
0 51	1 38	Wortley West Jcn. —	*184 76*	0 00 Wortley West Jcn.
3 15	4 02	**Bramley**		
4 77	5 64	**New Pudsey**		
C.M.M.				
191 18	8 30	Hammerton Street		
C.M.M.				
40 03	9 10	Mill Lane Jcn.		
40 27	9 34	**Bradford Interchange** →		*Hebden Bridge (39) - p.31*

[Bradford Forster Sq. (36) - p.32]

HEFFIELD - LEEDS via Barnsley (B.R. Table 34)

1. P.	M C		
8 40	0 00	**Sheffield**	→ *Retford (29) - p.18* *Doncaster (29) - p.22* *York (34) - p.33* *Derby (53) - p.45* *Nottingham (53) - p.47* *Manchester (29) - p.72*
8 37	0 37	Nunnery Main Line Jcn.	
9 34	0 74	**Attercliffe**	
1 06	2 46	Brightside Jcn.	→ ***Tinsley - p.23***
1 27	2 67	**Brightside**	
1 52	3 12	Wincobank Station Jcn.	
4 24	5 64	Ecclesfield West	
5 76	7 36	**Chapeltown**	
9 00	10 40	**Elsecar**	
0 45	12 05	**Wombwell**	
M.M.			
7 4	15 08	Quarry Jcn.	→ ***Mexborough - p.22***
6 54	16 01	**Barnsley**	→ *Huddersfield (34) - see below*
M.M.			
2 58	16 12	Barnsley Station Jcn.	
9 29	21 37	**Darton**	
7 33	23 31	Woolley Tunnels (South)	
M.M.			
1 53	23 14	Crigglestone Jcn.	*M. P.* *45 56* — **0 00** Crigglestone Jcn. *44 13* — **1 43** Horbury Station Jcn. (see p.30)
M.M.			
5 38	24 67	Horbury Jcn.	
7 43	26 72	Wakefield Kirkgate West Jcn.	
7 62	27 11	**Wakefield Kirkgate**	→ *Huddersfield Westgate (33) - p.50*
8 33	27 62	Turners Lane Jcn.	→ ***Calder Bridge Jcn. - p.34***
M.M.			
4 56	29 60	Goose Hill Jcn.	→ ***Oakenshaw South Jcn. - p.34***
5 11	30 15	**Normanton**	
6 00	31 04	Altofts Jcn.	→ ***Whitwood Jcn. - p.34***
6 34	31 38	**Altofts**	
7 37	32 41	Methley Jcn.	
0 02	35 06	**Woodlesford**	
2 42	37 46	Stourton Jcn.	
5 20	40 24	Engine Shed Jcn.	*M. P.* *195 20* — **0 00** Engine Shed Jcn. *195 52* — **0 32** Whitehall Jcn. → *Bradford Int. (40) - p.28* *Ilkley/Skipton (36) - p.32*
M.M.			
0 05	40 57	Leeds North Jcn.	
M.M.			
0 70	40 62	Leeds West Jcn.	
0 47	41 05	**Leeds**	→ *See p.28 for table refs.*

ARNSLEY - HUDDERSFIELD (B.R. Table 34)

1 P	M C		
6 54	0 00	**Barnsley**	→ ***Mexborough - p.22*** *Sheffield/Leeds (34) - see above*
6 43	0 11	Barnsley Station Jcn.	
3 67	2 67	Dodworth LC	
2 21	4 33	**Silkstone Common**	
0 63	5 71	Oxspring Tunnel (East)	
M.M.			
3 42	7 30	Huddersfield Jcn.	
3 36	7 36	**Penistone**	
9 31	11 41	**Denby Dale**	
7 14	13 58	**Shepley**	
6 26	14 46	**Stocksmoor**	
4 25	16 47	**Brockholes**	
3 28	17 44	**Honley**	
1 18	19 54	**Lockwood**	
0 40	20 32	Springwood Jcn.	
M.M.			
5 60	20 72	**Huddersfield**	→ *Leeds (39) - p.31* *Manchester (39) - p.74*

HUDDERSFIELD - WAKEFIELD (B.R. Table 33)

M. P.	M C		M. P.	M C	
25 60	**0 00**	**Huddersfield**			
27 60	**2 00**	**Deighton**			
28 39	**2 59**	Bradley Jcn.		**0 00**	Bradley Jcn..
				1 17	Bradley Wood Jcn. (see p.31)
28 78	**3 18**	Heaton Lodge South Jcn.	*18 78*	**3 18**	Heaton Lodge S. Jcn.
			29 54	**3 74**	Heaton Lodge Jcn.
C.M.M.		**(via underpass)**	*C.M.M.*		
37 49	**4 14**	Heaton Lodge East Jcn.	*37 49*	**4 14**	Heaton Lodge E. Jcn.
38 32	**4 77**	**Mirfield**			
39 75	**6 40**	Thornhill LNW Jcn. (see p.31)			
				3 54	Liversedge
				1 73	Liversedge Jcn.
40 50	**7 15**	Thornhill Jcn.		**0 00**	Thornhill Jcn.
				0 76	Railway Street Gds.
41 43	**8 08**	Dewsbury East Jcn.		**0 00**	Dewsbury East Jcn.
42 64	**9 29**	Healey Mills			
44 13	**10 58**	Horbury Station Jcn. →			***Crigglestone Jcn. - p.29***
45 38	**12 03**	Horbury Jcn.			
				0 00	**Wakefield Westgate** (see p.28)
				0 17	Westgate South Jcn.
47 43	**14 08**	Wakefield Kirkgate West Jcn.		**0 37**	Kirkgate West Jcn.
47 62	**14 27**	**Wakefield Kirkgate**		**0 56**	**Wakefield Kirkgate**

→ *Barnsley/Leeds (34) - p.29* ←
Calder Bridge Jcn. - p.34

Exits from Leeds. *Left* is Leeds West Jcn., divergence to Gelderd Road Jcn. and Wakefield. *Centre right* is the spur from Leeds North Jcn. to Engine Shed Jcn. and Woodlesford, whilst *Right,* lines to Whitehall Jcn. and Bradford veer off. The train from which this photo was taken is crossing over to the Harrogate lines (*extreme right,* out of shot). *(David Maxey).*

UDDERSFIELD - LEEDS (B.R. Table 39)

HEATON LODGE FAST LINE + 8CH.

1. P.	M C			
				Barnsley (34) - p.29
5 60	0 00	**Huddersfield**	→	*Wakefield (33) - p.30*
7 60	2 00	**Deighton**		*Manchester (39) - p.74*
8 39	2 59	Bradley Jcn.	→	***Bradley Wood Jcn. - p.30***
8 78	3 18	Heaton Lodge South Jcn.		
V.M.				
7 49	4 14	Heaton Lodge East Jcn.	→	***Bradley Wood Jcn. - See Below***
8 32	4 77	**Mirfield**		
9 75	6 40	Thornhill LNW Jcn.		
V.M.				
2 38	6 49	**Ravensthorpe**		
3 62	8 03	**Dewsbury**		
5 09	9 30	**Batley**		
6 25	10 46	Morley Tunnel (South)		
8 27	12 48	**Morley**	**0 71**	Dunlop and Rankin
0 65	15 06	Farnley Bridge Jcn.	**0 00**	Farnley Bridge Jcn.
2 05	16 26	Holbeck East Jcn.		
2 23	16 44	Whitehall Jcn.	→	***Engine Shed Jcn. - p.29***
V.M.				
0 05	16 64	Leeds North Jcn.		
0 00	16 69	Leeds West Jcn.		
V.M.				
0 47	17 12	**Leeds**	→	*Doncaster (26/33) - p.28*
				Bradford Int. (40) - p.28
				Barnsley/Sheffield (34) - p.29
				Ilkley (36) - p.32
				Skipton (36) - p.32
				Harrogate/York (35) - p.32
				Goole (28) - p.35
				York/Hull (39) - p.36

VIA H/MILLS 28.21

ADFORD INTERCHANGE - HALIFAX & HEBDEN BRIDGE (B.R. Table 39)

1. P.	M C			
) 27	0 00	**Bradford Interchange**	→	*Leeds (40) - p.28*
9 79	0 28	Mill Lane Jcn.	**2 71**	Laisterdyke Yard
			1 38	Hall Lane LC
9 20	1 07	Bowling Jcn.	**0 00**	Bowling Jcn.
3 18	2 09	Bowling Tunnel (South)		
6 12	4 15	Wyke Tunnel (South)		
3 10	7 17	Beacon Hill Tunnel (East)		
2 38	7 79	**Halifax**		
1 36	8 71	Dryclough Jcn.	**0 00**	Dryclough Jcn.
			1 11	Greetland Jcn.
			1 75	Elland
			5 73	Bradley Wood Jcn.
			7 43	Heaton Lodge Jcn.
			7 63	Heaton Lodge E. Jcn. (see p.30 & above)
			1 55	Greetland Jcn.
9 22	11 05	Milner Royd Jcn.	**0 00**	Milner Royd Jcn.
3 51	11 56	**Sowerby Bridge**		
4 68	15 39	**Mytholmroyd**		
3 56	16 51	**Hebden Bridge**	→	*Manchester Victoria (39) - p.74*
2 03	18 24	***ER/LMR Boundary***		*Copy Pit/Blackburn (108) - p.85*

LEEDS & BRADFORD FORSTER SQUARE - ILKLEY (B.R. Table 36)

M. P.	M C	
20 47	0 00	**Leeds**
C.M.M.		
0 00	0 23	Leeds West Jcn.
0 05	0 28	Leeds North Jcn.
C.M.M.		
195 54	0 48	Whitehall Jcn. (see p.29)
196 19	1 13	Wortley Jcn.
201 79	6 73	Apperley Jcn.
205 22	10 16	**Guiseley**
206 53	11 47	**Menston**
208 02	12 76	**Burley in Wharfdale**
210 21	15 15	**Ben Rhydding**
211 23	16 17	**Ilkley**

M. P.	M C	
208 58	0 00	**Bradford Forster Square**
206 01	2 57	Shipley Bradford Jcn.
205 73	2 65	**Shipley**
205 58	3 00	Shipley Leeds Jcn.
C.M.M.		
3 41	3 13	Guiseley Jcn.
2 29	4 25	**Baildon**
C.M.M.		
205 22	7 29	**Guiseley**
206 53	8 60	**Menston**
208 02	10 09	**Burley in Wharfdale**
210 21	12 28	**Ben Rhydding**
211 23	13 30	**Ilkley**

LEEDS - SKIPTON (B.R. Table 36)

M. P.	M C		
	0 00	**Leeds**	
195 54	0 48	Whitehall Jcn. (see p.29)	
196 19	1 13	Wortley Jcn.	
201 79	6 73	Apperley Jcn.	
205 45	10 39	Guiseley Jcn.	
205 58	10 52	Leeds Jcn.	
205 71	10 65	**Shipley**	
205 76	10 70	Shipley Bingley Jcn.	
206 51	11 45	**Saltaire**	
208 68	13 62	**Bingley**	
209 45	14 39	**Crossflatts**	
212 06	17 00	**Keighley**	
212 18	17 12	Keighley Station Jcn. SB	
212 38	17 32	Keighley Station Jcn.	→ 212 38 Station Jcn. (K&WVR)
216 52	21 46	Kildwick Station LC	
219 05	23 79	***ER/LMR Boundary***	
221 21	26 15	**Skipton**	→ *Carnforth/Carlisle (36) - p.86*

Keighley & Worth Valley Railway

M. P.	M C	
4 70	4 62	End of line
4 60	4 52	**Oxenhope**
3 52	3 44	**Haworth**
2 66	2 58	**Oakworth**
2 00	1 72	**Damems**
1 30	1 22	**Ingrow West**
0 08	0 00	**Keighley**
0 08	0 32	**Keighley**
0 00	0 24	***BR/KWVR Boundary***
C.M.M.		
212 18	0 20	Station Jcn. SB
212 38	0 00	Station Jcn.

LEEDS - HARROGATE - YORK (B.R. Table 35)

M. P.	M C		
	0 00	**Leeds**	→ *Doncaster (26/33) - p.28* *Bradford Int. (40) - p.28* *Sheffield (34) - p.29* *Huddersfield (39) - p.31* *Goole (28) - p.35* *York/Hull (39) - p.36*
M. P.			
	0 48	Whitehall Jcn. (see p.29)	
0 14	1 13	Wortley Jcn.	
2 11	3 10	**Headingley**	
4 61	5 60	**Horsforth**	
7 76	8 75	Bramhope Tunnel (North)	
10 62	11 61	**Weeton**	
14 03	15 02	**Pannal**	
C.M.M.			
20 38	18 23	**Harrogate**	
18 27	20 34	**Starbeck**	
16 54	22 07	**Knaresborough**	
14 47	24 14	Oakley Farm LC	
10 20	28 41	**Cattal**	
8 61	30 00	**Hammerton**	
5 10	33 51	Hessay LC	
2 74	35 67	**Poppleton**	
1 50	37 11	Skelton Jcn.	→ ***York Yards - p.33***
0 00	38 61	**York**	→ *ECML (North) KEY PLAN - p.26* *Scarborough (39) - p.37*

VIA GASCOIGNE WD/SELBY 53m 02ch
VIA CUDWORTH/CASTLEFORD 53m 14ch.

HEFFIELD - YORK (B.R. Table 34)

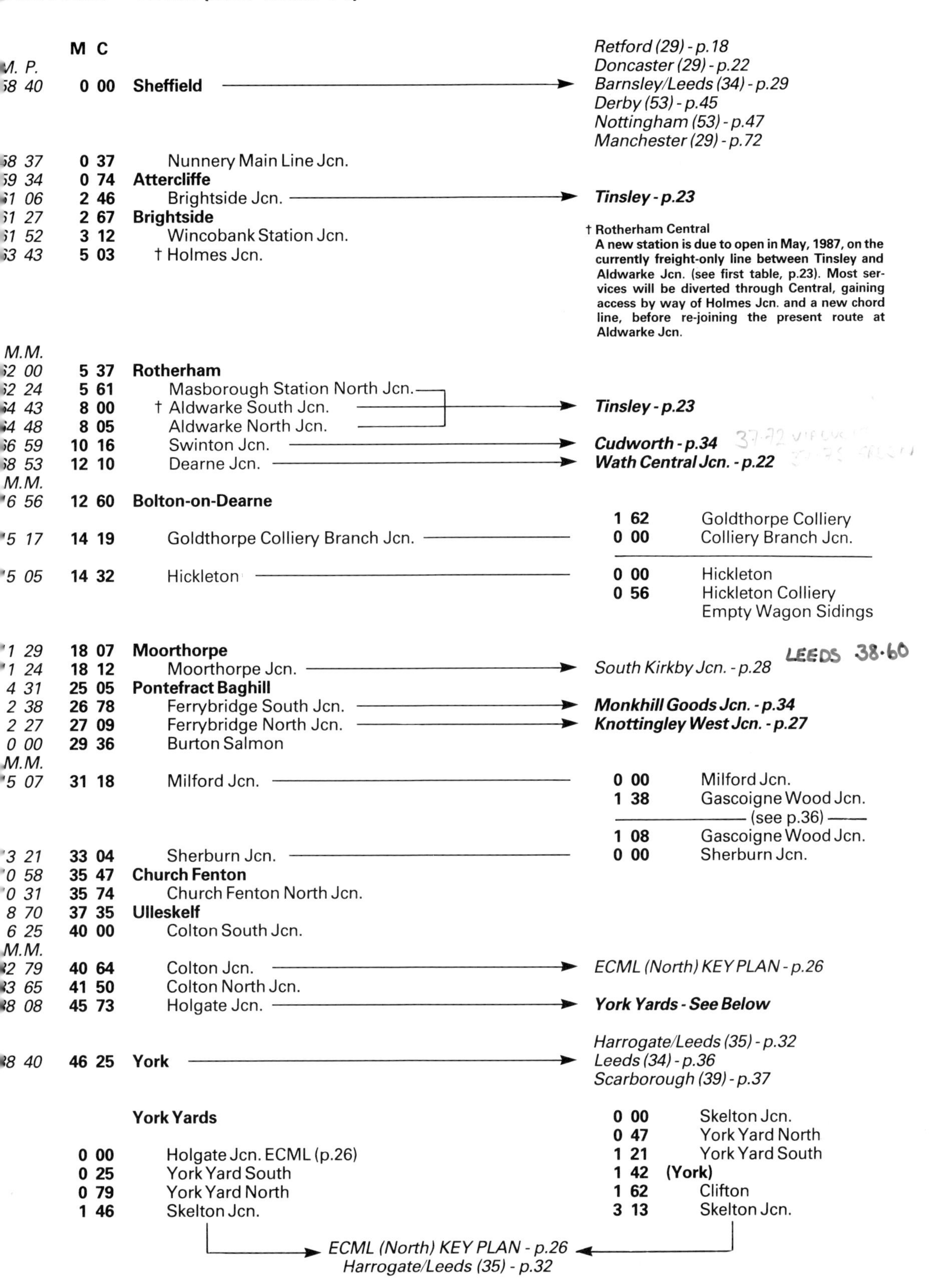

M. P.	M C		
58 40	0 00	**Sheffield** →	*Retford (29) - p.18* *Doncaster (29) - p.22* *Barnsley/Leeds (34) - p.29* *Derby (53) - p.45* *Nottingham (53) - p.47* *Manchester (29) - p.72*
58 37	0 37	Nunnery Main Line Jcn.	
59 34	0 74	**Attercliffe**	
61 06	2 46	Brightside Jcn. →	***Tinsley - p.23***
61 27	2 67	**Brightside**	
61 52	3 12	Wincobank Station Jcn.	
63 43	5 03	† Holmes Jcn.	
M.M.			
62 00	5 37	**Rotherham**	
62 24	5 61	Masborough Station North Jcn. →	***Tinsley - p.23***
64 43	8 00	† Aldwarke South Jcn. →	***Tinsley - p.23***
64 48	8 05	Aldwarke North Jcn. →	***Tinsley - p.23***
66 59	10 16	Swinton Jcn. →	***Cudworth - p.34***
68 53	12 10	Dearne Jcn. →	***Wath Central Jcn. - p.22***
M.M.			
76 56	12 60	**Bolton-on-Dearne**	
75 17	14 19	Goldthorpe Colliery Branch Jcn.	1 62 Goldthorpe Colliery 0 00 Colliery Branch Jcn.
75 05	14 32	Hickleton	0 00 Hickleton 0 56 Hickleton Colliery Empty Wagon Sidings
71 29	18 07	**Moorthorpe**	LEEDS 38·60
71 24	18 12	Moorthorpe Jcn. →	*South Kirkby Jcn. - p.28*
4 31	25 05	**Pontefract Baghill**	
2 38	26 78	Ferrybridge South Jcn. →	***Monkhill Goods Jcn. - p.34***
2 27	27 09	Ferrybridge North Jcn. →	***Knottingley West Jcn. - p.27***
0 00	29 36	Burton Salmon	
M.M.			
75 07	31 18	Milford Jcn.	0 00 Milford Jcn. 1 38 Gascoigne Wood Jcn. (see p.36) 1 08 Gascoigne Wood Jcn. 0 00 Sherburn Jcn.
73 21	33 04	Sherburn Jcn.	
70 58	35 47	**Church Fenton**	
70 31	35 74	Church Fenton North Jcn.	
8 70	37 35	**Ulleskelf**	
6 25	40 00	Colton South Jcn.	
M.M.			
82 79	40 64	Colton Jcn. →	*ECML (North) KEY PLAN - p.26*
83 65	41 50	Colton North Jcn.	
88 08	45 73	Holgate Jcn. →	***York Yards - See Below***
88 40	46 25	**York** →	*Harrogate/Leeds (35) - p.32* *Leeds (34) - p.36* *Scarborough (39) - p.37*

† Rotherham Central
A new station is due to open in May, 1987, on the currently freight-only line between Tinsley and Aldwarke Jcn. (see first table, p.23). Most services will be diverted through Central, gaining access by way of Holmes Jcn. and a new chord line, before re-joining the present route at Aldwarke Jcn.

York Yards

M C	
0 00	Holgate Jcn. ECML (p.26)
0 25	York Yard South
0 79	York Yard North
1 46	Skelton Jcn.

M C	
0 00	Skelton Jcn.
0 47	York Yard North
1 21	York Yard South
1 42	**(York)**
1 62	Clifton
3 13	Skelton Jcn.

→ *ECML (North) KEY PLAN - p.26* ←
Harrogate/Leeds (35) - p.32

Aldwarke - Cudworth - Normanton - Milford Jcn.

M. P.	M C	Location		Connection	
164 48	**0 00**	Aldwarke North Jcn. →		***Tinsley - p.23*** *Sheffield/York (34) - p.33*	
166 59	**2 11**	Swinton Jcn.			
172 68	**8 20**	Dearne Valley North Jcn. —		**0 00**	Dearne Valley N. Jcn.
				2 64	Grimethorpe Colliery
175 03	**10 35**	Cudworth Station			
178 28	**13 60**	Royston Jcn.	*M. P.*		
181 70	**17 22**	Oakenshaw South Jcn. —	*181 70*	**0 00**	Oakenshaw South Jcn
			183 04	**1 14**	Crofton East Jcn.
					(see below)
			C.M.M.		
181 77	**17 29**	Oakenshaw South Jcn. —	*49 41*	**0 00**	Oakenshaw South Jcn
			48 76	**0 45**	Oakenshaw Jcn.
					(see below)
184 56	**20 08**	Goose Hill Jcn. →		*Kirkgate (34) - p.29*	
185 11	**20 43**	**Normanton**			
C.M.M.					
23 57	**21 32**	Altofts Jcn. →		*Leeds (34) - p.29*	
22 04	**23 05**	Whitwood Jcn. →		*Leeds (28) - p.35*	
21 01	**24 08**	Castleford West Jcn.			
20 79	**24 10**	**Castleford** →		*Goole (28) - p.35*	
			C.M.M.		
20 39	**24 50**	Castleford East Jcn. —	*6 17*	**0 00**	Castleford East Jcn.
			4 43	**1 54**	Ledston Station
			3 22	**2 75**	Allerton Main
17 52	**27 37**	Fairburn Tunnel (West)			
15 07	**30 02**	Milford Jcn. →		***Gascoigne Wood Jcn. - p.33*** *York (34) - p.33*	

Wakefield Kirkgate - Crofton, Monkhill & Ferrybridge Jcns.

Westgate/Huddersfield (33) - p.30 ↑ (from Wakefield Kirkgate)

Sheffield/Leeds (34) - p.29 ↑ (from Turners Lane Jcn.)

M. P.	M C	Location	Connection	
47 62	**0 00**	**Wakefield Kirkgate**	**0 00**	Turners Lane Jcn.
48 28	**0 46**	Calder Bridge Jcn. —	**0 50**	Calder Bridge Jcn.
48 76	**1 14**	Oakenshaw Jcn. →	***Oakenshaw South Jcn.*** - See Above	
49 40	**1 58**	Crofton West Jcn. →	***Hare Park Jcn. - p.28***	
50 23	**2 41**	Crofton East Jcn. →	***Oakenshaw South Jcn.*** - See Above	
53 71	**6 09**	Featherstone LC		
56 36	**8 54**	Pontefract West Jcn.		
56 48	**8 66**	**Pontefract Monkhill** →	*Leeds/Goole (28) - p.35*	
C.M.M.				
3 06	**9 61**	Pontefract Monkhill Goods Jcn.		
2 38	**10 29**	Ferrybridge South Jcn. →	*York (34) - p.33*	

GOOLE - GILBERDYKE (B.R. Table 29)

M. P.	M C	Location	Connection
6 46	**0 00**	**Goole** →	*Doncaster (29) - p.24*
5 06	**1 40**	Goole Bridge	
3 49	**2 77**	**Saltmarshe**	
0 00	**6 46**	Gilberdyke Jcn.	
C.M.M.			
16 76	**6 57**	**Gilberdyke** →	*Leeds/Hull (39) - p.36*

EEDS - GOOLE (B.R. Table 28)

M. P.	M C	Station	Connections
20 47	**0 00**	**Leeds**	*Doncaster (26/33) - p.28* *Bradford Int. (40) - p.28* *Barnsley/Sheffield (34) - p.29* *Huddersfield (39) - p.31* *Ilkley/Skipton (36) - p.32* *Harrogate/York (35) - p.32* *York/Hull (39) - p.36*
.M.M.			
0 00	**0 23**	Leeds West Jcn.	
0 05	**0 28**	Leeds North Jcn.	
.M.M.			
95 20	**0 61**	Engine Shed Jcn.	***Whitehall Jcn. - p.29***
92 42	**3 39**	Stourton Jcn.	
90 02	**5 79**	**Woodlesford**	
87 37	**8 44**	Methley Jcn.	*Kirkgate/Sheffield - p.29*
.M.M.			
22 04	**9 55**	Whitwood Jcn.	***Altofts Jcn. - p.34***
21 01	**10 58**	Castleford West Jcn.	
20 79	**10 60**	**Castleford**	***Milford Jcn. - p.34***
		(REV.)	
20 79	**0 00**	**Castleford**	
.M.M.			
0 00	**0 02**	Castleford West Jcn.	***Altofts Jcn. - p.34***
.M.M.			
56 36	**3 23**	Pontefract West Jcn.	***Crofton Jcns. - p.34***
56 48	**3 35**	**Pontefract Monkhill**	
57 43	**4 30**	Pontefract Monkhill Goods Jcn.	***Ferrybridge South Jcn. - p.34***
58 20	**5 07**	Knottingley West Jcn.	***Ferrybridge North Jcn. - p.27***
58 37	**5 24**	**Knottingley**	
58 70	**5 57**	Knottingley East Jcn.	***Knottingley South Jcn. - p.27***
61 08	**7 75**	Sudforth Lane LC	
62 55	**9 42**	**Whitley Bridge**	
64 39	**11 26**	**Hensall**	
65 66	**12 53**	Drax Branch Jcn.	**0 00** Drax Branch Jcn. **4 16** Drax Power Station
68 10	**14 77**	**Snaith**	
70 75	**17 62**	**Rawcliffe**	
.M.M.			
0 64	**20 39**	Goole Engine Shed Jcn.	
0 00	**21 23**	Potters Grange Jcn.	
.M.M.			
6 46	**21 62**	**Goole**	*Doncaster (29) - p.24*

Wath Central. With the erstwhile motive power depot and yard in the background class 37 no. 37135 heads away from the sidings complex with empty ballast wagons during September 1977. Behind the photographer's right is the spur to Dearne Jcn. and the Sheffield - York via Pontefract main line. *(A.R. Kaye).*

LEEDS - YORK & HULL (B.R. Table 39)

M. P.	M C	Location	Connections
20 47	0 00	**Leeds** →	*Doncaster (26/33) - p.28* *Bradford Int. (40) - p.28* *Barnsley/Sheffield (34) - p.29* *Huddersfield (39) - p.31* *Ilkley/Skipton (36) - p.32* *Harrogate/York (35) - p.32* *Goole (28) - p.35*
19 44	1 03	Richmond Hill Tunnel (West)	
18 74	1 53	Neville Hill West Jcn.	(see branch below)
16 11	4 36	**Cross Gates**	
13 23	7 24	**Garforth**	
10 69	9 58	**Micklefield**	
10 63	9 64	Micklefield Station Jcn.	(see branch below)
7 57	12 70	**South Milford**	
6 27	14 20	Gascoigne Wood Jcn. →	***Milford/Sherburn Jcns. - p.33***
4 43	16 04	Hambleton West Jcn.	
3 34	17 13	Hambleton East Jcn. →	***Hambleton S. & N. Jcns. - p.27***
0 36	20 11	Selby West Jcn. →	***Selby Canal Jcn. - See Below***
C.M.M.			
31 12	20 47	Selby South Jcn. →	*Doncaster (26) - See Below*
30 79	20 60	**Selby**	
28 02	23 57	Hemingbrough LC	
25 03	26 56	**Wressle**	
22 27	29 32	**Howden**	
19 23	32 36	**Eastrington**	
17 07	34 52	Gilberdyke Jcn. →	*Goole (29) - p.34*
16 76	34 63	**Gilberdyke**	
14 33	37 26	**Broomfleet**	
10 38	41 21	**Brough**	
8 46	43 13	**Melton Halt**	
7 42	44 17	**Ferriby**	
4 64	46 75	**Hessle**	
1 74	49 65	Hessle Road Jcn. (see p.37)	
0 73	50 66	Anlaby Road Jcn.	(see branch below)
0 18	51 41	West Parade Jcn.	
0 00	51 59	**Hull** →	*Scarborough (32) - p.37*

Neville Hill West Jcn. branch:

M C	Location
0 00	Neville Hill W. Jcn.
1 21	Hunslet East

Micklefield Station Jcn. branch:

C.M.M.	M C	Location
15 62	9 64	Micklefield Stn. Jcn.
10 58	14 68	**Church Fenton**
10 31	15 15	Church Fenton N. Jcn.
8 70	16 56	**Ulleskelf**
C.M.M.		
182 79	20 05	Colton Jcn. ECML (see page 26)
188 40	25 46	**York** VIA METHLEY to

Anlaby Road Jcn. branch:

M C	Location
0 00	Anlaby Road Jcn.
0 24	West Parade N. Jcn. ↓

DONCASTER - SELBY (B.R. Table 26)

M. P.	M C	Location	Connections
155 77	0 00	**Doncaster** (see p.26) →	*ECML (South) KEY PLAN - p.15* *ECML (North) KEY PLAN - p.26*
169 16	13 19	Temple Hirst Jcn.	
172 76	16 79	Brayton Jcn.	(see branch below)
173 59	17 62	Selby Canal Jcn.	(see branch below)
174 11	18 14	Selby South Jcn.	
C.M.M.			
30 79	18 27	**Selby**	*Leeds/Hull (39) - See Above*

Brayton Jcn. branch:

C.M.M.	M C	Location
8 51	0 00	Brayton Jcn.
6 33	2 18	Barlow Tip

Selby Canal Jcn. branch:

M C	Location
0 00	Selby Canal Jcn.
0 32	Selby West Jcn.

Hessle Road Jcn. - Walton Street Jcn. & Hull Docks

M. P.	M C	Location		M C	Location
0 00	0 00	Hessle Road Jcn. (see p.36)			
0 57	0 57	Boothferry Park			
M.M.					
4 59	0 78	Springbank South Jcn.	———	0 00	Springbank South Jcn.
				0 45	Springhead Yard
4 20	1 37	Springbank North Jcn.	———	0 00	Springbank North Jcn.
				0 25	Walton Street Jcn. (see below)
0 41	5 16	Bridges Jcn.	———	0 00	Bridges Jcn.
0 15	5 42	Alexandra Dock (stop board)		1 50	King George Dock

HULL - BRIDLINGTON - SCARBOROUGH (B.R. Table 32)

M. P.	M C	Location		Connection
0 00	0 00	**Hull**	———►	*Selby/Leeds (39) - p.36*
	0 18	West Parade Jcn.		
	0 72	West Parade North Jcn.	———►	***Anlaby Jcn. - p.36***
	1 29	Walton Street Jcn.	———►	***Springbank North Jcn. - See Above***
	3 72	**Cottingham**		
	6 51	Beverley Parks LC		
	8 16	**Beverley**		
	11 16	**Arram**		
	13 53	Beswick LC		
	16 19	**Hutton Cranswick**		
	19 38	**Driffield**		
	21 44	**Nafferton**		
	25 45	Burton Agnes LC		
	28 54	Carnaby LC		
	30 72	**Bridlington**		
	32 25	Sewerby LC		
	34 43	**Bempton**		
	37 34	Speeton LC		
	41 51	**Hunmanby**		
	44 30	**Filey**		
46 72	46 72	Lebberston Road LC		
M.M.				
38 63	50 43	Seamer West Jcn.		
39 17	50 77	**Seamer**		
42 06	53 66	**Scarborough**		

SCARBOROUGH - YORK (B.R. Table 39)

M. P.	M C	Location		M C	Connection
42 06	0 00	**Scarborough**			
39 17	2 69	**Seamer**			
38 63	3 32	Seamer West Jcn.			
34 34	7 52	Ganton LC			
32 68	9 18	Weaverthorpe Station LC			
29 32	12 54	Heslerton Station LC			
25 42	16 44	Rillington Station LC			
21 12	20 74	**Malton**			***North York. Moors Railway - p.40***
15 01	27 05	Kirkham Abbey LC			
11 48	30 38	Barton Hill LC			
7 52	34 34	Common Road LC		1 53	Foss Islands
4 18	37 68	Haxby LC		0 15	Rowntree Halt
1 09	40 77	Burton Lane Jcn.	———	0 00	Burton Lane Jcn.
0 00	42 06	**York**	———►		*ECML (North) KEY PLAN - p.26* *Harrogate/Leeds (35) - p.32* ***York Yards - p.33***

Castle Hills Jcn. - Redmire

M. P.	M C	
44 10	**0 00**	**Darlington** (see p.26)
30 63	**13 27**	Castle Hills Jcn.

M. P.	M C	
29 76	**0 00**	**Northallerton** (p.26)
30 63	**0 67**	Castle Hills Jcn.

M. P.	M C	
0 00	**0 00**	Castle Hills Jcn.
C.M.M.		
1 49	**1 29**	Yafforth LC
2 71	**2 51**	Ainderby LC
4 26	**4 06**	Scruton LC
5 62	**5 42**	Leeming Bar LC
6 34	**6 14**	Aiskew LC
7 43	**7 23**	Bedale LC
9 55	**9 35**	Crakehall LC
13 17	**12 77**	Finghall Lane LC
19 65	**19 45**	Wensley LC
22 34	**22 14**	Redmire

Longlands Jcn. - Eaglescliffe

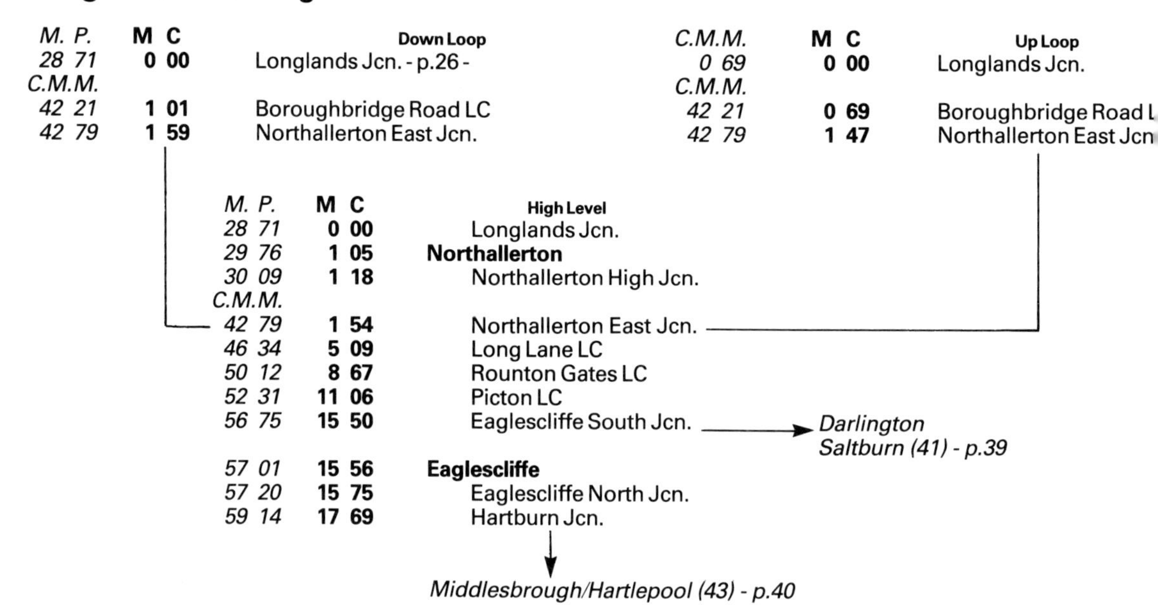

Down Loop

M. P.	M C	
28 71	**0 00**	Longlands Jcn. - p.26 -
C.M.M.		
42 21	**1 01**	Boroughbridge Road LC
42 79	**1 59**	Northallerton East Jcn.

Up Loop

C.M.M.	M C	
0 69	**0 00**	Longlands Jcn.
C.M.M.		
42 21	**0 69**	Boroughbridge Road L
42 79	**1 47**	Northallerton East Jcn

High Level

M. P.	M C	
28 71	**0 00**	Longlands Jcn.
29 76	**1 05**	**Northallerton**
30 09	**1 18**	Northallerton High Jcn.
C.M.M.		
42 79	**1 54**	Northallerton East Jcn.
46 34	**5 09**	Long Lane LC
50 12	**8 67**	Rounton Gates LC
52 31	**11 06**	Picton LC
56 75	**15 50**	Eaglescliffe South Jcn. → *Darlington Saltburn (41) - p.39*
57 01	**15 56**	**Eaglescliffe**
57 20	**15 75**	Eaglescliffe North Jcn.
59 14	**17 69**	Hartburn Jcn.

↓ *Middlesbrough/Hartlepool (43) - p.40*

DARLINGTON - BISHOP AUCKLAND (B.R. Table 41)

M. P.	M C		
44 10	**0 00**	**Darlington**	→ *Middlesbrough (41) - p.39*
44 36	**0 26**	Darlington North Jcn.	→ *ECML KEY PLAN - p.26*
44 58	**0 48**	Parkgate Jcn.	
C.M.M.			
0 49	**1 23**	**North Road**	
0 75	**1 49**	Hopetown Jcn.	
3 57	**4 31**	Whiley Hill LC	
5 08	**5 62**	**Heighington**	
6 30	**7 04**	**Newton Aycliffe**	
8 28	**9 02**	**Shildon**	
9 42	**10 16**	Shildon Tunnel (North)	
11 23	**11 77**	Bishop Auckland Jcn.	→ ***Eastgate - p.39***
11 27	**12 01**	**Bishop Auckland**	

M C	
0 00	Hopetown Jcn.
0 34	Nickstream

Darlington - Eastgate

M. P.	M C	
	0 00	**Darlington** (see p.38)
11 23	11 77	Bishop Auckland Jcn.
13 31	14 05	Etherley GF
M.M.		
1 14	16 35	Witton-le-Wear LC
7 43	22 64	Wolsingham
9 77	25 18	Broadwood LC
13 30	28 51	Unthank LC
15 79	31 20	Eastgate APCM

DARLINGTON - MIDDLESBROUGH - SALTBURN (B.R. Table 41)

M. P.	M C		
0 00	0 00	**Darlington**	→ *ECML (North) KEY PLAN - p.26*; *Bishop Auckland (41) - p.38*
	0 29	Darlington South Jcn.	
	3 65	**Dinsdale**	
	5 43	**Tees-side Airport**	
	8 09	**Allens West Halt**	
	8 58	Eaglescliffe South Jcn.	→ *Northallerton - p.38*
	8 63	**Eaglescliffe**	
	9 02	Eaglescliffe North Jcn.	
	10 76	Bowesfield Jcn.	→ *Hartlepool (43) - p.40*
	11 63	**Thornaby**	
	15 00	**Middlesbrough**	→ *Whitby (42) - See Below*
	15 23	Guisborough Jcn.	
	16 06	**Cargo Fleet**	
	17 40	**South Bank**	
	18 03	Beam Mill Jcn.	
	18 41	**Grangetown**	
	18 76	Grangetown Jcn.	
	19 32	Shell Jcn.	
	20 05	Redcar Oil Terminal Jcn. (Tod Point)	
	20 56	**British Steel Redcar**	
	22 64	**Redcar Central**	
	23 60	**Redcar East**	
	25 31	**Longbeck**	
	25 65	**Marske**	
	27 05	Saltburn West Jcn.	
27 57	27 57	**Saltburn**	

C.M.M.	M C	
57 20	9 02	Eaglescliffe N. Jcn.
59 14	10 76	Hartburn Jcn.

M C	
0 00	Beam Mill Jcn.
0 64	Slag Road LC (Lackenby)

M C	
0 00	Grangetown Jcn.
1 47	Shell Refinery

M. P.	M C	
27 05	0 00	Saltburn West Jcn.
33 64	6 64	Crag Hall
34 29	7 24	B.R. Boundary
36 77	9 72	Grinkle Tunnel (W.)
38 50	11 45	Boulby Potash Sdgs.

MIDDLESBROUGH - WHITBY (B.R. Table 42)

M. P.	M C	
15 00	0 00	**Middlesbrough**
M.M.		
0 00	0 23	Guisborough Jcn.
2 56	2 79	**Ormesby**
3 60	4 03	**Gypsy Lane**
4 27	4 50	**Nunthorpe**
8 14	8 37	**Great Ayton**
10 62	11 05	**Battersby** (continued overleaf)

MIDDLESBROUGH - WHITBY (B.R. Table 42) continued

	M C		
	0 00	**Middlesbrough**	
C.M.M.		*(see p.39)*	
12 03	11 05	**Battersby**	
13 64	12 66	**Kildale Halt**	
17 71	16 73	**Commondale Halt**	
19 38	18 40	**Castleton Moor**	
20 74	19 76	**Danby**	
24 43	23 45	**Lealholm**	
26 50	25 52	**Glaisdale**	
28 17	27 19	**Egton**	
29 59	28 61	**Grosmont**	
C.M.M.			
24 44	28 68	Grosmont Jcn.	→ North Yorkshire Moors Railway
27 63	32 07	**Sleights**	
29 31	33 55	**Ruswarp**	
30 62	35 06	**Whitby**	

North Yorkshire Moors Railway

M C	
17 72	**Pickering**
11 75	**Levisham**
8 24	**Newtondale Halt**
3 33	**Goathland**
0 00	**Grosmont LC**
0 27	**Grosmont LC**
0 00	Grosmont Jcn.

MIDDLESBROUGH - HARTLEPOOL (B.R. Table 43)

	M C		
M. P.			
15 00	0 00	**Middlesbrough**	→ *Darlington/Saltburn (41) - p.39*
11 63	3 17	**Thornaby**	
C.M.M.			
0 44	4 04	Bowesfield Jcn.	
C.M.M.			
59 14	4 48	Hartburn Jcn.	→ *Northallerton - p.38*
60 04	5 38	**Stockton**	
60 47	6 01	North Shore Jcn.	→ 0 00 North Shore Jcn.; 0 76 Stockton F.L.T. GF
61 71	7 25	Norton Jcn. South	
62 19	7 53	Norton Jcn. East	→ ***Norton Jcn. West - p.41***
63 69	9 23	Billingham Jcn.	→ ***Seal Sands - See Below***
64 47	10 01	**Billingham**	
67 28	12 62	**Greatham**	
68 60	14 14	Seaton Snook Jcn.	→ 0 00 Seaton Snook Jcn.; 1 51 Seaton-on-Tees
69 36	14 70	**Seaton Carew**	
70 06	15 40	Cliff House	→ 0 00 Cliff House; 0 67 End of Branch
71 55	17 09	**Hartlepool**	→ *Newcastle (43) - p.41*

Billingham Jcn. - Haverton & Seal Sands

M C		
0 00	Billingham Jcn.	
1 13	Belasis Lane Jcn.	→ 0 00 Belasis Lane Jcn.; 1 53 Haverton South
3 05	Port Clarence GF	
3 25	Philips Siding Jcn. GF	
5 01	Seal Sands Branch Jcn.	
6 44	Monsanto Sidings Jcn.	
7 43	***B.R. Boundary***	
7 49	Seal Sands Storage LC	

HARTLEPOOL - NEWCASTLE (B.R. Table 43)

M. P.	M C	Location	Connection
71 55	0 00	**Hartlepool**	→ *Middlesbrough (43) - p.40*
73 49	1 74	Cemetary North Jcn.	
78 58	7 03	Horden	
80 35	8 60	Easington	
84 11	12 36	Dawdon Jcn.	→ ***Seabanks - See Below***
84 44	12 69	**Seaham**	
85 24	13 49	Hall Dene LC	
87 63	16 08	Ryhope Grange Jcn.	→ ***Hawthorne / Hendon - See Below***
89 60	18 05	**Sunderland**	
90 26	18 51	Monkwearmouth	→ ***Austin Shipyard - See Below***
91 33	19 58	**Seaburn**	
93 17	21 42	**East Boldon**	
95 12	23 37	**Boldon Colliery**	
95 19	23 44	Boldon Colliery Jcn.	→ ***Bolden Colliery NCB - See Below***
98 07	26 32	Pelaw Jcn.	→ ***Simonside - See Below***
98 16	26 41	Pelaw Jcn.	→ ***Ferryhill - See Below***
99 00	27 25	**Heworth**	
100 68	29 13	Park Lane Jcn.	KEB +29c
101 33	29 58	High Level Bridge Jcn.	→ ***Newcastle Central Area - p.42***
C.M.M.			
0 14	30 04	Newcastle East Jcn.	
0 00	30 18	**Newcastle**	→ *ECML (North) KEY PLAN - pp.26/27*

M C	Location
0 00	Dawdon Jcn.
0 72	Seabanks
1 63	End of Branch

M C	Location
0 00	Boldon Colliery Jcn.
0 58	Green Lane Jcn.
2 25	Boldon Colliery NCB

M C	Location
0 00	Ryhope Grange Jcn.
2 77	Seaton LC
5 67	Hawthorne Coking Plant (B.R. Boundary)

M C	Location
0 00	Pelaw Jcn.
1 41	Hepburn
2 71	Jarrow
4 10	Simonside Wagon Works

M C	Location
0 00	Ryhope Grange Jcn.
1 28	Londonderry Jcn.
1 53	Henson

M C	Location
0 00	Kelloe Bank Foot Jcn. ECML
0 73	West Cornforth LC
3 03	Kelloe Bank Foot North End

M C	Location
0 00	Monkwearmouth
0 13	Wearmouth Colliery Jcn.
0 62	Southwick Goods Yard GF
1 37	Austin & Pickersgill Shipyard

Norton Jcns. - Ferryhill South - Tursdale Jcn. - Pelaw

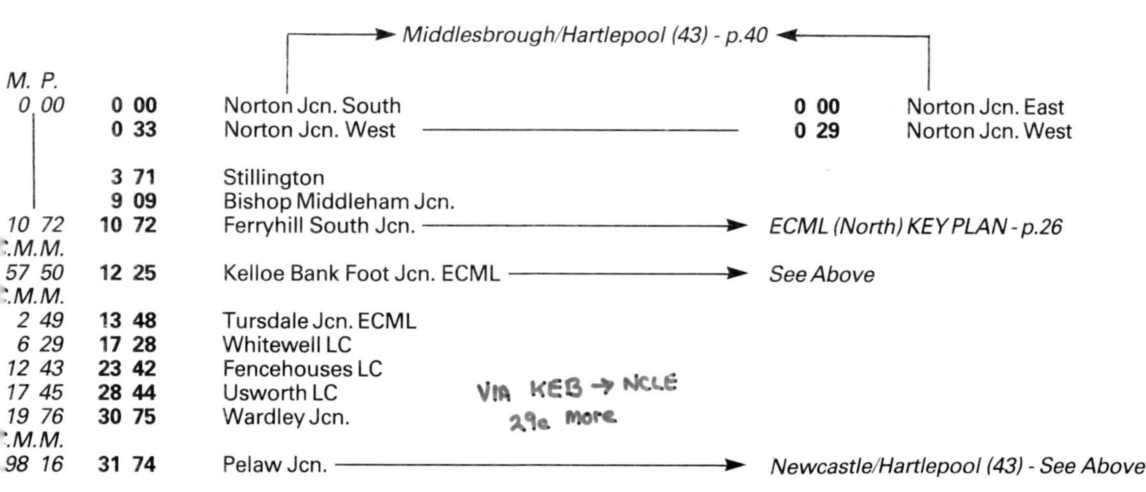

→ *Middlesbrough/Hartlepool (43) - p.40* ←

M. P.	M C	Location	Connection
0 00	0 00	Norton Jcn. South	
	0 33	Norton Jcn. West	
	3 71	Stillington	
	9 09	Bishop Middleham Jcn.	
10 72	10 72	Ferryhill South Jcn.	→ *ECML (North) KEY PLAN - p.26*
C.M.M.			
57 50	12 25	Kelloe Bank Foot Jcn. ECML	→ *See Above*
C.M.M.			
2 49	13 48	Tursdale Jcn. ECML	
6 29	17 28	Whitewell LC	
12 43	23 42	Fencehouses LC	
17 45	28 44	Usworth LC	VIA KEB → NCLE 29c more
19 76	30 75	Wardley Jcn.	
C.M.M.			
98 16	31 74	Pelaw Jcn.	→ *Newcastle/Hartlepool (43) - See Above*

M C	Location
0 00	Norton Jcn. East
0 29	Norton Jcn. West

NEWCASTLE - CARLISLE (B.R. Table 48)

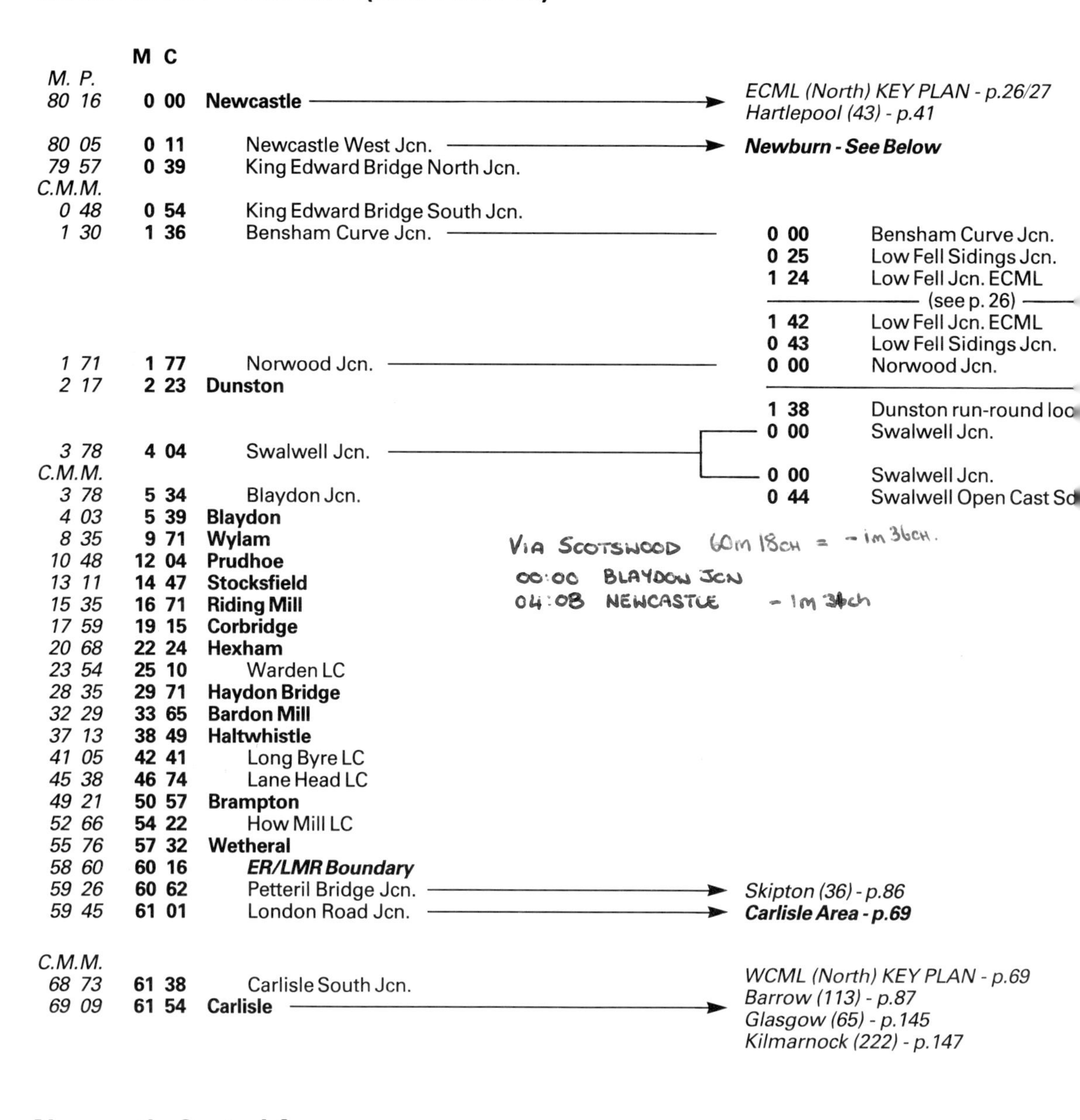

M. P.	M C	Location	Connections
80 16	0 00	**Newcastle**	*ECML (North) KEY PLAN - p.26/27* *Hartlepool (43) - p.41*
80 05	0 11	Newcastle West Jcn.	***Newburn - See Below***
79 57	0 39	King Edward Bridge North Jcn.	
C.M.M.			
0 48	0 54	King Edward Bridge South Jcn.	
1 30	1 36	Bensham Curve Jcn.	
1 71	1 77	Norwood Jcn.	
2 17	2 23	**Dunston**	
3 78	4 04	Swalwell Jcn.	
C.M.M.			
3 78	5 34	Blaydon Jcn.	
4 03	5 39	**Blaydon**	
8 35	9 71	**Wylam**	
10 48	12 04	**Prudhoe**	
13 11	14 47	**Stocksfield**	
15 35	16 71	**Riding Mill**	
17 59	19 15	**Corbridge**	
20 68	22 24	**Hexham**	
23 54	25 10	Warden LC	
28 35	29 71	**Haydon Bridge**	
32 29	33 65	**Bardon Mill**	
37 13	38 49	**Haltwhistle**	
41 05	42 41	Long Byre LC	
45 38	46 74	Lane Head LC	
49 21	50 57	**Brampton**	
52 66	54 22	How Mill LC	
55 76	57 32	**Wetheral**	
58 60	60 16	***ER/LMR Boundary***	
59 26	60 62	Petteril Bridge Jcn.	*Skipton (36) - p.86*
59 45	61 01	London Road Jcn.	***Carlisle Area - p.69***
C.M.M.			
68 73	61 38	Carlisle South Jcn.	*WCML (North) KEY PLAN - p.69*
69 09	61 54	**Carlisle**	*Barrow (113) - p.87* *Glasgow (65) - p.145* *Kilmarnock (222) - p.147*

M C	Location
0 00	Bensham Curve Jcn.
0 25	Low Fell Sidings Jcn.
1 24	Low Fell Jcn. ECML
	(see p. 26)
1 42	Low Fell Jcn. ECML
0 43	Low Fell Sidings Jcn.
0 00	Norwood Jcn.

M C	Location
1 38	Dunston run-round loo
0 00	Swalwell Jcn.

M C	Location
0 00	Swalwell Jcn.
0 44	Swalwell Open Cast Sc

VIA SCOTSWOOD 60m 18ch = -1m 36ch.
00:00 BLAYDON JCN
04:08 NEWCASTLE -1m 36ch

Newcastle Central Area

M C	M C	Location
	0 00	**Newcastle**
From	0 14	Newcastle East Jcn.
Park	0 40	High Level Bridge Jcn.
Lane	0 56	Greensfield Jcn.
0 62	0 70	King Edward Bge. E. Jcn.
0 75	1 03	King Edward Bge. N. Jcn.
1 23	1 31	Newcastle West Jcn.
1 34	1 42	**Newcastle**
29c MORE		
	0 00	Riverside Jcn. (p.27)
	1 08	St. Peters GF
	2 48	Walker Tunnel (South)
	4 29	Carville LC

M C	Location	M C
	(see p.41)	M C
	Park Lane Jcn.	0 0
	Greensfield Jcn.	0 4
0 70	K.E.B. East Jcn.	0 6
1 08	K.E.B. South Jcn.	1 0

M C	Location
0 00	Newcastle West Jcn.
2 77	Scotswood Tunnel (E.)
5 33	Newburn

Benton North - Bedlington - Morpeth Jcns.
Bedlington - Blythe & Lynemouth

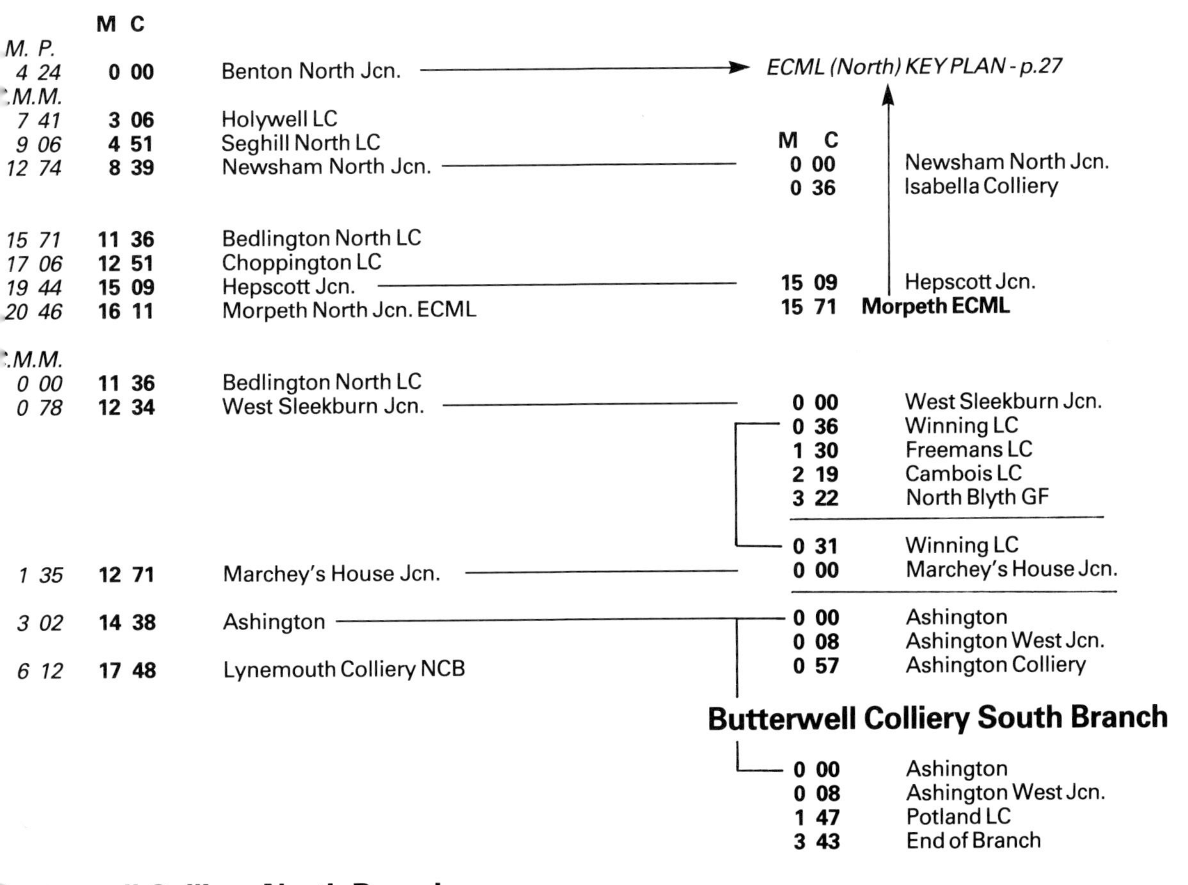

M C
M. P.
4 24 0 00 Benton North Jcn.
ECML (North) KEY PLAN - p.27
C.M.M.
7 41 3 06 Holywell LC
9 06 4 51 Seghill North LC
12 74 8 39 Newsham North Jcn.
M C
0 00 Newsham North Jcn.
0 36 Isabella Colliery
15 71 11 36 Bedlington North LC
17 06 12 51 Choppington LC
19 44 15 09 Hepscott Jcn.
20 46 16 11 Morpeth North Jcn. ECML
15 09 Hepscott Jcn.
15 71 Morpeth ECML
C.M.M.
0 00 11 36 Bedlington North LC
0 78 12 34 West Sleekburn Jcn.
0 00 West Sleekburn Jcn.
0 36 Winning LC
1 30 Freemans LC
2 19 Cambois LC
3 22 North Blyth GF
0 31 Winning LC
0 00 Marchey's House Jcn.
1 35 12 71 Marchey's House Jcn.
3 02 14 38 Ashington
6 12 17 48 Lynemouth Colliery NCB
0 00 Ashington
0 08 Ashington West Jcn.
0 57 Ashington Colliery
Butterwell Colliery South Branch
0 00 Ashington
0 08 Ashington West Jcn.
1 47 Potland LC
3 43 End of Branch

Butterwell Colliery North Branch

M C	
0 00	Butterwell Jcn. ECML
0 48	End of Branch

Callerton Branch

M C	
0 00	Benton North Jcn. (p.27)
0 34	Benton (T.W.M.)*
0 71	Four Lane Ends (T.W.M.)*
1 37	Long Benton (T.W.M.)*
1 65	Gosforth East Jcn.
2 47	Regent Centre East Jcn. (Gosforth West Jcn.)
2 54	Regent Centre (T.W.M.)*
3 21	Wansbeck Road (T.W.M.)*
3 47	Fawdon Station LC
4 49	Brunton Lane Jcn.
4 69	Bank Foot Jcn.
6 34	Callerton LC
7 00	Callerton I.C.I.

Tyne and Wear Metro - p.158

SECTION II - LONDON MIDLAND REGION

(a) Midland Main Line

ST. PANCRAS - DERBY & SHEFFIELD (B.R. Table 53)

KEY PLAN

M. P. / From Moorgate M C	M C	Location	Connection
0 00	0 00	**St. Pancras**	→ *Nottingham (53) - p.47*
	0 59	Dock Jcn. South	
	0 79	Camden Road Tunnels (South)	
	1 42	**Kentish Town**	→ *Moorgate (52) - See Below*
	1 70	Engine Shed Jcn.	
	2 13	Carlton Road Jcn.	→ ***Junction Road Jcn. - p.12***
	3 34	Belsize Tunnels (West)	
5 70	4 00	**West Hampstead Midland**	
6 79	5 09	**Cricklewood**	
7 09	5 19	Cricklewood Curve Jcn.	→ ***Dudding Hill Jcn. - p.54***
7 74	6 04	Brent Curve Jcn.	
8 69	6 79	**Hendon**	*Hertford North (24) - p.15*
9 62	7 72	Silkstream Jcn.	
11 18	9 28	**Mill Hill Broadway**	
13 28	11 38	Elstree Tunnels (South)	
14 25	12 35	**Elstree**	
17 07	15 17	**Radlett**	
21 61	19 71	**St. Albans City**	
26 41	24 51	**Harpenden**	
32 09	30 19	**Luton** (see below)	
34 45	32 55	**Leagrave**	
39 11	37 21	**Harlington**	
42 14	40 24	**Flitwick**	
44 09	42 19	Ampthill Tunnels (South)	
50 53	48 63	Kempston Road Jcns.	
51 06	49 16		
51 55	49 65	**Bedford Midland**	→ *Bletchley (64) - p.52*

M C	Location
0 00	**Moorgate**
0 35	**Barbican**
0 62	**Farringdon**
1 55	**Kings Cross Midland City**
3 40	**Kentish Town**
4 03	Carlton Road Jcn.
5 24	Belsize Tunnels (West)

(see left-hand column for mileages to Bedford)

M. P.	M C	Location	Connection
49 78	49 78	Bedford North Jcn.	
	56 45	Sharnbrook	
	59 00	Wymington Tunnel South (goods line only)	
	65 11	**Wellingborough**	
	68 22	Finedon Station	
	72 01	**Kettering**	
	74 46	Glendon South Jcn.	→ Corby line (see below)
	78 39	Desborough North	
	82 74	**Market Harborough**	
	86 42	East Langton	
	88 71	Kibworth	
	90 41	Wistow	
	93 70	Kilby Bridge	
	95 41	Wigston South Jcn.	→ ***Glen Parva Jcn. - p.46***
	95 71	Wigston North Jcn.	
	97 45	Knighton South Jcn.	→ ***Coalville - p.45***
99 07	99 07	**Leicester**	→ *Peterborough/Nuneaton (18) - p.46*

M. P.	M C	Location
74 46	0 00	Glendon South Jcn.
79 25	4 59	Corby North
82 01	7 35	Corby Tunnel (North)
87 30	12 64	Glaston Tunnel (South
90 18	15 52	Manton Jcn. (see p.46

M. P.	M C	Location
31 75	0 49	Vauxhall Sidings
32 32	0 12	Luton East Jcn.
C.M.M.		
30 12	0 07	Luton South Jcn.
30 19	0 00	**Luton**

M. P.	M C	Location
31 75	0 00	Vauxhall Sidings
32 32	0 37	Luton East Jcn.
32 43	0 48	Bute Street South
33 00	1 05	Bute Street North
34 45	2 50	Chaul Street LC
37 52	5 57	Portland Cement GF
37 78	6 03	Dunstable (buffer stop)

M. P.	M	C	Location	Connections
0 00	0	00	**St. Pancras**	
	99	07	**Leicester**	
	103	78	Syston South Jcn.	
	104	25	Syston North Jcn.	→ ***Syston East Jcn. - p.46***
	108	19	Mountsorrel GF	
	111	22	Loughborough Chord Jcn.	→ ***Hotchley Hill - See Below***
	111	46	**Loughborough**	
	118	36	Ratcliffe Jcn.	
	119	16	Trent South Jcn.	→ ***Toton - p.47*** *Nottingham (53) - p.47* *Trent East Jcn. - p.47*
	119	58	Sheet Stores Jcn.	→ ***Stenson Jcn. - p.48***
	120	28	**Long Eaton**	
22 19	122	19	Draycott GF	
M.M.	125	67	**Spondon**	
27 54	128	23	London Road Jcn.	*Sinfin (54) - p.49*
27 68	128	37	**Derby**	→ *Birmingham (80) - p.49* *Crewe (80) - p.63*
29 06	129	55	St. Mary's North Jcn.	
31 06	131	55	Little Eaton Jcn.	→ ***Denby - p.49***
32 79	133	48	Duffield Jcn.	→ ***Wirksworth - p.49***
33 08	133	57	**Duffield**	
35 55	136	24	**Belper**	
37 61	138	30	Ambergate Jcn.	→ *Matlock (54) - p.49*
39 47	140	16	Wingfield Tunnel (South)	
46 21	146	70	Clay Cross Tunnel (South)	
M.M.				
42 10	148	38	Clay Cross South Jcn.	→ *Nottingham (53) - p.47*
42 31	148	59	Clay Cross North Jcn.	
44 15	150	43	***LMR/ER Boundary***	
46 20	152	48	**Chesterfield**	
46 59	153	07	Tapton Jcn.	→ ***Barrow Hill/Woodhouse - p.19***
51 44	157	72	**Dronfield**	
52 49	158	77	Bradway Tunnel (South)	
53 73	160	21	Dore South Jcn.	
54 50	160	78	Dore Station Jcn.	→ ***Dore West Jcn. - p.72***
58 40	164	68	**Sheffield**	→ *Retford (29) - p.18* *Doncaster (29) - p.22* *Leeds (34) - p.29* *York (34) - p.33* *Manchester (29) - p.72*

M. P.	M	C	Location	M. P.	Branch M C	Branch location
97 45	0	00	Knighton South Jcn. (see p.44)			
94 65	7	20	Desford LC			
2 13	14	48	Coalville Jcn.		0 00	Coalville Jcn.
3 05	15	40	Mantle Lane Sidings		0 62	Coalfields Farm GF
20 67	23	22	Moira West Jcn.			
24 20	26	55	Swadlincote GF		0 00	Swadlincote GF
25 17	27	52	Drakelow Curve East Jcn.		2 34	Cadley Hill GF
59 59	28	14	Drakelow Curve West Jcn.			
6 40	28	75	Birmingham Curve Jcn.	126 40	28 75	Birmingham Curve Jcn.
				127 19	29 54	Branston Jcn.
27 00	29	35	Leicester Curve Jcn.			→ *Derby/Birmingham (80) - p.49*

Great Central Railway

M	C	Location
0	00	**Loughborough Central**
2	20	**Quorn & Woodhouse**
5	40	**Rothley**
7	60	**Belgrave & Birstall** (proposed)

M	C	Location
0	00	Loughborough Chord Jcn.
3	00	East Leake Tunnel (S)
5	15	Hotchley Hill

PETERBOROUGH - LEICESTER - BIRMINGHAM (B.R. Table 18)

M. P.	M C	Location	Connections
79 29	**0 00**	**Peterborough**	*Ely/Norwich (18) - p.9* *ECML (South) KEY PLAN - p.14* *Spalding/Lincoln (19) - p.16*
79 34	**3 05**	Werrington Jcn.	
C.M.M.			
16 71	**5 42**	Helpston Jcn.	
12 75	**9 38**	Uffington LC	
10 11	**12 22**	**Stamford**	
6 60	**15 53**	Ketton LC	
6 14	**16 19**	***ER/LMR Boundary***	
4 11	**18 22**	Luffenham Jcn. LC	
C.M.M.			
90 23	**22 33**	Manton Jcn.	***Corby - p.44***
93 61	**25 71**	**Oakham**	
96 67	**28 77**	Ashwell LC	
101 53	**33 63**	Saxby Jcn.	
105 22	**37 32**	**Melton Mowbray**	
C.M.M.			
113 36	**38 00**	Melton Jcn.	(see branch below)
110 17	**41 19**	Frisby LC	
107 05	**44 31**	Rearsby LC	
104 22	**47 14**	Syston East Jcn.	(see branch below)
103 78	**47 38**	Syston South Jcn.	
99 07	**52 29**	**Leicester**	*St. Pancras/Sheffield (53) - p.45*
97 45	**53 71**	Knighton South Jcn.	***Coalville - p.45***
C.M.M.			
15 31	**55 45**	Wigston North Jcn.	
14 68	**56 08**	**South Wigston**	
14 57	**56 19**	Glen Parva Jcn.	(see branch below)
11 64	**59 12**	**Narborough**	
10 04	**60 72**	Croft Sidings	
4 00	**66 76**	**Hinckley**	
0 58	**70 18**	Midland Jcn. (see below)	
C.M.M.			
96 69	**70 74**	Nuneaton South Jcn.	
97 10	**71 15**	**Nuneaton**	*WCML (South) KEY PLAN - p.55*
C.M.M.			
10 18	**71 41**	Nuneaton North Jcn.	
9 59	**72 00**	Abbey Jcn.	(see Nuneaton flyover below)
6 55	**75 04**	Arley Tunnel (East)	
2 04	**79 55**	Daw Mill	
C.M.M.			
31 69	**81 59**	Whitacre Jcn.	***Kingsbury Jcn. - p.49***
34 43	**84 33**	Water Orton East Jcn.	*Derby (56) - p.49*
34 54	**84 44**	**Water Orton**	
35 15	**85 05**	Water Orton West Jcn.	***Park Lane Jcn. - p.62***
36 14	**86 04**	Castle Bromwich Jcn.	***Park Lane Jcn. - p.62***
38 18	**88 08**	Bromford Bridge	
40 60	**90 50**	Landor Street Jcn.	***St. Andrew's Jcn. - p.58***
41 26	**91 16**	Grand Jcn.	*Leamington (116) - p.58*
C.M.M.			
112 05	**91 27**	Proof House Jcn. (Derby lines)	
112 19	**91 41**	Proof House Jcn.	*Aston - p.59/60*
112 73	**92 15**	**Birmingham New Street**	*See p.57 for Table Refs.*

M. P.	M C	Location
105 70	**0 00**	Melton Jcn.
107 42	**1 52**	Holywell Jcn. GF (Sou
111 22	**5 32**	Old Dalby GF
116 58	**10 68**	Stanton Tunnel GF
120 29	**14 39**	Edwalton (end of line)

M C	Location
0 00	Syston East Jcn.
0 17	Syston North Jcn.

M C	Location
0 50	Wigston South Jcn.
0 00	Glen Parva Jcn.

Nuneaton flyover

M. P.	M C	Location
11 31	**70 18**	Midland Jcn.
9 59	**71 70**	Abbey Jcn.

(10 chains shorter)

T. PANCRAS - NOTTINGHAM & SHEFFIELD (B.R. Table 53)

M. P.	M C	Location	Connection
0 00	**0 00**	**St. Pancras** (see pp.44/45)	
	119 16	Trent South Jcn.	→ ***Toton - See Below***
	119 67	Trent East Jcn.	→ ***Sheet Stores Jcn. - See Below***
	121 02	Attenborough Jcn.	→ ***Meadow Lane Jcn. - See Below***
	121 70	**Attenborough**	
	123 22	**Beeston**	
5 27	**125 27**	Lenton South Jcn.	→ ***Lenton North Jcn. - See Below***
M.M.			
4 22	**125 64**	Mansfield Jcn.	*Grantham (27) - p.48*
3 39	**126 47**	**Nottingham** *(REV.)*	→ *Newark (30) - p.48*
3 39	**0 00**	**Nottingham**	
4 22	**0 63**	Mansfield Jcn.	**0 27** Lenton South Jcn.
4 56	**1 17**	Lenton North Jcn.	**0 00** Lenton North Jcn.
5 55	**2 16**	Radford Jcn.	→ ***Linby/Calverton - p.48***
M.M.			
5 09	**7 17**	Trowell Jcn. (see below)	
7 31	**9 39**	Bennerley Jcn. GF	
9 69	**11 77**	**Langley Mill**	
2 76	**15 04**	Codnor Park Jcn.	
33 30	**15 38)**	(Riddings Jcn.)	

Midland Railway Centre

M. P.	M C	Location
132 76	**0 00**	Codnor Park Jcn.
133 19	**0 23**	Ironville Jcn.
133 26	**0 30**	**Ironville**
135 07	**2 11**	**Swanwick Junction**
135 57	**2 61**	**Butterley**
136 05	**3 09**	**Hammersmith**
136 13	**3 17**	End of line

is proposed to relay the curve from Ironville Jcn. to Riddings Jcn. (25 ains) and continue M.R.C. passenger services to a B.R. interchange sta- on at Pye Bridge (M.P. 133 32). A further station (Golden Valley Halt) is also anned between Ironville and Swanwick Junction at M.P. 134 20.

M. P.	M C	Location	Connection
3 69	**15 77**	Pye Bridge Jcn.	→ ***Shirebrook - p.20***
6 07	**18 15**	**Alfreton & Mansfield Parkway**	
6 67	**18 75**	Blackwell South Jcn.	
7 13	**19 21**	Tibshelf & Blackwell Branch Jcn.	→ ***Sutton Colliery - p.48***
2 10	**24 18**	Clay Cross South Jcn.	→ *Derby (53) - p.45*
2 31	**24 39**	Clay Cross North Jcn.	
4 15	**26 23**	***LMR/ER Boundary***	
6 20	**28 28**	**Chesterfield**	
6 59	**28 67**	Tapton Jcn.	→ *Barrow Hill/Woodhouse - p.19*
1 44	**33 52**	**Dronfield**	
2 49	**34 57**	Bradway Tunnel (South)	
3 73	**36 01**	Dore South Jcn.	
4 50	**36 58**	Dore Station Jcn.	→ ***Dore West Jcn. - p.72***
8 40	**40 48**	**Sheffield**	→ *Retford (29) - p.18* *Doncaster (29) - p.22* *Leeds (34) - p.29* *York (34) - p.33* *Manchester (29) - p.72*

M. P.	M C	Location	Connection
9 16	**0 00**	Trent South Jcn.	
9 69	**0 53**	Trent East Jcn.	
0 53	**1 37**	Long Eaton Town LC	
1 26	**2 10**	Toton Jcn. (see below)	
1 64	**2 48**	Toton Centre	
3 73	**4 57**	Stanton Gate SF	
5 09	**5 73**	Trowell Jcn.	→ *Sheffield (53) - See Above*

M C	Location
0 00	Sheet Stores Jcn. (see p.45)
0 41*	Trent East Jcn.
0 43* *	Trent East Jcn.

*** to Nottingham Line**
**** to Toton line**

M C	Location
0 00	Stanton Gate SF
3 13	West Hallam Colliery

Toton flyover line

M. P.	M C	Location	Connection
9 16	**0 00**	Trent South Jcn.	
0 55	**1 39**	Meadow Lane Jcn.	**0 00** Meadow Lane Jcn.
1 36	**2 20**	Toton Jcn.	

M C	Location
0 62	Attenborough Jcn. ↑
0 00	Meadow Lane Jcn.

NOTTINGHAM - GRANTHAM (B.R. Table 27)

M. P.	M C	Station		Connection
123 39	**0 00**	**Nottingham**	→	*St. Pancras/Sheffield (53) - p.47*
C.M.M.				
0 00	**0 16**	Nottingham East Jcn.		
2 35	**2 51**	Netherfield Jcn.	→	*Newark (30) - See Below*
C.M.M.				
125 17	**2 78**	**Netherfield**	—	**0 00** Netherfield **2 14** Gedling Colliery
124 32	**3 63**	Colwick Estates GF	—	**0 00** Colwick Estates GF **0 39** Exchange Sidings **1 65** End of Branch
123 66	**4 29**	Rectory Jcn.	—	**0 00** Rectory Jcn. **1 63** Cotgrave Colliery
123 08	**5 07**	**Radcliffe**		
119 39	**8 56**	**Bingham**		
		(see page 17)		
105 38	**22 57**	**Grantham**		

NOTTINGHAM - NEWARK (B.R. Table 30)

M. P.	M C	Station		Connection
123 39	**0 00**	**Nottingham**	→	*St. Pancras/Sheffield (53) - p.47* *Grantham (27) - See Above*
C.M.M.				
0 00	**0 16**	Nottingham East Jcn.		
2 35	**2 51**	Netherfield Jcn.		
2 78	**3 14**	**Carlton**		
4 77	**5 13**	**Burton Joyce**		
7 27	**7 43**	**Lowdham**		
9 45	**9 61**	**Thurgarton**		
10 55	**10 71**	**Bleasby**		
12 46	**12 62**	**Fiskerton**		
13 13	**13 29**	**Rolleston**		
14 20	**14 36**	Staythorpe Crossing LC		
16 32	**16 48**	***LMR/ER Boundary***		
16 78	**17 14**	**Newark Castle**	→	*Lincoln (30) - p.18*

M. P.	M C	Location		Connection
125 55	**0 00**	Radford Jcn.	→	*Nottingham/Trent - p.47*
127 60	**0 05**	Lincoln Street Crossing LC		
129 35	**3 60**	Bulwell Forest Crossing LC		
130 06	**4 31**	Bestwood Park Jcn.	—	*M. P.* *130 06* **4 31** Bestwood Park Jcn. *136 60* **11 05** Calverton Colliery
131 32	**5 57**	Hucknall Colliery Sidings		
132 24	**6 49**	Linby Colliery Sidings		
132 69	**7 14**	Linby LC		

M. P.	M C	Location		Connection
137 13	**0 00**	Tibshelf & Blackwell Branch Jcn.	→	*Toton/Nottingham - p.47*
140 34	**3 21**	Sutton Colliery Jcn.		
141 74	**4 61**	Sutton Colliery		

M. P.	M C	Location		Connection
119 58	**0 00**	Sheet Stores Jcn.	→	*Toton/Nottingham - p.47*
123 23	**3 45**	Castle Donington		
132 12	**12 34**	Stenson Jcn.	→	*Birmingham (56) - p.49*

ERBY - BIRMINGHAM (B.R. Table 80)

1. P.	M C		M. P.	M C	
					St. Pancras/Sheffield (53) - p.45
7 68	0 00	**Derby** →			*Crewe (80) - p.63*
M.M.					*Matlock (54) - See Below*
0 00	0 14	London Road Jcn.			
1 16	1 30	**Peartree**			
1 27	1 41	Melbourne Jcn.	131 15	1 41	Melbourne Jcn.
			130 73	1 63	**Sinfin North**
			130 37	2 19	**Sinfin Central**
			129 79	2 57	End of line
4 50	4 64	Stenson Jcn. →			***Sheet Stores Jcn. - p.48***
5 14	5 28	North Stafford Jcn.			
8 54	8 68	Clay Mills Jcn. LC			
0 67	11 01	**Burton on Trent**			
1 17	11 31	Leicester Curve Jcn. →			***Coalville - p.45***
2 15	12 29	Branston Jcn.			
6 30	16 44	Wichnor Jcn. →			***Lichfield - See Below***
9 40	19 54	Elford GF			
3 58	23 72	**Tamworth** (WCML - p.55)			
5 47	25 61	**Wilnecote**		4 39	Baddesley Colliery GF
8 26	28 40	Kingsbury SF		0 00	Kingsbury SF
			M. P.		
9 39	29 53	Kingsbury Jcn.	29 39	29 53	Kingsbury Jcn.
M.M.			31 69	32 03	Whitacre Jcn.
4 43	33 37	Water Orton East Jcn.	34 43	34 57	Water Orton East Jcn.
4 54	33 48	**Water Orton**			
M.M.		(see p.46)			
2 73	41 19	**Birmingham New Street** →			*See p.57 for Table Refs*

ERBY - MATLOCK (B.R. Table 54)

1. P.	M C		M. P.	M C	
7 68	0 00	**Derby**			
9 06	1 18	St. Mary's North Jcn. North			
1 06	3 18	Little Eaton Jcn.	131 06	0 00	Little Eaton Jcn.
			135 46	4 40	Denby North LC
2 79	5 11	Duffield Jcn.	132 79	0 00	Duffield Jcn.
3 08	5 20	**Duffield**	133 08	0 09	Duffield
			138 08	5 09	Iridgehay LC
			141 21	8 22	Wirksworth
			141 45	8 46	Wirksworth Incline GF
			142 01	9 02	Wirksworth Incline
5 55	7 67	**Belper**			
7 61	9 73	Ambergate Jcn. →			*Sheffield (53) - p.45*
8 18	10 30	**Ambergate**			
0 13	12 25	**Whatstandwell**			
3 10	15 22	**Cromford**			
3 73	16 05	**Matlock Bath**			
5 00	17 12	**Matlock**			

1. P.	M C		M C	
3 25	0 00	Wichnor Jcn. (see above)		
1 16	2 09	Rodidge LC		
9 74	3 31	Brookhay LC		
8 15	5 10	Lichfield T.V. Jcn.	0 00	Lichfield T.V. Jcn.
			0 19	High Level Goods Loop Jcn. (see p.55)
6 61	6 44	**Lichfield City** →		*Birmingham/Redditch (55) - p.59*

SECTION II - LONDON MIDLAND REGION

(b) West London & Outer Suburbs

MARYLEBONE - BANBURY (B.R. Table 115)

M. P.	M C	Location	Connections
205 77	**0 00**	**Marylebone**	
204 40	**1 37**	St. John's Wood Tunnel (North)	
C.M.M.			
6 31	**5 11**	Neasden South Jcn. →	*Aylesbury (114) - p.51* ***Neasden Jcn. - p.54***
5 00	**6 42**	**Wembley Complex**	
3 52	**7 70**	**Sudbury and Harrow Road**	
2 57	**8 67**	**Sudbury Hill, Harrow**	
1 57	**9 67**	**Northolt Park**	
0 09	**11 35**	Northolt Jcn. East	
0 00	**11 42**	Northolt Jcn. →	*Paddington (115) - p.92*
C.M.M.			
0 07	**11 49**	**South Ruislip**	
1 68	**13 30**	**West Ruislip**	
4 50	**16 12**	**Denham**	
5 42	**17 04**	**Denham Golf Club**	
7 18	**18 60**	**Gerrards Cross**	
9 74	**21 36**	**Seer Green**	
11 41	**23 03**	**Beaconsfield**	
13 12	**24 54**	Whitehouse Tunnel (East)	
16 29	**27 71**	**High Wycombe**	
21 27	**32 69**	**Saunderton**	
24 50	**36 12**	**Princes Risborough** →	***Chinnor/Thame - See opposite pag***; Aylesbury branch (below)
C.M.M.			
0 00	**45 31**	Former Ashendon Jcn.	
2 29	**47 60**	Brill Tunnel (South)	
9 27	**54 58**	**Bicester**	
15 13	**60 44**	Ardley Tunnel (South)	
C.M.M.			
81 12	**63 60**	Aynho Jcn.	
82 55	**65 23**	**Kings Sutton**	
86 16	**68 64**	**Banbury** →	*Birmingham (116) - p.58* *Paddington (116) - p.93*

C.M.M.	M C	Location
42 33	**36 12**	**Princes Risborough**
43 57	**37 36**	**Monks Risborough**
45 14	**38 73**	**Little Kimble**
C.M.M.		
38 08	**43 14**	Aylesbury South
38 13	**43 19**	**Aylesbury** ↓ *Marylebone (114) - p.51*

Princes Risborough. The signalbox controlling movements onto the Chinnor/Thame branches (going off behind the box) appears behind 25178 as it rolls into the down platform, having arrived light engine from Aylesbury on the 14th October 1980. *(A.O. Wynn).*

MARYLEBONE - AYLESBURY (B.R. Table 114) & Bletchley

M. P.	M C		
5 77	0 00	**Marylebone**	
4 40	1 37	St John's Wood Tunnel (North)	
0 66	5 11	Neasden South Jcn.	→ *Banbury (115) - p.50*
M.M.			
9 13	8 72	***LMR/L.R.T. Boundary***	
9 18	8 77	Harrow on the Hill South Jcn.	
9 39	9 18	**Harrow on the Hill**	
0 08	9 67	Harrow North Jcn.	
5 28	15 07	**Moor Park**	
6 28	16 07	Watford South Jcn.	
6 57	16 36	Watford North Jcn.	
7 37	17 16	**Rickmansworth**	
9 53	19 32	**Chorley Wood**	
1 67	21 46	**Chalfont & Latimer**	
3 70	23 49	**Amersham**	
5 21	25 00	***L.R.T./LMR Boundary***	
9 00	28 59	**Great Missenden**	
3 55	33 34	**Wendover**	
5 75	35 54	**Stoke Mandeville**	
8 08	37 67	Aylesbury South	→ *Princes Risborough (115) - p.50*
8 13	37 72	**Aylesbury**	
M.M.			
1 50	44 27	Quainton Road	
7 63	48 14	Calvert GFs	
7 05	48 72		
M.M.			
2 57	49 46	Claydon L.N.E. Jcn.	→ ***Oxford - See Below***
1 18	51 05	Claydon LC	
2 78	59 25	Swanbourne Sidings	
M.M.			
0 68	62 27	Bletchley flyover summit	— **62 27** Bletchley flyover summit **63 30** Denbigh Hall South Jcn. ↓ *WCML KEY PLAN - p.55*
M.M.			
0 76	63 07	Fenny Stratford Flyover Jcn.	
1 13	63 24	**Fenny Stratford**	→ *Bedford (64) - p.52*

M. P.	M C		
	0 00	Fenny Stratford Flyover Jcn.	**0 00** Denbigh Hall South Jcn.
	0 60	Bletchley flyover summit	— **1 03** Bletchley flyover summit
2 78	3 62	Swanbourne Sidings	
1 18	12 02	Claydon LC	
2 57	13 41	Claydon L.N.E. Jcn.	→ ***Aylesbury - See Above***
7 12	17 76	Launton LC	
8 00	18 64	***LMR/WR Boundary***	
9 31	20 15	Bicester London Road LC	
9 71	20 55	Central Ordnance Depot GF	
5 22	26 06	Islip GF	
7 54	28 38	Banbury Road GF	
M.M.			
4 45	30 73	Oxford North Jcn.	
3 41	31 77	**Oxford**	→ *Paddington/Banbury (116) - p.93* *Worcester/Hereford (126) - p.94*

M C		M C	
0 00	**Princes Risborough**	0 00	**Princes Risborough**
2 65	Wain Hall LC	1 48	Bledlow LC
3 57	Chinnor	5 60	Thame

BLETCHLEY - BEDFORD MIDLAND (B.R. Table 64)

M. P.	M C	Location	Connection
46 46	0 00	**Bletchley**	→ *WCML (South) KEY PLAN - p.55*
C.M.M.			
0 76	1 00	Fenny Stratford Flyover Jcn.	→ ***Aylesbury/Oxford - p.51***
1 13	1 17	**Fenny Stratford**	
2 05	2 09	**Bow Brickhill**	
4 11	4 15	**Woburn Sands**	
5 06	5 10	**Aspley Guise**	
6 60	6 64	**Ridgmont**	
8 52	8 56	**Lidlington**	
10 02	10 06	**Millbrook**	
11 18	11 22	**Stewartby**	
11 74	11 78	Forders Sidings	
12 76	13 00	**Kempston Hardwick**	
16 03	16 07	**Bedford St. Johns**	
C.M.M.			
49 65	16 67	**Bedford Midland**	→ *St. Pancras/Sheffield (53) - p.44*

WATFORD JUNCTION - ST. ALBANS ABBEY (B.R. Table 61)

M. P.	M C	Location
0 15	0 00	**Watford Junction** (Platform 11)
0 78	0 63	**Watford North**
1 66	1 51	**Garston**
3 37	3 22	**Bricket Wood**
5 02	4 67	**Park Street**
6 45	6 30	**St. Albans Abbey**

WATFORD JUNCTION - CROXLEY GREEN (B.R. Table 62)

M. P.	M C	Location	Connection
17 58	0 00	**Watford Junction**	→ *WCML (South) KEY PLAN - p.55* *Euston (59) - p.53*
16 67	0 71	**Watford High Street**	
C.M.M.			
0 08	1 03	Watford High Street Jcn.	
0 14	1 09	Croxley Green Jcn.	— 0 00 Croxley Green Jcn. 0 23 Croxley Green Depot
C.M.M.			
17 07	1 52	Watford Stadium	
17 32	1 77	**Watford West**	
18 09	2 54	**Croxley Green**	

BROAD STREET - CAMDEN JCN. (formerly B.R. Tables 58/59)

M. P.	M C	Location	Connection
0 00	0 00	**Broad Street** - see note p.53	
	1 79	**Dalston Junction**	
	2 21	Dalston Western Jcn.	→ *Liverpool Street (58) - p.12*
	2 70	**Canonbury**	→ *North Woolwich (6/58) - p.12*
	3 11	Canonbury Jcn.	→ ***Finsbury Park - p.15***
	3 36	**Highbury & Islington**	
	3 74	**Caledonian Road & Barnsbury**	
	4 64	Camden Road East Jcn.	→ ***Freight Terminal Jcn. - p.15***
	5 01	**Camden Road**	→ *Richmond (58) - p.53*
	5 09	Camden Road Jcn.	
	5 49	**Primrose Hill**	
5 79	5 79	Camden Jcn.	→ *Watford Jcn. (58/59) - p.53*

USTON - WATFORD JUNCTION (B.R. Tables 58 & 59)

via D.C. Lines

M C (from Liverpool Street)	M C			M C	
	0 00	**Euston** (see p.55)		0 00	**Liverpool Street** (see p.12)
				6 40	**Camden Road**
	0 62	Park Street Tunnels (South)		6 48	Camden Road Jcn.
				7 08	**Primrose Hill**
	1 54	Camden Jcn.	———	7 38	Camden Jcn.
8 08	2 24	Primrose Hill Tunnel (West)			
8 17	2 33	**South Hampstead**			
8 65	3 01	**Kilburn High Road**			
9 39	3 55	**Queens Park**			
10 25	4 41	**Kensal Green**			
				0 26	Kensal Green Jcn.
11 20	5 36	**Willesden Junction L.L.**	———	0 00	**Willesden Junction L.L.**
11 72	6 08	**Harlesden**			
12 68	7 04	**Stonebridge Park**			
13 73	8 09	**Wembley Central**			
14 53	8 69	**North Wembley**			
15 19	9 35	**South Kenton**			
16 08	10 24	**Kenton**			
17 14	11 30	**Harrow & Wealdstone**			
18 29	12 45	**Headstone Lane**			
19 09	13 25	**Hatch End**			
20 41	14 57	**Carpenders Park**			
21 68	16 04	**Bushey**			
22 39	16 55	Watford High Street Jcn.	——→		*Croxley Green (62) - p.52*
22 51	16 67	**Watford High Street**			
23 42	17 58	**Watford Junction**	——→		*St. Albans Abbey (61) - p.52* *WCML (South) KEY PLAN - p.55*

Broad Street to Dalston Western Jcn. finally closed in July, 1986. Services from Watford Junction and Richmond (SR) have been diverted into Liverpool Street via the new Graham Road curve (Navarino Jcn. to Reading Lane Jcn. - see p.12).
The 0m. 00c shown for Broad Street on p.52 refers to the original buffer stops.

CHMOND (SR) - CAMDEN ROAD (B.R. Table 58)

	M C			M C	
M. P.					
2 39	0 00	**Richmond**	——→		*Waterloo/Reading (147) - p.115*
1 10	1 29	**Kew Gardens**			
0 05	2 34	**Gunnersbury**			
M.M.					
3 12	2 43	***SR/LMR Boundary***			
2 63	2 72	Bollo Lane Jcn. LC			
2 52	3 03	South Acton Jcn.	——→		***Kew East Jcn. - p.54***
2 48	3 07	**South Acton**			
1 70	3 65	**Acton Central**			***West London Jcn.***
0 65	4 70	Acton Wells Jcn.	——→		***Acton East Jcn. - p.54***
M.M.					***Cricklewood***
0 34	5 12	Former Old Oak Jcn.			
M.M.					
5 48	5 46	Willesden High Level Jcn.	——→		***Mitre Bridge Jcn. - p.54***
5 39	5 55	**Willesden Junction H.L.**			
				1 00	Willesden Jcn. (see p.54)
5 17	5 77	Kensal Green Jcn.	———	0 00	Kensal Green Jcn.
4 41	6 53	**Kensal Rise**			
3 71	7 23	**Brondesbury Park**			
3 36	7 58	**Brondesbury**			
2 75	8 19	**West Hampstead**			
2 44	8 50	**Finchley Road**			
1 53	9 41	**Hampstead Heath**			
1 15	9 79	Gospel Oak Jcn.	———	9 79	Gospel Oak Jcn.
1 10	10 04	**Gospel Oak**		10 02	**Gospel Oak** ↓
0 42	10 52	**Kentish Town West**			
M.M.					*Barking (2) - p.12*
5 09	11 15	Camden Road Jcn.			
5 01	11 23	**Camden Road**	——→		*Liverpool St. (58) - p.12* *N. Woolwich (6/58) - p.12*

West London Freight Lines

1. Kew East Jcn. - Willesden, Neasden & Cricklewood

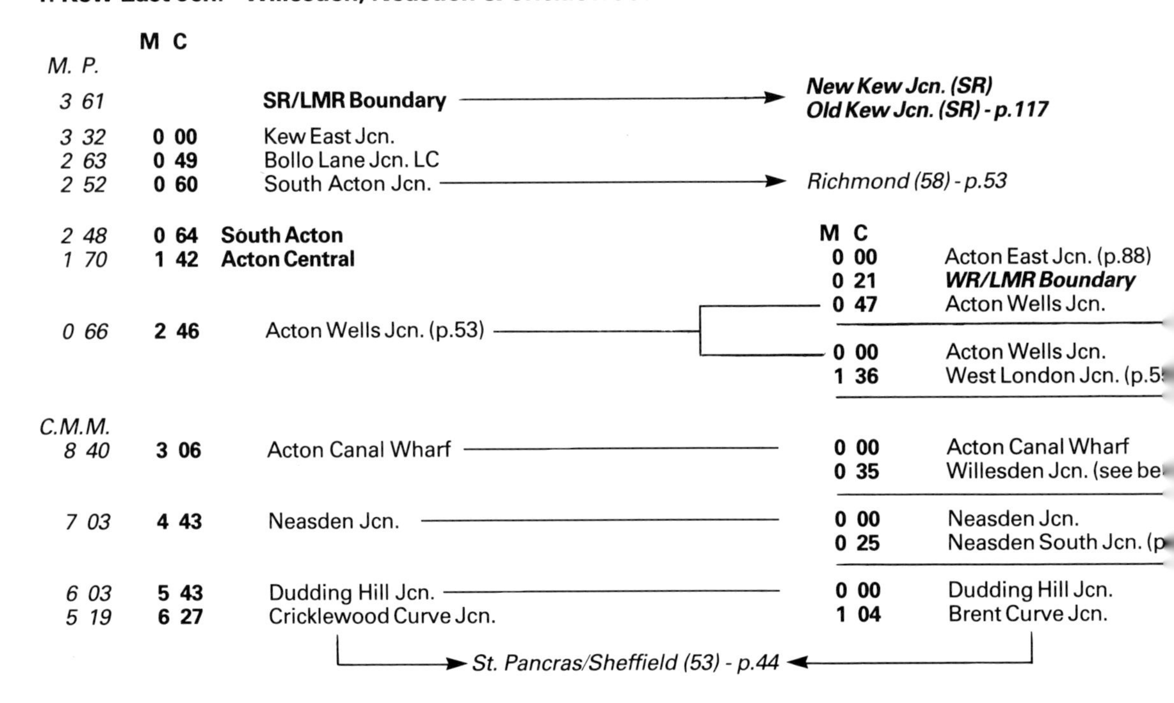

M. P.	M C	Location	Connection
3 61		**SR/LMR Boundary**	→ ***New Kew Jcn. (SR)*** ***Old Kew Jcn. (SR) - p.117***
3 32	**0 00**	Kew East Jcn.	
2 63	**0 49**	Bollo Lane Jcn. LC	
2 52	**0 60**	South Acton Jcn.	→ *Richmond (58) - p.53*
2 48	**0 64**	**South Acton**	
1 70	**1 42**	**Acton Central**	
0 66	**2 46**	Acton Wells Jcn. (p.53)	
C.M.M.			
8 40	**3 06**	Acton Canal Wharf	
7 03	**4 43**	Neasden Jcn.	
6 03	**5 43**	Dudding Hill Jcn.	
5 19	**6 27**	Cricklewood Curve Jcn.	→ *St. Pancras/Sheffield (53) - p.44*

M C	Location
0 00	Acton East Jcn. (p.88)
0 21	***WR/LMR Boundary***
0 47	Acton Wells Jcn.
0 00	Acton Wells Jcn.
1 36	West London Jcn. (p.5
0 00	Acton Canal Wharf
0 35	Willesden Jcn. (see be
0 00	Neasden Jcn.
0 25	Neasden South Jcn. (p
0 00	Dudding Hill Jcn.
1 04	Brent Curve Jcn. → *St. Pancras/Sheffield (53) - p.44*

2. Kensington Olympia - Old Oak & Willesden

M. P.	M C	Location	Connection
2 54	**0 00**	**Kensington Olympia**	→ ***Stewarts Lane - p.118*** *Brighton Lines - p.118* *Clapham Junction (149) - p.116*
0 66	**1 68**	North Pole Jcn.	
0 29	**2 25**	Mitre Bridge Jcn.	
C.M.M.			
5 23	**2 54**	West London Jcn.	
5 65	**3 16**	Willesden Jcn. WCML - p.55	

M C	Location
1 68	North Pole Jcn.
2 13	***LMR/WR Boundary***
2 38	Old Oak East Jcn. - p.8
2 25	Mitre Bridge Jcn.
2 68	Willesden H.L. Jcn. - p

3. Willesden Jcns., Carriage Sidings - Wembley Central

M. P.	M C	Location	Connection
5 65*	**0 00**	Willesden Jcn. WCML - p.55	
5 72*	**0 07**	Willesden Jcn.	→ ***Acton Canal Wharf - See Above***
5 73*			
C.M.M.			
0 72	**0 08**	Willesden Jcn.	
1 33	**0 49**	High Level Sidings	
2 00	**1 16**	Willesden Carriage Sidings South	
2 50	**1 66**	Willesden Carriage Sidings North	
C.M.M.			
7 28	**2 14**	Wembley Central WCML	
8 04	**2 70**	**Wembley Central**	

M. P.	Location
6 01*	Willesden Jcn.
5 01	Kensal Green Jcn. - p.!

*** Note different mileages**

SECTION II - LONDON MIDLAND REGION

(c) West Coast Main Line (South)

USTON - CREWE (B.R. Table 65)

KEY PLAN

M.P.	M C	Location	Connections
0 00	**0 00**	**Euston**	
	0 62	Park Street Tunnels (South)	
	1 36	Camden Jcns.	*Watford Jcn.* (59) - p.53
	1 54		*Primrose Hill* (59) - p.53
	2 27	Primrose Hill Tunnels (West)	
	4 45	Kensal Green Tunnels (East)	
	5 23	West London Jcn.	***Acton Wells Jcn. - p.54*** ***Mitre Bridge Jcn. - p.54***
	5 65	Willesden Jcn.	***Acton Canal Wharf - p.54*** ***Kensal Green Jcn. - p.54***
	6 41	Brent Sidings	
	8 04	**Wembley Central**	
	11 30	**Harrow & Wealdstone**	
	15 79	**Bushey**	
	17 35	**Watford Junction**	*Euston (59) - p.53* *St. Albans Abbey (61) - p.52* *Croxley Green (62) - p.52*
	19 40	F.L. Watford Tunnels (North)	
	19 42	**S.L.**	
	20 74	**Kings Langley**	
	23 06	**Apsley**	
	24 39	**Hemel Hempstead**	
	27 75	**Berkhamsted**	
	31 53	**Tring**	
	36 08	**Cheddington**	
	40 14	**Leighton Buzzard**	
	46 46	**Bletchley**	*Bedford (64) - p.52*
	47 52	Denbigh Hall South Jcn.	***Aylesbury/Bicester - p.51***
	49 65	**Milton Keynes**	
	52 33	**Wolverton**	
	56 47	Hanslope Jcn.	*Northampton (66) - p.57*
	61 74	Milton LC	
	64 43	Banbury Lane LC	
	68 09	Stowe Hill Tunnel (South)	
	76 64	Kilsby Tunnel (South)	
	82 26	Rugby South Jcn.	*Northampton (66) - p.57*
	82 40	**Rugby**	*Birmingham (65/66) - p.57*
	83 18	Trent Valley Jcn.	***Southam - p.57***
	96 68	Nuneaton South Jcns.	***Coventry - p.57***
	96 69		*Leicester (18) - p.46*
	97 10	**Nuneaton**	
	97 36	Nuneaton North Jcn.	*Birmingham (18) - p.46*
	102 17	**Atherstone**	
	106 37	**Polesworth**	
	110 12	**Tamworth L.L.**	*Derby/B'ham (80) - p.49*
	116 23	**Lichfield Trent Valley**	
	116 28	High Level Goods Loop Jcn.	***Lichfield T.V. Jcn. - p.49***
	124 22	**Rugeley**	
	124 39	Rugeley North Jcn.	***Walsall - p.60***
	127 08	Colwich Jcn.	*Stoke (65) - p.62*
	130 47	Whitehouse Jcn.	
	133 32	Stafford No. 4	*Wolverhampton (69) - p.62*
3 43	**133 43**	**Stafford**	

 KEY PLAN

M. P.	M C		
0 00	0 00	**Euston**	
	133 43	**Stafford**	
	138 72	**Norton Bridge**	
	139 00	Norton Bridge North Jcn.	→ *Stoke (69) - p.62*
	149 74	Madeley Jcn.	→ ***Silverdale/Holditch - See Below***
	156 16	Basford Hall Jcn.	→ ***Independent Lines - See Below***
	157 60	Crewe South Jcn.	
158 00	158 00	**Crewe**	→ *Stoke/Derby (80) - p.63* *Shrewsbury (87) - p.66* *Chester/Holyhead (83) - p.67* *WCML (North) KEY PLAN - p.68*

Crewe Independent Lines

M. P.	M C		M. P.
156 16	0 00	Basford Hall Jcn. (see above)	
156 41	0 25	Sorting Sidings South	
157 24	1 08	Sorting Sidings North	157 24 157 60
157 64	1 48	Salop Goods Jcn.	157 64 158 26
157 71	1 55	Salop Goods Jcn.	
157 73	1 57	Salop Goods Jcn.	157 73
158 16	2 00	Tunnel Entrance South	158 16 158 58
158 76	2 60	Sydney Bridge Jcn.	→ *Manchester Picc. (81) - p.70*

Stoke (80) - p.63 ↑

M C	
0 00	North Stafford Jcn.
1 04	Sorting Sidings Sth.

M C	
1 08	Sorting Sidings Nth.
1 44	Gresty Lane Jcn.

↓ *Shrewsbury (87) - p.66*

Chester Independent Lines

M C	
1 44	Salop Goods Jcn.
2 06	Crewe North Jcn.

↓ *Chester (83) - p.66*

Salop Lines

M C	
0 00	Gresty Lane Jcn.
0 37	Salop Goods Jcn.

Liverpool Independent Lines

M C	
1 57	Salop Goods Jcn.
2 00	Tunnel Entrance Sth.
2 42	Crewe Coal Yard

↓ *WCML (North) KEY PLAN - p.68*

C.M.M.	M C	
	0 00	Madeley Jcn.
7 36	0 28	Madeley Chord Jcn.
5 61	2 03	Keele Tunnel (South)
4 32	3 32	Silverdale Tunnel (South)
3 45	4 19	Silverdale
2 01	5 63	Apedale Jcn.
C.M.M.		
0 00	5 66	Apedale LC
0 31	6 17	Holditch Colliery

USTON - BIRMINGHAM & WOLVERHAMPTON (B.R. Tables 65/66/69)

M. P.	M C	Location	Connection
0 00	**0 00**	**Euston**	
		(see p.55)	
	56 47	Hanslope Jcn.	→ Northampton line (below)
	82 26	Rugby South Jcn.	→
	82 40	**Rugby**	→
	83 10	Trent Valley Jcns.	
	83 18	Trent Valley Jcns.	
	93 71	Leamington Jcn.	
	93 79	**Coventry**	→ *Leamington/Banbury (116) - p.58*
	94 19	Nuneaton Jcn.	→ Nuneaton line (below)
	95 28	**Canley**	
	97 40	**Tile Hill**	
	99 36	**Berkswell**	
	102 61	**Hampton-in-Arden**	
	104 55	**Birmingham International**	
	106 33	**Marston Green**	
	108 00	**Lea Hall**	
	109 08	**Stechford**	
	109 12	Stechford North Jcn.	→ Aston line (below)
	110 79	**Adderley Park**	
	111 72	Grand Jcn.	→ Curzon Street (below)
12 19	**112 19**	Proof House Jcn.	
.M.M.			
0 05	**112 73**	**Birmingham New Street**	→ *Peterborough (18) - p.46*; *Derby (80) - p.49*; *Banbury (116) - p.58*; *Stratford-upon-Avon (71) - p.58*; *Lichfield/Redditch (55) - p.59/60*; *Walsall (70) - p.60*; *Kidderminster (67) - p.61*; *Bristol (131) - p.95*
0 19	**113 07**	New St. North Tunnel (East)	
2 06	**114 74**	Soho South Jcn.	→ Soho loop (below)
2 38	**115 26**	Soho North Jcn.	→
3 30	**116 18**	**Smethwick Rolfe Street**	
3 64	**116 52**	Galton Jcn.	→ *Kidderminster (67) - p.61*
5 33	**118 21**	**Sandwell & Dudley**	
7 29	**120 17**	**Dudley Port**	
8 16	**121 04**	**Tipton**	
8 45	**121 33**	Bloomfield Jcn.	
9 46	**122 34**	**Coseley**	
12 60	**125 48**	Crane Street Jcn.	→ ***Portobello Jcn. - p.62***
12 69	**125 57**	**Wolverhampton**	→ *Stafford (69) - p.62*; *Shewsbury (74) - p.64*

M C	Location
56 47	Hanslope Jcn.
64 00	Huntsbury Hill Tunnel (Sth.)
65 68	**Northampton**
75 37	**Long Buckby**
78 27	Watford Lodge Tunnel (Sth.)
84 53	Rugby South Jcn.
84 67	**Rugby**
0 00	Nuneaton Jcn.
3 20	Three Spires Jcn.
4 71	Hawkesbury Lane LC
9 53	Nuneaton South Jcn.
9 75	**Nuneaton**

↓ *WCML (South) KEY PLAN - p.55*

M C	Location
0 00	Stechford North Jcn.
2 61	Aston (Stechford Jcn.)
2 69	**Aston** (see pp.59/60)
0 00	Grand Jcn.
0 17	Curzon Street
0 00	Soho South Jcn.
0 33	Soho East Jcn.
2 32	Perry Barr West Jcn.
2 71	Perry Barr North Jcn.
	(see p.60)
2 50	Perry Bar South Jcn.
2 21	Perry Bar West Jcn.
0 22	Soho East Jcn.
0 00	Soho North Jcn.

BANBURY - BIRMINGHAM (B.R. Table 116)

M. P.	M C	Station	Connection
*0 05**	0 05*	**Paddington** * see note - p.88 (see p.93)	
	75 21	**Heyford**	
	76 40	***WR/LMR Boundary***	
	81 12	Aynho Jcn.	→ *Marylebone (115) - p.50*
	82 55	**Kings Sutton**	
	86 16	**Banbury**	
	88 21	Little Bourton LC	
	92 25	Claydon Crossing	
	94 76	Fenny Compton	
	99 13	Greaves Sidings	
	106 25	**Leamington Spa**	→ Coventry line (below)
	108 02	**Warwick**	
	112 14	**Hatton**	→ *Stratford-on-Avon (71) - See Below*
	112 51	Hatton North Jcn.	
	116 31	**Lapworth**	
	118 75	**Dorridge**	
	120 66	**Widney Manor**	
	122 25	**Solihull**	
	124 11	**Olton**	
	125 08	**Acocks Green**	
	125 73	Tyseley South Jcn.	
	126 05	**Tyseley**	→ *Stratford (71) - p.59*
126 59	126 59	Small Heath South Jcn.	→ *Moor Street (71) - p.59*
C.M.M.			
41 44	128 11	Bordesley Jcn.	→ ***Kings Norton - p.60***
41 18	128 37	St. Andrew's Jcn.	→ Landor Street line (below)
C.M.M.			
41 26	129 09	Grand Jcn.	
C.M.M.			
112 05	129 20	Proof House Jcn. (Derby lines)	
112 19	129 34	Proof House Jcn.	
112 73	130 08	**Birmingham New Street**	→ *Peterborough (18) - p.46*; *Derby (80) - p.49*; *Euston/Wolverhampton (66/69) - p.5*; *Lichfield/Redditch (55) - p.59/60*; *Walsall (70) - p.60*; *Kidderminster (67) - p.61*; *Bristol (131) - p.95*

M. P.	M C	Station
	106 25	**Leamington Spa**
3 73	110 79	Kenilworth Jcns.
4 47	111 53	Kenilworth Jcns.
8 45	115 51	Leamington Jcn.
C.M.M.		
93 79	115 59	**Coventry** (see p.57)
112 73	134 53	**Birmingham New Street**

M. P.	M C	Station
41 18	0 00	St Andrew's Jcn.
40 60	0 38	Landor Street Jcn. (see p.46)

STRATFORD-UPON-AVON - LEAMINGTON (B.R. Table 71)

M. P.	M C	Station	Connection
8 77	0 00	**Stratford-upon-Avon**	
11 49	2 52	**Wilmcote**	
12 58	3 61	Bearley Jcn.	→ *Moor Street (71) - p.59*
13 19	4 22	**Bearley**	
16 38	7 41	**Claverdon**	
17 62	8 65	Hatton West Jcn.	→ Hatton line (below)
18 16	9 19	**Hatton**	
C.M.M.			
108 02	13 31	**Warwick**	
106 25	15 08	**Leamington Spa**	

M. P.	M C	Station
17 62	8 65	Hatton West Jcn.
18 18	9 21	Hatton North Jcn. (see above)

TRATFORD-UPON-AVON - BIRMINGHAM MOOR STREET (B.R. Table 71)

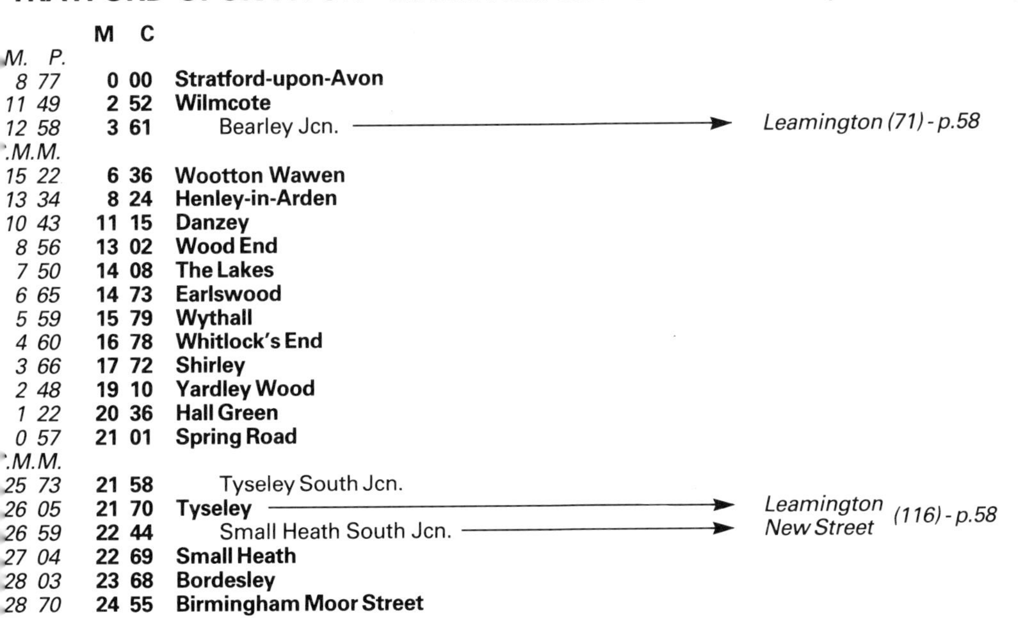

M. P.	M C	Station	Connection
8 77	0 00	**Stratford-upon-Avon**	
11 49	2 52	**Wilmcote**	
12 58	3 61	Bearley Jcn.	→ *Leamington (71) - p.58*
.M.M.			
15 22	6 36	**Wootton Wawen**	
13 34	8 24	**Henley-in-Arden**	
10 43	11 15	**Danzey**	
8 56	13 02	**Wood End**	
7 50	14 08	**The Lakes**	
6 65	14 73	**Earlswood**	
5 59	15 79	**Wythall**	
4 60	16 78	**Whitlock's End**	
3 66	17 72	**Shirley**	
2 48	19 10	**Yardley Wood**	
1 22	20 36	**Hall Green**	
0 57	21 01	**Spring Road**	
.M.M.			
25 73	21 58	Tyseley South Jcn.	
26 05	21 70	**Tyseley**	→ *Leamington (116) - p.58*
26 59	22 44	Small Heath South Jcn.	→ *New Street (116) - p.58*
27 04	22 69	**Small Heath**	
28 03	23 68	**Bordesley**	
28 70	24 55	**Birmingham Moor Street**	

ICHFIELD CITY - BIRMINGHAM NEW STREET (B.R. Table 55)

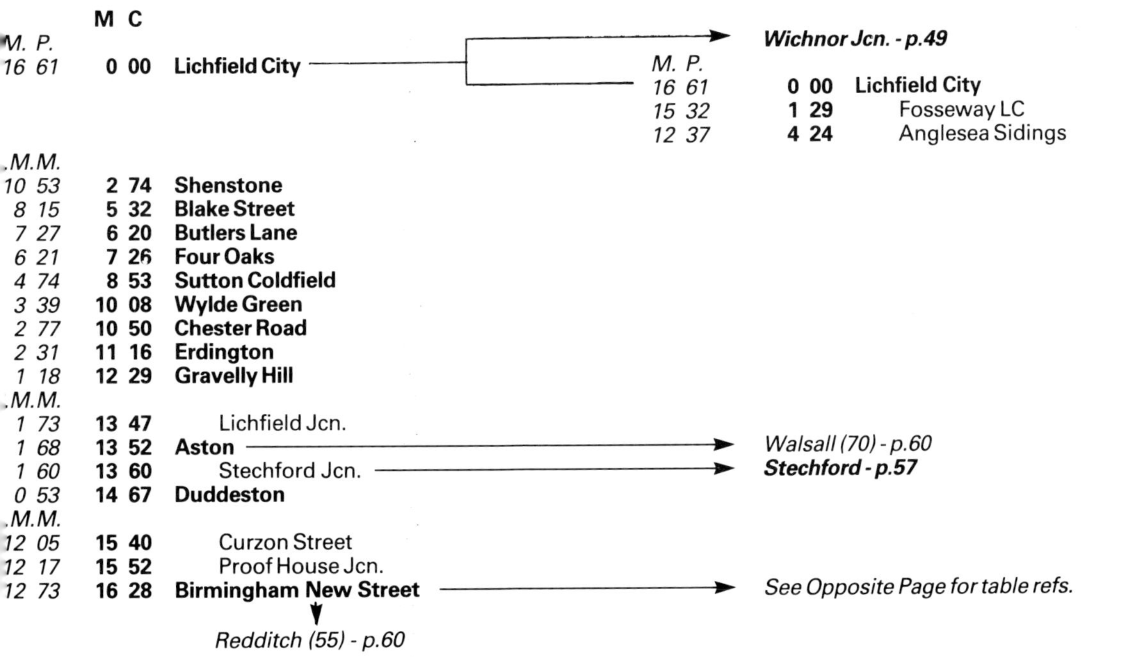

M. P.	M C	Station	Connection
16 61	0 00	**Lichfield City**	→ ***Wichnor Jcn. - p.49***
.M.M.			
10 53	2 74	**Shenstone**	
8 15	5 32	**Blake Street**	
7 27	6 20	**Butlers Lane**	
6 21	7 26	**Four Oaks**	
4 74	8 53	**Sutton Coldfield**	
3 39	10 08	**Wylde Green**	
2 77	10 50	**Chester Road**	
2 31	11 16	**Erdington**	
1 18	12 29	**Gravelly Hill**	
.M.M.			
1 73	13 47	Lichfield Jcn.	
1 68	13 52	**Aston**	→ *Walsall (70) - p.60*
1 60	13 60	Stechford Jcn.	→ ***Stechford - p.57***
0 53	14 67	**Duddeston**	
.M.M.			
12 05	15 40	Curzon Street	
12 17	15 52	Proof House Jcn.	
12 73	16 28	**Birmingham New Street**	→ *See Opposite Page for table refs.*; ↓ *Redditch (55) - p.60*

Branch from Lichfield City:

M. P.	M C	Station
16 61	0 00	**Lichfield City**
15 32	1 29	Fosseway LC
12 37	4 24	Anglesea Sidings

BIRMINGHAM NEW STREET - REDDITCH (B.R. Table 55)

M. P.	M C	
0 05	0 00	**Birmingham New Street**
C.M.M.		
42 35	0 16	New Street Jcn.
43 18	0 79	**Five Ways**
44 73	2 54	**University**
45 50	3 31	**Selly Oak**
46 58	4 39	**Bournville**
47 20	5 01	Lifford West Jcn.**
47 64	5 45	**Kings Norton**
C.M.M.		
46 77	5 63	Kings Norton Jcn.
48 12	6 78	**Northfield**
49 12	7 78	**Longbridge**
49 21	8 07	Halesowen Jcn.
50 34	9 20	Cofton Sidings
51 67	10 53	**Barnt Green**
53 47	12 33	**Alvechurch**
56 61	15 47	**Redditch**

M. P.	M C	
112 73	0 00	**Birmingham New Street**
112 19	0 54	Proof House Jcn.
41 18	1 51	St. Andrews Jcn. (see
41 44	1 77	Bordesley Jcn.
43 47	4 00	Moseley Tunnel (N.)
*46 11	6 44	Lifford East Jcn.
46 59	7 12	**Kings Norton**
46 77	7 30	Kings Norton Jcn.
*46 11	0 00	Lifford East Jcn.
**46 36	0 25	Lifford West Jcn.
51 67	10 53	**Barnt Green**
52 40	11 26	***LMR/WR Boundary***

Bristol (131) - p.95

BIRMINGHAM NEW STREET - WALSALL (B.R. Table 70)

M. P.	M C		
112 73	0 00	**Birmingham New Street**	*See p.58 for table refs.*
112 17	0 56	Proof House Jcn.	
C.M.M.			
0 00	0 68	Curzon Street	
0 53	1 41	**Duddeston**	
1 60	2 48	Stechford Jcn.	***Stechford - p.57***
1 68	2 56	**Aston**	
1 73	2 61	Lichfield Jcn.	*Lichfield City (55) - p.59*
2 45	3 33	**Witton**	
3 33	4 21	**Perry Barr**	
3 44	4 32	Perry Barr South Jcn.	
4 10	4 78	Perry Barr North Jcn.	***Perry Barr West Jcn. - p.57***
4 76	5 64	**Hamstead**	
6 74	7 62	Charlmont Road LC	
8 20	9 08	Bescot Down Yard	
8 47	9 35	**Bescot**	
C.M.M.			
0 01	9 38	Bescot Jcn.	***Bescot Curve Jcn. - p.61*** ***Darlaston Jcn. - p.62***
C.M.M.			
5 42	10 22	Pleck Jcn.	
6 29	11 09	**Walsall**	***Water Orton - p.62*** ***Rugeley - See Below***

M. P.	M C		
6 29	0 00	**Walsall**	
C.M.M.			
0 00	0 50	Rycroft Jcn.	***Water Orton - p.62***
2 06	2 56	Bloxwich LC	
9 12	9 62	Hednesford	
14 52	15 22	**Rugeley**	
C.M.M.			
124 39	15 39	Rugeley North Jcn.	*WCML (South) KEY PLAN - p.55*

IRMINGHAM NEW STREET - KIDDERMINSTER - WORCESTER (B.R. Table 67)

M. P.	M C	Location	
0 05	0 00	**Birmingham New Street**	→ *See p.58 for Table Refs.*
0 19	0 14	New Street North Tunnel (East)	
2 06	2 01	Soho South Jcn.	
2 38	2 33	Soho North Jcn.	→ Soho South Jcn. .57
3 30	3 25	**Smethwick Rolfe Street**	
3 64	3 59	Galton Jcn.	→ *Wolverhampton (69) - p.57*
M.M.			
33 32	4 03	Smethwick Jcn.	— 0 00 Smethwick Jcn. / 1 48 Handsworth
33 37	4 08	**Smethwick West**	
34 46	5 17	**Langley Green**	
36 14	6 65	**Rowley Regis**	
37 30	8 01	**Old Hill**	
38 65	9 36	**Cradley Heath**	
40 14	10 65	**Lye**	
M.M.			
42 51	11 57	Stourbridge Jcn.	
45 25	12 03	**Stourbridge Junction** (see below)	
40 29	13 79	**Hagley**	
38 51	15 57	**Blakedown**	
35 46	18 62	**Kidderminster**	
35 17	19 11	Kidderminster Jcn.	
31 72	22 36	**Hartlebury**	
30 40	23 68	***LMR/WR Boundary***	
26 26	28 02	Droitwich Spa Jcn.	
26 10	28 18	**Droitwich Spa**	→ *Bristol/Birmingham (131) - p.95*
0 78	33 30	Tunnel Jcn.	— 33 30 Tunnel Jcn. / 34 08 **Worcester Foregate St.**
0 46	33 62	Shrub Hill Jcn.	
0 31	33 77	**Worcester Shrub Hill**	→ *Oxford/Hereford (117) - p.94*
M. P.			

Severn Valley Railway

M. P.	M C	Location
149 74	0 00	**Bridgnorth**
147 59	2 15	**Eardington**
145 33	4 41	**Hampton Loade**
144 08	5 66	Alveley Sidings
143 21	6 53	**Highley**
142 15	7 59	Kinlet & Billingsley
140 74	9 00	**Arley**
138 77	10 77	**Northwood Halt**
137 32	12 42	Bewdley Jcn. (North)
137 28	12 46	**Bewdley**
137 12	12 62	Bewdley Jcn. (South)
136 32	13 42	**Foley Park Halt**
135 18	14 56	Kidderminster Jcn.
135 46	15 04	**Kidderminster** (S.V.R.)

NEW ST - LANDORE JN VIA UNIVERSITY/CAMP HILL = 10m 57ch

M. P.	M C	Location	
2 25	0 00	**Stourbridge Junction**	— 0 00 **Stourbridge Junction** / 0 49 **Stourbridge Town**
2 51	0 26	Stourbridge Jcn.	
4 33	2 08	Kingswinford Jcn.	— see branch below
7 37	5 12	Dudley Tunnel (South)	
M.M.			
0 00	5 75	Dudley	
3 26	9 21	Wednesbury LC	
4 73	10 68	Bescot Curve Jcn.	— 0 00 Bescot Curve Jcn. / 0 37 Bescot Jcn. (see p.60)
5 44	11 39	Pleck Jcn.	→ ***Darlaston Jcn. - p.62***
6 29	12 24	**Walsall**	→ ***Water Orton - p.62*** / ***Rugeley - p.60***

M. P.	M C	Location
144 33	0 00	Kingswinford Jcn.
145 13	0 60	Bromley GF
145 73	1 40	Pensnett GF

Bushbury & Crane Street Jcns. (Wolverhampton) - Walsall & Water Orton

M. P.	M C	Location		
15 32	**0 00**	Bushbury Jcns.	→	*Stafford (69)* — See Below
15 23	**0 09**		→	***Oxley Jcn.***

M. P.	M C	Location
1 59	**0 00**	Crane Street Jcn. (see p.57)
1 34	**0 25**	Heath Town Jcn.
C.M.M.		
12 64	**1 55**	Portobello Jcn.
9 65	**4 54**	Darlaston Jcn.
C.M.M.		
5 44	**5 55**	Pleck Jcn.
6 29	**6 40**	**Walsall**

M. P.	M C	Location
12 64	**2 48**	Portobello Jcn.
9 65	**5 47**	Darlaston Jcn.
C.M.M.		
5 44	**6 48**	Pleck Jcn.
6 29	**7 33**	**Walsall**

Bescot/Birmingham (70) - p.60
Rugeley - p.60
Stourbridge Jcn. - p.61

M. P.	M C	Location
9 65	**0 00**	Darlaston Jcn.
8 50	**1 15**	Bescot Jcn. (see p.60)

M. P.	M C	Location	
6 29	**0 00**	**Walsall**	
C.M.M.			
47 53	**0 42**	Ryecroft Jcn.	→ ***Rugeley - p.60***
44 73	**3 22**	Aldridge	
40 14	**8 01**	Sutton Park GF	
36 04	**12 11**	Park Lane Jcn.	
35 15	**13 00**	Water Orton West Jcn.	

C.M.M.	M C	Location
0 00	**12 11**	Park Lane Jcn.
C.M.M.		
36 14	**12 69**	Castle Bromwich Jcn.

Peterborough (18) — *p.46* — *Birmingham (18)*
Derby (56) — *p.49*

WOLVERHAMPTON - STAFFORD - STOKE ON TRENT (B.R. Table 69)

M. P.	M C	Location	
12 69	**0 00**	**Wolverhampton**	→ *Birmingham/Euston (65/69) - p.57*; *Shrewsbury/Chester (74) - p.64*
13 32	**0 43**	Wolverhampton North Jcn.	
C.M.M.			
15 32	**1 54**	Bushbury Jcn.	
19 71	**6 13**	Four Ashes	
22 74	**9 16**	Littleton Colliery SF	
23 32	**9 54**	**Penkridge**	
C.M.M.			
133 04	**14 72**	Stafford No. 4 Jcn.	
133 43	**15 31**	**Stafford**	→ *WCML (South) KEY PLAN - pp..55/56*
138 72	**20 60**	**Norton Bridge**	
C.M.M.			
3 56	**20 68**	Norton Bridge North Jcn.	
0 08	**24 36**	**Stone**	
C.M.M.			
27 00	**24 44**	Stone Jcn.	
24 45	**26 79**	**Barlaston**	
24 00	**27 44**	**Wedgwood**	
20 36	**31 08**	Stoke Jcns.	→ *Derby/Crewe (80) - p.63*
20 33	**31 11**		→ ***Oakamoor/Caldon p.63***
20 00	**31 44**	**Stoke-on-Trent**	→ *Manchester Picc. (65/69) - p.71*

M. P.	M C	Location
	1 11	Oxley Jcn.
15 23	**0 09**	Bushbury (Oxley) Jcn.
15 32	**0 00**	Bushbury Jcn. (see above)

M. P.	M C	Location
38 61	**0 00**	Colwich Jcn.
35 50	**3 11**	Hixon LC
28 64	**9 77**	Ashby-by-Stone LC
27 00	**11 61**	Stone Jcn.

DERBY - STOKE ON TRENT - CREWE (B.R. Table 80)

M. P.	M C	Location	Connections
27 68	0 00	**Derby**	*St. Pancras/Sheffield (53) - p.45* *Birmingham (80) p.49* *Matlock (54) - p.49*
M.M.			
0 00	0 14	London Road Jcn.	
1 16	1 30	**Peartree**	
1 27	1 41	Melbourne Jcn.	*Sinfin (54) - p.49*
4 50	4 64	Stenson Jcn.	***Sheet Stores Jcn. - p.48***
M.M.			
30 10	5 28	North Stafford Jcn.	
26 69	8 49	Egginton Jcn.	see branch below
22 53	12 65	Scropton LC	
19 62	15 56	Dovefields LC	
16 29	19 09	**Uttoxeter**	
13 32	22 06	Bramshall LC	
9 57	25 61	Upper Leigh LC	
7 08	28 30	Cresswell Jcn.	see branch below
5 19	30 19	**Blyth Bridge**	
3 49	31 69	Meir Tunnel (East)	
1 71	33 47	**Longton**	
M.M.			
0 36	35 38	Stoke Jcns.	***Oakamoor/Caldon - See Below***
0 33	35 41	Stoke Jcns.	
0 00	35 74	**Stoke-on-Trent**	*Stafford (69) - p.62* *Manchester Piccadilly (69) - p.70*
8 64	37 10	**Etruria**	
7 03	38 71	**Longport**	
M.M.			
0 00	42 25	**Kidsgrove**	
2 39	44 64	**Alsager**	
4 77	47 22	Barthomley LC	
7 70	50 15	North Stafford Jcn.	***Sorting Sidings South - p.56***
M.M.			
7 60	50 57	Crewe South Jcn.	
8 00	50 77	**Crewe**	*WCML (South) KEY PLAN - p.56* *Shrewsbury (87) - p.66* *Chester/Holyhead (83) - p.67* *WCML (North) KEY PLAN - p.68* *Manchester Piccadilly (81) - p.70*

Egginton Jcn. branch:

M. P.	M C	Location
26 69	0 00	Egginton Jcn. - Up
26 67	0 02	Egginton Jcn. - Down
26 63 / *153 52*	0 06	Access Jcn. (REV.)
148 30	5 28	Mickleover Sidings
148 12	5 46	End of Line

Cresswell Jcn. branch:

M C	Location
3 73	Cheadle
0 00	Cresswell Jcn.

Foxfield Steam Railway

M. P.	M C	Location
0 23	0 00	Foxfield Wood
0 75	0 52	**Dilhorne Park**
2 70	2 47	**Caverswall Road**
3 32	3 09	Blyth Bridge West (End of line)

Stoke-on-Trent - Oakamoor & Caldon Quarry

M. P.	M C	Location
0 00	0 00	**Stoke-on-Trent**
M.M.		
0 00	0 33	Stoke Jcn.
M.M.		
0 00	4 04	Milton Jcn.
3 11	7 15	Endon LC
6 65	10 69	Leek Brook Jcn. (REV.)
M.M.		
7 57	0 00	Leek Brook Jcn.
6 45	1 12	**Cheddleton**
2 40	5 17	Boltons Sidings LC
0 07	7 50	Oakamooor, B.I.S. Siding

Leek Brook Jcn. branch:

M C	Location
0 00	Leek Brook Jcn.
3 20	Apesford LC
8 08	Caldon Quarry

WOLVERHAMPTON - SHREWSBURY - CHESTER (B.R. Table 74)

M. P.	M C		
12 69	**0 00**	**Wolverhampton**	→ *Birmingham/Euston (65/69) - p.57*
C.M.M.			
143 52	**0 43**	Wolverhampton North Jcn.	→ *Stafford/Stoke (69) - p.62*
C.M.M.			
143 02	**1 16**	Oxley (Stafford Road) Jcn.	→ ***Bushbury Jcn. - p.62***
145 66	**4 00**	**Bilbrook**	
146 41	**4 55**	**Codsall**	
149 38	**7 52**	**Albrighton**	
150 69	**9 03**	**Cosford**	
154 24	**12 38**	**Shifnal**	
156 26	**14 40**	Madeley Jcn.	**0 00** Madeley Jcn. **6 09** Ironbridge P.S.
157 40	**15 54**	**Telford Central**	
158 31	**16 45**	**Oakengates**	
159 43	**17 57**	New Hadley	
160 76	**19 10**	Stafford Jcn.	**0 00** Stafford Jcn. **2 18** Donnington GF
161 21	**19 35**	**Wellington**	
163 70	**22 04**	Alscott GF	
171 15	**29 29**	Abbey Foregate Jcn.	**0 00** Abbey Foregate Jcn. **0 25** English Bridge Jcn. ↓
171 39	**29 53**	Severn Bridge Jcn.	
171 46	**29 60**	**Shrewsbury**	→ *Aberystwyth (75) - p.65* *Pwllheli (76) - p.65* *Craven Arms/Crewe (87) - p.66*
171 54	**29 68**	Crewe Jcn.	
175 34	**33 48**	Leaton LC	
179 14	**37 28**	Baschurch LC	
183 26	**41 40**	Haughton Sidings	
187 67	**46 01**	Whittington LC	
189 40	**47 54**	Oswestry Branch Jcn.	**0 00** Oswestry Branch Jcn. **2 20** Davies & Metcalfe LC **5 70** Lynclys **8 15** Llanddu Jcn. **8 57** Blodwell ARC **8 76** Line blocked
189 50	**47 64**	**Gobowen**	

Llangollen Railway

M C	* Approximate mileages only
0 00	**Llangollen**
0 60	**Pentre Felin**
2 00	**Berwyn**
	Glyndyfrdwy
8 00	Carrog

M. P.	M C		
192 54	**50 68**	**Chirk**	
196 75	**55 09**	**Ruabon**	
199 76	**58 10**	Bersham Sidings	
201 42	**59 56**	Croes Newydd North Fork LC	**0 00** North Fork LC **1 02** Gatewen
201 66	**60 00**	**Wrexham General**	→ *Bidston (105) - p.83*
206 44	**64 58**	Rossett LC	
209 67	**68 01**	Balderton LC	
C.M.M.			
181 01	**70 24**	Saltney Jcn.	
179 48	**71 57**	Chester South Jcn.	**0 00** Chester South Jcn. **0 23** Chester North Jcn. ↓
179 29	**71 76**	Chester West Jcn.	→ *Hooton (107) - p.78*
179 10	**72 15**	**Chester**	→ *Crewe/Holyhead (83) - p.67* *Manchester Victoria (83) - p.78* *Manchester Piccadilly (98) - p.79*

SHREWSBURY - ABERYSTWYTH (B.R. Table 75) - PWLLHELI (B.R. Table 76)

M. P.	M C	
71 46	0 00	**Shrewsbury** → *Wolverhampton/Chester (74) - p.64* / *Craven Arms/Crewe (87) - p.66*
M.M.		
0 11	0 07	Severn Bridge Jcn.
0 28	0 24	English Bridge Jcn. → ***Abbey Foregate Jcn. - p.64***
M.M.		
0 00	0 64	Sutton Bridge Jcn.
8 76	9 60	Streeton Heath LC
10 25	11 09	Westbury LC
12 41	13 25	Plas-y-Court LC
M.M.		
32 27	18 11	Buttington LC
33 70	19 54	**Welshpool**
38 20	24 04	Forden LC
43 63	29 47	Abermule LC
47 58	33 42	**Newtown**
52 70	38 54	Llanidloes Road LC
53 31	39 15	**Caersws**
59 17	45 01	Carno LC
61 26	47 10	Talerddig
64 58	50 42	Llanbrynmair LC
70 04	55 68	Cemmes Road
75 04	60 68	**Machynlleth**
78 75	64 59	Dovey Jcn.
79 03	64 67	**Dovey Junction**
80 54	66 38	Gogarth
82 30	68 14	Abertafol
84 08	69 72	**Penhelig**
85 02	70 66	**Aberdovey**
88 56	74 40	**Tywyn***
91 09	76 73	**Tonfanau**
93 24	79 08	**Llangelynin**
95 19	81 03	**Llwyngwril**
97 72	83 56	**Fairbourne****
98 79	84 63	**Morfa Mawddach**
0 43	86 27	**Barmouth**
2 13	87 77	**Llanaber**
4 37	90 21	**Talybont**
5 56	91 40	**Dyffryn Ardudwy**
7 70	93 54	**Llanbedr**
8 46	94 30	**Pensarn**
9 17	95 01	**Llandanwg**
1 07	96 71	**Harlech**
3 55	99 39	**Tygwyn**
4 42	100 26	**Talsarnau**
5 63	101 47	**Llandecwyn**
6 47	102 31	**Penrhyndeudraeth**
7 58	103 42	**Minffordd**
9 73	105 57	**Porthmadog*****
4 74	110 58	**Criccieth**
9 29	115 13	**Penychain**
0 76	116 60	**Abererch**
2 70	118 54	**Pwllheli**

Welshpool & Llanfair Railway

M C	
0 00	**Welshpool Raven Square**
2 55	**Sylfaen**
3 64	**Castle Caereinion**
5 59	**Cyfronydd**
6 56	**Heniarth**
8 07	**Llanfair Caereinion**

M. P.	M C	
78 75	64 59	Dovey Jcn.
79 03	64 67	**Dovey Junction**
85 21	71 05	Ynyslas LC
87 27	73 11	**Borth**
90 02	75 66	Llandre Vicarage LC
94 56	80 40	Llanbadarn LC
95 60	81 44	**Aberystwyth**

ABERYSTWYTH - DEVIL'S BRIDGE (B.R. Table 73)

Vale of Rheidol Steam Railway

M. P.	M C	
0 15	0 00	**Aberystwyth**
1 17	1 02	**Llanbadarn**
2 26	2 11	**Glanrafon**
4 54	4 39	**Capel Bangor**
6 55	6 40	**Nantyronen**
7 53	7 38	**Aberffrwd**
9 22	9 07	**Rheidol Falls**
10 70	10 55	**Rhiwfron**
11 72	11 57	**Devil's Bridge**

**** Talyllyn Railway***

M C	
0 00	**Tywyn Wharf**
0 34	**Tywyn Pendre**
0 74	**Hendy Halt**
1 34	**Fach Goch Halt**
1 69	**Cynfal Halt**
2 13	**Rhydyronen**
2 38	**Tynllwyn-hen Halt**
3 15	**Brynglas**
4 72	**Dolgoch Falls**
5 25	**Quarry Siding Halt**
6 47	**Abergynolwyn**
7 28	**Nant Gwernol**

*****Welsh Highland Railway***

M C	
0 00	**Porthmadog**
0 43	**Pen-y-Mount Halt**
2 06	Pont Croesor (proposed)

Fairbourne Railway**

M C	
0 00	**Gorsaf Newydd** (Fairbourne)
0 33	**Traeth Mawr**
0 55	**Gorsafawddach a'idraigodanheddogleddollonpenrhynareurdraethceredigion**
1 56	**Pont Penrhyn**
2 04	**Porth Penrhyn**

[*Ffestiniog Railway - p.66*]

CRAVEN ARMS - SHREWSBURY - CREWE (B.R. Tables 87 & 129)

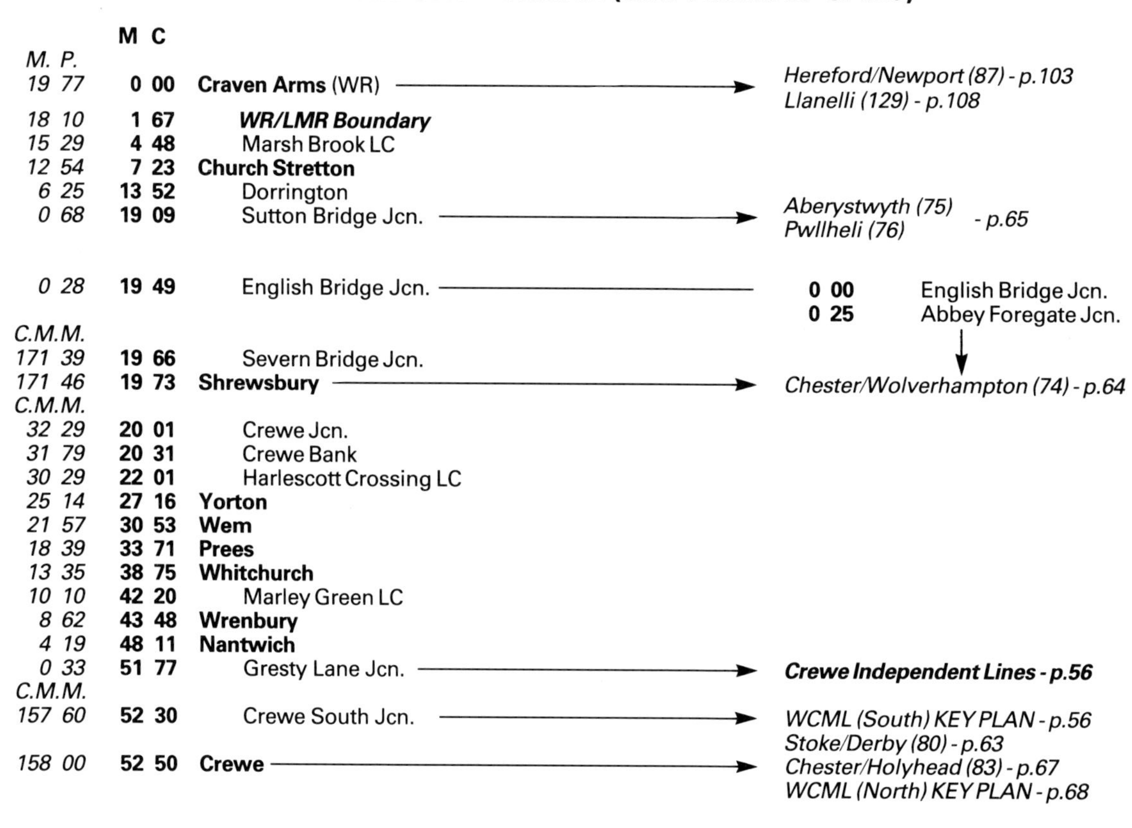

M. P.	M C		
19 77	0 00	**Craven Arms** (WR) →	*Hereford/Newport (87) - p.103* *Llanelli (129) - p.108*
18 10	1 67	***WR/LMR Boundary***	
15 29	4 48	Marsh Brook LC	
12 54	7 23	**Church Stretton**	
6 25	13 52	Dorrington	
0 68	19 09	Sutton Bridge Jcn. →	*Aberystwyth (75)* *Pwllheli (76)* - *p.65*
0 28	19 49	English Bridge Jcn. —	**0 00** English Bridge Jcn. **0 25** Abbey Foregate Jcn. ↓
C.M.M.			
171 39	19 66	Severn Bridge Jcn.	
171 46	19 73	**Shrewsbury** →	*Chester/Wolverhampton (74) - p.64*
C.M.M.			
32 29	20 01	Crewe Jcn.	
31 79	20 31	Crewe Bank	
30 29	22 01	Harlescott Crossing LC	
25 14	27 16	**Yorton**	
21 57	30 53	**Wem**	
18 39	33 71	**Prees**	
13 35	38 75	**Whitchurch**	
10 10	42 20	Marley Green LC	
8 62	43 48	**Wrenbury**	
4 19	48 11	**Nantwich**	
0 33	51 77	Gresty Lane Jcn. →	***Crewe Independent Lines - p.56***
C.M.M.			
157 60	52 30	Crewe South Jcn. →	*WCML (South) KEY PLAN - p.56*
158 00	52 50	**Crewe** →	*Stoke/Derby (80) - p.63* *Chester/Holyhead (83) - p.67* *WCML (North) KEY PLAN - p.68*

LLANDUDNO - BLAENAU FFESTINIOG (B.R. Table 84)

M. P.	M		
3 14	0 00	**Llandudno**	
1 22	1 72	**Deganwy**	
C.M.M.			
223 55	3 14	**Llandudno Junction** →	*Chester/Crewe* *Holyhead (83) - p. 67*
223 55	0 00	**Llandudno Junction**	
C.M.M.			
0 30	0 30	Llandudno Jcn.	
	1 42	**Glan Conwy**	
	5 12	**Tal-y-Cafn**	
	8 12	**Dolgarrog**	
	11 08	**Llanrwst**	
	15 02	**Betws-y-Coed**	
	19 28	**Pont-y-Pant**	
	20 62	**Dolwyddelan**	
	22 46	**Roman Bridge**	
24 33	24 33	Ffestiniog Tunnel (North)	
C.M.M.			
25 36	27 42	**Blaenau Ffestiniog**	
23 75	29 03	Fronlas LC	
18 54	34 24	Trawsfynydd C.E.G.B. Siding	

Festiniog Railway

M. P.	M C	
13 54 ½		End of Line
13 50	0 00	**Blaenau Ffestiniog**
12 10	1 40	**Tanygrisiau**
9 44	4 06	**Dduallt**
9 07	4 43	**Campbell's Platform**
7 35	6 15	**Tan-y-Bwlch**
6 19	7 31	**Plas Halt**
4 16	9 34	Rhiw Goch
3 09	10 41	**Penrhyn**
2 03	11 47	**Minffordd**
1 05	12 45	**Boston Lodge**
0 00	13 50	**Porthmadog**

(see p.65)

REWE - CHESTER - HOLYHEAD (B.R. Table 83)

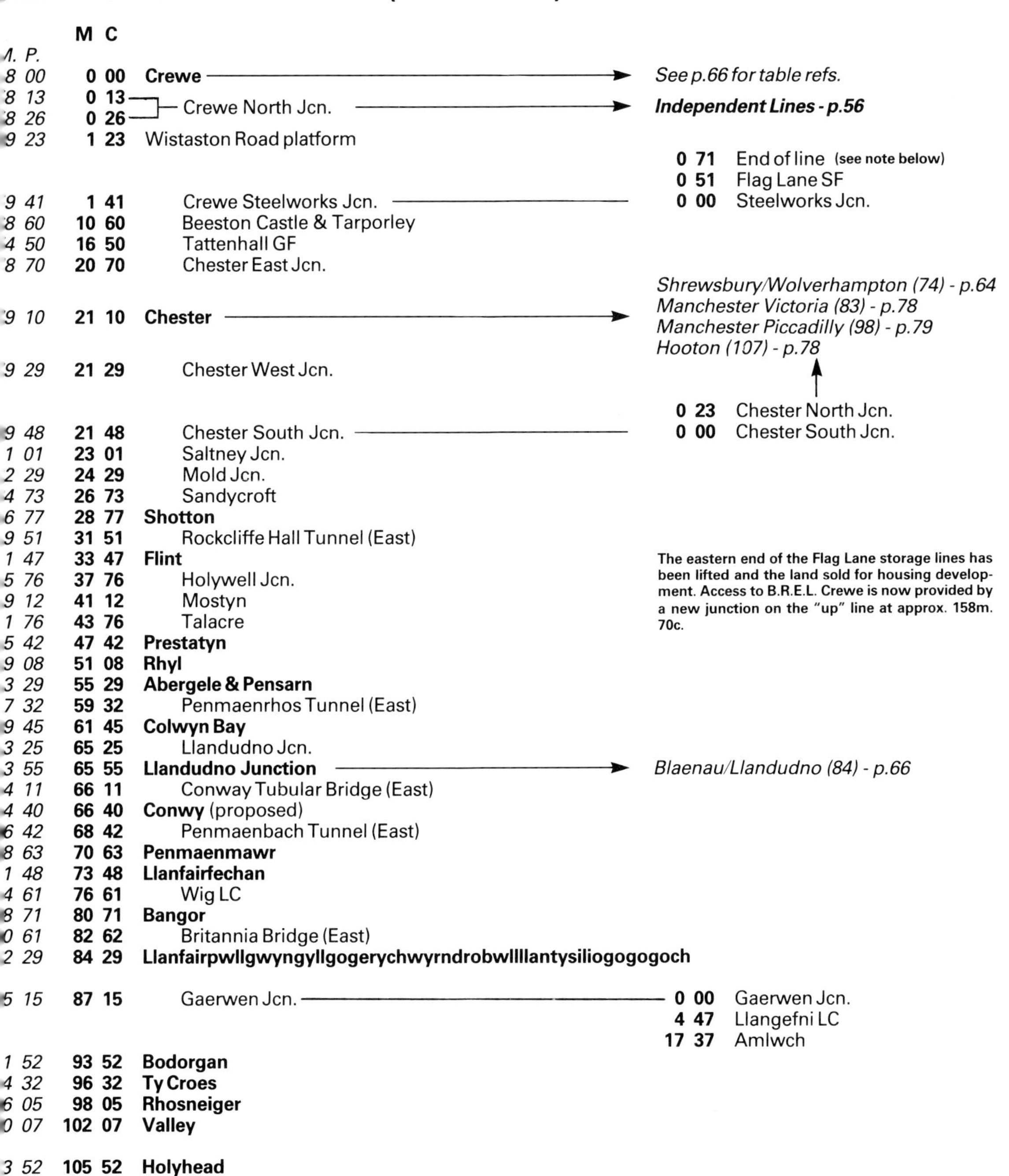

M. P.	M C		
8 00	**0 00**	**Crewe** →	*See p.66 for table refs.*
8 13	**0 13**	Crewe North Jcn. →	***Independent Lines - p.56***
8 26	**0 26**		
9 23	**1 23**	Wistaston Road platform	
			0 71 End of line (see note below)
			0 51 Flag Lane SF
9 41	**1 41**	Crewe Steelworks Jcn. —	**0 00** Steelworks Jcn.
8 60	**10 60**	Beeston Castle & Tarporley	
4 50	**16 50**	Tattenhall GF	
8 70	**20 70**	Chester East Jcn.	
9 10	**21 10**	**Chester** →	*Shrewsbury/Wolverhampton (74) - p.64* *Manchester Victoria (83) - p.78* *Manchester Piccadilly (98) - p.79* *Hooton (107) - p.78*
9 29	**21 29**	Chester West Jcn.	
			0 23 Chester North Jcn.
9 48	**21 48**	Chester South Jcn. —	**0 00** Chester South Jcn.
1 01	**23 01**	Saltney Jcn.	
2 29	**24 29**	Mold Jcn.	
4 73	**26 73**	Sandycroft	
6 77	**28 77**	**Shotton**	
9 51	**31 51**	Rockcliffe Hall Tunnel (East)	
1 47	**33 47**	**Flint**	
5 76	**37 76**	Holywell Jcn.	
9 12	**41 12**	Mostyn	
1 76	**43 76**	Talacre	
5 42	**47 42**	**Prestatyn**	
9 08	**51 08**	**Rhyl**	
3 29	**55 29**	**Abergele & Pensarn**	
7 32	**59 32**	Penmaenrhos Tunnel (East)	
9 45	**61 45**	**Colwyn Bay**	
3 25	**65 25**	Llandudno Jcn.	
3 55	**65 55**	**Llandudno Junction** →	*Blaenau/Llandudno (84) - p.66*
4 11	**66 11**	Conway Tubular Bridge (East)	
4 40	**66 40**	**Conwy** (proposed)	
6 42	**68 42**	Penmaenbach Tunnel (East)	
8 63	**70 63**	**Penmaenmawr**	
1 48	**73 48**	**Llanfairfechan**	
4 61	**76 61**	Wig LC	
8 71	**80 71**	**Bangor**	
0 61	**82 62**	Britannia Bridge (East)	
2 29	**84 29**	**Llanfairpwllgwyngyllgogerychwyrndrobwllllantysiliogogogoch**	
5 15	**87 15**	Gaerwen Jcn. —	**0 00** Gaerwen Jcn.
			4 47 Llangefni LC
			17 37 Amlwch
1 52	**93 52**	**Bodorgan**	
4 32	**96 32**	**Ty Croes**	
6 05	**98 05**	**Rhosneiger**	
0 07	**102 07**	**Valley**	
3 52	**105 52**	**Holyhead**	

The eastern end of the Flag Lane storage lines has been lifted and the land sold for housing development. Access to B.R.E.L. Crewe is now provided by a new junction on the "up" line at approx. 158m. 70c.

Snowdon Mountain Railway

M C	
0 00	**Llanberis**
1 09	**Hebron**
2 25	**Halfway**
3 30	**Clogwyn**
4 54	**Snowdon Summit**

SECTION II - LONDON MIDLAND REGION

(d) West Coast Main Line (North)

CREWE- CARLISLE (B.R. Table 65)

KEY PLAN

M. P.	M C	Location	Connection
0 00	**0 00**	**Euston**	
158 00	**158 00**	**Crewe**	*WCML (South) KEY PLAN - p.55/56*
	158 13	Crewe North Jcns.	*Chester/Holyhead (83) - p.67*
	158 16	Crewe North Jcns.	*Manchester Piccadilly (81) - p.70*
	158 58	Coal Yard Jcn.	***Independent Lines - p.56***
	161 17	Coppenhall	
	165 41	**Winsford**	
	169 64	**Hartford**	
	170 55	Hartford L.N.W. Jcn.	***Hartford C.L.C. Jcn. - See Below***
	172 38	**Acton Bridge**	
	174 22	Weaver Jcns. (up line)	*Liverpool (65/82) - p.80*
	175 20	Weaver Jcns. (down line)	
	177 40	Norton LC	
	180 24	Acton Grange Jcn.	
	181 76	Warrington South Jcn.	
	182 11	**Warrington Bank Quay**	
	183 20	Dallam Branch Jcn.	
	185 38	Winwick Jcns. (dn. slow line)	*Chester/Man. Vic. (83) - p.78*
185 47	**185 47**	Winwick Jcns. (fast lines)	
C.M.M.			
0 53	**187 77**	Golbourne Jcn.	***Lowton Jcn. - p.77***
2 42	**189 66**	Haydock Branch Jcn.	***Haydock Oil Sidings - See Below***
4 43	**191 67**	Bamfurlong Sidings Jcn.	***Ince Moss Jcn. - See Below***
5 18	**192 42**	Springs Branch Jcn.	***Bickershaw - See Below***
6 33	**193 57**	Wigan Station Jcn.	***Wigan Wallgate (95) - p.76***
6 47	**193 71**	**Wigan North Western**	*Liverpool (99) - p.77*
12 13	**199 37**	Blainscough	
14 18	**201 42**	Balshaw Lane Jcn.	
16 21	**203 45**	Euxton Jcn.	*Manchester Victoria (96) - p.76*
17 54	**204 78**	**Leyland**	
18 77	**206 21**	Farington Jcn.	***Lostock Hall Jcn. - See Below***
20 08	**207 32**	Farington Curve Jcn.	*Blackburn (108) - p.85* *Ormskirk (100A) - p.84*
21 39	**208 63**	Preston South Jcn.	
21 57	**209 01**	**Preston**	

M. P.	M C	Location
16 19	**0 00**	Acton Grange Jcn.
17 23	**1 04**	Walton Old Jcn. (see p.80)
C.M.M.		
181 76	**1 57**	Warrington South Jc **(5 chains longer)**

M C	Location
0 00	Hartford L.N.W. Jcn.
0 65	Hartford C.L.C. Jcn. (p.79)

M C	Location
0 00	Springs Branch Jcn.
2 76	Bickershaw Colliery

M C	Location
0 00	Haydock Branch Jcn.
2 10	Ashton-in-Mackerfield GF
2 59	Haydock Oil Sidings

M C	Location
0 00	Farington Jcn.
0 77	Lostock Hall Jcn. (p.85)

M C	Location
0 00	Bamfurlong Sidings Jcn.
0 60	Ince Moss Jcn. (p.77)

REWE- CARLISLE (B.R. Table 65) continued

M.M.	M C	Location	C.M.M.	M C	Connections
0 00	209 01	**Preston**			
0 33	209 34	Fylde Jcn. →			***Deepdale - p.84*** *Blackpool (96) - p.84*
3 70	212 71	Barton & Broughton South GF			
7 37	216 38	Brock LC			
9 29	218 30	Garstang & Catterall GF			
5 11	224 12	Bay Horse GF			
7 77	226 78	Oubeck			
M.M.					
0 00	229 79	**Lancaster**			
1 72	231 71	Morecambe South Jcn.			Morecambe (109) - p.85
3 10	233 09	Hest Bank LC			
6 08	236 07	Carnforth North Jcn. →	0 19	236 07	Carnforth North Jcn.
			0 31	236 19	**Carnforth** ↓ *Barrow (110) - p. 87.* *Skipton (36) - p.86*
9 08	249 07	**Oxenholme** →			*Windermere (111) - p.86*
4 20	254 19	Lambrigg GF			
6 21	256 20	Grayrigg			
8 05	258 04	Low Gill GF			
1 57	261 56	Tebay South			
2 21	262 20	Tebay North			
7 68	267 67	Shap Summit			
9 09	269 08	Shap Quarry (Hardendale)			
1 60	271 59	Harrisons Sidings GF			
6 74	276 73	Clifton & Lowther GF			
1 20	281 19	**Penrith**			
6 02	286 01	Plumpton No. 1 GF			
1 73	291 72	Southwaite GF			
7 59	297 58	Upperby Bridge Jcn. →			***Carlisle Area - See Below***
8 23	298 22	Upperby Jcn.			
8 73	298 72	Carlisle South Jcn.			
9 09	299 08	**Carlisle** →			*Newcastle (48) - p.42* *Skipton (36) - p.86* *Barrow (113) - p.87*
M.M.					
0 00	0 00	**Carlisle**			
	0 53	Caldew Jcn.			
	1 79	Kingmoor			
	4 28	Carlisle Yard Down Tower →			***Stainton/Brunthill - See Below***
	5 04	Carlisle Yard Up Tower			
	6 07	Floriston LC			
	7 64	Mossband Jcn. →			***Longtown - See Below***
	8 00	***LMR/ScR Boundary***			
8 57	8 57	Gretna Jcn. →			*Glasgow (65) - p.145* *Kilmarnock (222) - p.147*

M.M.	M C	Location
7 59	0 00	Upperby Bridge Jcn.
M.M.		
0 40	0 40	Upperby Jcn.
	1 07	Bog Jcn.
1 23	1 23	Rome Street Jcn.
	2 10	Caldew Jcn. *

*** Closed, but retained at Rome Street Jcn. for access to Metal Box works.**

M C	Location
0 00	London Road Jcn. (see p. 42/86)
0 34	Upperby Jcn.

M C	Location
0 00	London Road Jcn.
0 25	Bog Jcn.
0 40	former Forks Jcn.
0 69	Currock Jcn. (see p.87)

M C	Location
0 00	Carlisle Yard Down Tower
1 10	Stainton Jcn. (Stainton Tip)
2 01	Brunthill, Admiralty Sidings

M C	Location
0 00	Mossband Jcn.
1 03	Bush-on-Esk LC
1 75	Longtown Siding

CREWE- MANCHESTER PICCADILLY (B.R. Table 81)

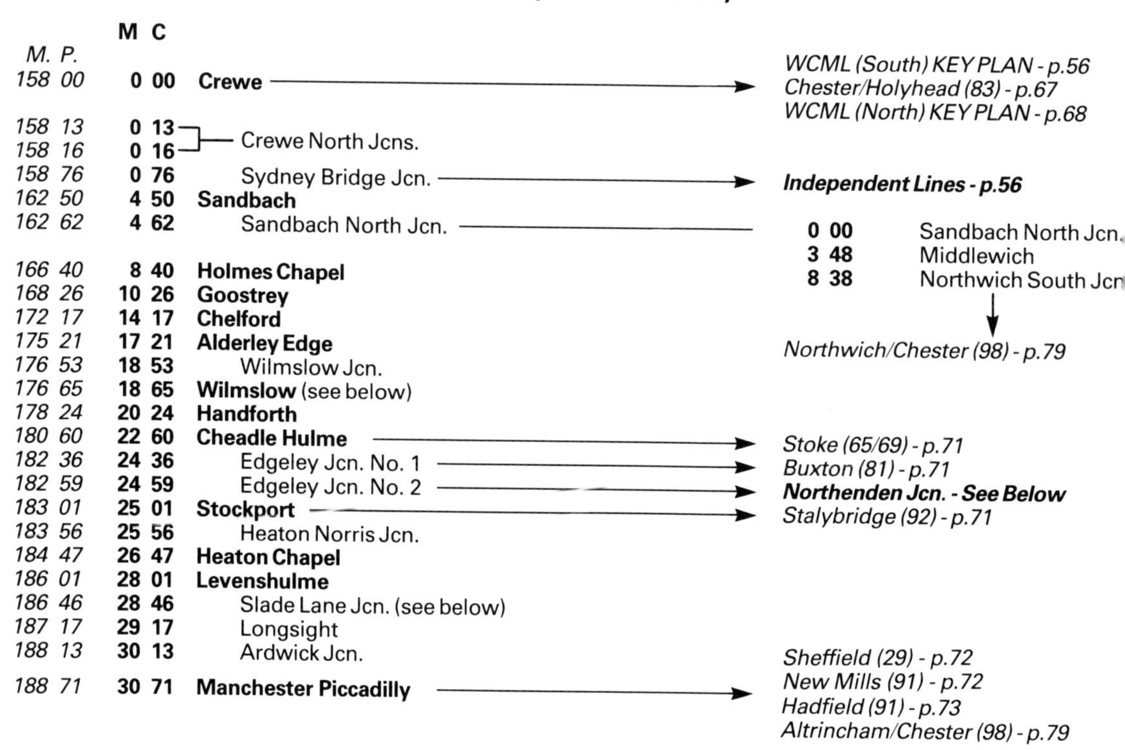

M. P.	M C	Station	Connections
158 00	0 00	**Crewe**	*WCML (South) KEY PLAN - p.56* *Chester/Holyhead (83) - p.67* *WCML (North) KEY PLAN - p.68*
158 13	0 13	Crewe North Jcns.	
158 16	0 16		
158 76	0 76	Sydney Bridge Jcn.	***Independent Lines - p.56***
162 50	4 50	**Sandbach**	
162 62	4 62	Sandbach North Jcn.	**0 00** Sandbach North Jcn. **3 48** Middlewich **8 38** Northwich South Jcn. *Northwich/Chester (98) - p.79*
166 40	8 40	**Holmes Chapel**	
168 26	10 26	**Goostrey**	
172 17	14 17	**Chelford**	
175 21	17 21	**Alderley Edge**	
176 53	18 53	Wilmslow Jcn.	
176 65	18 65	**Wilmslow** (see below)	
178 24	20 24	**Handforth**	
180 60	22 60	**Cheadle Hulme**	*Stoke (65/69) - p.71*
182 36	24 36	Edgeley Jcn. No. 1	*Buxton (81) - p.71*
182 59	24 59	Edgeley Jcn. No. 2	***Northenden Jcn. - See Below***
183 01	25 01	**Stockport**	*Stalybridge (92) - p.71*
183 56	25 56	Heaton Norris Jcn.	
184 47	26 47	**Heaton Chapel**	
186 01	28 01	**Levenshulme**	
186 46	28 46	Slade Lane Jcn. (see below)	
187 17	29 17	Longsight	
188 13	30 13	Ardwick Jcn.	
188 71	30 71	**Manchester Piccadilly**	*Sheffield (29) - p.72* *New Mills (91) - p.72* *Hadfield (91) - p.73* *Altrincham/Chester (98) - p.79*

WILMSLOW - MANCHESTER PICCADILLY via Styal (B.R. Table 81)

M. P.	M C	Station
0 00		Wilmslow Jcn.
0 12	0 00	**Wilmslow**
1 79	1 67	**Styal**
3 37	3 25	**Heald Green**
5 11	4 79	**Gatley**
6 25	6 13	**East Didsbury**
7 18	7 06	**Burnage**
8 07	7 75	**Mauldeth Road**
C.M.M.		
186 46	9 32	Slade Lane Jcn.
187 17	10 03	Longsight
188 13	10 79	Ardwick Jcn.
188 71	11 57	**Manchester Piccadilly**

M. P.	M C	Station	Connections
	0 00	Deansgate Jcn.	*Altrincham (98) - p.79*
30 12	0 33	Skelton Jcn. East	
33 52	3 73	Northenden Jcn.	
C.M.M.			
181 71	6 05	Cheadle Jcn.	
177 40	10 36	Hazel Grove High Level Jcn.	
176 33	11 43	Disley Tunnel (West)	
172 11	15 65	New Mills South Jcn.	*Sheffield (29) - p.72*

M. P.	M C	Station
27 20	0 00	Partington Jcn.
30 09	2 69	Skelton Jcn. West
30 12	2 72	Skelton Jcn. East
3 69	3 73	Northenden Jcn.
0 21	7 41	Edgeley Jcn. No. 1
0 00	7 62	Edgeley Jcn. No. 2 (see above)

STOKE-ON-TRENT - MANCHESTER PICCADILLY (B.R. Tables 65 & 69)

M.P.	M C		
20 00	**0 00**	**Stoke-on-Trent**	→ *Derby/Crewe (80) - p.63* *Wolverhampton (69) - p.62*
18 64	**1 16**	**Etruria**	
17 03	**2 77**	**Longport**	
.M.M.			
13 66	**6 31**	**Kidsgrove**	
11 30	**8 67**	Mow Cop LC	
8 12	**12 05**	**Congleton**	
4 67	**15 30**	North Roda GF	
0 20	**19 77**	**Macclesfield**	
.M.M.			
7 10	**22 43**	**Prestburn**	
5 15	**24 38**	**Adlington**	
2 79	**26 54**	**Poynton**	
1 49	**28 04**	**Bramhall**	
.M.M.			
80 60	**29 53**	**Cheadle Hulme** (see p.70)	
83 01	**31 74**	**Stockport**	
88 71	**37 64**	**Manchester Piccadilly**	→ *See p.70 for table refs.*

0 00	**Euston** (see p.55)	**0 00**
127 07	Colwich Jcn.	**127 07**
via Hixon		**via Stafford**
145 68	**Stoke-on-Trent**	**149 56**
183 52	**Manchester Picc.**	**187 40**

STOCKPORT - STALYBRIDGE (B.R. Table 92)

M. P.	M C		
83 01	**0 00**	**Stockport**	→ *Man. Picc./Crewe (81) - p.70*
.M.M.			
0 00	**0 55**	Heaton Norris Jcn.	
1 50	**2 25**	**Reddish South**	
3 39	**4 14**	**Denton**	
4 10	**4 65**	Denton Jcn.	→ **0 00** Denton Jcn. **2 61** Ashton Moss Sth. Jcn. **3 02** O.A. & G.B. Jcn. (see p.74)
4 68	**4 43**	Stockport Jcn.	
4 77	**5 52**	**Guide Bridge**	→ *Hadfield (91) - p.73*
.M.M.			
0 04	**5 65**	Ashton Jcn.	**0 18** Guide Bridge E. Jcn. ↑
0 22	**6 03**	Guide Bridge North Jcn.	→ **0 00** Guide Bridge N. Jcn.
.M.M.			
7 46	**7 69**	Stalybridge No. 2 Jcn.	
7 52	**7 75**	**Stalybridge**	→ *Huddersfield (39) - p.74*

MANCHESTER PICCADILLY - BUXTON (B.R. Table 81)

M. P.	M C		
	0 00	**Manchester Piccadilly** (see p.70)	
	5 70	**Stockport**	
0 00	**6 35**	Edgeley Jcn. No. 1	
0 62	**7 17**	**Davenport**	
2 20	**8 55**	**Hazel Grove**	
2 34	**8 69**	Hazel Grove East Jcn.	→ *Sheffield (29) - p.72*
4 25	**10 60**	**Middlewood**	
6 03	**12 38**	**Disley**	
7 50	**14 05**	**New Mills Newtown**	
8 62	**15 17**	**Furness Vale**	
10 05	**16 40**	**Whaley Bridge**	
13 69	**20 24**	**Chapel-en-le-Frith**	
16 12	**22 47**	**Dove Holes**	
18 68	**25 23**	Buxton Jcn.	— **0 00** Buxton Jcn. **4 70** Brigg's Siding
19 10	**25 45**	**Buxton**	→ ***Chinley - p.73***

MANCHESTER PICCADILLY - SHEFFIELD via Hazel Grove (B.R. Table 29)

	M C		Connections
	0 00	**Manchester Piccadilly** (see p. 70)	→ *Crewe (81) - p.70* *Stoke (69) - p.71* *Hadfield (81) - p.73* *Altrincham/Chester (98) - p.79*
M. P.	**5 70**	**Stockport**	
0 00	**6 35**	Edgeley Jcn. No. 1	
0 62	**7 17**	**Davenport**	
2 20	**8 55**	**Hazel Grove**	→ *Buxton (81) - p.71*
2 34	**8 69**	Hazel Grove East Jcn.	
C.M.M.			
177 40	**9 17**	Hazel Grove High Level Jcn.	→ ***Northenden Jcn. - p.70***
176 33	**10 24**	Disley Tunnel (West)	
172 11	**14 46**	New Mills South Jcn. (see below)	
169 48	**17 09**	**Chinley**	***Buxton - p.73*** ↑
C.M.M.			*M C*
174 00	**18 19**	Chinley North Jcn.	**0 57** Chinley South Jcn.
173 52	**18 47**	Chinley East Jcn.	— **0 00** Chinley East Jcn.
172 44	**19 55**	Cowburn Tunnel (West)	
169 23	**22 76**	**Edale**	
165 20	**26 79**	Earles Sidings	
164 26	**27 73**	**Hope**	
162 33	**29 66**	**Bamford**	
160 60	**31 39**	**Hathersage**	
158 70	**33 29**	**Grindleford**	
155 20	**36 79**	Totley Tunnel (East)	
155 15	**37 04**	***LMR/ER Boundary***	
C.M.M.			
0 00	**38 03**	Dore West Jcn.	— **0 00** Dore West Jcn.
0 27	**38 30**	**Dore**	**0 23** Dore South Jcn. (p.45
C.M.M.			
154 50	**38 61**	Dore Station Jcn.	
158 40	**42 51**	**Sheffield**	→ *Retford (29) - p.18* *Doncaster (29) - p.22* *Leeds/York (34) - pp.29/33* *Derby/Nottingham (53) - pp.45/47*

MANCHESTER PICCADILLY - NEW MILLS CENTRAL (B.R. Table 91)

	M C			M C		Connections
M. P.	**0 00**	**Manchester Piccadilly**				
0 52	**0 58**	Ardwick Jcn.				
0 61	**0 67**	**Ardwick**				
1 36	**1 42**	Ashburys West Jcn.				→ *Manchester Victoria (29) - p.74*
1 42	**1 48**	**Ashburys**				
C.M.M.			*M. P.*	**M C**		
46 24	**1 62**	Ashburys East Jcn.	*1 56*	**1 62**	Ashburys East Jcn. (see p.73)	
			6 15	**6 21**	Hyde Jcn.	
45 30	**2 56**	**Belle Vue**	*6 33*	**6 39**	**Hyde North**	
45 00	**3 06**	**Ryder Brow**	*7 27*	**7 33**	**Hyde Central**	
44 09	**3 77**	**Reddish North**	*8 70*	**8 76**	**Woodley**	
C.M.M.			*C.M.M.*			
180 35	**5 54**	**Brinnington**	*179 44*	**9 00**	Woodley Jcn.	
179 34	**6 55**	**Bredbury**				
178 33	**7 56**	Romiley Jcn.	*178 33*	**10 11**	Romiley Jcn.	
			178 31	**10 13**	**Romiley**	
178 31	**7 58**	**Romiley**	*178 31*	**0 00**	**Romiley**	
			C.M.M.			
177 23	**8 66**	Marple Wharf Jcn.	*11 02*	**1 08**	Marple Wharf Jcn.	
176 57	**9 32**	**Marple**	*10 04*	**2 06**	**Rose Hill**	
174 47	**11 42**	**Strines**				
173 11	**12 78**	**New Mills Central**				
172 11	**13 78**	New Mills South Jcn.				→ *Man. Picc./Sheffield - (see above)*

MANCHESTER PICCADILLY - GLOSSOP & HADFIELD (B.R. Table 91)

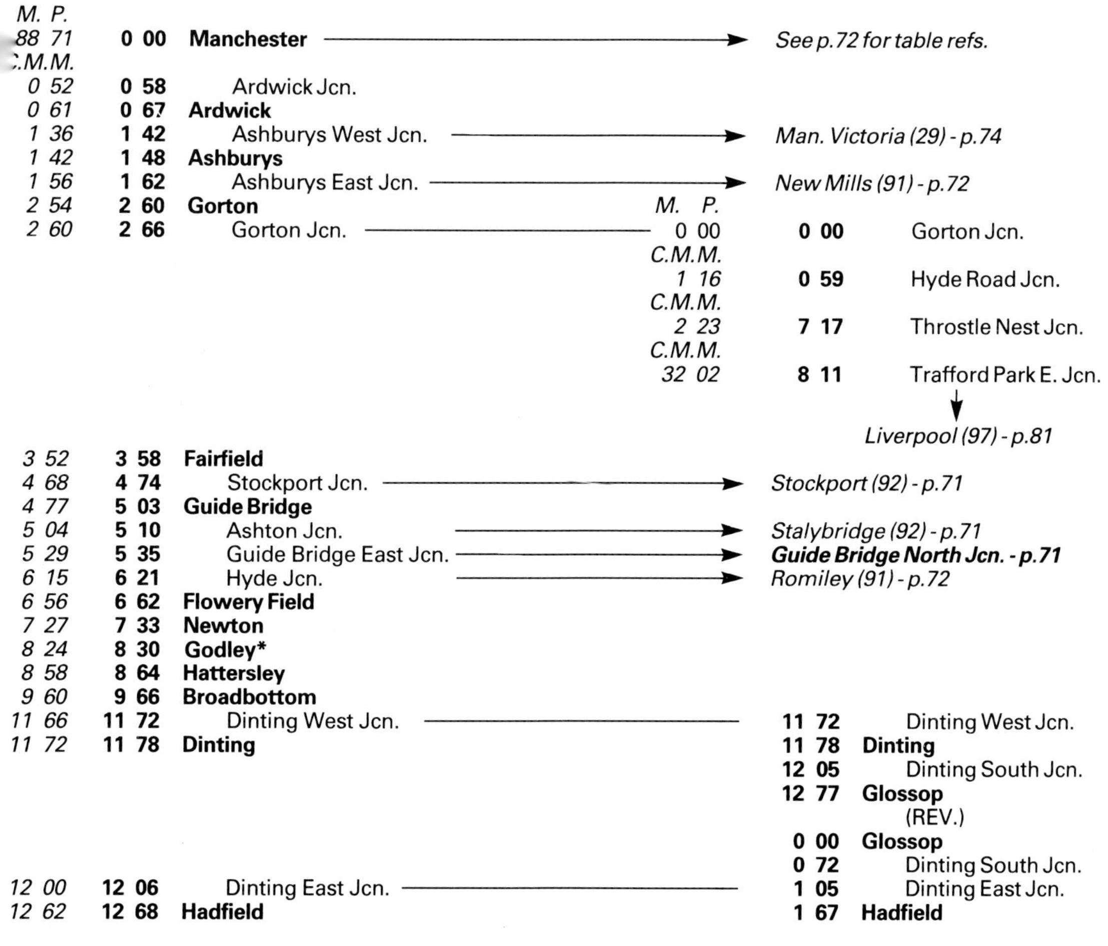

M. P.	M C	Location	Connection
88 71	0 00	**Manchester**	*See p.72 for table refs.*
C.M.M.			
0 52	0 58	Ardwick Jcn.	
0 61	0 67	**Ardwick**	
1 36	1 42	Ashburys West Jcn.	*Man. Victoria (29) - p.74*
1 42	1 48	**Ashburys**	
1 56	1 62	Ashburys East Jcn.	*New Mills (91) - p.72*
2 54	2 60	**Gorton**	
2 60	2 66	Gorton Jcn.	(see below)
3 52	3 58	**Fairfield**	
4 68	4 74	Stockport Jcn.	*Stockport (92) - p.71*
4 77	5 03	**Guide Bridge**	
5 04	5 10	Ashton Jcn.	*Stalybridge (92) - p.71*
5 29	5 35	Guide Bridge East Jcn.	***Guide Bridge North Jcn. - p.71***
6 15	6 21	Hyde Jcn.	*Romiley (91) - p.72*
6 56	6 62	**Flowery Field**	
7 27	7 33	**Newton**	
8 24	8 30	**Godley***	
8 58	8 64	**Hattersley**	
9 60	9 66	**Broadbottom**	
11 66	11 72	Dinting West Jcn.	(see below)
11 72	11 78	**Dinting**	
12 00	12 06	Dinting East Jcn.	(see below)
12 62	12 68	**Hadfield**	

M. P.	M C	Location
0 00	0 00	Gorton Jcn.
C.M.M.		
1 16	0 59	Hyde Road Jcn.
C.M.M.		
2 23	7 17	Throstle Nest Jcn.
C.M.M.		
32 02	8 11	Trafford Park E. Jcn.
		Liverpool (97) - p.81

M C	Location
11 72	Dinting West Jcn.
11 78	**Dinting**
12 05	Dinting South Jcn.
12 77	**Glossop** (REV.)
0 00	**Glossop**
0 72	Dinting South Jcn.
1 05	Dinting East Jcn.
1 67	**Hadfield**

A new Godley station is proposed between here and Hattersley. The present station will be re-named Godley East.

Chinley - Peak Forest - Buxton

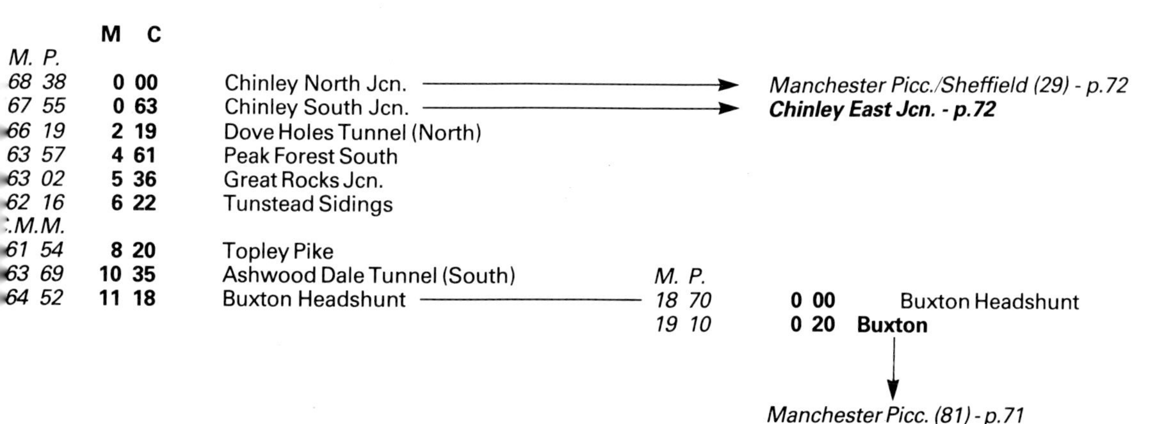

M. P.	M C	Location	Connection
68 38	0 00	Chinley North Jcn.	*Manchester Picc./Sheffield (29) - p.72*
67 55	0 63	Chinley South Jcn.	***Chinley East Jcn. - p.72***
66 19	2 19	Dove Holes Tunnel (North)	
63 57	4 61	Peak Forest South	
63 02	5 36	Great Rocks Jcn.	
62 16	6 22	Tunstead Sidings	
C.M.M.			
61 54	8 20	Topley Pike	
63 69	10 35	Ashwood Dale Tunnel (South)	
64 52	11 18	Buxton Headshunt	(see below)

M. P.	M C	Location
18 70	0 00	Buxton Headshunt
19 10	0 20	**Buxton**
		Manchester Picc. (81) - p.71

MANCHESTER VICTORIA - HUDDERSFIELD (B.R. Table 39)

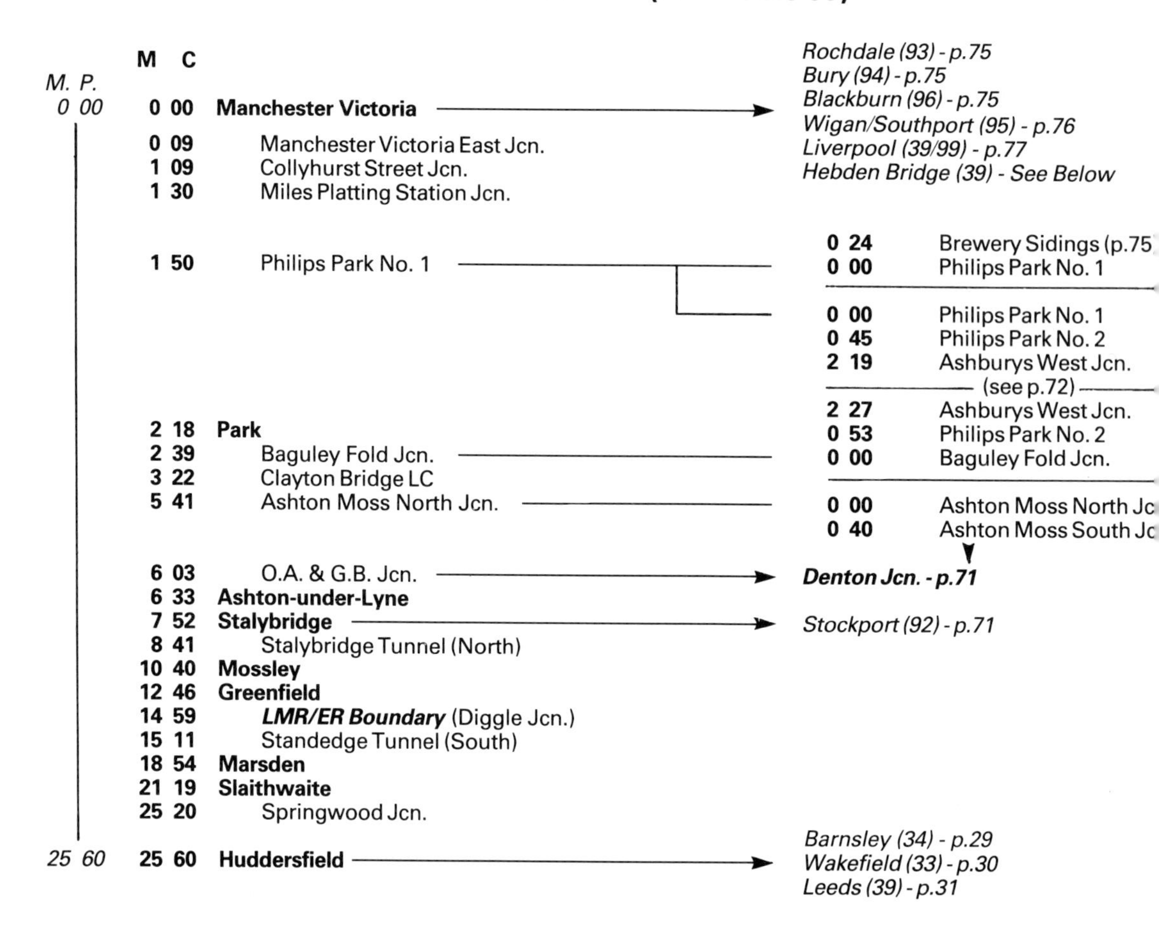

M. P.	M C	Location	Connections
			Rochdale (93) - p.75
			Bury (94) - p.75
0 00	**0 00**	**Manchester Victoria**	*Blackburn (96) - p.75*
			Wigan/Southport (95) - p.76
	0 09	Manchester Victoria East Jcn.	*Liverpool (39/99) - p.77*
	1 09	Collyhurst Street Jcn.	*Hebden Bridge (39) - See Below*
	1 30	Miles Platting Station Jcn.	
			0 24 Brewery Sidings (p.75
	1 50	Philips Park No. 1	**0 00** Philips Park No. 1
			0 00 Philips Park No. 1
			0 45 Philips Park No. 2
			2 19 Ashburys West Jcn.
			(see p.72)
			2 27 Ashburys West Jcn.
	2 18	**Park**	**0 53** Philips Park No. 2
	2 39	Baguley Fold Jcn.	**0 00** Baguley Fold Jcn.
	3 22	Clayton Bridge LC	
	5 41	Ashton Moss North Jcn.	**0 00** Ashton Moss North Jc
			0 40 Ashton Moss South Jc
	6 03	O.A. & G.B. Jcn.	***Denton Jcn. - p.71***
	6 33	**Ashton-under-Lyne**	
	7 52	**Stalybridge**	*Stockport (92) - p.71*
	8 41	Stalybridge Tunnel (North)	
	10 40	**Mossley**	
	12 46	**Greenfield**	
	14 59	***LMR/ER Boundary*** (Diggle Jcn.)	
	15 11	Standedge Tunnel (South)	
	18 54	**Marsden**	
	21 19	**Slaithwaite**	
	25 20	Springwood Jcn.	
			Barnsley (34) - p.29
25 60	**25 60**	**Huddersfield**	*Wakefield (33) - p.30*
			Leeds (39) - p.31

MANCHESTER VICTORIA - ROCHDALE - HEBDEN BRIDGE (B.R. Table 39)

M. P.	M C	Location	Connections
0 00	**0 00**	**Manchester Victoria**	
0 09	**0 09**	Manchester Victoria East Jcn.	
0 73	**0 73**	Cheetham Hill Jcn.	***Queens Road Jcn. - p.75***
C.M.M.			
2 21	**2 35**	Thorpes Bridge Jcn.	*Rochdale (93) - p.75*
4 00	**4 14**	**Moston**	
5 16	**5 30**	Middleton Jcn.	
5 74	**6 08**	**Mills Hill**	
8 53	**8 67**	Castleton East Jcn.	**0 00** Castleton East Jcn.
			0 37 Castleton North Jcn.
			1 15 Heywood GF
8 69	**9 03**	**Castleton**	
10 36	**10 50**	**Rochdale**	*Manchester Victoria (93) - p.75*
10 74	**11 08**	Rochdale Jcn.	
12 65	**12 79**	**Smithy Bridge**	
13 65	**13 79**	**Littleborough**	
16 64	**16 78**	Summit Tunnel (North)	
19 13	**19 27**	**Todmorden**	
19 61	**19 75**	Hall Royd Jcn.	*Copy Pit/Gannow Jcn. (108) - p.85*
22 03	**22 17**	***LMR/ER Boundary*** (Eastwood)	
23 56	**23 70**	**Hebden Bridge**	*Halifax/Bradford (39) - p.31*

MANCHESTER VICTORIA - ROCHDALE via Oldham (B.R. Table 93)

M.P.	M C	Location	Connections
0 00	0 00	**Manchester Victoria**	→ *See p.74 for table refs.*
	0 09	Manchester Victoria East Jcn.	
	1 09	Collyhurst Street Jcn.	
	1 30	Miles Platting Station Jcn.	
	1 38	**Miles Platting**	
	1 59	Brewery Sidings	→ ***Philips Park No. 1 - p.74***
	2 21	Thorpes Bridge Jcn.	→ *Rochdale (39) - p.74*
	2 54	**Dean Lane**	
	3 54	**Failsworth**	
	4 52	**Hollinwood**	
	6 28	**Oldham Werneth**	
	7 40	**Oldham Mumps**	
	8 14	**Derker**	
	8 38	**Royton**	
	10 05	**Shaw**	
	11 64	**New Hay**	
12 69	12 69	**Milnrow**	
C.M.M.			
10 74	14 16	Rochdale East Jcn.	
10 36	10 54	**Rochdale**	→ *Hebden Bridge (39) - p.74*

MANCHESTER VICTORIA - BURY (B.R. Table 94)

M.P.	M C	Location	Branch M C	Branch
				Rochdale (39) - p.74 ↑
0 00	0 00	**Manchester Victoria**		
C.M.M.	0 51	Collyhurst Tunnel (South)	0 00	Cheetham Hill Jcn.
1 21	1 38	Queens Road Jcn.	0 28	Queens Road Jcn.
1 56	1 73	**Woodlands Road**		
2 38	2 55	**Crumpsall**		
3 07	3 24	**Bowker Vale**		
3 76	4 13	**Heaton Park**		
4 34	4 51	**Prestwich**		
5 17	5 34	**Besses-o'-th'-Barn**		
5 74	6 11	**Whitefield**		
7 26	7 43	**Radcliffe**		
8 35	8 52	Hagside LC		
9 51	9 68	**Bury**		

MANCHESTER VICTORIA - BLACKBURN (B.R. Table 96)

M.P.	M C	Location	Branch M C	Branch / Connections
0 00	0 00	**Manchester Victoria**		
	0 38	Deal Street Jcn.		→ *Liverpool (39/99) - p.77*
	0 59	**Salford**		
		Windsor link - see note p.76		
		Salford Crescent		
	1 66	Windsor Bridge Jcn.	1 66	Windsor Bridge Jcn.
			2 21	**Pendleton**
			2 77	Brindle Heath Jcn.
	3 32	Agecroft Jcn.	3 36	Agecroft Jcn.
	4 57	**Clifton**		
	7 57	**Kearsley**		
	8 31	**Farnworth**		
	9 06	**Moses Gate**		
	10 50	**Bolton**		→ *Wigan Wallgate (95)*, *Preston (96)* - *p.76*
	10 55	Bolton West Jcn.		
	12 35	**Hall i' th' Wood**		
	13 47	**Bromley Cross**		
	15 19	Turton LC		
16 47	16 47	**Entwhistle**		
M.M.	20 27	**Darwen**		
10 11	24 08	Bolton Jcn.		
10 42	24 39	**Blackburn**		→ *Preston/Colne (108) - p.85*, ***Hellifield - p.85***

MANCHESTER VICTORIA & BOLTON - WIGAN WALLGATE - SOUTHPORT & KIRK
(B.R. Table

M.P.	M C	Location	Connections
0 00	0 00	**Manchester Victoria**	→ Huddersfield (39) - p.74; Hebden Bridge (39) - p.74; Rochdale (93) - p.75; Bury (94) - p.75; Blackburn (96) - p.75; Liverpool (39/99) - p.77
	0 38	Deal Street Jcn.	
	0 59	**Salford**	
		Windsor link - see note below	
		Salford Crescent	
	1 66	Windsor Bridge Jcn.	
	2 21	**Pendleton**	
	2 77	Brindle Heath Jcn.	
	4 74	**Swinton**	
	5 61	**Moorside**	
	7 33	**Walkden**	
	11 01	**Atherton**	
		Hag Fold (proposed)	
	12 57	**Daisy Hill**	
	14 64	Crow Nest Jcn.	→ 17 18 (M.P.)
	15 17	**Hindley**	
	16 70	**Ince**	
	17 44	Wigan Station Jcn.	→ 6 33 (C.M.M.)
	17 72	**Wigan Wallgate**	6 47 (C.M.M.)
	18 04	Wallgate Jcn.	→ C.M.M.
	20 46	**Gathurst**	19 24
	22 30	**Appley Bridge**	20 77
	24 49	**Parbold**	22 24
	26 10	**Hoscar**	24 35
	27 49	**Burscough Bridge**	29 40
	28 70	**New Lane**	
	30 78	**Bescar Lane**	
	32 44	Pool Hey LC	
	34 02	**Meols Cop**	
35 15	35 15	**Southport**	→ Liverpool Central (101) - p.83

Preston (96) - See Below

M. P.	M C	Location
10 50	0 00	**Bolton**
10 55	0 05	Bolton West Jcn.
13 39	2 69	Lostock Jcn.
15 25	4 55	**Westhoughton**
17 18	6 48	Crow Nest Jcn.
	9 56	**Wigan Wallgate**

C.M.M.	M C	Location
6 33	17 44	Wigan Station Jcn.
6 47	17 58	**Wigan North Western**

WCML (North) KEY PLAN - p.68

M C	Location
18 04	Wallgate Jcn.
19 64	**Pemberton**
21 37	**Orrell**
22 64	**Upholland**
24 75	**Rainford**
30 00	**Kirkby**

Liverpool Central (102) - p.84

MANCHESTER VICTORIA - BOLTON - PRESTON (B.R. Table 96)

M. P.	M C	Location	Connections
0 00	0 00	**Manchester Victoria** (see page 75)	
	10 50	**Bolton**	→ Blackburn (96) - p.75
	10 55	Bolton West Jcn.	
	13 39	Lostock Jcn.	→ Wigan Wallgate (95) - See Above
	17 14	**Blackrod**	
	17 27	Blackrod Jcn.	
	19 15	**Adlington**	
22 16	22 16	**Chorley**	
C.M.M.	24 18	Euxton R.O.F. GF	
16 21	25 30	Euxton Jcn.	
17 54	26 63	**Leyland**	
18 77	28 06	Farington Jcn.	→ ***Lostock Hall Jcn. - p.68***
20 08	29 17	Farington Curve Jcn.	→ Blackburn (108) - p.85; Ormskirk (100A) - p.84
21 39	30 48	Preston South Jcn.	
21 57	30 66	**Preston**	→ Blackpool (96) - p.84; WCML (North) KEY PLAN - p.69

The Windsor link, due to open in 1987, will allow Bolton and Wigan services to run into Manchester Piccadilly rather than Victoria. The full route wi Windsor Bridge Jcn., **Salford Crescent** (new station), Windsor link, Ordsall Lane Jcn., Castlefield Jcn. (see p.77/79), **Deansgate, Oxford Road, Manchester Piccadilly.**

LIVERPOOL LIME STREET - MANCHESTER VICTORIA (B.R. Tables 39 & 99)

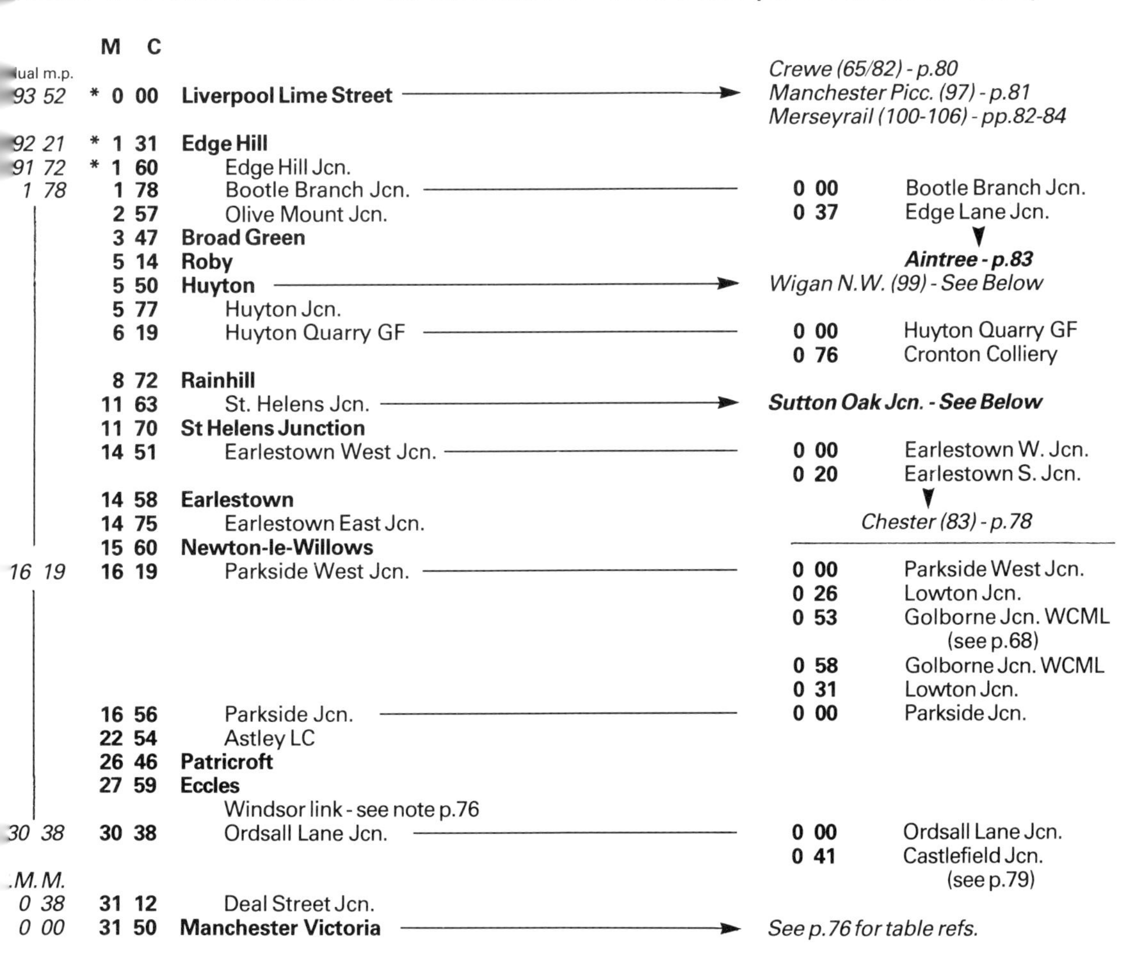

ual m.p.	M C			Connections
93 52	* 0 00	**Liverpool Lime Street**	→	*Crewe (65/82) - p.80* *Manchester Picc. (97) - p.81* *Merseyrail (100-106) - pp.82-84*
92 21	* 1 31	**Edge Hill**		
91 72	* 1 60	Edge Hill Jcn.		
1 78	1 78	Bootle Branch Jcn.	—	**0 00** Bootle Branch Jcn. **0 37** Edge Lane Jcn. ▼ ***Aintree - p.83***
	2 57	Olive Mount Jcn.		
	3 47	**Broad Green**		
	5 14	**Roby**		
	5 50	**Huyton**	→	*Wigan N.W. (99) - See Below*
	5 77	Huyton Jcn.		
	6 19	Huyton Quarry GF	—	**0 00** Huyton Quarry GF **0 76** Cronton Colliery
	8 72	**Rainhill**		
	11 63	St. Helens Jcn.	→	***Sutton Oak Jcn. - See Below***
	11 70	**St Helens Junction**		
	14 51	Earlestown West Jcn.	—	**0 00** Earlestown W. Jcn. **0 20** Earlestown S. Jcn. ▼ *Chester (83) - p.78*
	14 58	**Earlestown**		
	14 75	Earlestown East Jcn.		
	15 60	**Newton-le-Willows**		
16 19	16 19	Parkside West Jcn.	—	**0 00** Parkside West Jcn. **0 26** Lowton Jcn. **0 53** Golborne Jcn. WCML (see p.68) **0 58** Golborne Jcn. WCML **0 31** Lowton Jcn. **0 00** Parkside Jcn.
	16 56	Parkside Jcn.	—	
	22 54	Astley LC		
	26 46	**Patricroft**		
	27 59	**Eccles**		
		Windsor link - see note p.76		
30 38	30 38	Ordsall Lane Jcn.	—	**0 00** Ordsall Lane Jcn. **0 41** Castlefield Jcn. (see p.79)
.M.M.				
0 38	31 12	Deal Street Jcn.		
0 00	31 50	**Manchester Victoria**	→	*See p.76 for table refs.*

LIVERPOOL LIME STREET - WIGAN NORTH WESTERN (B.R. Table 99)

M. P.	M C			Connections
0 00	0 00	**Liverpool Lime Street** (see above)		
5 50	5 50	**Huyton**		
.M.M.	5 77	Huyton Jcn.		
1 57	7 69	**Prescot**		
2 47	8 59	**Eccleston Park**		
3 43	9 55	**Thatto Heath**		
5 12	11 24	St. Helens Station Jcn.	—	**0 00** St. Helens Stn. Jcn. **1 40** Sutton Oak Jcn. **1 75** St. Helens Jcn. (see above) **0 00** Sutton Oak Jcn. **4 04** Sutton Manor Colliery
5 24	11 36	**St. Helens Shaw Street**		
8 78	15 10	**Garswood**		
10 22	16 34	**Bryn**		
12 10	18 22	Ince Moss Jcn.	→	***Bamfurlong Sidings Jcn. - p.68***
.M.M.				
5 24	18 66	Springs Branch Jcn. WCML		
6 33	19 75	Wigan Station Jcn.	→	*Wigan Wallgate (95) - p.76*
6 47	20 09	**Wigan North Western**	→	*WCML (North) KEY PLAN - p.68*

VIA ARPLEY YARDS

MANCHESTER VICTORIA - CHESTER (B.R. Table 83)

M. P.	M C	Location	Connections
	0 00	**Manchester Victoria** →	*Huddersfield (39) - p.74* *Hebden Bridge (39) - p.74* *Rochdale (39/93) - p.74/75* *Bury (94) - p.75* *Blackburn (96) - p.75* *Wigan Wallgate (95) - p.76* *Preston (96) - p.76* *Liverpool (39/99) - p.77*
31 12	**0 38**	Deal Street Jcn.	
30 38	**1 12**	Ordsall Lane Jcn. →	***Castlefield Jcn. - p.77/79***
		Windsor Link - see note p.76	
27 59	**3 71**	**Eccles**	
26 46	**5 04**	**Patricroft**	
22 54	**8 76**	Astley LC	
16 56	**14 74**	Parkside Jcn.	
16 19	**15 31**	Parkside West Jcn. →	***Lowton Jcn. - p.77***
15 60	**15 70**	**Newton-le-Willows**	
C.M.M.			
187 10	**16 55**	Earlestown East Jcn.	
187 03	**16 62**	**Earlestown**	
186 74	**16 71**	Earlestown South Jcn. →	***Earlestown West Jcn. - p.77***
185 47	**18 18**	Winwick Jcns. (fast lines) →	*WCML (North) KEY PLAN - p.68*
185 38	**18 27**	Winwick Jcns. (down slow line)	
183 20	**20 45**	Dallam Branch Jcn.	
182 11	**21 54**	**Warrington Bank Quay**	
181 76	**21 69**	Warrington South Jcn. →	*Walton Old Jcn. - p.68* *Liverpool (65/82) - p.80*
C.M.M.			
16 19	**23 41**	Acton Grange Jcn.	
13 06	**26 54**	**Runcorn East**	
11 05	**28 55**	Frodsham Jcn. —	**1 54** Halton Jcn. (↑ Liverpool) **0 00** Frodsham Jcn.
9 68	**29 72**	**Frodsham**	
7 40	**32 20**	Helsby Jcn.	
7 34	**32 26**	**Helsby** →	*Hooton (107) - See Below*
2 57	**37 03**	Mickle Trafford Jcn. —	see branch below
C.M.M.			
178 70	**39 36**	Chester East Jcn.	
179 10	**39 56**	**Chester** →	*Shrewsbury (74) - p.64* *Crewe/Holyhead (83) - p.67* *Manchester Picc. (98) - p.79*

Mickle Trafford branch:

C.M.M.	M C	Location
35 34	**0 00**	Mickle Trafford Jcn.
C.M.M.		
0 00	**2 58**	
6 08	**8 66**	Dee Marsh Jcn. (see p.83)

CHESTER & HELSBY - HOOTON (B.R. Table 107)

M. P.	M C	Location
179 10	**0 00**	**Chester**
C.M.M.		
0 16	**0 19**	Chester West Jcn.
0 36	**0 39**	Chester North Jcn. — (**0 23** Chester South Jcn.; **0 00** Chester North Jcn.)
0 79	**1 02**	**Bache**
5 11	**5 14**	**Capenhurst**
7 68	**7 71**	Hooton Jcn.
8 07	**8 10**	**Hooton** ↓ *Rock Ferry/ Liverpool (106) - p.82*

M. P.	M C	Location
8 61	**0 00**	**Helsby**
8 12	**0 49**	West Cheshire Jcn. (see p.79)
6 44	**2 17**	**Ince & Elton**
6 04	**2 57**	**Stanlow & Thornton**
3 44	**5 17**	**Ellesmere Port**
1 47	**7 14**	**Little Sutton**
C.M.M.		
7 68	**8 58**	Hooton Jcn.
8 07	**8 77**	**Hooton**

MANCHESTER PICCADILLY - ALTRINCHAM - CHESTER (B.R. Table 98)

M. P.	M C		
0 13	0 00	**Manchester Piccadilly**	→ *Crewe (81) - p.70* *Stoke (69) - p.71* *Buxton (81) - p.71* *Sheffield (29) - p.72* *Hadfield (91) - p.73*
0 56	0 43	**Oxford Road**	
1 05	0 72	**Deansgate**	
.M.M.			
0 37	1 02	Castlefield Jcn.	**0 00** Castlefield Jcn. **0 41** Ordsall Lane Jcn. ↓ *Liverpool (39/99) - p.77* *Chester (83) - p.78*
1 17	1 62	Cornbrook Jcn.	→ *Liverpool (97) - p.81*
1 74	2 39	**Old Trafford**	
2 28	2 73	**Warwick Road**	
3 34	3 79	**Stretford**	
4 51	5 16	**Dane Road**	
5 11	5 56	**Sale**	
5 57	6 22	**Brooklands**	
6 55	7 20	**Timperley**	
7 06	7 51	Deansgate Jcn.	→ ***Skelton Jcn. - p.70***
7 30	7 75	**Navigation Road**	
7 61	8 26	**Altrincham**	
.M.M.			
8 36	9 12	**Hale**	
10 05	10 61	**Ashley**	
11 75	12 51	**Mobberley**	
14 36	15 12	**Knutsford**	
17 17	17 73	**Plumley**	
19 14	19 70	**Lostock Gralam**	
20 49	21 25	**Northwich**	
20 56	21 32	Sandbach Jcn.	**0 00** Sandbach Jcn. **0 28** Northwich South Jcn. (see p.70)
20 76	21 52	Northwich West Jcn.	**0 00** Northwich South Jcn. **0 29** Northwich West Jcn.
21 68	22 44	Hartford East Jcn.	**0 00** Hartford East Jcn. **0 22** Hartford North Jcn.
22 10	22 66	Hartford West Jcn.	**0 00** Hartford North Jcn. **0 22** Hartford West Jcn.
22 21	22 77	**Greenbank**	
23 09	23 65	Hartford C.L.C. Jcn.	→ ***Hartford L.N.W. Jcn. - p.68/80***
25 25	26 01	**Cuddington**	
28 02	28 58	**Delamere**	
31 05	31 61	**Mouldsworth**	**0 00** **Mouldsworth** **3 71** West Cheshire Jcn. (see p.78)
.M.M.			
2 57	36 10	Mickle Trafford Jcn.	
.M.M.			
78 70	38 43	Chester East Jcn.	
79 10	38 63	**Chester**	→ *See p.78 for table refs.*

CREWE - LIVERPOOL LIME STREET (B.R. Tables 65 & 82)

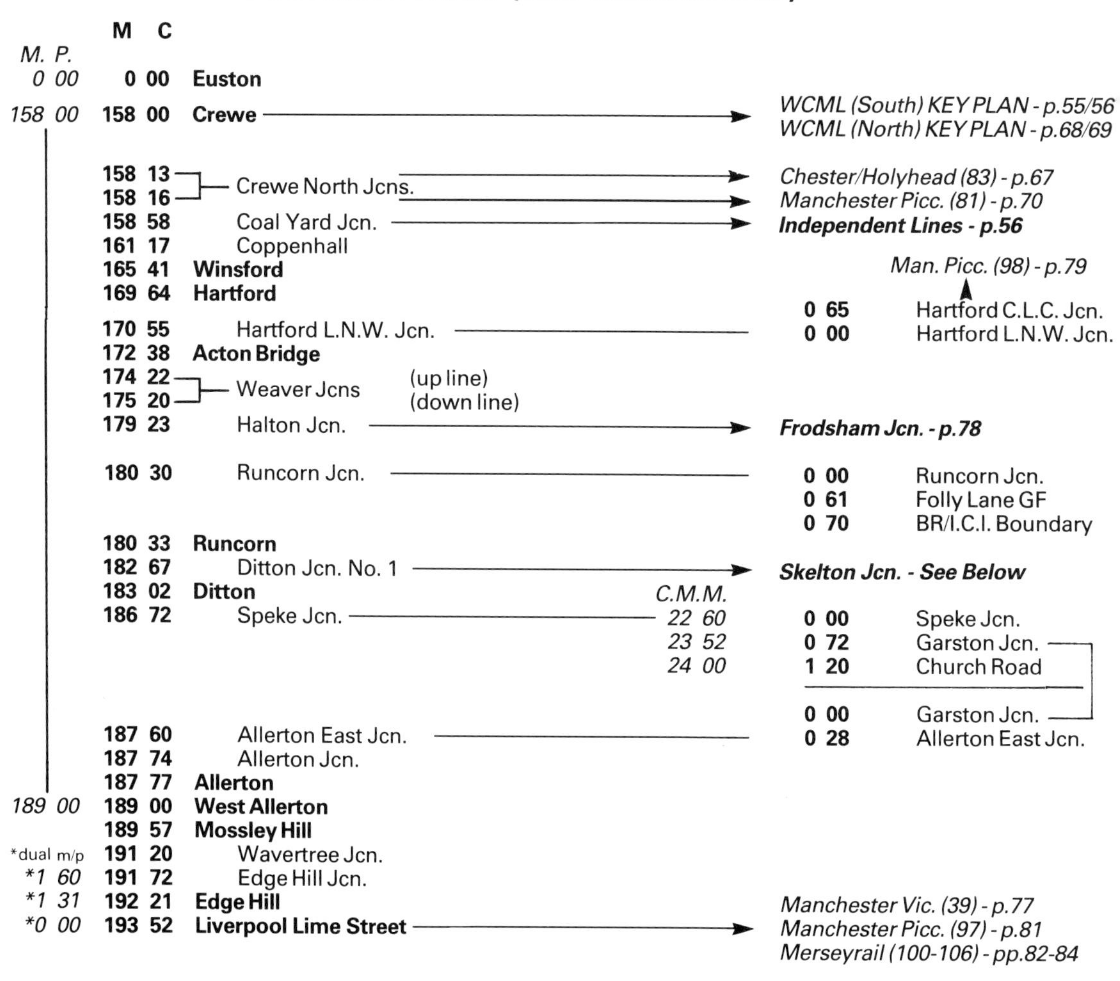

M C
M. P.
0 00 | 0 00 Euston
158 00 | 158 00 Crewe → WCML (South) KEY PLAN - p.55/56
WCML (North) KEY PLAN - p.68/69
158 13
158 16 Crewe North Jcns. → Chester/Holyhead (83) - p.67
Manchester Picc. (81) - p.70
158 58 Coal Yard Jcn. → Independent Lines - p.56
161 17 Coppenhall
165 41 Winsford
169 64 Hartford
Man. Picc. (98) - p.79
0 65 Hartford C.L.C. Jcn.
170 55 Hartford L.N.W. Jcn. — 0 00 Hartford L.N.W. Jcn.
172 38 Acton Bridge
174 22
175 20 Weaver Jcns (up line) (down line)
179 23 Halton Jcn. → Frodsham Jcn. - p.78
180 30 Runcorn Jcn. — 0 00 Runcorn Jcn.
0 61 Folly Lane GF
0 70 BR/I.C.I. Boundary
180 33 Runcorn
182 67 Ditton Jcn. No. 1 → Skelton Jcn. - See Below
183 02 Ditton
C.M.M.
186 72 Speke Jcn. — 22 60 | 0 00 Speke Jcn.
23 52 | 0 72 Garston Jcn.
24 00 | 1 20 Church Road
0 00 Garston Jcn.
187 60 Allerton East Jcn. — 0 28 Allerton East Jcn.
187 74 Allerton Jcn.
187 77 Allerton
189 00 | 189 00 West Allerton
189 57 Mossley Hill
*dual m/p | 191 20 Wavertree Jcn.
*1 60 | 191 72 Edge Hill Jcn.
*1 31 | 192 21 Edge Hill
*0 00 | 193 52 Liverpool Lime Street → Manchester Vic. (39) - p.77
Manchester Picc. (97) - p.81
Merseyrail (100-106) - pp.82-84

Ditton Jcn. - Skelton Jcns.

M. P.	M	C		
18 55	0	00	Ditton Jcn. No. 1	
17 53	1	02	Widnes West Deviation	
16 28	2	27	Carterhouse Jcn.	
14 46	4	09	Fiddlers Ferry P.S.	
13 37	5	18	Penketh Hall LC	
11 70	6	65	Monk's Siding LC	
11 03	7	52	Arpley Jcn.	→ 0 68 Arpley Jcn.; 0 00 Walton Old Jcn. → WCML (North) KEY PLAN - p.68
9 61	8	74	Latchford	
6 44	12	11	Statham LC	Closed
4 69	13	66	Lymm Lane LC	Closed
3 10	15	45	Dunham Massey LC	Closed
1 04	17	51	Sinderland Crossing LC	Closed
C.M.M.				
30 09	18	64	Skelton Jcn. West	→ Partington - p.70
30 12	18	67	Skelton Jcn. East	→ Northenden Jcn. - p.70

LIVERPOOL LIME STREET - HUNTS CROSS - WARRINGTON CENTRAL - MANCHESTER PICCADILLY (B.R. Table 97)

al m/p	M C		
3 52	*0 00	**Liverpool Lime Street** ⟶	*See p.80 for table refs.*
2 21	*1 31	**Edge Hill**	
1 72	*1 60	Edge Hill Jcn.	
1 20	2 32	Wavertree Jcn.	
9 57	3 75	**Mossley Hill**	
9 00	4 52	**West Allerton**	
7 77	5 55	**Allerton**	
M.M.			
0 00	5 58	Allerton Jcn.	
M.M.			
6 11	6 15	Hunts Cross West Jcn.	
7 07	7 11	**Hunts Cross** ⟶	*Liverpool Central (102) - p.84*
		Halewood (proposed)	
0 42	10 46	**Hough Green**	
2 20	12 24	**Widnes**	
5 67	15 71	**Sankey**	
8 34	18 38	**Warrington Central**	
0 13	20 17	**Padgate**	
1 44	21 48	**Birchwood**	
4 36	24 40	**Glazebrook**	
4 62	24 66	Glazebrook East Jcn.	
5 51	25 55	**Irlam**	
7 65	27 69	**Flixton**	
8 40	28 44	**Chassen Road**	
9 02	29 06	**Urmston**	
0 15	30 19	**Humphrey Park**	
0 68	30 72	**Trafford Park**	
1 70	31 74	Manchester United Football Ground	
2 02	32 06	Trafford Park East Jcn. ⟶	***Gorton Jcn. - p.73***
M.M.			
1 17	33 01	Cornbrook Jcn.	
M.M.			
1 15	33 61	Castlefield Jcn. ⟶	***Ordsall Lane Jcn. - p.79***
1 05	33 71	**Deansgate**	
0 56	34 20	**Oxford Road**	*Crewe (81) - p.70*
0 13	34 63	**Manchester Piccadilly** ⟶	*Stoke (69) - p.71*
			Buxton (81) - p.71
			Sheffield (29) - p.72
			Hadfield (91) - p.73
			Altrincham (98) - p.79

Hazel Grove East Jcn. 47567 *'Red Star'* swings down from the High Level Jcn. with the northbound 'European' on the 21st November, 1986. Opened earlier the same year, the Hazel Grove chord allows the diversion of Manchester-Sheffield trains via Stockport. In the foreground are the lines to and from Buxton; the bridge in the background carries the freight-only line to Northenden Jcn. (see pp.70/71/72). *(Steve Turner).*

MOORFIELDS - ROCK FERRY - HOOTON (B.R. Table 106)

M. P.	M C	
0 39	**0 00**	**Moorfields**
1 06	**0 47**	**Lime Street**
1 48	**1 09**	**Liverpool Central**
2 03	**1 44**	**James Street**
C.M.M.		*(see below)*
0 69	**1 62**	Mann Island Jcn.
1 60	**2 53**	Canning Street Jcn.
1 68	**2 61**	**Birkenhead, Hamilton Square**
1 72	**2 65**	Hamilton Square Jcn.
2 34	**3 27**	**Birkenhead Central**
2 64	**3 57**	**Green Lane**
C.M.M.		
13 43	**4 36**	**Rock Ferry** (through line)
12 36	**5 43**	**Bebington**
11 62	**6 17**	**Port Sunlight**
11 16	**6 63**	**Spital**
10 38	**7 41**	**Bromborough Rake**
9 76	**8 03*	**Bromborough**
8 07	**9 72**	**Hooton** ——→ *Chester/Helsby (107) - p.78*

M. P.	M C	
0 39	**3 16**	**Moorfields**
0 16	**2 73**	**James Street** (platform 1
0 00	**2 57**	Mann Island Jcn.
C.M.M.		
1 68	**1 58**	**Hamilton Square**
2 34	**1 12**	**Birkenhead Central**
2 64	**0 62**	**Green Lane**
3 46	**0 00**	**Rock Ferry** (Bay buffer stc

MOORFIELDS - WEST KIRBY (B.R. Table 104) & NEW BRIGHTON (B.R. Table 10

M. P.	M C	
0 39	**0 00**	**Moorfields**
1 06	**0 47**	**Lime Street**
1 48	**1 09**	**Liverpool Central**
2 03	**1 44**	**James Street**
C.M.M.		(see below)
0 69	**1 62**	Mann Island Jcn.
1 60	**2 53**	Canning Street Jcn.
1 68	**2 61**	**Hamilton Square** (platform 3)
1 72	**2 65**	Hamilton Square Jcn.
3 05	**3 78**	**Birkenhead Park**
3 75	**4 68**	**Birkenhead North**
4 40	**5 33**	Bidston East Jcn.
4 73	**5 66**	Bidston Dee Jcn.
4 75	**5 68**	**Bidston**
5 65	**6 58**	**Leasowe**
6 23	**7 16**	**Moreton**
8 13	**9 06**	**Meols**
8 69	**9 62**	**Manor Road**
9 32	**10 25**	**Hoylake**
10 36	**11 29**	**West Kirby**

M. P.	M C	
0 39	**10 06**	**Moorfields**
0 16	**9 63**	**James Street** (platform 1
0 00	**9 47**	Mann Island Jcn.
C.M.M.		
1 68	**8 48**	**Hamilton Square**
3 75	**6 41**	**Birkenhead North**
3 75	**4 68**	**Birkenhead North**
4 40	**5 33**	Bidston East Jcn.
4 74	**5 67**	Seacombe Jcn. (see p.83)
5 47	**6 40**	**Wallasey Village**
5 73	**6 66**	**Wallasey Grove Road**
7 05	**7 78**	**New Brighton**

Bidston - Rock Ferry via M.D.H.B. line

M. P.	M C	
4 75	**0 00**	**Bidston** ——→ *Wrexham (105) - p.83*
C.M.M.		
0 00	**0 35**	Bidston East Jcn.
0 18	**0 53**	Birkenhead North No. 2SB
0 36	**0 71**	Wallasey Bridge LC
0 43	**0 78**	***LMR/MDHB Boundary***
C.M.M.		
15 76	**1 74**	Duke Street LC
15 40	**2 65**	***MDHB/LMR Boundary***
15 29	**2 76**	Canning Street North SB
14 64	**3 41**	Haymarket Tunnel (North)
14 15	**4 10**	Green Lane SB
13 59	**4 46**	Rock Ferry North Jcn.
13 43	**4 62**	**Rock Ferry** (through line)

M C	
0 00	**James Street**
0 20	Paradise Jcn.
0 40	**Liverpool Central** (see p.83)

IDSTON - WREXHAM (B.R. Table 105)

M.P.	M C	Station	Connection
			M.D.H.B. line - p.82
4 75	0 00	**Bidston**	→ *West Kirby/Moorfields (104) - p.82*
M.M.			
0 08	0 03	Bidston Dee Jcn.	→ (see below)
1 66	1 61	**Upton**	
6 07	6 02	**Heswell**	
8 55	8 50	**Neston**	
13 77	13 72	Dee Marsh Jcn.	→ ***Mickle Trafford Jcn. - p.78***
14 12	14 07	**Hawarden Bridge**	
M.M.			
13 01	14 42	**Shotton**	
10 64	16 59	**Hawarden**	
8 67	18 56	**Buckley**	
7 41	20 02	**Penyfford**	
5 45	21 78	**Hope**	
4 73	22 50	**Caergwrle**	
4 20	23 23	**Cefn-y-Bedd**	
2 29	25 14	**Gwersyllt**	
0 49	26 74	**Wrexham General**	→ *Shrewsbury/Chester (74) - p.64*
0 01	27 42	**Wrexham Central**	

M C	Location
0 00	Bidston Dee Jcn.
0 39	Seacombe Jcn. (see p.82)

IVERPOOL CENTRAL - SOUTHPORT (B.R. Table 101)

M.P.	M C	Station	Connection
37 11	0 00	**Liverpool Central**	→ *West Kirby/Rock Ferry (104/6) - p.82* *Ormskirk (100) - p.84* *Hunts Cross/Kirkby (101/102) - p.84*
36 71	0 20	Paradise Jcn. (see p.82)	
36 46	0 45	**Moorfields (see p.82)**	
35 03	2 08	**Sandhills**	
M.M.			
1 41	2 16	Sandhills Jcn.	
2 06	2 61	**Bank Hall**	
2 33	3 08	Bootle Jcn.	→ (see below)
2 61	3 36	**Bootle Oriel Road**	
3 14	3 69	**Bootle New Strand**	
3 52	4 27	Marsh Lane Jcn.	→ (see below)
4 14	4 69	**Seaforth & Litherland**	
5 19	5 74	**Waterloo**	
6 28	7 03	**Blundellsands & Crosby**	
7 10	7 65	**Hall Road**	
9 04	9 59	**Hightown**	
11 13	11 68	**Formby**	
11 78	12 53	**Freshfield**	
14 67	15 42	**Ainsdale**	
16 26	17 01	**Hillside**	
17 27	18 02	**Birkdale**	
18 21	18 76	**Southport**	→ *Wigan Wallgate (95) - p.76*

Manchester Vic. (99) - p.77 ↑

M.P.	M C	Location
2 57	**0 00**	Olive Mount Jcn.
C.M.M.		
0 51	**0 43**	Edge Lane Jcn. (p.77)
C.M.M.		
2 33	**4 77**	Bootle Jcn.
2 61	**5 25**	**(Oriel Road)**
3 14	**5 58**	**(New Strand)**
C.M.M.		
34 50	**6 16**	Marsh Lane Jcn.
32 46	**8 20**	Sefton Jcn.
C.M.M.		
0 43	**8 67**	Aintree Excursion Platform

M.P.	M C	Location
5 05	**0 00**	Bootle Jcn.
5 41	**0 36**	Alexandra Dock GF
7 12	**2 07**	Seaforth F.L.T.

LIVERPOOL CENTRAL - ORMSKIRK / HUNTS CROSS - KIRKBY
(B.R. Tables 100, 101 & 102)

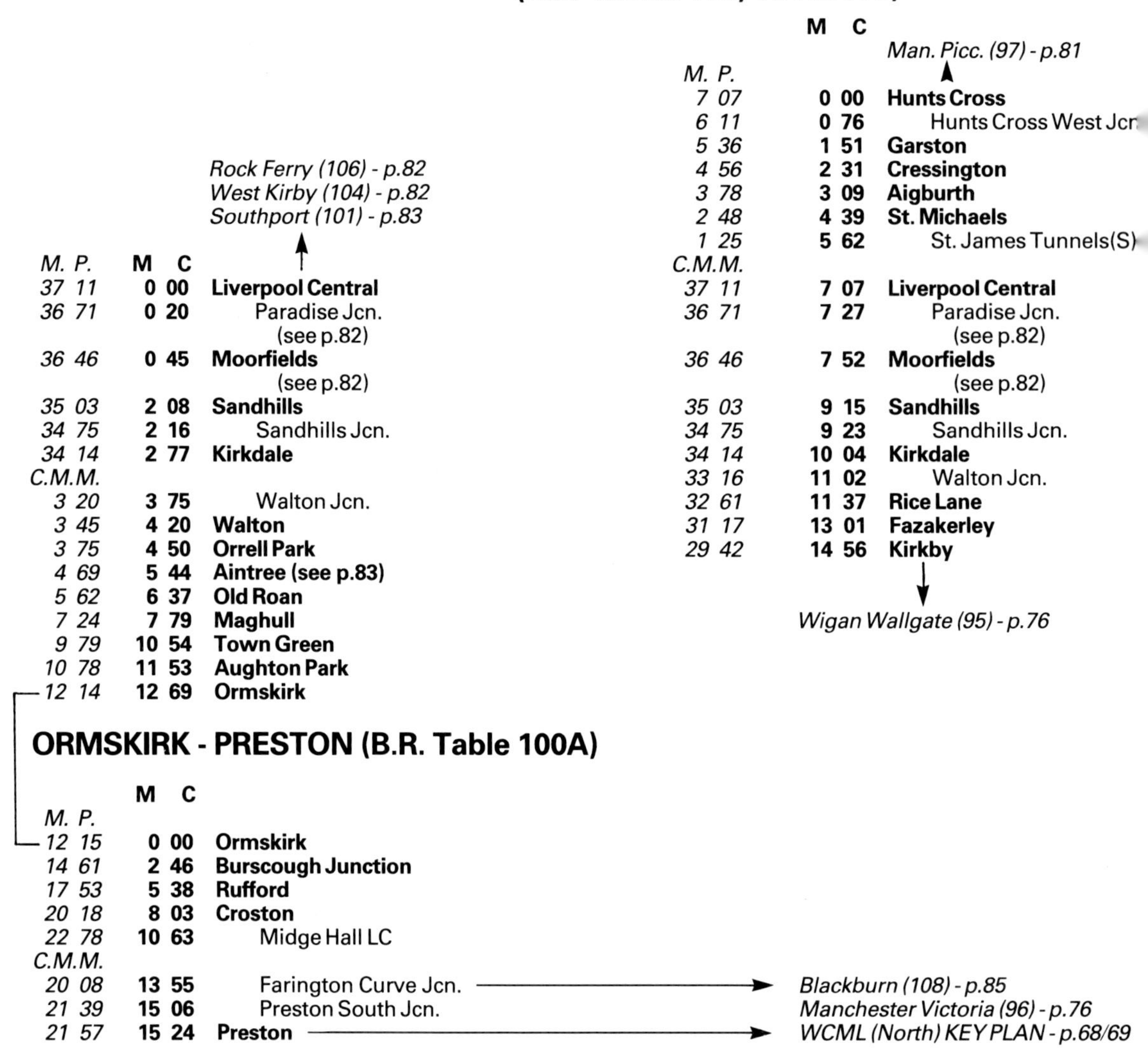

Rock Ferry (106) - p.82
West Kirby (104) - p.82
Southport (101) - p.83
↑

M. P.	M C	
37 11	**0 00**	**Liverpool Central**
36 71	**0 20**	Paradise Jcn. (see p.82)
36 46	**0 45**	**Moorfields** (see p.82)
35 03	**2 08**	**Sandhills**
34 75	**2 16**	Sandhills Jcn.
34 14	**2 77**	**Kirkdale**
C.M.M.		
3 20	**3 75**	Walton Jcn.
3 45	**4 20**	**Walton**
3 75	**4 50**	**Orrell Park**
4 69	**5 44**	**Aintree (see p.83)**
5 62	**6 37**	**Old Roan**
7 24	**7 79**	**Maghull**
9 79	**10 54**	**Town Green**
10 78	**11 53**	**Aughton Park**
12 14	**12 69**	**Ormskirk**

Man. Picc. (97) - p.81
↑

M. P.	M C	
7 07	**0 00**	**Hunts Cross**
6 11	**0 76**	Hunts Cross West Jcn
5 36	**1 51**	**Garston**
4 56	**2 31**	**Cressington**
3 78	**3 09**	**Aigburth**
2 48	**4 39**	**St. Michaels**
1 25	**5 62**	St. James Tunnels(S)
C.M.M.		
37 11	**7 07**	**Liverpool Central**
36 71	**7 27**	Paradise Jcn. (see p.82)
36 46	**7 52**	**Moorfields** (see p.82)
35 03	**9 15**	**Sandhills**
34 75	**9 23**	Sandhills Jcn.
34 14	**10 04**	**Kirkdale**
33 16	**11 02**	Walton Jcn.
32 61	**11 37**	**Rice Lane**
31 17	**13 01**	**Fazakerley**
29 42	**14 56**	**Kirkby**

↓
Wigan Wallgate (95) - p.76

ORMSKIRK - PRESTON (B.R. Table 100A)

M. P.	M C		
12 15	**0 00**	**Ormskirk**	
14 61	**2 46**	**Burscough Junction**	
17 53	**5 38**	**Rufford**	
20 18	**8 03**	**Croston**	
22 78	**10 63**	Midge Hall LC	
C.M.M.			
20 08	**13 55**	Faringtion Curve Jcn. →	*Blackburn (108) - p.85*
21 39	**15 06**	Preston South Jcn.	*Manchester Victoria (96) - p.76*
21 57	**15 24**	**Preston** →	*WCML (North) KEY PLAN - p.68/69*

PRESTON - BLACKPOOL (B.R. Table 96)

M. P.	M C	
0 00	**0 00**	**Preston**
	0 33	Fylde Jcn.
	5 17	**Salwick**
	7 67	**Kirkham & Wesham**
	8 28	Kirkham North Jcn.
	10 09	Weeton
	12 32	Singleton
14 31	**14 31**	**Poulton-le-Fylde**
	14 40	Poulton Jcn.
	16 32	**Layton**
	17 49	**Blackpool North**

M. P.	M C	
14 40	**0 00**	Poulton Jcn.
16 71	**2 31**	Burn Naze
18 77	**4 37**	Wyre Power Station

M C	
0 00	Fylde Jcn.
1 30	Deepdale Jcn. LC

M C	
8 28	Kirkham North Jcn.
11 09	**Moss Side**
13 56	**Lytham**
14 75	**Ansdell & Fairhaven**
16 51	**St. Annes-on-the-Sea**
18 34	**Squires Gate**
	Blackpool Pleasure Beach (proposed)
20 01	**Blackpool South**

PRESTON - BLACKBURN - COLNE (B.R. Table 108)

M. P.	M C		Connections
			WCML (North) KEY PLAN - p.68/69
			Manchester Victoria (96) - p.76
21 57	**0 00**	**Preston** →	*Ormskirk (100A) - p.84*
21 39	**0 18**	Preston South Jcn.	*Blackpool (96) - p.84*
C.M.M.			
0 00	**1 49**	Farington Curve Jcn.	
1 20	**2 69**	**Lostock Hall**	
1 42	**3 11**	Lostock Hall Jcn. →	***Farington Jcn. - p.68***
2 32	**4 01**	**Bamber Bridge**	
5 27	**6 76**	Hoghton LC	
7 43	**9 12**	**Pleasington**	
8 50	**10 19**	**Cherry Tree**	
9 24	**10 73**	**Mill Hill**	
10 11	**11 60**	Bolton Jcn.	
10 42	**12 11**	**Blackburn** →	*Manchester Victoria (96) - p.75*
11 09	**12 58**	Daisyfield Jcn.	
13 26	**14 75**	**Rishton**	
14 76	**16 45**	**Church & Oswaldtwistle**	
15 68	**17 37**	**Accrington**	
17 36	**19 05**	**Huncoat**	
18 73	**20 42**	**Hapton**	
20 05	**21 54**	Rose Grove West Jcn.	
20 30	**21 79**	**Rose Grove**	
21 03	**22 52**	Gannow Jcn. →	*Hebden Bridge (108) - See Below*
21 38	**23 07**	**Burnley Barracks**	
21 77	**23 46**	**Burnley Central**	
24 15	**25 64**	**Brierfield**	
25 35	**27 04**	**Nelson**	
27 41	**29 10**	**Colne**	

Branch from Blackburn:

M. P.	M C	
10 42	**0 00**	**Blackburn**
11 09	**0 47**	Daisyfield Jcn.
13 71	**3 29**	Wilpshire Tunnel (S)
21 40	**10 78**	Clitheroe
21 60	**11 18**	Horrocksford Jcn.
28 57	**18 15**	Gisburn Tunnel (W.)
34 68	**24 26**	**Hellifield**

Carlisle/Carnforth (36) - p.86

Branch from Rose Grove West Jcn.:

M C	
0 00	Rose Grove West Jcn.
1 55	Padiham CEGB Sidings

PRESTON - HEBDEN BRIDGE (B.R. Table 108)

M. P.	M C		Connections
	0 00	**Preston**	
10 42	**12 11**	**Blackburn**	
20 30	**21 79**	**Rose Grove**	
21 03	**22 52**	Gannow Jcn.	
21 68	**23 37**	**Burnley, Manchester Road**	
23 06	**24 55**	Townley Tunnel (West)	
25 52	**27 21**	Holme Tunnel (West)	
26 22	**27 71**	Copy Pit GF	
28 76	**30 45**	Kitson Wood Tunnel (West)	
C.M.M.			
19 61	**32 23**	Hall Royd Jcn.	
22 03	**34 45**	***LMR/ER Boundary*** (Eastwood)	*Halifax/Bradford (39/108) - p.31*
23 56	**36 18**	**Hebden Bridge** →	*Manchester Victoria (39) - p.74*

LANCASTER - MORECAMBE (B.R. Table 109)

M. P.	M C		Connections
0 00	**0 00**	**Lancaster** →	*WCML (North) KEY PLAN - p.69*
C.M.M.			
0 00	**1 72**	Morecambe South Jcn	
0 44	**2 36**	Bare Lane Jcn.	
0 57	**2 49**	**Bare Lane**	
1 74	**3 66**	Morecambe Jcn.	
2 27	**4 19**	**Morecambe**	

M C	
0 00	Hest Bank LC
1 30	Bare Lane Jcn.

M C	
0 00	**Morecambe**
0 33	Morecambe Jcn.
3 06	Heysham Moss Sdgs.
4 38	Heysham Harbour

SKIPTON - CARLISLE & CARNFORTH (B.R. Table 36)

M. P.	M C	Location	Connection
221 21	0 00	**Skipton**	→ *Leeds (36) - p.32*
221 35	0 14	Skipton Station North Jcn.	→ ***Swinden - See Below***
224 79	3 58	**Gargrave**	
231 15	9 74	**Hellifield**	→ ***Blackburn - p.85***
232 41	11 20	**Long Preston**	
234 40	13 19	Settle Jcn.	→ Carnforth line (below)
236 30	15 09	**Settle**	
238 54	17 33	Stainforth Tunnel (Sth.)	
242 37	21 16	Horton	
247 20	25 79	Ribblehead	
249 25	28 04	Blea Moor Tunnel (Sth.)	
253 32	32 11	Dent	
254 11	32 70	Rise Hill Tunnel (Sth.)	
256 55	35 34	Garsdale	
259 57	38 36	Ais Gill Summit	
264 23	43 02	Birkett Tunnel (Sth.)	
266 40	45 19	Kirkby Stephen	
269 00	47 59	Crosby Garrett Tunnel (Sth.)	
273 13	51 72	Helm Tunnel (Sth.)	
277 22	56 01	**Appleby**	
277 34	56 13	Appleby North Jcn.	→ Warcop branch (below)
284 55	63 34	Culgaith LC	
288 23	67 02	Langwathby	
290 63	69 42	Long Meg Sidings	
292 50	71 29	Lazonby	
295 42	74 21	Baron Wood No. 1 Tunnel (Sth.)	
298 16	76 75	Armathwaite	
299 55	78 34	Low House Crossing LC	
302 77	81 56	Howe & Co's Sidings	
C.M.M.			
59 26	85 71	Petteril Bridge Jcn.	
59 45	86 10	London Road Jcn.	→ ***Carlisle Area - p.69***
C.M.M.			
68 73	86 47	Carlisle South Jcn.	
69 09	86 63	**Carlisle**	→ *Newcastle (48) - p.42* *WCML (North) KEY PLAN - p.69* *Barrow (113) - p.87* *Glasgow (65) - p.145* *Kilmarnock (222) - p.147*

M. P.	M C	Location
234 40	13 19	Settle Jcn.
236 27	15 06	**Giggleswick**
241 79	20 58	**Clapham**
246 23	25 02	**Bentham**
249 42	28 21	**Wennington**
C.M.M.		
9 01	28 67	Melling Tunnel (Sth.)
C.M.M.		
0 25	37 37	Carnforth East Jcn. (see p.87)
C.M.M.		
0 38	37 58	Carnforth Station Jcn
0 31	37 65	**Carnforth** ↓ *WCML (North) KEY PLAN - p.69*, *Barrow (110) - p.87*

M C	Location
0 00	Appleby North Jcn.
0 38	Appleby East LC
6 20	Warcop

C.M.M.	M C	Location
222 68	0 00	Skipton Station North Jcn.
221 07	1 61	Haw Tunnel (Sth.)
C.M.M.		
0 00	2 04	Embsay Jcn.
5 17	7 21	Rylstone LC
7 10	9 14	Swinden, Spencers Siding

OXENHOLME - WINDERMERE (B.R. Table 111)

M. P.	M C	Location
19 08	0 00	**Oxenholme** (see p.69)
C.M.M.		
2 05	2 09	**Kendal**
4 02	4 06	**Barneside**
6 52	6 56	**Staveley**
10 20	10 24	**Windermere**

Lakeside & Haverthwaite Railway

M. P.	M C	Location
4 48	0 00	**Haverthwaite**
6 60	2 12	**Newby Bridge**
8 00	3 32	**Lakeside**

CARNFORTH - BARROW-IN-FURNESS (B.R. Table 110)

M. P.	M C	Location	Connections	M C	Location
0 31	0 00	**Carnforth**	→		*Skipton (36) - p.86*
0 38	0 07	Carnforth Station Jcn.		0 00	Carnforth East Jcn. (see p.86)
0 67	0 36	Carnforth F. & M. Jcn.	—	0 27	F. & M. Jcn.
3 55	3 24	**Silverdale**			
6 29	5 78	**Arnside**			
9 31	9 00	**Grange-over-Sands**			
11 27	10 76	**Kents Bank**			
13 48	13 17	**Cark**			
17 55	17 24	Plumpton Jcn.	—	0 00	Plumpton Jcn.
19 28	18 77	**Ulverston**		0 48	Glaxo Siding
22 53	22 22	Lindal Tunnel (North)			
23 67	23 34	**Dalton**			
24 38	24 07	Dalton Jcn.	—	0 00	Dalton Jcn.
27 13	26 62	**Roose**		0 76	Park South Jcn. (see below)
27 57	27 26	Salthouse Jcn.			
29 05	28 54	**Barrow-in-Furness**			

BARROW-IN-FURNESS -CARLISLE (B.R. Table 113)

M. P.	M C	Location	Connections
29 05	0 00	**Barrow-in-Furness**	
32 76	3 71	Park South Jcn.	→ ***Dalton Jcn. - See Above***
35 03	5 78	**Askam**	
38 19	9 14	**Kirkby-in-Furness**	
40 40	11 35	**Foxfield**	
42 34	13 29	**Green Road**	
45 07	16 02	**Millom**	
48 12	19 07	**Silecroft**	
53 37	24 32	**Bootle**	
57 79	28 74	**Ravenglass**	
59 78	30 73	**Drigg**	
62 12	33 07	**Seascale**	
63 76	34 71	**Sellafield**	
65 76	36 71	**Braystones**	
67 32	38 27	**Nethertown**	
70 22	41 17	**St. Bees**	
73 78	44 73	**Corkickle**	
74 66	45 61	**Whitehaven**	
C.M.M.			
0 16	45 68	Bransty	
1 41	47 13	**Parton**	
4 50	50 22	**Harrington**	
6 69	52 41	**Workington**	
8 19	53 71	Siddick Jcn.	— 0 00 Siddick Jcn.
10 42	56 14	**Flimby**	1 03 Calva Jcn.
C.M.M.			4 38 Buckhill
0 21	57 78	**Maryport**	
7 73	65 50	**Aspatria**	
16 20	73 77	**Wigton**	
23 43	81 20	**Dalston**	
26 74	84 51	Currock Jcn.	→ ***Carlisle Area - p.69***
C.M.M.			
68 73	85 33	Carlisle South Jcn.	*Newcastle (48) - p.42* *WCML (North) KEY PLAN - p.69*
69 09	85 49	**Carlisle**	→ *Skipton (36) - p.86* *Glasgow (65) - p.145* *Kilmarnock (222) - p.147*

Ravenglass & Eskdale Railway

M C	Location
0 00	**Ravenglass**
1 08	**Muncaster Mill**
1 48	**Miteside Halt**
4 16	**Irton Road**
4 64	**The Green**
6 40	**Beckfoot**
6 75	**Eskdale** (Dalgarth)

SECTION III - WESTERN REGION

(a) London - West of England

PADDINGTON - BRISTOL TEMPLE MEADS - PENZANCE (B.R. Tables 127 & 135)

KEY PLAN

M. P.	M	C	Location	Connection
*0 05**	**0**	**05**	***Paddington**	
(see note)	**0**	**61**	Subway Jcn.	
	1	**20**	**Westbourne Park**	
	1	**33**	Portobello Jcn.	
	1	**73**	Ladbroke Grove	
	2	**64**	Old Oak Common East Jcn.	→ *Kensington Olympia (LMR) - p.54*
	3	**20**	Old Oak Common West Jcn.	→ *South Ruislip (115) - p.92*
	4	**16**	Acton East Jcn.	→ ***Acton Wells Jcn. - p.54***
	4	**21**	**Acton Main Line**	
	4	**54**	Acton Goods Yard GF	
	5	**56**	**Ealing Broadway**	→ *Greenford (118) - p.92*
	6	**41**	**West Ealing**	
	6	**56**	West Ealing Jcn.	
	7	**28**	**Hanwell**	→ ***Drayton Green Jcn. - p.92***
	9	**06**	**Southall**	
	9	**57**	Southall West Jcn.	→ ***Brentford Goods - see below***
	10	**71**	**Hayes & Harlington**	
	13	**17**	**West Drayton**	→ ***Colnbrook - see below***
	14	**60**	**Iver**	
	16	**18**	**Langley**	
	17	**03**	Dolphin Jcns.	
	17	**40**		
	18	**36**	**Slough**	→ **0 00 Slough**; **2 63 Windsor & Eton Central**
	20	**77**	**Burnham**	
	22	**39**	**Taplow**	
	24	**19**	**Maidenhead**	→ *Marlow (120) - p.92*
	29	**29**	Ruscombe Jcns.	
	29	**60**		
	31	**01**	**Twyford**	→ *Henley-on-Thames (121) - p.92*
	34	**02**	Sonning GF	
	35	**40**	Reading New Jcn.	
	35	**78**	**Reading**	→ *Guildford (124) - p.115*; *Waterloo (147) - p.115*; *Basingstoke (158) - p.113*
	36	**17**	Westbury Line Jcn.	→ *Westbury (122/135) - p.91*
	36	**76**	Reading West Jcn.	→ ***Oxford Road Jcn. - p.113***
	38	**52**	**Tilehurst**	
	41	**43**	**Pangbourne**	
	44	**60**	**Goring & Streatley**	
	48	**37**	**Cholsey**	
	51	**20**	Moreton Cutting Jcns.	
	51	**53**		
	52	**58**	Didcot East Jcn. (up line)	
	52	**66**	Didcot East Jcn. (down line)	
*53 10**	**53**	**10**	**Didcot Parkway**	→ *Banbury (116) - p.93*; *Worcester/Hereford (126) - p.94*

M	C	Location
0	**00**	**Southall**
2	**70**	Brentford Goods

M	C	Location
0	**00**	**West Drayton**
3	**09**	Colnbrook LC
3	**60**	End of Branch

***NOTE: According to B.R. records, there is a 5 chains error at Paddington (a chain or so more since the recent re-building). Paddington is shown as Om. 05c. on all tables so that mileages tie up with lineside mile-posts.**

PADDINGTON - BRISTOL TEMPLE MEADS - PENZANCE continued

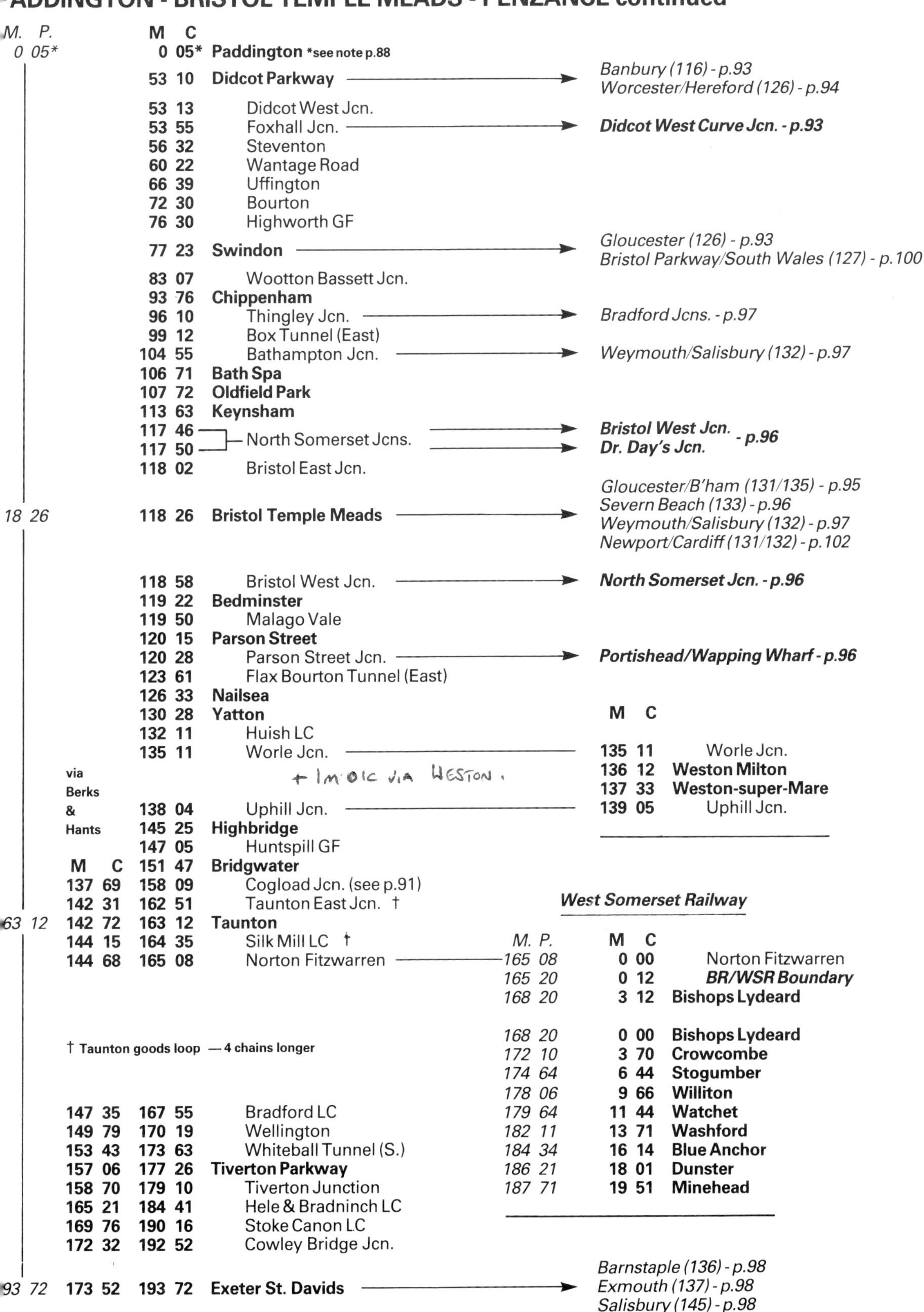

M. P.	M C (via Berks & Hants)	M C	Location	Connections
0 05*		0 05*	**Paddington** *see note p.88	
		53 10	**Didcot Parkway**	*Banbury (116) - p.93* *Worcester/Hereford (126) - p.94*
		53 13	Didcot West Jcn.	
		53 55	Foxhall Jcn.	***Didcot West Curve Jcn. - p.93***
		56 32	Steventon	
		60 22	Wantage Road	
		66 39	Uffington	
		72 30	Bourton	
		76 30	Highworth GF	
		77 23	**Swindon**	*Gloucester (126) - p.93* *Bristol Parkway/South Wales (127) - p.100*
		83 07	Wootton Bassett Jcn.	
		93 76	**Chippenham**	
		96 10	Thingley Jcn.	*Bradford Jcns. - p.97*
		99 12	Box Tunnel (East)	
		104 55	Bathampton Jcn.	*Weymouth/Salisbury (132) - p.97*
		106 71	**Bath Spa**	
		107 72	**Oldfield Park**	
		113 63	**Keynsham**	
		117 46	North Somerset Jcns.	***Bristol West Jcn.*** - ***p.96***
		117 50	North Somerset Jcns.	***Dr. Day's Jcn.*** - ***p.96***
		118 02	Bristol East Jcn.	
18 26		118 26	**Bristol Temple Meads**	*Gloucester/B'ham (131/135) - p.95* *Severn Beach (133) - p.96* *Weymouth/Salisbury (132) - p.97* *Newport/Cardiff (131/132) - p.102*
		118 58	Bristol West Jcn.	***North Somerset Jcn. - p.96***
		119 22	**Bedminster**	
		119 50	Malago Vale	
		120 15	**Parson Street**	
		120 28	Parson Street Jcn.	***Portishead/Wapping Wharf - p.96***
		123 61	Flax Bourton Tunnel (East)	
		126 33	**Nailsea**	
		130 28	**Yatton**	
		132 11	Huish LC	
		135 11	Worle Jcn.	
			+ 1m 01c via Weston.	
		138 04	Uphill Jcn.	
		145 25	**Highbridge**	
		147 05	Huntspill GF	
		151 47	**Bridgwater**	
	137 69	158 09	Cogload Jcn. (see p.91)	
	142 31	162 51	Taunton East Jcn. †	
63 12	142 72	163 12	**Taunton**	
	144 15	164 35	Silk Mill LC †	
	144 68	165 08	Norton Fitzwarren	West Somerset Railway
	147 35	167 55	Bradford LC	
	149 79	170 19	Wellington	
	153 43	173 63	Whiteball Tunnel (S.)	
	157 06	177 26	**Tiverton Parkway**	
	158 70	179 10	Tiverton Junction	
	165 21	184 41	Hele & Bradninch LC	
	169 76	190 16	Stoke Canon LC	
	172 32	192 52	Cowley Bridge Jcn.	
93 72	173 52	193 72	**Exeter St. Davids**	*Barnstaple (136) - p.98* *Exmouth (137) - p.98* *Salisbury (145) - p.98*

† Taunton goods loop — 4 chains longer

M C	Location
135 11	Worle Jcn.
136 12	**Weston Milton**
137 33	**Weston-super-Mare**
139 05	Uphill Jcn.

West Somerset Railway

M. P.	M C	Location
165 08	0 00	Norton Fitzwarren
165 20	0 12	***BR/WSR Boundary***
168 20	3 12	**Bishops Lydeard**
168 20	0 00	**Bishops Lydeard**
172 10	3 70	**Crowcombe**
174 64	6 44	**Stogumber**
178 06	9 66	**Williton**
179 64	11 44	**Watchet**
182 11	13 71	**Washford**
184 34	16 14	**Blue Anchor**
186 21	18 01	**Dunster**
187 71	19 51	**Minehead**

PADDINGTON - BRISTOL TEMPLE MEADS - PENZANCE continued

M. P.	M C (via B&H)	M C	Location	Connection
0 05*		0 05*	**Paddington** *see note - p.88	
118 26		118 26	**Bristol Temple Meads**	
193 72	173 52	193 72	**Exeter St. Davids**	
	174 46	194 66	**Exeter St. Thomas**	
	178 39	198 59	Exminster	
	182 16	202 36	**Starcross**	
	184 14	204 34	**Dawlish Warren**	
	185 67	206 07	**Dawlish**	
	186 14	206 34	Kennaway Tunnel N.	
	186 33	206 53	Coryton Tunnel N.	
	186 46	206 66	Phillot Tunnel N.	
	186 52	206 72	Clerks Tunnel N.	
	186 79	207 19	Parson's Tunnel N.	
	188 58	208 78	**Teignmouth**	
	193 45	213 65	Newton Abbot East	→ Heathfield branch
	193 66	214 06	**Newton Abbot**	
	194 69	215 09	Aller Jcn. (see above)	
	202 27	222 47	Dart Valley GF	→ Dart Valley Railway
	202 43	222 63	**Totnes**	
	209 40	229 60	Brent GF	
	214 79	235 19	Ivybridge East GF	
	218 70	239 10	Hemerdon GF	
	222 49	242 69	Tavistock Jcn. GF	
	223 62	244 02	Laira Jcn.	→ ***Plymouth Friary, Plymstock, Cattewater* - p.99**
	224 15	244 35	Lipson Jcn.	
245 75	225 55	245 75	**Plymouth**	
C.M.M.				
248 28	226 75	247 15	**Devonport**	
248 60	227 27	247 47	**Dockyard**	
249 30	227 77	248 17	**Keyham**	
250 00	228 47	248 67	St. Budeaux Jcn.	→ *Gunnislake (139) - p.99*
250 15	228 62	249 02	**St. Budeaux Ferry Road**	
251 26	229 73	250 13	**Saltash**	
256 24	234 71	255 11	**St. Germans**	
261 61	240 28	260 48	**Menheniot**	
264 66	243 33	263 53	**Liskeard**	→ *Looe (140) - p.99*
270 01	248 48	268 68	Largin	
274 03	252 50	272 70	**Bodmin Parkway**	
277 34	256 01	276 21	**Lostwithiel**	→ ***Carne Point - p.99***
281 69	260 36	280 56	**Par**	→ *Newquay (142) - p.99*
286 26	264 73	285 13	**St. Austell**	
288 56	267 23	287 43	Burngullow Jcn.	→ ***Parkandillack - p.99***
297 50	276 17	296 37	Polperro Tunnel (East)	
300 57	279 24	299 44	**Truro**	→ *Falmouth (143) - p.99*
301 25	279 72	300 12	Penwithers Jcn.	
306 09	284 56	304 76	Chacewater GF	
309 68	288 35	308 55	**Redruth**	
313 40	292 70	312 27	**Camborne**	
319 32	297 79	318 19	**Hayle**	
320 67	299 34	319 54	**St. Erth**	→ *St. Ives (144) - p.99*
325 12	303 59	323 79	Long Rock LC	
326 50	305 17	325 37	**Penzance**	

M C	Location	via B&H
215 09	Aller Jcn.	194 69
219 10	**Torre**	198 70
220 04	**Torquay**	199 64
222 12	**Paignton**	201 72
222 22	Paignton South LC	

Torbay & Dartmouth Railway

M. P.	M C	Location
222 07	0 00	**Paignton Queens Park** (buffer stop)
222 22	0 15	Paignton South L C
222 67	0 60	**Goodrington Sands**
225 00	2 73	**Churston**
228 64	6 57	**Kingswear** (buffer stop)

M C	Location
3 20	Heathfield
0 00	Newton Abbot East

Dart Valley Railway

M. P.	M C	Location
7 05	0 00	Buffer stop
6 77	0 08	**Buckfastleigh**
6 77	0 00	**Buckfastleigh**
3 25	3 52	**Staverton Bridge**
0 30	6 47	Riverside GF
0 22	6 55	**Totnes Riverside**

ADDINGTON - TAUNTON via Westbury (B.R. Tables 122/135)

("Berks. & Hants." line)

M. P.	M	C		
0 05*	0	05*	**Paddington** *see note - p.88	
	35	78	**Reading** →	*Basingstoke (158) - p.113* *Guildford (124) - p.115* *Waterloo (147) - p.115*
	36	17	Westbury Line Jcn.	
	36	37	Oxford Road Jcn. →	***Reading West Jcn. - p.113***
	36	75	**Reading West**	
	37	62	Southcote Jcn.	
	41	22	**Theale**	
	44	63	**Aldermaston**	
	46	56	**Midgham**	
	49	51	**Thatcham**	
	52	39	Newbury Racecourse	
	53	06	**Newbury**	
	56	09	Hamstead LC	
	58	42	**Kintbury**	
	61	47	**Hungerford**	
	66	29	**Bedwyn**	
	70	07	Savernake GF	
	75	26	**Pewsey**	
	78	73	Woodborough Sidings GF	
	88	06	Lavington GF	
	94	45	Heywood Road Jcn. (see below)	
94 77	94	77	Westbury East Loop Jcn. —	0 00 Westbury East Loop Jcn. 0 35 Hawkeridge Jcn.
.M.M.				
09 54	95	37	Westbury North Jcn. →	*Salisbury/Bristol (132) - p.97*
09 64	95	47	**Westbury**	
10 12	95	75	Westbury South Jcn.	
11 18	97	01	Fairwood Jcn. —	(see Westbury avoiding line)
14 40	100	23	Clink Road Jcn. —	(see Frome avoiding line)
15 17	101	00	Frome North Jcn. (see below)	
15 44	101	27	**Frome**	
16 57	102	40	Blatchbridge Jcn. —	(see Frome avoiding line)
20 67	106	50	East Somerset Jcn. —	(see East Somerset Railway)
26 13	111	76	**Bruton**	
29 46	115	29	**Castle Cary**	
.M.M.				
15 38	115	38	Castle Cary Jcn. (p.97)	
26 59	126	59	Somerton Tunnel (East)	
34 79	134	79	Athelney LC	
.M.M.				
58 09	137	69	Cogload Jcn.	
62 51	142	31	Taunton East Jcn.	
63 12	142	72	**Taunton** →	*Bristol/Exeter (135) - p.89*

Westbury avoiding line

M	C	
94	45	Heywood Road Jcn.
97	02	Fairwood Jcn. (1 chain longer)

Frome avoiding line

M	C	
100	23	Clink Road Jcn.
102	25	Blatchbridge Jcn. (15 chains shorter)

East Somerset Railway

M. P.	M	C	
0 04	0	00	East Somerset Jcn.
	3	46	Merehead Quarry Jcn. GF
	4	53	Merehead West
	5	53	**Cranmore**
6 00	5	76	***BR/ESR Boundary***
	6	03	**Cranmore West**
	6	49	**Merryfield Lane**
	7	38	Mendip Vale (end of line)

M. P.	M	C	
0 00	0	00	Frome North Jcn.
	2	38	Somerset Quarries North GF
	2	51	Bedlam Tunnel (East)
	2	76	Great Elm Tunnel (East)
	3	56	Murdercombe Tunnel (North)
4 00	4	00	Whatley Quarry GF

M	C	
0	00	Merehead Quarry Jcn. GF
1	54	Merehead Quarry

M	C	
0	00	Merehead Quarry Jcn. GF
1	07	Merehead West
1	33	Whites Crossing Siding (REV.)
2	15	Merehead Quarry

EALING BROADWAY - GREENFORD (B.R. Table 118)

M. P.	M C	Station	Connection
5 51	0 00	**Ealing Broadway**	→ *Paddington/Reading - p.88*
6 36	0 65	**West Ealing**	
6 56	1 05	West Ealing Jcn.	
7 03	1 32	Drayton Green Jcn.	—
7 07	1 36	**Drayton Green**	
7 44	1 73	**Castle Bar Park**	
8 24	2 53	**South Greenford**	
8 45	2 74	Greenford South Jcn.	—
8 65	3 14	LRT Bay Jcn.	
8 76	3 25	Greenford West Jcn.	→ *Paddington (115) - See Below*
9 06	3 35	**Greenford**	

M C	Station
	↑ *Paddington/Reading - p.88*
0 00	**Hanwell**
0 36	Drayton Green Jcn.

M C	Station
0 00	Greenford South Jcn.
0 25	Greenford East Jcn.
	↓ *Paddington (115) - See Below*

PADDINGTON - BANBURY via Greenford (B.R. Table 115)

M. P.	M C	Station	Connection
0 05*	0 05	**Paddington** *See note - p.88	
|	1 20	**Westbourne Park**	
|	3 20	Old Oak Common West Jcn.	
|	4 65	Park Royal GF	
|	7 15	Greenford East Jcn.	→ *Ealing Broadway (118) - See Above*
|	7 48	Greenford West Jcn.	
|	9 30	***WR/LMR Boundary***	
10 06*	10 06	Northolt Jcn. East	
C.M.M.			
0 00	10 13	Northolt Jcn.	→ *Marylebone / Banbury (115) - p.50*
0 07	10 20	**South Ruislip**	
16 29	26 42	**High Wycombe**	
24 50	34 63	**Princes Risborough**	
C.M.M.			
9 27	53 29	**Bicester**	
C.M.M.			
86 16	67 35	**Banbury**	→ *Birmingham (116) - p.58* *Paddington (116) - p.93*

MAIDENHEAD - MARLOW (B.R. Table 120)

M. P.	M C	Station
24 19	0 00	**Maidenhead** (see p.88)
25 36	1 17	**Furze Platt**
27 12	2 73	**Cookham**
28 55	4 36	**Bourne End**
C.M.M.		
0 18	4 52	Brooksby LC
2 54	7 08	**Marlow**

TWYFORD - HENLEY-ON-THAMES (B.R. Table 121)

M. P.	M C	Station
31 01	0 00	**Twyford** (see p.88)
32 68	1 67	**Wargrave**
33 66	2 65	**Shiplake**
35 50	4 49	**Henley-on-Thames**

PADDINGTON - BANBURY via Didcot (B.R. Table 116)

	M C				
*0 05**	**0 05***	**Paddington** (see note - p.88) →	*West of England KEY PLAN - pp.88-90*		
	35 78	**Reading** →	*Westbury (122/135) - p.91* *Basingstoke (158) - p.113* *Waterloo (147) - p.115* *Guildford (124) - p.115*		
	52 58	Didcot East Jcn. (up line) †			
	52 66	Didcot East Jcn. (down line) †			
	53 10	**Didcot Parkway**			
	53 13	Didcot West Jcn.		**0 31**	Foxhall Jcn. (see p.89)
	53 51	Didcot West Curve Jcn. —		**0 00**	Didcot West Curve Jcn.
	53 74	Didcot North Jcn. †			
	54 48	Appleford LC			
	55 16	**Appleford**			
	56 17	**Culham**			
	58 35	**Radley**		**2 53**	Morris Cowley
	61 08	Kennington Jcn. —		**0 00**	Kennington Jcn.
	63 41	**Oxford**			
	64 45	Oxford North Jcn. →	***Bletchley - p.51***		
	66 32	Wolvercot Jcn. →	*Worcester/Hereford (126) - p.94*		
	70 34	Bletchington GF			
	72 40	**Tackley**			
	75 21	**Heyford**			
	76 40	***WR/LMR Boundary***			
	81 12	Aynho Jcn. →	*Marylebone (115) - p.50*		
	82 55	**Kings Sutton**			
86 16	**86 16**	**Banbury** →	*Birmingham (116) - p.58*		

† **Didcot avoiding line - 9 chains shorter**

SWINDON - GLOUCESTER (B.R. Table 126)

M. P.	M C				
77 23	**0 00**	**Swindon** →	*Paddington (127/135) - p.89* *Bristol Parkway/S. Wales (127) - p.100*		
79 00	**1 57**	Bremmell Sidings GF			
31 09	**3 66**	Purton LC			
36 74	**9 51**	Minety LC			
90 79	**13 56**	**Kemble**			
94 50	**17 27**	Sapperton Short Tunnel (South)			
95 74	**18 51**	Sapperton Long Tunnel (North)			
98 64	**21 41**	St. Mary's LC			
02 13	**24 70**	**Stroud**			
04 74	**27 51**	**Stonehouse**			
M.M.					
99 68	**29 51**	Standish Jcn. →	*Bristol (131) - p.95*		
M.M.					
04 10	**34 59**	Tuffley —		**0 00**	Tuffley
				2 21	Quedgeley Depot Sdgs. GF
M.M.					
13 03	**35 61**	Gloucester Yard Jcn. →	*Birmingham (131) - p.95*		
13 56	**36 34**	Horton Road LC			
13 61	**36 39**	Horton Road Jcn. →	*Barnwood Jcn. - p.95*		
14 04	**36 62**	**Gloucester** →	*Newport (131) - p.102*		

PADDINGTON - WORCESTER & HEREFORD (B.R. Table 126)

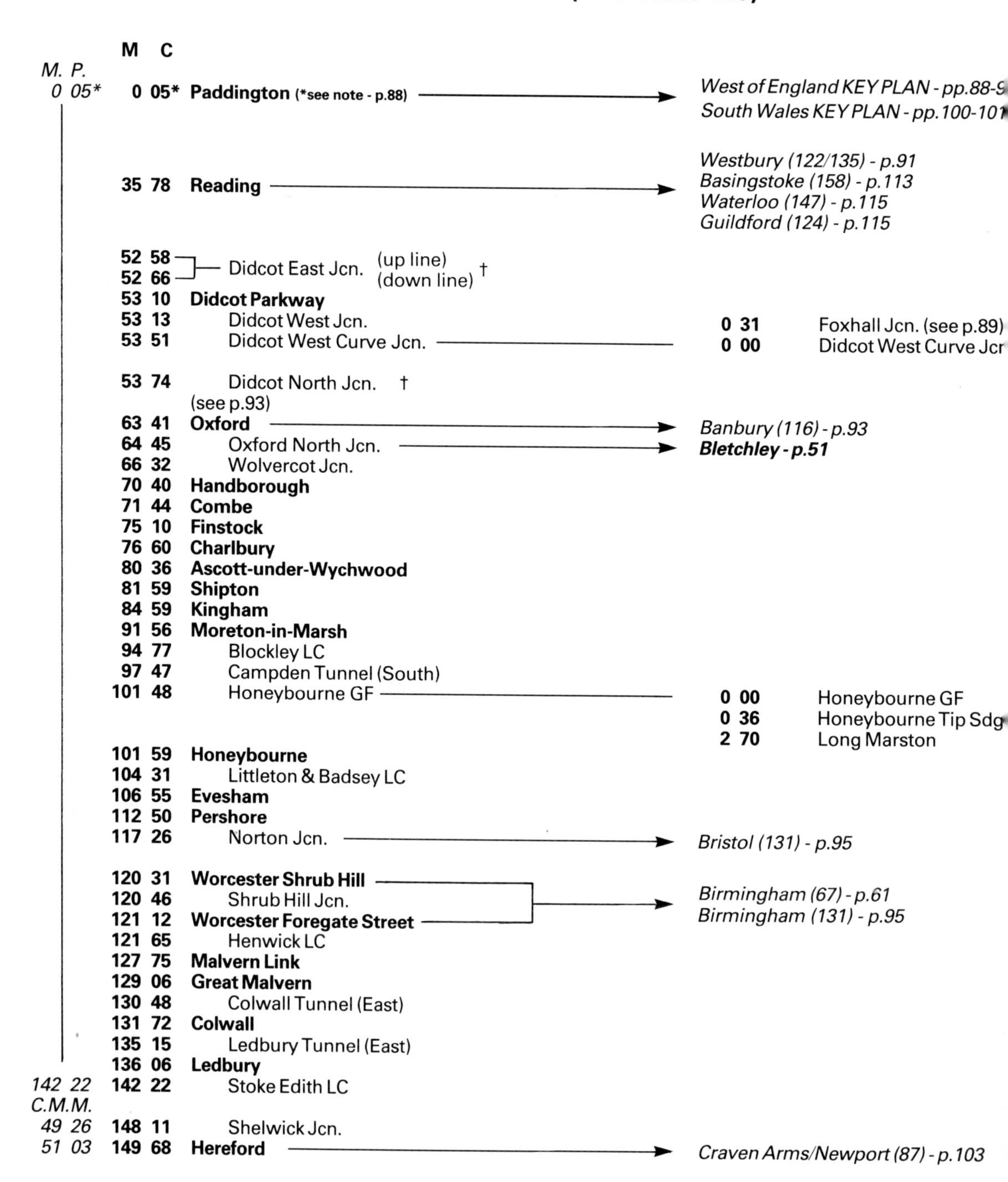

M C
M. P.
0 05* 0 05* Paddington (*see note - p.88)
West of England KEY PLAN - pp.88-9
South Wales KEY PLAN - pp.100-101
35 78 Reading
Westbury (122/135) - p.91
Basingstoke (158) - p.113
Waterloo (147) - p.115
Guildford (124) - p.115
52 58 Didcot East Jcn. (up line) †
52 66 (down line)
53 10 Didcot Parkway
53 13 Didcot West Jcn.
53 51 Didcot West Curve Jcn.
0 31 Foxhall Jcn. (see p.89)
0 00 Didcot West Curve Jcn
53 74 Didcot North Jcn. †
(see p.93)
63 41 Oxford
Banbury (116) - p.93
64 45 Oxford North Jcn.
Bletchley - p.51
66 32 Wolvercot Jcn.
70 40 Handborough
71 44 Combe
75 10 Finstock
76 60 Charlbury
80 36 Ascott-under-Wychwood
81 59 Shipton
84 59 Kingham
91 56 Moreton-in-Marsh
94 77 Blockley LC
97 47 Campden Tunnel (South)
101 48 Honeybourne GF
0 00 Honeybourne GF
0 36 Honeybourne Tip Sdg
2 70 Long Marston
101 59 Honeybourne
104 31 Littleton & Badsey LC
106 55 Evesham
112 50 Pershore
117 26 Norton Jcn.
Bristol (131) - p.95
120 31 Worcester Shrub Hill
120 46 Shrub Hill Jcn.
121 12 Worcester Foregate Street
Birmingham (67) - p.61
Birmingham (131) - p.95
121 65 Henwick LC
127 75 Malvern Link
129 06 Great Malvern
130 48 Colwall Tunnel (East)
131 72 Colwall
135 15 Ledbury Tunnel (East)
136 06 Ledbury
142 22 142 22 Stoke Edith LC
C.M.M.
49 26 148 11 Shelwick Jcn.
51 03 149 68 Hereford
Craven Arms/Newport (87) - p.103

† Didcot avoiding line - 9 chains shorter

BRISTOL - BIRMINGHAM (B.R. Tables 131 & 135)

101m 12ch Via Worcest/ 101m 12ch Kidd/Stour.

M. P.	M C	Location	Connections
18 26	0 00	**Bristol Temple Meads**	→ *Paddington/Exeter (127/135) - p.89*; *Weymouth/Salisbury (132) - p.97*; *Newport/Cardiff (131/132) - p.102*
.M.M.			
0 31	0 24	Bristol East Jcn.	
0 53	0 46	Dr. Day's Jcn.	→ ***North Somerset Jcn. - p.96***
1 04	0 77	**Lawrence Hill**	
1 19	1 12	Lawrence Hill GF	→ ***Avonside - p.96***
1 50	1 43	**Stapleton Road**	
2 03	1 76	Narroways Hill Jcn.	→ *Severn Beach (133) - p.96*
.M.M.			
13 01	4 43	Filton Jcn.	→ ***Filton West Jcn. - p.96***
11 79	5 45	Stoke Gifford Jcn.	
11 62	5 62	**Bristol Parkway**	→ *Paddington/South Wales (127) - p.100*
.M.M.			
21 26	10 32	Westerleigh Jcn.	
20 03	11 55	Yate South GF	
19 54	12 04	Yate Middle GF	
16 12	15 46	Wickwar Tunnel (South)	
13 13	18 45	Charfield GF	
07 70	23 68	Berkeley Road Jcn.	
01 47	30 11	Stonehouse GF	
99 68	31 70	Standish Jcn.	→ *Swindon (126) - p.93*
.M.M.			
94 10	36 78	Tuffley	→ ***Quedgeley - p.93***

M C	Location
2 19	Westerleigh C.C.E. Sdgs.
0 00	Yate South GF

M C	Location
0 00	Yate Middle GF
2 47	Latteridge LC
5 46	Tytherington Tunnel (S)
6 24	Tytherington

M C	Location
0 00	Berkeley Road Jcn.
2 04	Berkeley GF
4 13	Sharpness

M. P.	M C	Location	M C (*via Gloucester & Worcester*)	Location
93 08	38 00	Gloucester Yard Jcn.	38 00	Gloucester Yard Jcn.
			39 01	**Gloucester** (pp.93/102) (REV.)
			39 24	Horton Road Jcn.
92 21	38 67	Barnwood Jcn.	39 78	Barnwood Jcn.
86 58	44 30	**Cheltenham Spa**	45 41	**Cheltenham Spa**
84 23	46 65	Swindon Road LC	47 76	Swindon Road LC
79 47	51 41	Ashchurch GF	52 52	Ashchurch GF
74 51	56 37	Eckington GF	57 48	Eckington GF
70 51	60 37	Pirton LC	61 48	Pirton LC
68 60	62 28	Abbotswood Jcn.	63 39	Abbotswood Jcn.
			64 21	Norton Jcn. (see p.94)
66 42	64 46	Spetchley GF	67 26	**Worcester Shrub Hill**
62 60	68 28	Oddingley LC	67 73	Tunnel Jcn.
62 12	68 76	Dunhampstead LC	73 05	**Droitwich Spa** (see p.61)
			73 21	Droitwich Spa Jcn.
57 43	73 45	Stoke Works Jcn.	77 20	Stoke Works Jcn.
55 30	75 58	**Bromsgrove**	79 33	**Bromsgrove**
52 57	78 31	Blackwell Summit	82 06	Blackwell Summit
52 40	78 48	***WR/LMR Boundary***	82 23	***WR/LMR Boundary***
51 67	79 21	**Barnt Green**	82 76	**Barnt Green**

+1m 47c via C/Hill → B.N.S

via Selly Oak - see p.60

M C	Location	M C	Location
89 74	**Birmingham New Street**	93 49	**Birmingham New Street**

Peterborough (18) - p.46
Derby (80) - p.49
Euston/Wolverhampton (65) - p.57
Banbury (116) - p.58

Stratford-upon-Avon (71) - p.58
Lichfield/Redditch (55) - p.59/60
Walsall (70) - p.60
Kidderminster (67) - p.61

BRISTOL - SEVERN BEACH (B.R. Table 133) & Avonmouth Loop

M. P.	M C	Location
118 26	**0 00**	**Bristol Temple Meads** → *Paddington/Exeter (127/135) - p.89*; *Weymouth/Salisbury (132) - p.97*
C.M.M.		
0 31	**0 24**	Bristol East Jcn.
0 53	**0 46**	Dr. Day's Jcn.
1 04	**0 77**	**Lawrence Hill**
1 19	**1 12**	Lawrence Hill GF
1 50	**1 43**	**Stapleton Road**
2 03	**1 76**	Narroways Hill Jcn.
2 68	**2 61**	**Montpelier**
3 25	**3 18**	**Redland**
3 72	**3 65**	**Clifton Down**
6 00	**5 73**	**Sea Mills**
7 50	**7 43**	**Shirehampton**
9 02	**8 75**	**Avonmouth**
C.M.M.		
16 00	**9 25**	St. Andrews Jcn. LC
15 37	**9 68**	**St. Andrews Road**
14 38	**10 67**	Hallen Marsh Jcn.
C.M.M.		
114 12	**15 17**	Charlton Tunnel (West)
113 12	**16 17**	North Filton
112 78	**16 31**	Filton West Jcn.
112 04	**17 25**	Stoke Gifford Jcn.
111 62	**17 47**	**Bristol Parkway**

M C	Location
0 00	North Somerset Jcn.
0 23	Dr. Day's Jcn. (see below)

M C	Location
0 00	Lawrence Hill GF
0 42	Barton Street LC
1 08	Avonside Wharf

M. P.	M C	Location
2 03	**1 76**	Narroways Hill Jcn.
4 50	**4 43**	Filton Jcn. (to Parkway - p.95)
4 64	**4 57**	**Filton**
4 66	**4 59**	Filton Jcn.
5 41	**5 34**	Filton West Jcn.

M. P.	M C	Location
14 38	**10 67**	Hallen Marsh Jcn.
11 62	**13 43**	**Severn Beach**

M. P.	M C	Location
112 78	**16 31**	Filton West Jcn.
C.M.M.		
0 00	**16 71**	Patchway Jcn.
C.M.M.		
5 77	**17 15**	**Patchway**

Paddington (127) —— *p.100* —— *South Wales (127)*

Bristol Temple Meads - St. Philip's Marsh, Ashton Gate & Wapping Wharf

M. P.	M C	Location
118 26	**0 00**	**Bristol Temple Meads**
118 58	**0 32**	Bristol West Jcn.
119 22	**0 76**	**Bedminster**
119 50	**1 24**	Malago Vale
120 15	**1 69**	**Parson Street**
120 28	**2 02**	Parson Street Jcn. → *Weston/Exeter (127/135) - p.89*
121 18	**2 72**	Ashton Jcn.
C.M.M.		
0 65	**3 33**	Ashton Bridge LC
0 53	**3 45**	Cumberland Road LC
0 00	**4 18**	Wapping Wharf

M. P.	M C	Location
118 26	**0 00**	**Bristol Temple Meads**
118 02	**0 24**	Bristol East Jcn.
117 50	**0 56**	North Somerset Jcn. (to Dr. Day's - see above
117 46	**0 60**	North Somerset Jcn.
C.M.M.		
0 34	**1 14**	St. Philip's Marsh
1 08	**1 68**	Bristol West Jcn.

Weston/Exeter (127/135) - p.89

M. P.	M C	Location
121 18	**2 72**	Ashton Jcn.
121 30	**3 04**	Ashton Gate
129 64	**11 38**	Portishead

WEYMOUTH & SALISBURY - BRISTOL via Westbury (B.R. Table 132)

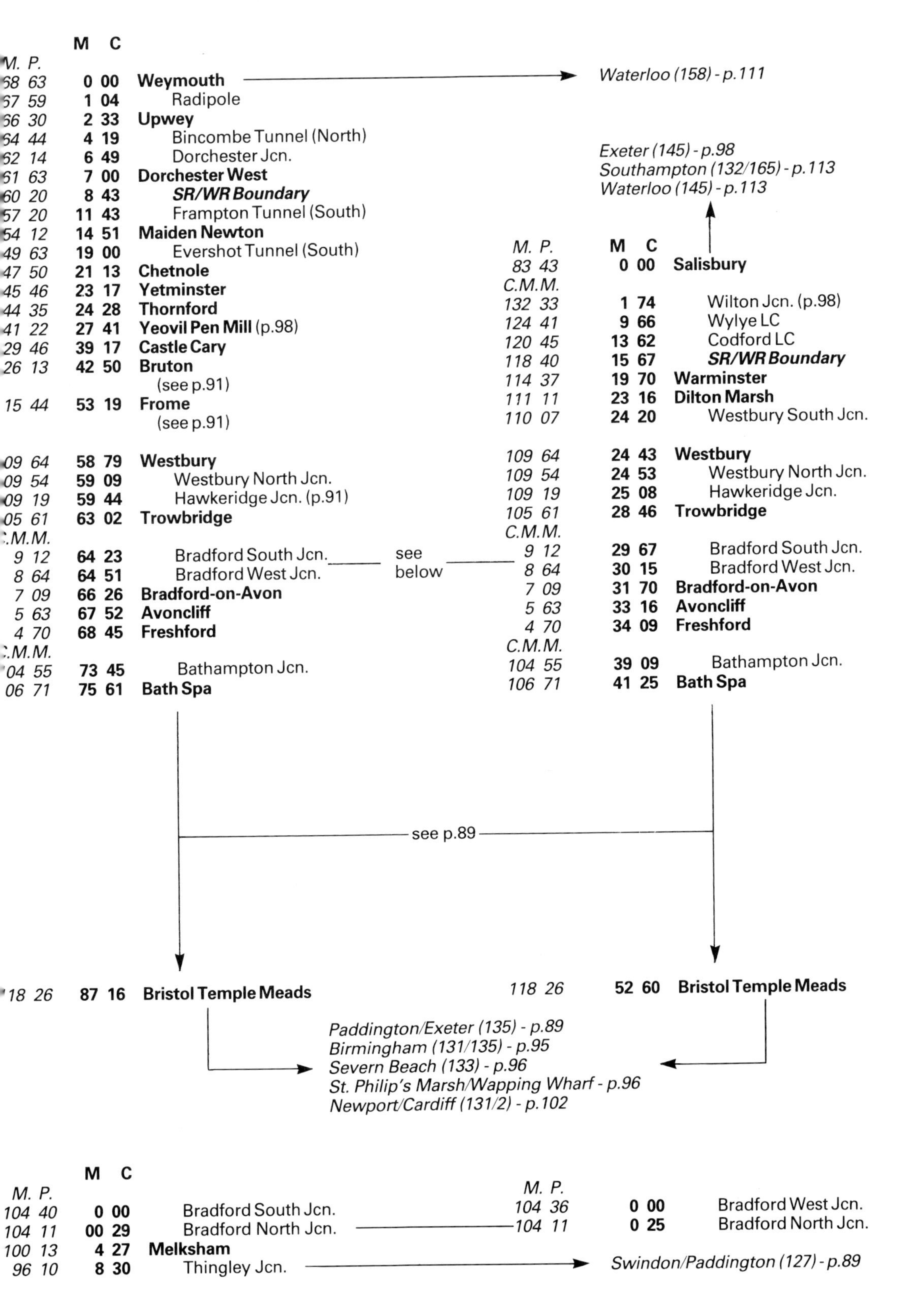

M. P.	M	C	Station	
68 63	0	00	**Weymouth**	→ *Waterloo (158) - p.111*
67 59	1	04	Radipole	
66 30	2	33	**Upwey**	
64 44	4	19	Bincombe Tunnel (North)	
62 14	6	49	Dorchester Jcn.	
61 63	7	00	**Dorchester West**	
60 20	8	43	***SR/WR Boundary***	
57 20	11	43	Frampton Tunnel (South)	
54 12	14	51	**Maiden Newton**	
49 63	19	00	Evershot Tunnel (South)	
47 50	21	13	**Chetnole**	
45 46	23	17	**Yetminster**	
44 35	24	28	**Thornford**	
41 22	27	41	**Yeovil Pen Mill** (p.98)	
29 46	39	17	**Castle Cary**	
26 13	42	50	**Bruton** (see p.91)	
15 44	53	19	**Frome** (see p.91)	
09 64	58	79	**Westbury**	
09 54	59	09	Westbury North Jcn.	
09 19	59	44	Hawkeridge Jcn. (p.91)	
05 61	63	02	**Trowbridge**	
C.M.M.				
9 12	64	23	Bradford South Jcn.	— see below —
8 64	64	51	Bradford West Jcn.	
7 09	66	26	**Bradford-on-Avon**	
5 63	67	52	**Avoncliff**	
4 70	68	45	**Freshford**	
C.M.M.				
04 55	73	45	Bathampton Jcn.	
06 71	75	61	**Bath Spa**	
			see p.89	
18 26	87	16	**Bristol Temple Meads**	

Exeter (145) - p.98
Southampton (132/165) - p.113
Waterloo (145) - p.113

M. P.	M	C	Station
83 43	0	00	**Salisbury**
C.M.M.			
132 33	1	74	Wilton Jcn. (p.98)
124 41	9	66	Wylye LC
120 45	13	62	Codford LC
118 40	15	67	***SR/WR Boundary***
114 37	19	70	**Warminster**
111 11	23	16	**Dilton Marsh**
110 07	24	20	Westbury South Jcn.
109 64	24	43	**Westbury**
109 54	24	53	Westbury North Jcn.
109 19	25	08	Hawkeridge Jcn.
105 61	28	46	**Trowbridge**
C.M.M.			
9 12	29	67	Bradford South Jcn.
8 64	30	15	Bradford West Jcn.
7 09	31	70	**Bradford-on-Avon**
5 63	33	16	**Avoncliff**
4 70	34	09	**Freshford**
C.M.M.			
104 55	39	09	Bathampton Jcn.
106 71	41	25	**Bath Spa**
118 26	52	60	**Bristol Temple Meads**

Paddington/Exeter (135) - p.89
Birmingham (131/135) - p.95
Severn Beach (133) - p.96
St. Philip's Marsh/Wapping Wharf - p.96
Newport/Cardiff (131/2) - p.102

M. P.	M	C	Station	
104 40	0	00	Bradford South Jcn.	
104 11	00	29	Bradford North Jcn.	
100 13	4	27	**Melksham**	
96 10	8	30	Thingley Jcn.	→ *Swindon/Paddington (127) - p.89*

M. P.	M	C	Station
104 36	0	00	Bradford West Jcn.
104 11	0	25	Bradford North Jcn.

SALISBURY - EXETER (B.R. Table 145) / EXMOUTH - EXETER (B.R. Table 137)

M. P.	M C	
83 43	**0 00**	**Salisbury**
85 37	**1 74**	Wilton Jcn.
86 25	**2 62**	Wilton
92 39	**8 76**	Teffont Mill LC
94 75	**11 32**	Tisbury Quarry LC
96 14	**12 51**	**Tisbury**
97 11	**13 48**	Tisbury West LC
105 23	**21 60**	**Gillingham**
107 44	**24 01**	Buckhorn Weston Tunnel (East)
109 41	**25 78**	Ashford LC
112 02	**28 39**	**Templecombe**
117 40	**33 77**	***SR/WR Boundary***
118 04	**34 41**	**Sherborne**
122 31	**38 68**	Yeovil Jcn.
122 48	**39 05**	**Yeovil Junction**
131 33	**47 70**	**Crewkerne**
134 04	**50 41**	Hewish LC
139 32	**55 69**	Chard Junction LC
144 41	**60 78**	**Axminster**
148 05	**64 42**	Seaton Junction
152 45	**69 02**	Honiton Tunnel (East)
154 60	**71 17**	**Honiton**
159 24	**75 61**	**Feniton**
163 02	**79 39**	**Whimple**
165 20	**81 57**	Crannaford LC
168 40	**84 77**	**Pinhoe**
170 21	**86 58**	Exmouth Jcn.
170 72	**87 29**	**St. James Park**
171 30	**87 67**	**Exeter Central**
C.M.M.		
193 72	**88 49**	**Exeter St. Davids**

Salisbury → *Bristol (132) - p.97*, *Southampton (132/165) - p.113*, *Waterloo (145) - p.113*

Wilton Jcn. →

M C	
0 00	Wilton Jcn.
0 21	Quidhampton

Yeovil Jcn. →

Westbury/Bristol (132) - p.97 ↑

M C	
0 00	**Yeovil Pen Mill**
1 42	Yeovil Jcn.

M. P.	M C	
9 30	**0 00**	**Exmouth**
7 28	**2 02**	**Lympstone**
6 20	**3 10**	**Lympstone Commando**
5 67	**3 43**	**Exton**
4 23	**5 07**	**Topsham**
2 71	**6 39**	Newcourt
0 34	**8 76**	**Polsloe Bridge**
0 00	**9 30**	Exmouth Jcn.
C.M.M.		
170 72	**10 01**	**St. James Park**
171 30	**10 39**	**Exeter Central**
C.M.M.		
193 72	**11 21**	**Exeter St. Davids**

EXETER - BARNSTAPLE (B.R. Table 136) & Meldon Quarry

M. P.	M C	
193 72	**0 00**	**Exeter St. Davids**
C.M.M.		
173 50	**1 20**	Cowley Bridge Jcn.
176 51	**4 21**	**Newton St. Cyres**
179 26	**6 76**	**Crediton**
179 32	**7 02**	Crediton Jcn.
180 09	**7 59**	Salmon Pool LC
182 72	**10 42**	**Yeoford**
185 67	**13 37**	**Copplestone**
187 40	**15 10**	**Morchard Road**
189 65	**17 35**	**Lapford**
193 54	**21 24**	**Eggesford**
197 51	**25 21**	**Kings Nympton**
200 38	**28 08**	**Portsmouth Arms**
204 52	**32 22**	**Umberleigh**
207 02	**34 52**	**Chapelton**
211 25	**38 75**	**Barnstaple**
211 42	**39 12**	Barnstaple GF

Exeter St. Davids → *Paddington/Bristol (135) - p.89*, *Paignton/Penzance (135) - p.90*

Crediton Jcn. →

M. P.	M C	
179 32	**7 02**	Crediton Jcn.
180 09	**7 59**	Salmon Pool LC
182 72	**10 42**	**(Yeoford)**
197 25	**24 75**	Okehampton
198 76	**26 46**	Meldon Quarry GF
199 07	**26 57**	Meldon Quarry

aira Jcn. - Plymouth Friary - Cattewater - Plymstock

M. P.	M C	
4 02	0 00	Laira Jcn. — see p.90
4 27	0 25	Goods Branch LC
4 45	0 43	Mount Gould Jcn.
	1 54	Plymouth Friary
0 00	0 00	Plymouth Friary
	0 43	Cattewater Jcn.
	1 16	Maxwell Road LC
	1 43	Conoco LCs
	1 49	Conoco LCs
1 59	1 59	Cattewater Harbour

M C	
0 00	Lipson Jcn.
0 34	Mount Gould Jcn.
1 45	Plymouth Friary
0 00	Plymouth Friary
0 43	Cattewater Jcn.
0 78	B.R. Boundary
1 29	Plymstock

LYMOUTH - GUNNISLAKE .R. Table 139)

M. P.	M C	
5 75	0 00	**Plymouth**
M.M.		
8 28	1 20	**Devonport**
8 60	1 52	**Dockyard**
9 30	2 22	**Keyham**
7 22	2 72	St. Budeaux Jcn.
7 02	3 12	**St. Budeaux Victoria Road**
5 79	4 15	Ernesettle South GF
2 69	7 25	**Bere Ferrers**
0 05	10 09	**Bere Alston**
M.M.		(REV.)
0 04	10 09	**Bere Alston**
1 55	11 60	**Calstock**
4 48	14 53	**Gunnislake**

LISKEARD - LOOE (B.R. Table 140)

M. P.	M C	
8 67	0 00	**Liskeard**
6 63	2 04	**Coombe**
5 03	3 64	**St. Keyne**
3 58	5 09	**Causland**
2 29	6 38	**Sandplace**
0 19	8 48	**Looe**

Lostwithiel - Carne Point

M. P.	M C	
277 34	0 00	**Lostwithiel**
277 54	0 20	Lostwithiel Jcn.
281 11	3 57	Golant LC
282 20	4 66	Carne Point

AR - NEWQUAY (B.R. Table 142)

M. P.	M C	
31 57		Par Jcn.
31 69	0 00	**Par**
39 19	0 30	St. Blazey
33 15	1 26	Pontsmill GF
35 78	4 09	**Luxulyan**
37 43	5 54	Goonbarrow Jcn. (see below)
38 03	6 14	**Bugle**
90 40	8 51	**Roche**
92 32	10 43	Tregoss Moor LC
94 17	12 28	St. Dennis Jcn.
96 11	14 22	**St. Columb Road**
98 48	16 59	Coswarth LC
00 16	18 27	**Quintrel Downs**
02 32	20 43	**Newquay**
02 50	20 61	Newquay GF

M. P.	M C	
37 54	0 00	Goonbarrow Jcn.
39 13	1 50	Carbis Wharf

M. P.	M C	
38 56	0 00	Burngullow Jcn.
91 31	2 55	Drinnick Mill
93 60	5 04	Parkandillack

TRURO - FALMOUTH (B.R. Table 143)

M. P.	M C	
300 57	0 00	**Truro**
301 25	0 48	Penwithers Jcn.
302 68	2 11	Sparnock Tunnel (N.)
304 78	4 21	**Perranwell**
306 40	5 63	Perran Tunnel (S.)
309 08	8 31	**Penryn**
311 13	10 36	**Penmere**
312 09	11 32	**The Dell**
312 46	11 69	**Falmouth**

ST. ERTH - ST. IVES (B.R. Table 144)

M. P.	M C	
320 77	0 00	**St. Erth** (Branch Platform)
321 49	0 52	**Lelant Saltings**
322 06	1 09	**Lelant**
323 78	3 01	**Carbis Bay**
325 13	4 16	**St. Ives**

SECTION III - WESTERN REGION

(b) South Wales

PADDINGTON - FISHGUARD HARBOUR (B.R. Table 127)

KEY PLAN

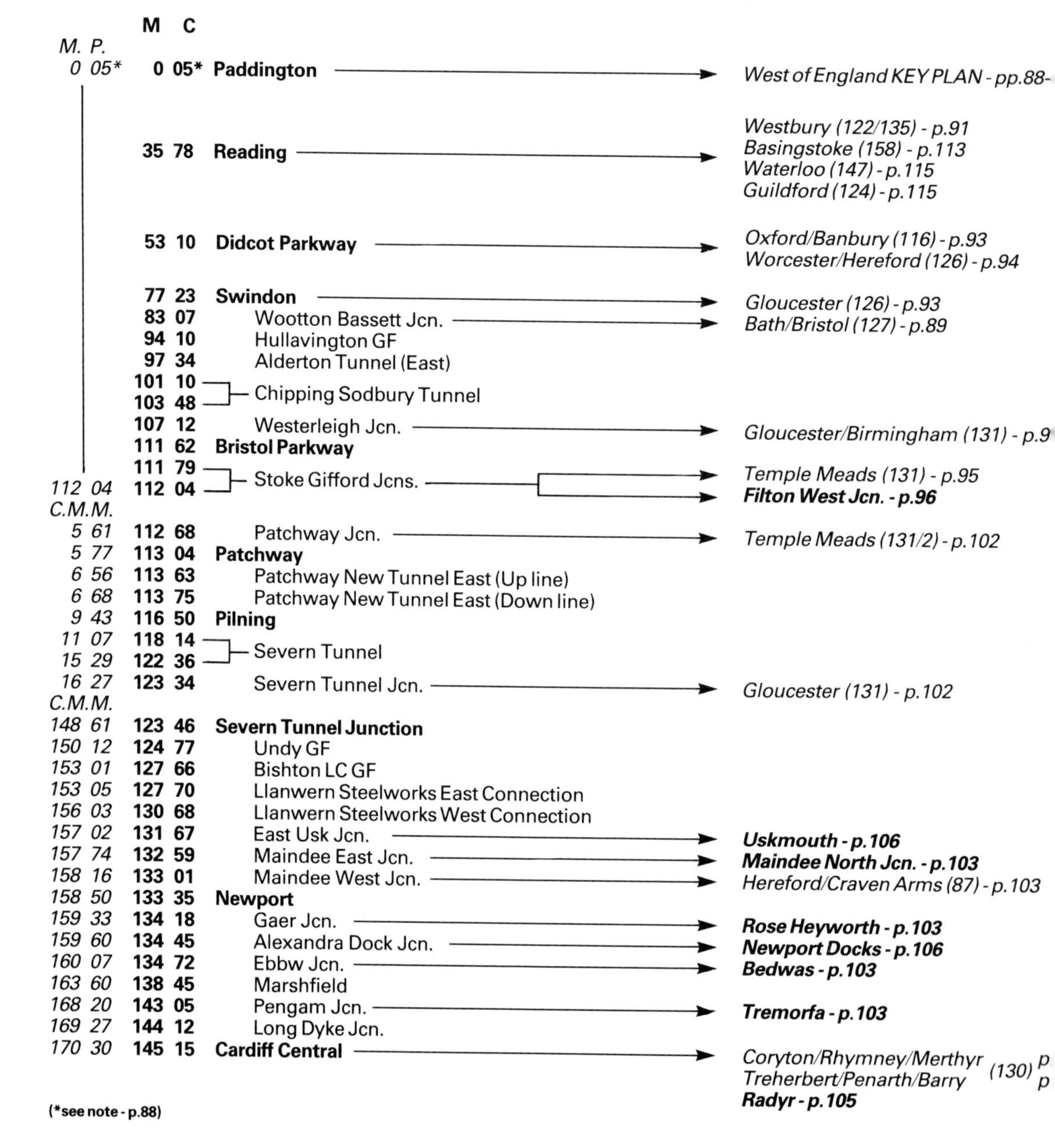

M C
M. P.
0 05* 0 05* Paddington
West of England KEY PLAN - pp.88-
35 78 Reading
Westbury (122/135) - p.91
Basingstoke (158) - p.113
Waterloo (147) - p.115
Guildford (124) - p.115
53 10 Didcot Parkway
Oxford/Banbury (116) - p.93
Worcester/Hereford (126) - p.94
77 23 Swindon
Gloucester (126) - p.93
83 07 Wootton Bassett Jcn.
Bath/Bristol (127) - p.89
94 10 Hullavington GF
97 34 Alderton Tunnel (East)
101 10
103 48
Chipping Sodbury Tunnel
107 12 Westerleigh Jcn.
Gloucester/Birmingham (131) - p.9
111 62 Bristol Parkway
111 79
112 04 112 04
Stoke Gifford Jcns.
Temple Meads (131) - p.95
Filton West Jcn. - p.96
C.M.M.
5 61 112 68 Patchway Jcn.
Temple Meads (131/2) - p.102
5 77 113 04 Patchway
6 56 113 63 Patchway New Tunnel East (Up line)
6 68 113 75 Patchway New Tunnel East (Down line)
9 43 116 50 Pilning
11 07 118 14
15 29 122 36
Severn Tunnel
16 27 123 34 Severn Tunnel Jcn.
Gloucester (131) - p.102
C.M.M.
148 61 123 46 Severn Tunnel Junction
150 12 124 77 Undy GF
153 01 127 66 Bishton LC GF
153 05 127 70 Llanwern Steelworks East Connection
156 03 130 68 Llanwern Steelworks West Connection
157 02 131 67 East Usk Jcn.
Uskmouth - p.106
157 74 132 59 Maindee East Jcn.
Maindee North Jcn. - p.103
158 16 133 01 Maindee West Jcn.
Hereford/Craven Arms (87) - p.103
158 50 133 35 Newport
159 33 134 18 Gaer Jcn.
Rose Heyworth - p.103
159 60 134 45 Alexandra Dock Jcn.
Newport Docks - p.106
160 07 134 72 Ebbw Jcn.
Bedwas - p.103
163 60 138 45 Marshfield
168 20 143 05 Pengam Jcn.
Tremorfa - p.103
169 27 144 12 Long Dyke Jcn.
170 30 145 15 Cardiff Central
Coryton/Rhymney/Merthyr (130) p
Treherbert/Penarth/Barry p
Radyr - p.105

(*see note - p.88)

ADDINGTON - SWANSEA - FISHGUARD HARBOUR (cont.) (B.R. Tables 127 & 128)

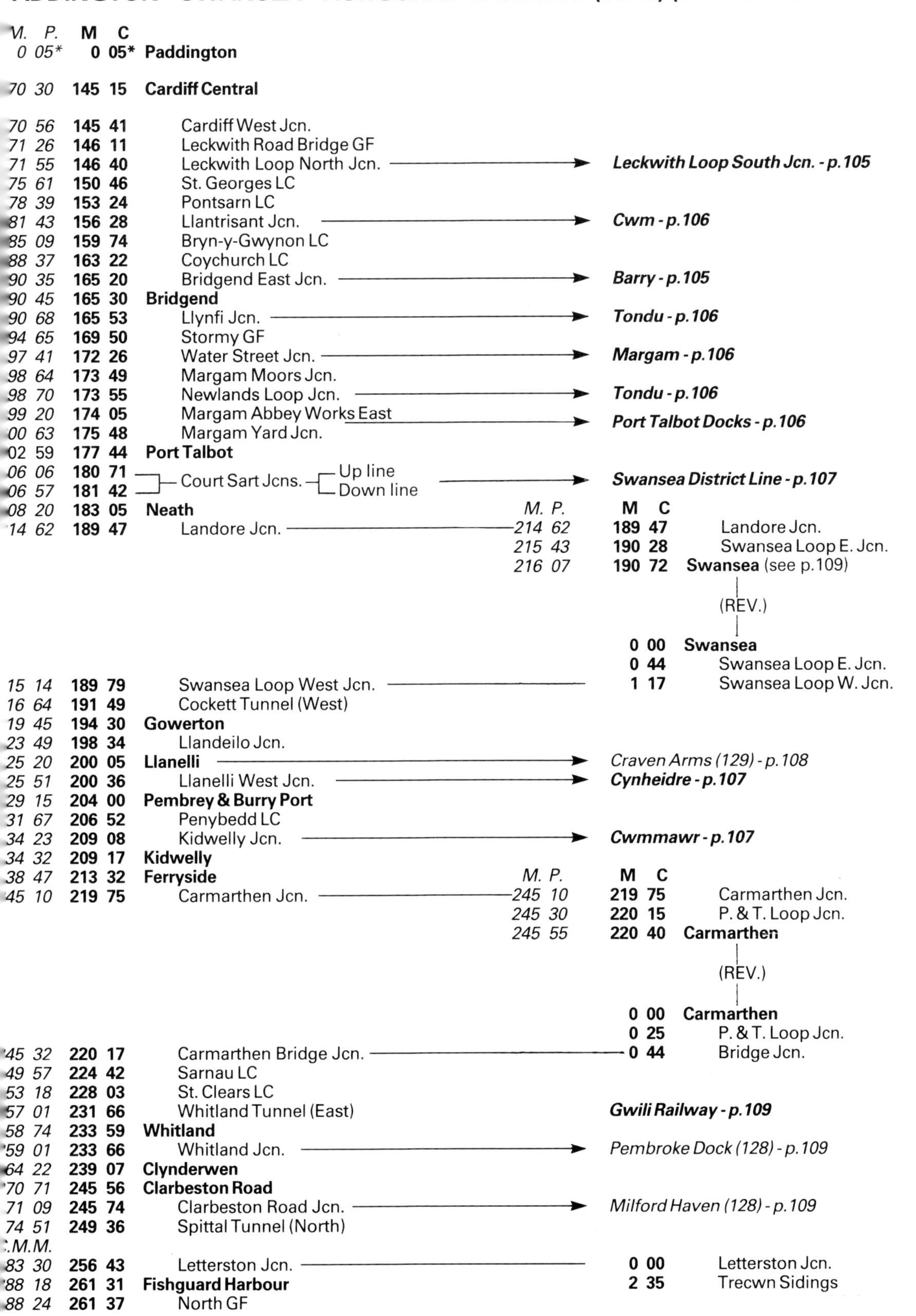

M. P.	M C		
*0 05**	**0 05***	**Paddington**	
70 30	**145 15**	**Cardiff Central**	
70 56	**145 41**	Cardiff West Jcn.	
71 26	**146 11**	Leckwith Road Bridge GF	
71 55	**146 40**	Leckwith Loop North Jcn.	→ ***Leckwith Loop South Jcn. - p.105***
75 61	**150 46**	St. Georges LC	
78 39	**153 24**	Pontsarn LC	
81 43	**156 28**	Llantrisant Jcn.	→ ***Cwm - p.106***
85 09	**159 74**	Bryn-y-Gwynon LC	
88 37	**163 22**	Coychurch LC	
90 35	**165 20**	Bridgend East Jcn.	→ ***Barry - p.105***
90 45	**165 30**	**Bridgend**	
90 68	**165 53**	Llynfi Jcn.	→ ***Tondu - p.106***
94 65	**169 50**	Stormy GF	
97 41	**172 26**	Water Street Jcn.	→ ***Margam - p.106***
98 64	**173 49**	Margam Moors Jcn.	
98 70	**173 55**	Newlands Loop Jcn.	→ ***Tondu - p.106***
99 20	**174 05**	Margam Abbey Works East	→ ***Port Talbot Docks - p.106***
00 63	**175 48**	Margam Yard Jcn.	
02 59	**177 44**	**Port Talbot**	
06 06	**180 71**	Court Sart Jcns. – Up line	→ ***Swansea District Line - p.107***
06 57	**181 42**	Court Sart Jcns. – Down line	
08 20	**183 05**	**Neath**	
14 62	**189 47**	Landore Jcn.	→ see Swansea branch below
15 14	**189 79**	Swansea Loop West Jcn.	→ Swansea Loop W. Jcn. (1 17)
16 64	**191 49**	Cockett Tunnel (West)	
19 45	**194 30**	**Gowerton**	
23 49	**198 34**	Llandeilo Jcn.	
25 20	**200 05**	**Llanelli**	→ *Craven Arms (129) - p.108*
25 51	**200 36**	Llanelli West Jcn.	→ ***Cynheidre - p.107***
29 15	**204 00**	**Pembrey & Burry Port**	
31 67	**206 52**	Penybedd LC	
34 23	**209 08**	Kidwelly Jcn.	→ ***Cwmmawr - p.107***
34 32	**209 17**	**Kidwelly**	
38 47	**213 32**	**Ferryside**	
45 10	**219 75**	Carmarthen Jcn.	→ see Carmarthen branch below
45 32	**220 17**	Carmarthen Bridge Jcn.	→ Bridge Jcn. (0 44)
49 57	**224 42**	Sarnau LC	
53 18	**228 03**	St. Clears LC	
57 01	**231 66**	Whitland Tunnel (East)	***Gwili Railway - p.109***
58 74	**233 59**	**Whitland**	
59 01	**233 66**	Whitland Jcn.	→ *Pembroke Dock (128) - p.109*
64 22	**239 07**	**Clynderwen**	
70 71	**245 56**	**Clarbeston Road**	
71 09	**245 74**	Clarbeston Road Jcn.	→ *Milford Haven (128) - p.109*
74 51	**249 36**	Spittal Tunnel (North)	
:.M.M.			
83 30	**256 43**	Letterston Jcn.	→ Letterston Jcn. (0 00)
88 18	**261 31**	**Fishguard Harbour**	
88 24	**261 37**	North GF	

M. P.	M C	
214 62	**189 47**	Landore Jcn.
215 43	**190 28**	Swansea Loop E. Jcn.
216 07	**190 72**	**Swansea** (see p.109)
		(REV.)
	0 00	**Swansea**
	0 44	Swansea Loop E. Jcn.
	1 17	Swansea Loop W. Jcn.

M. P.	M C	
245 10	**219 75**	Carmarthen Jcn.
245 30	**220 15**	P. & T. Loop Jcn.
245 55	**220 40**	**Carmarthen**
		(REV.)
	0 00	**Carmarthen**
	0 25	P. & T. Loop Jcn.
	0 44	Bridge Jcn.

M C	
0 00	Letterston Jcn.
2 35	Trecwn Sidings

BRISTOL TEMPLE MEADS - NEWPORT & CARDIFF (B.R. Tables 131 & 132)

M. P.	M C		
118 26	**0 00**	**Bristol Temple Meads** →	*Paddington/Exeter (135) - p.89* *Gloucester/Birmingham (131) - p.9* *Severn Beach (133) - p.96* ***St. Philip's Marsh/Wapping - p.96*** *Weymouth/Salisbury (132) - p.97*
C.M.M.			
0 31	**0 24**	Bristol East Jcn.	
0 53	**0 46**	Dr. Day's Jcn. →	***North Somerset Jcn. - p.96***
1 04	**0 77**	**Lawrence Hill**	
1 19	**1 12**	Lawrence Hill GF →	***Avonside - p.96***
1 50	**1 43**	**Stapleton Road**	
2 03	**1 76**	Narroways Hill Jcn.	
4 50	**4 43**	Filton Jcn. →	*Parkway - p.95*
4 64	**4 57**	**Filton**	
4 66	**4 59**	Filton Jcn. →	***Filton West Jcn. - p.95***
5 61	**5 54**	Patchway Jcn. →	*Parkway - p.100*
5 77	**5 70**	**Patchway**	
9 43	**9 36**	**Pilning**	
C.M.M.			
148 61	**16 32**	**Severn Tunnel Junction**	*See p.100 for intermediates and Table Refs.*
158 50	**26 21**	**Newport**	
170 30	**38 01**	**Cardiff Central**	

GLOUCESTER - NEWPORT & CARDIFF (B.R. Table 131)

M. P.	M C		
114 04	**0 00**	**Gloucester** →	*Swindon (126) - p.93* *Bristol/Birmingham (131) - p.95*
115 42	**1 38**	Over Jcn.	
120 66	**6 62**	Broken Cross LC	
125 08	**11 04**	Newnham Tunnel (North)	
128 22	**14 18**	Awre LC	
132 36	**18 32**	Naas LC	
133 21	**19 17**	Lydney GF	
133 37	**19 33**	**Lydney**	
136 14	**22 10**	Woolaston LC	
140 52	**26 48**	Wye Valley Jcn.	
141 33	**27 29**	**Chepstow**	
146 76	**32 72**	Caldicot LC GF	
148 02	**33 78**	**Caldicot**	
148 61	**34 57**	**Severn Tunnel Junction**	*See p.100 for intermediates & Table*
158 50	**44 46**	**Newport**	
170 30	**56 26**	**Cardiff Central**	

Over Jcn. branch:

M C	
0 00	Over Jcn.
1 06	Llanthony Yard

Dean Forest Railway

C.M.M.	M C	
8 00	**0 00**	Lydney GF
8 33	**0 33**	***BR/DFR Boundary***
8 40	**0 40**	Lydney Lakeside
8 73	**0 73**	Lydney Town Halt
9 31	**1 31**	Middle Forge Jcn.
9 55	**1 55**	Norchard High Level
10 60	**2 60**	Tufts Bridge
11 21	**3 21**	Whitecroft Halt
12 25	**4 25**	Parkend
12 44	**4 44**	End of line

The above table shows the proposed future layout of the D.F.R. At present, running is confined within the Norchard Steam Centre - Norchard Low Level to Middle Forge - a distance of 33 chains.

Wye Valley Jcn. branch:

M C	
0 00	Wye Valley Jcn.
1 35	Tiddenham Tunnel (S
2 60	Tintern Quarry

Caldicot LC GF branches:

M C	
1 60	Caerwent
0 00	Caldicot LC GF

M C	
0 00	Caldicot LC GF
1 08	Sudbrook Pumping S

CRAVEN ARMS - HEREFORD - NEWPORT (B.R. Table 87)

M. P.	M C		M. P.	M C	
19 77	**0 00**	**Craven Arms** →			*Shrewsbury/Crewe (87) - p.66* *Llanelli (129) - p.108*
20 01	**0 04**	Craven Arms GF			
22 68	**2 71**	Onibury LC			
25 20	**5 23**	Bromfield LC			
27 42	**7 45**	**Ludlow**			
30 49	**10 52**	Ashford Bowdler LC			
32 02	**12 05**	Woofferton			
38 36	**18 39**	**Leominster**			
42 68	**22 71**	Dinmore Tunnel (North)			
46 65	**26 68**	Moreton-on-Lugg LC			
49 26	**29 39**	Shelwick Jcn.			
50 53	**30 56**	Brecon Curve Jcn.		**0 00**	Brecon Curve Jcn.
				0 19	Barton Curve
51 03	**31 06**	**Hereford** →			*Worcester (126) - p.94*
M.M.					
3 15	**35 37**	Red Hill Tunnel (North)			
5 37	**37 49**	Tram Inn LC			
11 14	**43 26**	Pontrilas			
22 75	**55 17**	**Abergavenny**	M. P.		
			27 46	**0 00**	Glascoed
30 52	**62 74**	Little Mill Jcn.	29 30	**1 64**	Little Mill Jcn.
32 19	**64 41**	**Pontypool**			
34 22	**66 44**	Chapel Lane GF			
35 13	**67 35**	**Cwmbran**			
41 33	**73 55**	Maindee North Jcn.		**0 00**	Maindee North Jcn.
M.M.				**0 32**	Maindee East Jcn.
58 16	**74 08**	Maindee West Jcn.			*Paddington/Fishguard (127) - p.100*
58 50	**74 42**	**Newport** →			*Bristol T.M. (131/2) - p.102*

Gaer & Ebbw Jcns. - Rose Heyworth, Ebbw Vale, Oakdale & Bedwas

M. P.	M C	
59 33	**0 00**	Gaer Jcn. (see p.100)
M.M.		
1 02	**0 71**	Park Jcn.

M. P.	M C	
160 07	**0 00**	Ebbw Jcn. (p.100)
C.M.M.		
1 02	**0 62**	Park Jcn.

M. P.	M C	
1 02	**0 00**	Park Jcn.
3 32	**2 30**	Rogerstone GF
6 15	**5 13**	Lime Kiln Sidings LC
9 45	**8 43**	Celynen GFs
10 06	**9 04**	Celynen GFs
14 21	**13 19**	Aberbeeg Jcn. (see below)
17 30	**16 28**	Rose Heyworth
17 74	**16 72**	End of line

M. P.	M C	
6 15	**5 13**	Lime Kiln Sidings LC
C.M.M.		
2 69	**8 35**	Pantyresk LC
4 10	**9 56**	Cwmdoes LC
4 67	**10 33**	Penar Jcn.
6 69	**12 35**	Thomas LC
7 48	**13 14**	Colliers Arms (Oakdale)
7 61	**13 27**	End of line

M. P.	M C	
14 21	**0 00**	Aberbeeg Jcn.
15 67	**1 46**	Graig Fawr North GF
16 44	**2 23**	Cwm North GF
18 35	**4 14**	Waunllwyd GF
18 59	**4 38**	End of line (Ebbw Vale)

M. P.	M C	
1 02	**0 00**	Park Jcn.
C.M.M.		
1 35	**2 38**	Rhiwderin LC
3 50	**4 53**	Machen Quarry GFs
4 45	**5 48**	Machen Quarry GFs
6 58	**7 61**	Trethomas
8 06	**9 09**	Bedwas

M. P.	M C	
68 20	**0 00**	Pengam Jcn. (p.100)
M.M.		
3 76	**0 76**	Tidal Sidings GF
4 38	**1 38**	Tremorfa Works GF
4 54	**1 54**	Splott Jcn. (BR/BTDB Boundary)

CARDIFF CENTRAL - CORYTON & RHYMNEY (B.R. Table 130)

M. P.	M C	
170 30	0 00	**Cardiff Central** → *South Wales KEY PLAN - pp.100/10*
C.M.M.		
0 00	0 12	Cardiff East Jcn.
C.M.M.		
0 66	0 23	Queen Street South Jcn.
1 08	0 56	**Cardiff Queen Street**
1 17	0 65	Queen Street North Jcn.
3 32	2 75	Heath Jcn.
3 52	3 15	**Heath High Level**
4 61	4 24	**Llanishen**
5 46	5 09	**Lisvane & Thornhill**
6 00	5 43	**Cefn Onn**
7 14	6 57	Caerphilly Tunnel (North)
8 21	7 64	**Caerphilly**
8 69	8 32	**Aber**
10 71	10 34	**Llanbradach**
13 41	13 04	Ystrad Mynach South
13 60	13 23	**Ystrad Mynach**
13 72	13 35	Ystrad Mynach North
14 53	14 16	**Hengoed**
16 30	15 73	**Pengam**
17 35	16 78	**Gilfach Fargoed**
18 07	17 50	**Bargoed**
19 31	18 74	**Brithdir**
20 40	20 03	**Tirphill**
22 65	22 28	**Pontlottyn**
23 68	23 31	**Rhymney**
23 80	23 43	End of line

M. P.	M C	
0 02	0 00	**Cardiff Bute Road**
0 66	0 64	Queen Street S. Jcn.
1 08	1 06	**Cardiff Queen Street**

C.M.M.	M C	
0 16	2 75	Heath Jcn.
0 29	3 08	**Heath Low Level**
1 37	4 17	**Birchgrove**
1 78	4 58	**Rhiwbina**
2 25	5 05	**Whitchurch**
2 57	5 37	**Coryton**

M. P.	M C	
13 41	13 04	Ystrad Mynach Sout
C.M.M.		
12 55	14 58	Nelson East GF
13 53	15 56	Nelson & Llancaiach
20 40	22 43	Cwmbargoed
20 75	22 78	End of line

	M C	
13 53	0 00	Nelson & Llancaiach
14 47	0 74	Taff Merthyr Colliery
14 68	1 15	End of line

	M C	
13 72	0 00	Ystrad Mynach Nort
14 71	0 79	Penrhiwfelin GF
15 08	1 16	End of line

CARDIFF CENTRAL - MERTHYR TYDFIL (B.R. Table 130)

M. P.	M C	
170 30	0 00	**Cardiff Central** → *South Wales KEY PLAN - pp.100/10*
C.M.M.		
1 08	0 56	**Cardiff Queen Street**
1 17	0 65	Queen Street North Jcn. → *Coryton/Rhymney (130) - See Abov*
1 60	1 28	**Cardiff Cathays**
2 35	2 03	Maindy Bridge GF
4 27	3 75	**Llandaff**
5 23	4 71	Radyr Jcn. → ***Penarth Curve Jcns. - p.105***
5 32	5 00	**Radyr**
7 20	6 68	Walnut Tree Jcn.
7 24	6 72	**Taff Wells**
9 53	9 21	**Treforest Estate**
10 57	10 25	Maesmawr
12 00	11 48	**Treforest**
12 69	12 37	**Pontypridd** → *Treherbert (130) - p.105*
13 09	12 57	Pontypridd Jcn.
15 40	15 08	Stormstown Jcn.
16 20	15 68	Abercynon Jcn.
16 25	15 73	**Abercynon**
17 73	17 41	**Quaker's Yard**
19 41	19 09	Black Lion
19 77	19 45	**Merthyr Vale**
21 69	21 37	**Troed-y-rhiw**
23 03	22 51	**Pentre-bach**
24 51	24 19	**Merthyr Tydfil**

M C	
6 68	Walnut Tree Jcn.
9 21	Nantgarw

M C	
15 08	Stormstown Jcn.
16 49	Ynysybwl

M. P.	M C	
16 20	15 68	Abercynon Jcn.
18 20	17 68	Penrhiwceiber
19 76	19 44	Mountain Ash GF
21 22	20 70	Abercwmboi
C.M.M.		
22 44	23 47	Aberdare
27 15	28 18	Hirwaun

CARDIFF CENTRAL - TREHERBERT (B.R. Table 130)

M. P.	M C		
170 30	0 00	**Cardiff Central**	
			(see p.104)
C.M.M.			
12 69	12 37	**Pontypridd**	
13 09	12 57		Pontypridd Jcn.
14 72	14 40	**Trehafod**	
16 13	15 61	**Porth** ———	
17 41	17 09	**Dinas**	
18 03	17 51	**Tonypandy**	
19 07	18 55	**Llwynypia**	
20 05	19 53	**Ystrad Rhondda**	
20 76	20 44	**Ton Pentre**	
22 02	21 50	**Treorchy**	
22 70	22 38	**Ynyswen**	
23 54	23 22	**Treherbert**	
23 57	23 25		Treherbert Station GF

M. P.	M C		
16 13	0 00	**Porth**	
22 44	6 31		Maerdy Colliery GF

CARDIFF CENTRAL - PENARTH & BARRY ISLAND (B.R. Table 130)

M. P.	M C			
170 30	0 00	**Cardiff Central**		
C.M.M.				
0 10	0 26		Cardiff West Jcn.	
0 25	0 41		Radyr Branch Jcn. ——→	***Radyr***
0 47	0 63		Penarth Curve South Jcn. ——→	***Penarth Curve N. Jcn.*** ***- See Below***
0 73	1 09	**Grangetown**		
2 29	2 45		Cogan Jcn. ———	
2 41	2 57	**Cogan**		
		Eastbrook		
4 18	4 34	**Dinas Powis**		
6 10	6 26	**Cadoxton**		
6 78	7 14	**Barry Docks**		
8 07	8 23	**Barry**		
8 16	8 32		Barry Jcn. ——→	***Bridgend - See Below***
8 70	9 06	**Barry Island**		
8 75	9 11		Barry Island GFs	

C.M.M.	M C		
0 01	2 45		Cogan Jcn.
0 57	3 21	**Dingle Road**	
1 12	3 56	**Penarth**	

Radyr Branch Jcn. (Cardiff) - Radyr Jcn.

M. P.	M C			
0 25	0 00		Radyr Branch Jcn. (see above)	
0 47	0 22		Penarth Curve North Jcn. ———	
0 63	0 38	Ninian Park		
0 69	0 44		Leckwith Loop South Jcn. ———	
1 58	1 33		Ely Paper Mills GF	
4 02	3 57		Radyr Quarry Jcn.	
C.M.M.				
5 23	4 16		Radyr Jcn. ——→	*Merthyr (130) - p.104* *Treherbert (130) - See Above*

M C	
0 00	Penarth Curve S. Jcn.
0 25	Penarth Curve N. Jcn.

M C	
0 00	Leckwith Loop S. Jcn.
0 26	Leckwith Loop N. Jcn.
	(see p.101)

Barry Jcn. - Bridgend (Vale of Glamorgan line)

M. P.	M C			
0 00	0 00		Barry Jcn. ——→	*Cardiff Central (130) - See Above*
|	3 21		Rhoose GF	
|	5 36		Aberthaw Cement GF	
|	8 31		St. Athan	
|	13 26		Llandow	
18 00	18 00		Fords Sidings GF	
C.M.M.				
90 35	18 78		Bridgend East Jcn.	
90 45	19 17	**Bridgend** ——→		*Cardiff/Swansea (127) - p.101*

Bridgend - Tondu - Maesteg, Blaengarw & Ogmore Vale

	M C	
M. P.		
190 68	**0 00**	Bridgend Llynfi Jcn. (see p.101)
C.M.M.		
2 70	**2 59**	Tondu

2 70	**0 00**	Tondu
4 45	**1 55**	Gelli Las GF
4 73	**2 33**	Ely Paper Mill GF
8 20	**5 30**	Maesteg (old platform)
8 41	**5 51**	Llynfi South GF
8 59	**5 69**	Llynfi North GF

C.M.M.		
0 00	**0 00**	Tondu
	1 47	New Mills LC
	4 79	Caedu LC
	5 49	Ogmore Vale South LC
	6 29	Wyndham Pits GFs
	6 67	Wyndham Pits GFs
7 10	**7 10**	Nantymoel

	M C	
C.M.M.		
0 00	**0 00**	Tondu
C.M.M.		
0 08	**0 63**	Brynmenyn LC
2 03	**2 58**	Llangeiner LC
4 30	**5 05**	Pontycwmmer
5 16	**5 71**	Blaengarw (BR/NCB Boundary)

Tondu - Margam

M. P.	M C	
0 00	**0 00**	Tondu
1 05	**1 05**	Fountain LC
C.M.M.		
7 41	**2 43**	Cefn Jcn.
6 56	**3 28**	Mill Pitt
3 34	**6 50**	Newlands Jcn.
2 41	**7 43**	Margam Abbey Works East (see below & p.101)

M. P.	M C	
3 34	**6 50**	Newlands Jcn.
2 77	**7 07**	Newlands Loop Jcn. (see p.101)

Water Street Jcn. - Margam - Port Talbot Docks

	M C	
M. P.		
197 41	**0 00**	Water Street Jcn. (see p.101)
C.M.M.		
2 41	**1 70**	Margam Abbey Works East (p.101)
0 79	**3 32**	Margam Yard Jcn. (p.101)
C.M.M.		
0 56	**5 07**	Port Talbot Docks (BR/BTDB Boundary)

0 00	Water Street Jcn.
1 57	Margam Sorting Sidin
1 70	Margam Abbey Works

M. P.		
159 60	**0 00**	Alexandra Dock Jcn. (p.100)
160 24	**0 44**	East Mendalgief
160 27	**0 47**	Newport Docks (BR/BTDB Boundary)

0 00	Alexandra Dock Jcn.
1 37	Newport Dock Street

0 00	East Usk Jcn. (p.100)
2 23	Alpha Steel GF
2 42	Monsanto GF
2 74	Uskmouth

0 00	Llantrisant Jcn. (p.101
0 47	Mwyndy Jcn.
3 28	Cwm Llantwit Colliery

Court Sart Jcns. - Morlais & Hendy Jcns. (Swansea District line)

***NOTE: Court Sart Jcn. (Up line) is now known as Briton Ferry Up Flying Loop Jcn.!**

M. P.	M C	
17 33	**0 00**	*Court Sart Jcn. (Up line)
18 07	**0 54**	Court Sart Junction (Down line) - p.101
C.M.M.		
0 46	**1 63**	Dynevor Jcn.
C.M.M.		
1 24	**2 39**	Jersey Marine North Jcn.
0 57	**3 06**	Llandarcy GF
C.M.M.		
1 08	**3 63**	Lonlas Tunnel (South)
2 25	**5 00**	Felin Fran GF
4 04	**6 59**	Llangyfelach Tunnel (East)
6 45	**9 20**	Penllergaer Tunnel (East)
8 67	**11 42**	Graig Merthyr Colliery GFs
9 04	**11 59**	Graig Merthyr Colliery GFs
9 34	**12 09**	Grovesend Colliery Loop GF
10 05	**12 60**	Morlais East Jcn.
10 67	**13 42**	Morlais Jcn. → *Llanelli/Craven Arms (129) - p.108*

M. P.	M C	
19 16	**1 63**	Dynevor Jcn.
C.M.M.		
44 19	**2 71**	Jersey Marine S. Jcn.
46 66	**5 38**	Burrows Sidings
48 09	**6 61**	Swansea Eastern Depot
48 13	**6 65**	End of Branch

C.M.M.	M C	
2 26	**0 00**	Jersey Marine S. Jcn.
1 24	**1 02**	Jersey Marine N. Jcn.

M C	
0 00	Felin Fran GF
1 36	Clydach-on-Tawe North

M C	
0 75	End of line (Brynlliw)
0 00	Grovesend Loop GF

	M C	
0 00	**12 60**	Morlais East Jcn.
0 46	**13 26**	Hendy Jcn.

Llanelli/Craven Arms (129) - p.108

Jersey Marine South Jcn. - Onllwyn & Aberpergwm

M. P.	M C	
44 19	**0 00**	Jersey Marine South Jcn. (see above)
C.M.M.		
0 01	**3 02**	Neath & Brecon Jcn.
3 75	**6 76**	Blaenant GF
10 20	**13 21**	Onllwyn
10 34	**13 35**	End of Branch

M. P.	M C	
41 17	**3 02**	Neath & Brecon Jcn.
33 44	**10 55**	Aberpergwm Colliery

Llanelli - Cynheidre

M. P.	M C	
25 51	**0 00**	Llanelli West Jcn. (see p.101)
M.M.		
0 23	**0 21**	Florries (Old Castle) LC
1 19	**1 17**	Lake View LC
2 02	**2 00**	Felin Foel LCs
2 13	**2 11**	Felin Foel LCs
6 29	**6 27**	Cynheidre

Kidwelly - Coedbach & Cwmmawr

M. P.	M C	
234 23	**0 00**	Kidwelly Jcn. (p.101)
C.M.M.		
0 48	**1 31**	Coedbach Washery
C.M.M.		
5 28	**2 47**	Parc-y-Llong LC
7 65	**5 04**	Pontyates LC
11 00	**8 19**	Pontyberem LC
12 04	**9 23**	Hirwaun LC
12 44	**9 63**	Cwmmawr

NOTE: Court Sart Jcn. (Up line) is now known as Briton Ferry Up Flying Loop Jcn.

LLANELLI - CRAVEN ARMS (B.R. Table 129) (Central Wales line)

	M C		
M. P.			
225 20	**0 00**	**Llanelli** →	*South Wales KEY PLAN - p.101*
C.M.M.			
0 00	**1 51**	Llandeilo Jcn.	
1 07	**2 58**	**Bynea**	
3 01	**4 52**	**Llangennech**	
3 48	**5 19**	Morlais Jcn. →	***Swansea District Line - p.107***
4 54	**6 25**	Hendy Jcn.	
5 26	**6 77**	**Pontardulais**	
10 01	**11 52**	Pantyffynnon Jcn. →	***Gwaun Cae-Gurwen Abernant - See Below***
10 08	**11 59**	**Pantyffynnon**	
11 21	**12 72**	**Ammanford**	
12 28	**13 79**	Brynmarlais LC	
13 08	**14 59**	**Llandebie**	
13 77	**15 48**	Cilyrychen LC	
17 16	**18 67**	**Ffairfach**	
18 09	**19 60**	**Llandeilo**	
22 14	**23 65**	Glanrhyd LC	
23 59	**25 30**	**Llangadog**	
25 40	**27 11**	**Llanwrda**	
28 15	**29 66**	Llandovery South GF	
29 24	**30 75**	**Llandovery**	
C.M.M.			
54 55	**35 50**	**Cynghordy**	
51 45	**38 60**	Sugar Loaf Tunnel (South)	
48 03	**42 22**	**Llanwrtyd Wells**	
44 47	**45 58**	**Llangammarch Wells**	
42 69	**47 36**	**Garth**	
39 39	**50 66**	**Cilmery**	
37 40	**52 65**	**Builth Road**	
31 73	**58 32**	**Llandrindod Wells**	
28 21	**62 04**	**Pen-y-bont**	
25 26	**64 79**	**Dolau**	
21 55	**68 50**	**Llanbister Road**	
18 57	**71 48**	**Llangynllo**	
17 79	**72 26**	Llangynllo Tunnel (North)	
14 69	**75 36**	**Knucklas**	
12 23	**78 02**	**Knighton**	
8 04	**82 21**	**Bucknell**	
5 09	**85 16**	**Hopton Heath**	
2 46	**87 59**	**Broome**	
C.M.M.			
20 01	**90 36**	Craven Arms GF	
19 77	**90 40**	**Craven Arms** →	*Shrewsbury/Crewe (87) - p.66* *Hereford/Newport (87) - p.103*

Pantyffynnon - Gwaun Cae-Gurwen & Abernant

	M C		C.M.M.	M C	
M. P.					
10 01	**0 00**	Pantyffynnon Jcn. (see above)			
11 07	**1 06**	Ammanford LC			
13 53	**3 52**	Cawdor LC			
14 71	**4 70**	Raven LC			
15 78	**5 77**	Abernant Jcn. —	*0 00*	**5 77**	Abernant Jcn.
16 18	**6 17**	Gwaun Cae-Gurwen Colliery Sidings	*2 29*	**8 26**	Abernant
16 39	**6 38**	Gwaun Cae-Gurwen Colliery LC			
16 67	**6 66**	End of line			

SWANSEA - CARMARTHEN - PEMBROKE DOCK (B.R. Table 128)

M. P.	M C	M C		
216 07	0 00		**Swansea**	→ *South Wales KEY PLAN - p.101*
C.M.M.				
0 53	0 44		Swansea Loop East Jcn.	
C.M.M.				
215 14	1 17		Swansea Loop West Jcn.	
219 45	5 48		**Gowerton**	
225 20	11 23		**Llanelli**	→ *Craven Arms (129) - p.108*
229 15	15 18		**Pembrey & Burry Port**	
234 32	20 35		**Kidwelly**	
238 47	24 50		**Ferryside**	
245 10	31 13		Carmarthen Jcn.	→ *Carmarthen Avoiding line - p.101*
245 30	31 33		P & T Loop Jcn.	
245 55	31 58		**Carmarthen**	
C.M.M.			(REV.)	
0 19	32 03		P & T Loop Jcn.	
C.M.M.				
245 32	32 22		Carmarthen Bridge Jcn.	
258 74	45 64	0 00	**Whitland**	
259 01	45 71	0 07	Whitland Jcn.	
264 08	50 78	5 14	**Narberth**	
269 62	56 52	10 68	**Kilgetty**	
270 41	57 31	11 47	**Saundersfoot**	
274 58	61 48	15 64	**Tenby**	
275 71	62 61	16 77	**Penally**	
279 09	65 79	20 15	**Manorbier**	
282 50	69 40	23 56	**Lamphrey**	
284 11	71 01	25 17	**Pembroke**	
285 06	71 76	26 12	Pembroke Tunnel (South)	
286 26	73 16	27 32	**Pembroke Dock**	

Gwili Railway Company

M. P.	M C	
247 15		*End of line*
248 74		Siding
249 10		
249 11	0 00	**Bronwydd Arms**
250 20	1 09	**Cwmdwyfran Halt**
250 50	1 39	**Penybont Halt**
250 70	1 59	**Llwyfan Cerrig**
252 14	3 03	Cynwyl Elfed - **proposed**
255 15	6 04	Llanpumpsaint - **proposed**

SWANSEA - CARMARTHEN - MILFORD HAVEN (B.R. Table 128)

M. P.	M C	M C		
	0 00		**Swansea**	See Above & p.101
	31 58		**Carmarthen**	See Above & p.101
258 74	45 64		**Whitland**	See Above & p.101
264 22	51 12		**Clunderwen**	
270 71	57 61	0 00	**Clarbeston Road**	→ *Fishguard Harbour (127/8) - p.101*
271 09	57 79	0 18	Clarbeston Road Jcn.	
274 34	61 24	3 43	Crundale LC	
276 03	62 73	5 12	**Haverfordwest**	
279 09	65 79	8 18	Winsel LC	
280 67	67 57	9 76	**Johnston**	
282 00	68 70	11 09	Gulf Oil Branch Jcn.	See Below
283 12	70 02	12 21	Herbrandston Jcn.	See Below
284 65	71 55	13 74	**Milford Haven**	
284 69	71 59	13 78	South GF	

M.M.	M C	
0 00	0 00	Gulf Oil Branch Jcn.
2 35	2 35	Gulf Refinery, Waterston

M.M.	M C	
0 00	0 00	Herbrandston Jcn.
	1 06	Amoco Jcn. GF (Robeston Sidings)
	1 60	St. Botolphs LC
2 34	2 34	Esso Refinery

SECTION IV - SOUTHERN REGION

(a) South Western Division

WATERLOO - WEYMOUTH (B.R. Table 158)

KEY PLAN

M. P.	M C	Location	Connections
			Reading (147) - p.115
0 00	0 00	**Waterloo** →	*City line (150) - p.117*
			Waterloo East (207) - p.130
	1 29	**Vauxhall**	
	2 50	**(Queenstown Road)**	
	2 65	Queens Road Box	
	3 17	West London Jcn.	
	3 63	Clapham Jcn. 'A'	*Kensington (149) - p.116*
	3 74	**Clapham Junction** →	***Stewarts Lane - p.118***
	5 46	**Earlsfield**	*Victoria (186) - p.119*
	6 28	Wimbledon Staff Halt	
	7 12	Wimbledon 'A'	***Point Pleasant Jcn. - p.116***
	7 19	**Wimbledon** →	*Streatham - p.125*
			West Croydon (179) - p.126
			Sutton - p.125
	7 49	Wimbledon West Jcn.	
	8 51	**Raynes Park** →	*Chessington/Epsom (152) - p.116*
	9 62	**New Malden** →	*Twickenham/Shepperton (152) - p.*
	10 78	**Berrylands**	
	12 03	**Surbiton** →	*Effingham/Guildford (152) - p.114*
			Hampton Court (152) - p.116
	13 27	Hampton Court Jcn. (Up line)	
	13 34	Guildford New Line Jcn. (Down)	
	14 31	**Esher**	
	15 73	**Hersham**	
	17 06	**Walton-on-Thames**	
	19 12	**Weybridge** →	*Staines (147) - p.118*
	20 23	Byfleet Jcn. →	*Addlestone Jcn. - p.118*
	20 32	**Byfleet & New Haw**	
	21 54	**West Byfleet**	
	24 27	**Woking** →	*Portsmouth Harbour (156) - p.112*
	24 62	Woking Jcn.	
	27 79	**Brookwood**	
	29 39	Pirbright Jcns (Up line) →	*Alton (156) - p.114*
	29 48	Pirbright Jcns (Down line)	
	33 17	**Farnborough**	
	36 38	**Fleet**	
	39 66	**Winchfield**	
	42 13	**Hook**	
	47 55	Basingstoke G.W.R. Jcn.	
	47 61	**Basingstoke** →	*Reading (158) - p.113*
			Salisbury (145) - p.113
	50 21	Worting Jcn.	
	54 02	Steventon	
	55 58	Litchfield Tunnel (North Portals)	
	57 17	Popham No. 1 Tunnel (North Portals)	
	57 35	Popham No. 2 Tunnel (North Portals)	
	58 04	**Micheldever**	
	60 13	Weston	
	62 45	Wallers Ash Tunnel (South)	
66 39	66 39	**Winchester**	

WATERLOO - WEYMOUTH (B.R. Table 158) cont.

M. P.	M C	Location	Connections
0 00	**0 00**	**Waterloo**	
66 39	**66 39**	**Winchester**	
	69 50	**Shawford**	
	72 46	Allbrook Jcn.	*Fareham (165) - p.112*
	73 35	**Eastleigh** →	***Romsey - p.113***
	74 04	Eastleigh South Jcn.	***Eastleigh TMD - p.113***
	74 66	**Southampton Parkway**	
	75 56	**Swaythling**	
	77 10	**St. Denys**	
	77 54	Mount Pleasant LC	
	78 15	Northam Jcn. →	***So'ton Eastern Docks - See Below***
	78 52	Southampton Tunnel (East)	
			So'ton Western Docks - See Below
	79 19	**Southampton** →	*Portsmouth (132/165) - p.112*
	79 75	Millbrook Jcn.	*Salisbury (132/165) - p.113*
	80 11	**Millbrook**	
	81 70	**Redbridge**	
	81 76	Redbridge Jcn.	
	82 43	**Totton**	
	82 62	Fawley line Jcn.	(see Fawley branch)
	83 72	Ashurst LC	
	85 34	**Lyndhurst Road**	
	88 06	**Beaulieu Road**	
	92 66	**Brockenhurst**	(see Lymington branch)
	93 60	Lymington Jcn.	
	95 45	**Sway**	
	98 44	**New Milton**	
	101 05	**Hinton Admiral**	
	104 28	**Christchurch**	
	106 24	**Pokesdown**	
	108 02	**Bournemouth**	
	110 47	Branksome Jcn.	
	110 51	**Branksome**	(see Bournemouth C.S. branch)
	111 76	**Parkstone**	
	113 62	**Poole**	
	115 77	**Hamworthy**	
	116 01	Hamworthy Jcn.	(see Hamworthy Goods branch)
	118 61	**Holton Heath**	
	120 70	**Wareham**	
	121 77	Worgret Jcn.	(see Furzebrook branch)
	122 78	Holme LC	
	124 12	Stoke LC	
	125 69	**Wool**	
	126 56	East Burton LC	
	130 24	**Moreton**	
	131 17	Woodsford LCs	
	131 77	Woodsford LCs	
35 70	**135 70**	**Dorchester South**	
M.M.			
32 14	**136 15**	Dorchester Jcn. →	*Westbury (132) - p.97*
34 44	**138 45**	Bincombe Tunnel (North)	
36 30	**140 31**	**Upwey**	
37 59	**141 60**	Radipole	
38 34	**142 35**	Weymouth Quay Jcn.	(see Weymouth Quay branch)
38 63	**142 64**	**Weymouth**	

M C	Location
0 00	Fawley line Jcn.
3 26	Marchwood LC
8 60	Fawley GF

M. P.	M C	Location
92 66	**0 00**	**Brockenhurst**
93 60	**0 74**	Lymington Jcn.
96 61	**3 75**	Ampress Works
97 15	**4 71**	**Lymington Town**
98 15	**5 29**	**Lymington Pier**

M C	Location
0 74	Bournemouth C.S.
0 04	Branksome Jcn.
0 00	**Branksome**

M C	Location
0 00	Hamworth Jcn.
2 04	Hamworthy Goods

M C	Location
0 00	Worgret Jcn.
2 48	Furzebrook Sidings

M C	Location
142 35	Weymouth Quay Jcn.
143 66	Weymouth Quay

M C	Location
0 00	Northam Jcn.
0 67	Canute Road LC
1 56	Southampton Ocean Terminal

M C	Location
0 00	**Southampton**
0 55	Millbrook Dock Entrance
2 66	So'ton Western Docks (Berth 105)

WATERLOO - PORTSMOUTH HARBOUR (B.R. Table 156)

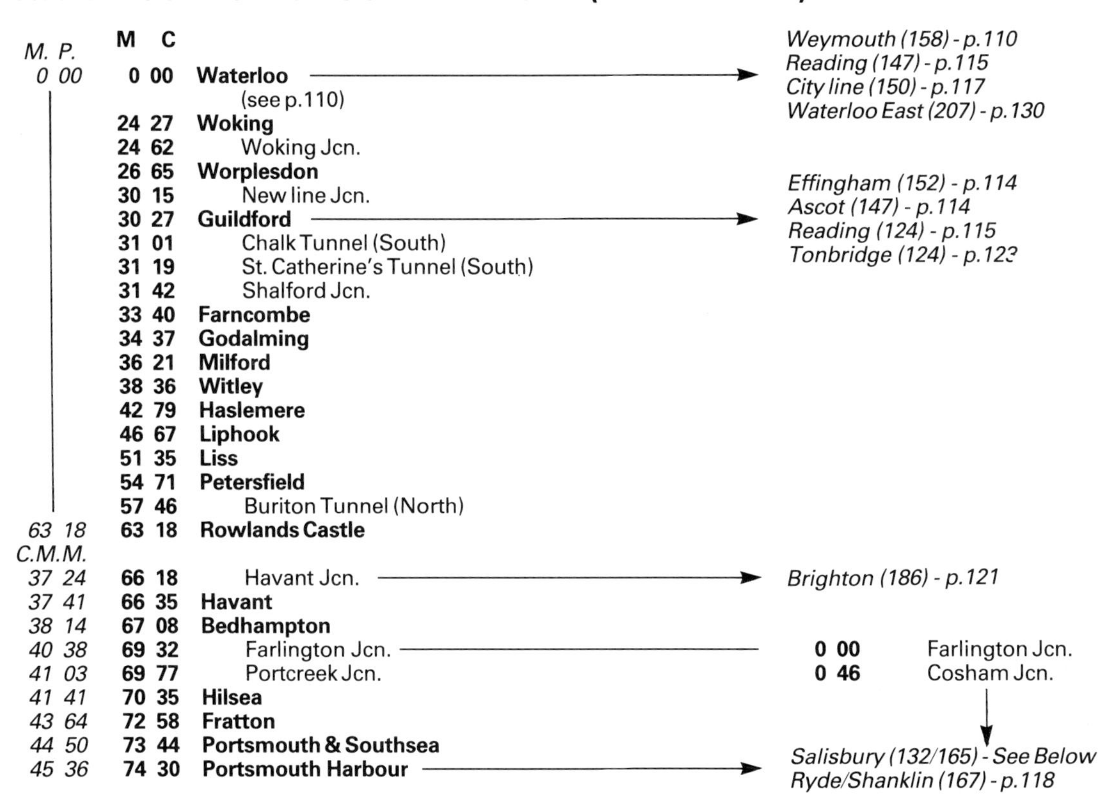

M. P.	M C	Location	Connections
0 00	**0 00**	**Waterloo** (see p.110)	*Weymouth (158) - p.110* *Reading (147) - p.115* *City line (150) - p.117* *Waterloo East (207) - p.130*
	24 27	**Woking**	
	24 62	Woking Jcn.	
	26 65	**Worplesdon**	
	30 15	New line Jcn.	
	30 27	**Guildford**	*Effingham (152) - p.114* *Ascot (147) - p.114* *Reading (124) - p.115* *Tonbridge (124) - p.123*
	31 01	Chalk Tunnel (South)	
	31 19	St. Catherine's Tunnel (South)	
	31 42	Shalford Jcn.	
	33 40	**Farncombe**	
	34 37	**Godalming**	
	36 21	**Milford**	
	38 36	**Witley**	
	42 79	**Haslemere**	
	46 67	**Liphook**	
	51 35	**Liss**	
	54 71	**Petersfield**	
	57 46	Buriton Tunnel (North)	
63 18	**63 18**	**Rowlands Castle**	
C.M.M.			
37 24	**66 18**	Havant Jcn.	*Brighton (186) - p.121*
37 41	**66 35**	**Havant**	
38 14	**67 08**	**Bedhampton**	
40 38	**69 32**	Farlington Jcn.	**0 00** Farlington Jcn.
41 03	**69 77**	Portcreek Jcn.	**0 46** Cosham Jcn.
41 41	**70 35**	**Hilsea**	
43 64	**72 58**	**Fratton**	
44 50	**73 44**	**Portsmouth & Southsea**	*Salisbury (132/165) - See Below*
45 36	**74 30**	**Portsmouth Harbour**	*Ryde/Shanklin (167) - p.118*

PORTSMOUTH HARBOUR - SALISBURY (B.R. Tables 132/165)

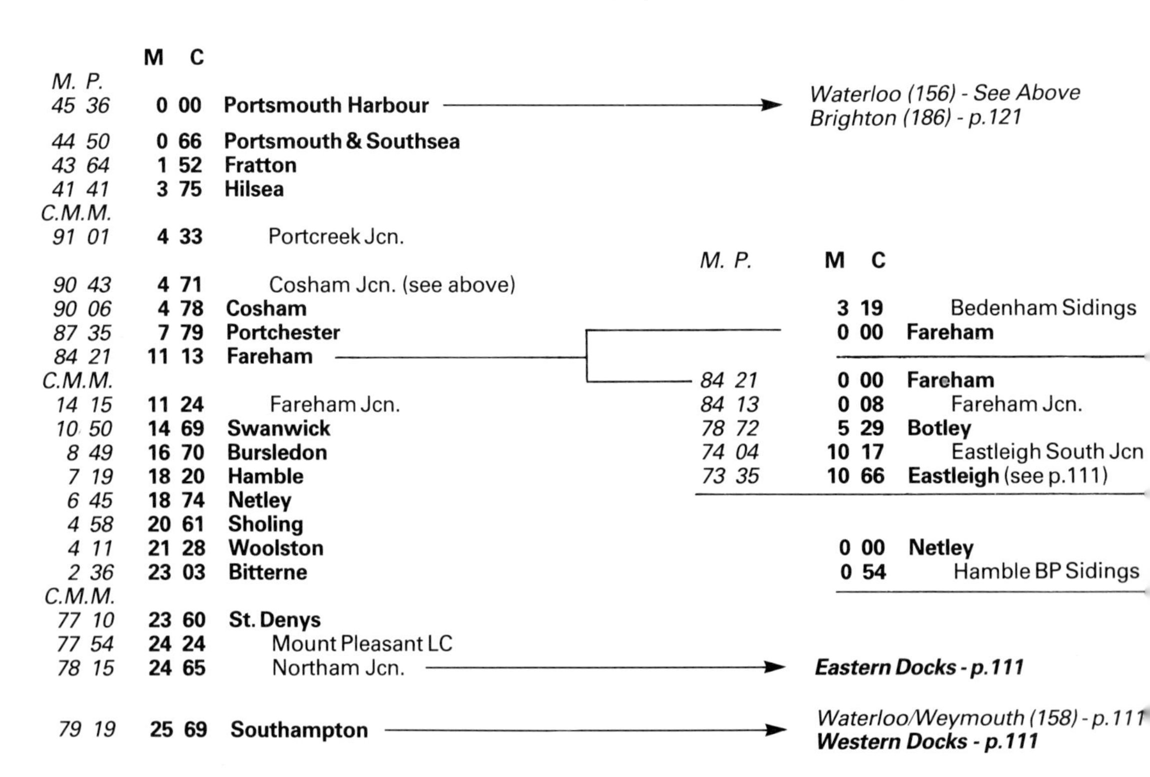

M. P.	M C	Location	Connections
45 36	**0 00**	**Portsmouth Harbour**	*Waterloo (156) - See Above* *Brighton (186) - p.121*
44 50	**0 66**	**Portsmouth & Southsea**	
43 64	**1 52**	**Fratton**	
41 41	**3 75**	**Hilsea**	
C.M.M.			
91 01	**4 33**	Portcreek Jcn.	
90 43	**4 71**	Cosham Jcn. (see above)	
90 06	**4 78**	**Cosham**	
87 35	**7 79**	**Portchester**	
84 21	**11 13**	**Fareham**	
C.M.M.			
14 15	**11 24**	Fareham Jcn.	
10 50	**14 69**	**Swanwick**	
8 49	**16 70**	**Bursledon**	
7 19	**18 20**	**Hamble**	
6 45	**18 74**	**Netley**	
4 58	**20 61**	**Sholing**	
4 11	**21 28**	**Woolston**	
2 36	**23 03**	**Bitterne**	
C.M.M.			
77 10	**23 60**	**St. Denys**	
77 54	**24 24**	Mount Pleasant LC	
78 15	**24 65**	Northam Jcn.	***Eastern Docks - p.111***
79 19	**25 69**	**Southampton**	*Waterloo/Weymouth (158) - p.111* ***Western Docks - p.111***

M. P.	M C	Location
	3 19	Bedenham Sidings
	0 00	**Fareham**

M. P.	M C	Location
84 21	**0 00**	**Fareham**
84 13	**0 08**	Fareham Jcn.
78 72	**5 29**	**Botley**
74 04	**10 17**	Eastleigh South Jcn
73 35	**10 66**	**Eastleigh** (see p.111)

M C	Location
0 00	**Netley**
0 54	Hamble BP Sidings

PORTSMOUTH HARBOUR - SALISBURY (B.R. Tables 132/165) cont.

M.P.	M C	
	0 00	**Portsmouth Harbour**
M. P.		
79 19	25 69	**Southampton**
80 11	26 61	**Millbrook**
81 70	27 60	**Redbridge**
M.M.		
23 31	27 66	Redbridge Jcn.
M.M.		
80 47	33 13	**Romsey** →
84 21	36 67	**Dunbridge**
88 10	40 56	**Dean**
95 61	48 23	Laverstock South Jcn. →
M.M.		
82 36	48 47	Salisbury Tunnel Jcn.
83 43	49 54	**Salisbury** →

M.P.	M C	
	0 00	**Eastleigh**
	0 49	Eastleigh South Jcn.
		via Depot Loop
	1 60	**Eastleigh**
		(see p.111)
73 35	0 00	**Eastleigh**
79 24	5 69	Halterworth LC
80 47	7 12	**Romsey**

M C	
0 00	Laverstock South Jcn.
0 34	Laverstock North Jcn. (see below)

Waterloo (145) - See Below
Bristol (132) - p.97
Exeter (145) - p.98

WATERLOO - SALISBURY (B.R. Table 145)

M.P.	M C		
0 00	0 00	**Waterloo** (see p.110)	
	24 27	**Woking**	→ *Portsmouth Harbour (156) - p.112*
	47 61	**Basingstoke**	→ *Reading (158) - See Below*
	50 21	Worting Jcn.	
	55 42	**Overton**	
	59 08	**Whitchurch**	
	66 19	**Andover** →	
	67 61	Red Post Jcn.	
	72 49	**Grateley**	
	82 05	Laverstock North Jcn.	
	82 36	Salisbury Tunnel Jcn.	
83 43	83 43	**Salisbury**	→ *Bristol (132) - p.97*; *Exeter (145) - p.98*; *Portsmouth (132/165) - See Above*

M.P.	M C	
66 19	0 00	**Andover**
C.M.M.		
0 00	1 42	Red Post Jcn.
1 74	3 36	Weyhill
5 64	7 26	Ludgershall
6 09	7 51	*Horse Dock — Buffer stops
6 26	7 68	*Hedge End Sdg. — Buffer stops
6 33	7 75	*Stop Board (REME Sdg.)

* NOTE: Three separate sidings

BASINGSTOKE - READING (B.R. Table 158)

M.P.	M C		
M. P.			
47 61	0 00	**Basingstoke**	→ *Waterloo/Weymouth (158) - p.110*
M.M.			
51 33	0 06	Basingstoke G.W.R. Jcn.	
46 41	4 18	**Bramley**	
43 14	8 25	**Mortimer**	
37 76	13 43	***SR/WR Boundary***	
37 62	13 57	Southcote Jcn.	
36 75	14 44	**Reading West**	
36 37	15 02	Oxford Road Jcn. →	
36 17	15 22	Westbury line Jcn.	
35 78	15 41	**Reading**	→ *West of England KEY PLAN - p.88*; *Waterloo (147) - p.115*; *Guildford (124) - p.115*

M C	
0 00	Oxford Road Jcn.
0 41	Reading West Jcn. (p.88)

WATERLOO - GUILDFORD via Cobham (B.R. Table 152)

M. P.	M C			
0 00	**0 00**	**Waterloo**		
	7 19	**Wimbledon**	see p.110 for intermediates & Table Refs.	
	12 03	**Surbiton**		
	13 27	Hampton Court Jcn. (Up line)	→	*Hampton Court (152) - p.116*
	13 34	Guildford New line Jcn. (Down)		
	14 04	**Hinchley Wood**		
	15 11	**Claygate**		
	16 79	**Oxshott**		
	18 63	**Cobham**		
	21 10	**Effingham Junction**	→	*Epsom (152) - p.116*
	22 12	**Horsley**		
	25 26	**Clandon**		
	28 47	**London Road (Guildford)**		
29 58	**29 58**	New line Jcn.		
C.M.M.				
30 27	**29 70**	**Guildford**	→	*Portsmouth (156) - p.112* *Ascot (147) - See Below* *Reading (124) - p.115* *Tonbridge/Gatwick (124) - p.123*

GUILDFORD - ASCOT (B.R. Table 147)

M. P.	M C			
30 27	**0 00**	**Guildford**		
34 29	**4 12**	**Wanborough**		
C.M.M.				
49 18	**6 07**	**Ash**	→	*Reading (124) - p.115*
50 01	**6 70**	Aldershot South Jcn.		
50 43	**7 32**	Aldershot North Jcn.	—	**0 00** Aldershot North Jcn **0 36** Government Sidings
C.M.M.				
35 00	**8 72**	**Aldershot** (REV.)	→	*Alton (156) - See Below*
33 40	**10 32**	Aldershot North Jcn.		
32 38	**11 34**	**Ash Vale**	→	*Woking/Waterloo (156) - See Below*
C.M.M.				
40 57	**11 42**	Ash Vale Jcn.		
37 48	**14 51**	**Frimley**		
35 30	**16 69**	**Camberley**		
32 08	**20 11**	**Bagshot**		
28 79	**23 20**	**Ascot**	→	*Waterloo/Reading (147) - p.115*

WATERLOO - ALTON (B.R. Table 156)

M. P.	M C		
0 00	**0 00**	**Waterloo**	
	12 03	**Surbiton**	See p.110 for intermediates
	24 27	**Woking**	
	27 79	**Brookwood**	
	29 39	Pirbright Jcn. (Up line)	
	29 48	Pirbright Jcn. (Down line)	
	32 30	Ash Vale Jcn.	
	32 38	**Ash Vale (see above)**	
	33 40	Aldershot North Jcn.	
35 00	**35 00**	**Aldershot (see above)**	
C.M.M.			
40 33	**38 06**	**Farnham**	
44 24	**41 77**	**Bentley**	
49 13	**46 66**	**Alton**	

Mid-Hants Railway

M. P.	M C	
49 13	**0 00**	**Alton**
50 24	**1 11**	Butts Jcn.
53 48	**4 35**	**Medstead & Four Marks**
56 34	**7 21**	**Ropley**
59 24	**10 11**	**Alresford**

WATERLOO - READING (B.R. Table 147)

M. P.	M C		
0 00	0 00	**Waterloo**	*Weymouth (158) - p.110* *City line (150) - p.117* *Waterloo East (207) - p.130*
	1 29	**Vauxhall**	
	2 50	**Queenstown Road**	
	3 17	West London Jcn.	
	3 63	Clapham Junction 'A'	*Kensington (149) - p.116*
	3 74	**Clapham Junction**	***Stewarts Lane - p.118*** *Victoria (186) - p.119*
	4 60	**Wandsworth Town**	
	5 09	Point Pleasant Jcn.	***Wimbledon - p.116***
	5 72	**Putney**	
	7 07	**Barnes**	*Hounslow (147) - p.117*
	8 21	**Mortlake**	
	9 03	**North Sheen**	
	9 57	**Richmond**	*Camden Road (LMR) (58) - p.53*
	10 66	**St. Margarets**	
	11 22	**Twickenham**	*Waterloo (152) - p.117*
	12 43	**Whitton**	
	13 03	Whitton Jcn.	*Hounslow Jcn. - p.117*
	13 35	Feltham Jcn.	
	14 68	**Feltham**	
	17 40	**Ashford**	
	19 02	**Staines**	*Windsor (147) - p.118*
	21 02	**Egham**	
	23 15	**Virginia Water**	*Weybridge (147) - p.118*
	25 11	**Longcross**	
	26 71	**Sunningdale**	
	28 79	**Ascot**	*Guildford (147) - p.114*
32 24	32 24	**Bracknell**	
M.M.			
62 08	36 51	**Wokingham**	*Guildford (124) - See Below*
64 10	38 53	**Winnersh**	
64 72	39 35	**Winnersh Triangle**	
66 01	40 44	**Earley**	
67 00	41 43	***SR/WR Boundary***	
67 76	42 39	Reading Spur Jcn.	
68 68	43 31	**Reading** (Platform 4a/4b)	*West of England KEY PLAN - p.88* *Basingstoke (158) - p.113*

READING - GUILDFORD (B.R. Table 124)

M. P.	M C		
68 68	0 00	**Reading** (Platform 4a/4b)	
67 76	0 72	Reading Spur Jcn.	
67 00	1 68	***WR/SR Boundary***	
66 01	2 67	**Earley**	
64 72	3 76	**Winnersh Triangle**	
64 10	4 58	**Winnersh**	
62 08	6 60	**Wokingham**	*Waterloo (147) - See Above*
58 66	10 02	**Crowthorne**	
57 22	11 46	**Sandhurst**	
55 58	13 10	**Blackwater**	
53 16	15 57	**Farnborough North**	
51 18	16 67	**North Camp**	
50 01	18 67	Aldershot South Jcn.	
49 18	19 50	**Ash**	*Aldershot/Ascot (147) - p.114*
M.M.			
34 29	21 45	**Wanborough**	
30 27	25 57	**Guildford**	*Waterloo/Portsmouth (156) - p.112* *Waterloo via Cobham (152) - p.114* *Tonbridge/Gatwick (124) - p.123*

M C	
0 00	**Reading** (Main Line)
0 38	Reading New Jcn.
0 77	Reading Spur Jcn.
25 62	**Guildford**

WATERLOO - CHESSINGTON & EPSOM / EFFINGHAM & HORSHAM (B.R. Tables 152/178)

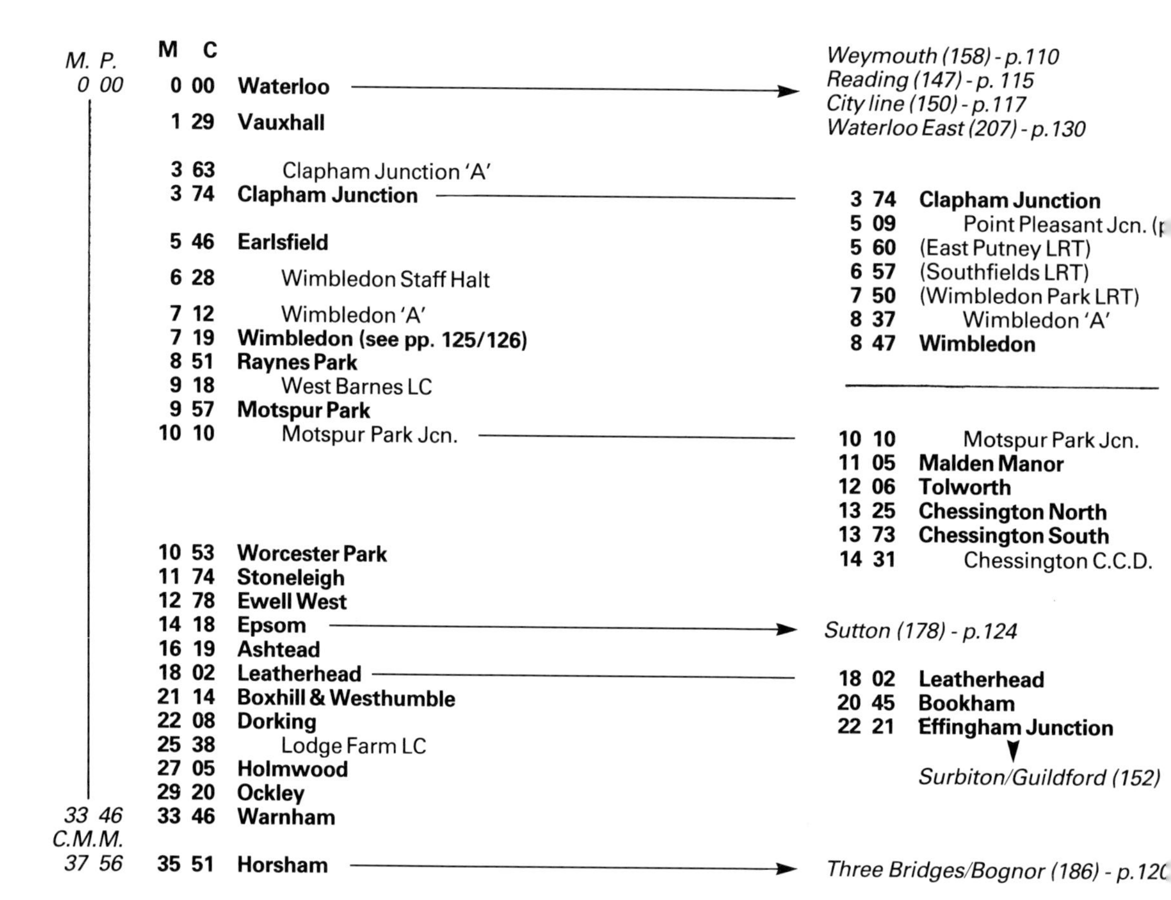

M. P.
0 00
M C
0 00 Waterloo
1 29 Vauxhall
3 63 Clapham Junction 'A'
3 74 Clapham Junction
5 46 Earlsfield
6 28 Wimbledon Staff Halt
7 12 Wimbledon 'A'
7 19 Wimbledon (see pp. 125/126)
8 51 Raynes Park
9 18 West Barnes LC
9 57 Motspur Park
10 10 Motspur Park Jcn.
10 53 Worcester Park
11 74 Stoneleigh
12 78 Ewell West
14 18 Epsom
16 19 Ashtead
18 02 Leatherhead
21 14 Boxhill & Westhumble
22 08 Dorking
25 38 Lodge Farm LC
27 05 Holmwood
29 20 Ockley
33 46 33 46 Warnham
C.M.M.
37 56 35 51 Horsham
Weymouth (158) - p.110
Reading (147) - p. 115
City line (150) - p.117
Waterloo East (207) - p.130
3 74 Clapham Junction
5 09 Point Pleasant Jcn. (
5 60 (East Putney LRT)
6 57 (Southfields LRT)
7 50 (Wimbledon Park LRT)
8 37 Wimbledon 'A'
8 47 Wimbledon
10 10 Motspur Park Jcn.
11 05 Malden Manor
12 06 Tolworth
13 25 Chessington North
13 73 Chessington South
14 31 Chessington C.C.D.
Sutton (178) - p.124
18 02 Leatherhead
20 45 Bookham
22 21 Effingham Junction
Surbiton/Guildford (152)
Three Bridges/Bognor (186) - p.12

WATERLOO - HAMPTON COURT (B.R. Table 152)

M. P.	M C	
0 00	0 00	**Waterloo**
		(see p.110)
	12 03	**Surbiton**
	12 28	Hampton Court Jcns. (Down line)
	13 27	Hampton Court Jcns. (Up line)
	14 01	**Thames Ditton**
14 76	14 76	**Hampton Court**

CLAPHAM JUNCTION - KENSINGTON OLYMPIA (B.R. Table 149)

M. P.	M C		
3 74	0 00	**Clapham Junction** (Windsor Lines)	→ *Brighton Lines - p.118*
3 63	0 11	Clapham Junction 'A'	
C.M.M.			
2 49	0 13	***SR/LMR Boundary***	
2 28	0 34	Latchmere Jcn.	→ *Stewarts Lane - p.118*
C.M.M.			
2 54	3 17	**Kensington Olympia**	→ *Old Oak/Willesden - p.54*

WATERLOO - SHEPPERTON & TWICKENHAM (B.R. Table 152)

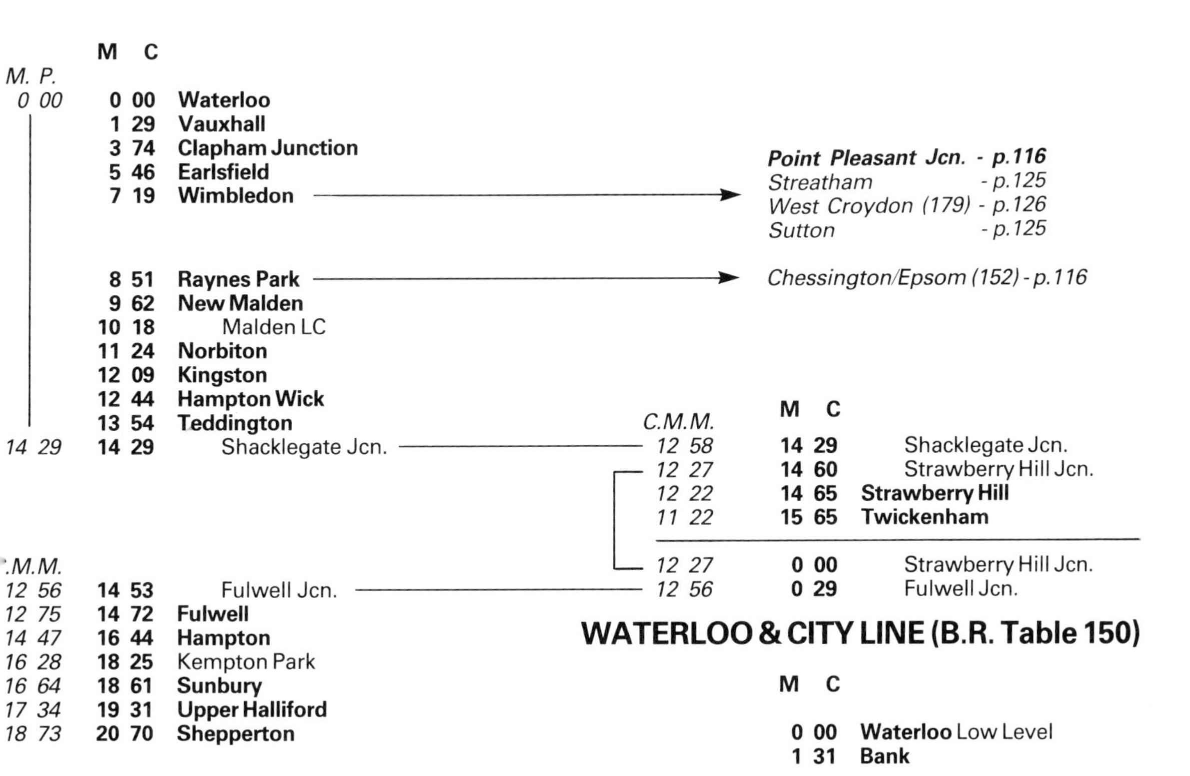

M C
M. P.
0 00 0 00 Waterloo
1 29 Vauxhall
3 74 Clapham Junction
5 46 Earlsfield
7 19 Wimbledon
Point Pleasant Jcn. - p.116
Streatham - p.125
West Croydon (179) - p.126
Sutton - p.125
8 51 Raynes Park
Chessington/Epsom (152) - p.116
9 62 New Malden
10 18 Malden LC
11 24 Norbiton
12 09 Kingston
12 44 Hampton Wick
13 54 Teddington
14 29 14 29 Shacklegate Jcn.
C.M.M.
12 58
12 27
12 22
11 22
M C
14 29 Shacklegate Jcn.
14 60 Strawberry Hill Jcn.
14 65 Strawberry Hill
15 65 Twickenham
12 27 0 00 Strawberry Hill Jcn.
12 56 0 29 Fulwell Jcn.
C.M.M.
12 56 14 53 Fulwell Jcn.
12 75 14 72 Fulwell
14 47 16 44 Hampton
16 28 18 25 Kempton Park
16 64 18 61 Sunbury
17 34 19 31 Upper Halliford
18 73 20 70 Shepperton
WATERLOO & CITY LINE (B.R. Table 150)
M C
0 00 Waterloo Low Level
1 31 Bank

WATERLOO - HOUNSLOW & WHITTON (B.R. Table 147)

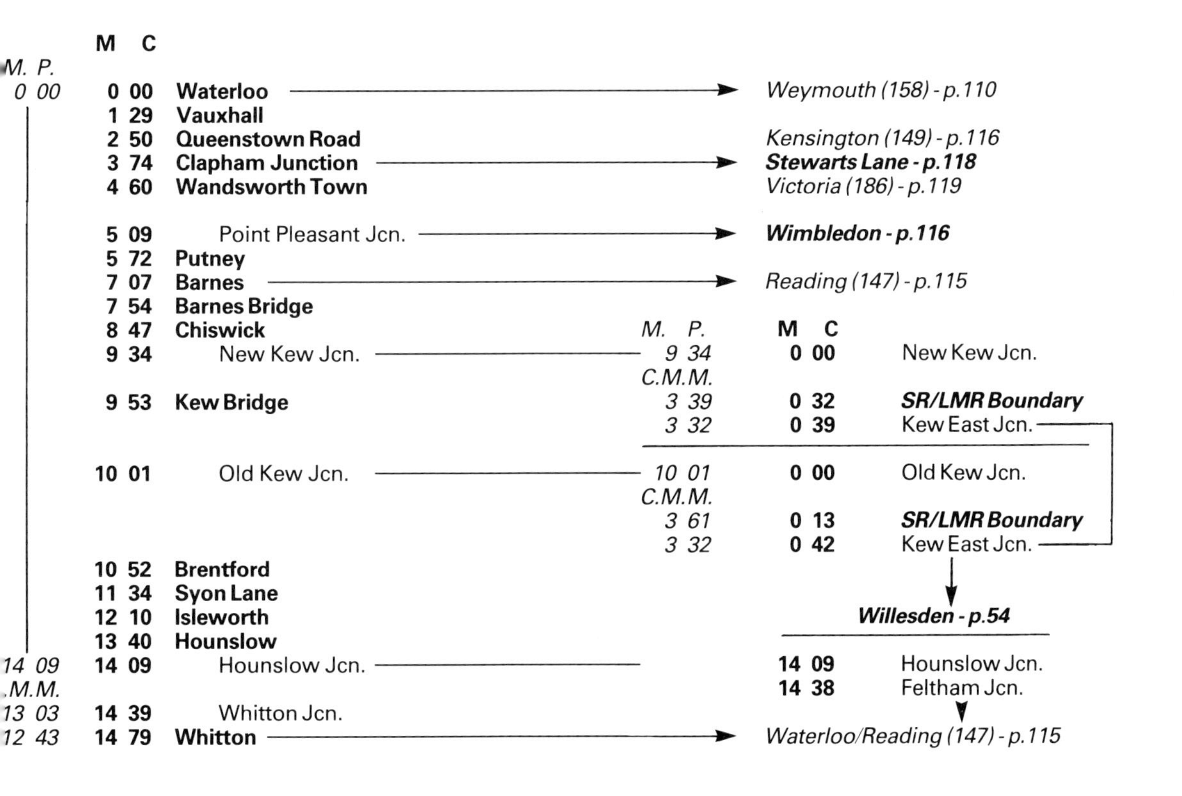

M C
M. P.
0 00 0 00 Waterloo
Weymouth (158) - p.110
1 29 Vauxhall
2 50 Queenstown Road
Kensington (149) - p.116
3 74 Clapham Junction
Stewarts Lane - p.118
4 60 Wandsworth Town
Victoria (186) - p.119
5 09 Point Pleasant Jcn.
Wimbledon - p.116
5 72 Putney
7 07 Barnes
Reading (147) - p.115
7 54 Barnes Bridge
8 47 Chiswick
9 34 New Kew Jcn.
M. P.
9 34
M C
0 00 New Kew Jcn.
C.M.M.
9 53 Kew Bridge
3 39 0 32 SR/LMR Boundary
3 32 0 39 Kew East Jcn.
10 01 Old Kew Jcn.
10 01 0 00 Old Kew Jcn.
C.M.M.
3 61 0 13 SR/LMR Boundary
3 32 0 42 Kew East Jcn.
10 52 Brentford
11 34 Syon Lane
12 10 Isleworth
13 40 Hounslow
Willesden - p.54
14 09 14 09 Hounslow Jcn.
14 09 Hounslow Jcn.
14 38 Feltham Jcn.
C.M.M.
13 03 14 39 Whitton Jcn.
12 43 14 79 Whitton
Waterloo/Reading (147) - p.115

WATERLOO & STAINES - WINDSOR & WEYBRIDGE (B.R. Table 147)

M. P.	M C			M C	
				0 51	Staines West Oil Sdgs
0 00	0 00	**Waterloo**		0 00	**Staines**
	3 74	**Clapham Junction** (see p.115)			
	19 02	**Staines**	→	19 02	**Staines**
21 02	21 02	**Egham**		21 40	**Wraysbury**
C.M.M.				22 48	**Sunnymeads**
24 65	23 15	**Virginia Water**		23 63	**Datchet**
22 25	25 55	**Chertsey**		25 48	**Windsor & Eton Riverside**
20 71	27 09	**Addlestone**			
19 74	28 06	Addlestone Jcn.	→	0 00	Addlestone Jcn.
				0 71	Byfleet Jcn.
19 12	28 68	**Weybridge**	→		*Waterloo/Weymouth (158) - p.110*

RYDE PIER HEAD - SHANKLIN (B.R. Table 167)

M. P.	M C		
		Portsmouth Harbour	→ *Waterloo (156) - p.112* *Salisbury (132/165) - p.112* *Brighton (186) - p.121*
0 00	0 00	**Ryde Pier Head**	
	0 32	**Ryde Esplanade**	
	1 19	**Ryde St. John's Road**	
	2 14	Smallbrook	
	4 55	**Brading**	
	6 42	**Sandown**	
8 29	8 29	**Shanklin**	

Kensington Olympia - Stewarts Lane - Victoria/Factory Jcn.

M. P.	M C		M. P.	M C	
2 54	0 00	**Kensington Olympia**	→		*Old Oak/Willesden - p.54* *Clapham Junction (149) - p.116*
C.M.M.					
2 28	2 63	Latchmere Jcn.	2 28	2 63	Latchmere Jcn.
C.M.M.			C.M.M.		
2 27	3 07	***LMR/SR Boundary***	3 31	2 79	***LMR/SR Boundary***
2 11	3 23	Culvert Road Jcn.	3 01	3 29	**Clapham Junction** (p.119) (Brighton Lines)
1 66	3 48	Longhedge Jcn.	0 39	3 48	Longhedge Jcn.
1 36	2 78	Stewarts Lane	0 00	4 07	Factory Jcn. (p. 126/127)
0 73	4 41	Battersea Pier Jcn.			
0 00	5 34	**Victoria**			

Clapham Junction - Stewarts Lane - Victoria

M. P.	M C		M. P.	M C	
3 74	0 00	**Clapham Junction** (p.115) (Windsor Lines)	2 57	0 00	**Clapham Junction** (p.119) (Brighton Lines)
3 63	0 11	Clapham Jcn. 'A'	C.M.M.		
C.M.M.			2 20	0 53	Pouparts Jcn. (p.119)
2 11	0 63	Culvert Road Jcn.			
1 66	1 08	Longhedge Jcn.	1 66	1 07	Longhedge Jcn.
1 36	1 38	Stewarts Lane			
0 73	2 01	Battersea Pier Jcn.			
0 00	2 74	**Victoria**	→		*Brighton (186) - p.119* *Ramsgate (212) - p.127*

SECTION IV - SOUTHERN REGION

(b) Central Division

VICTORIA - BRIGHTON Via Quarry Line (B.R. Table 186)

KEY PLAN

M. P.	M C	Location	Connections
0 00	**0 00**	**Victoria**	*Ramsgate (212) - p.127* *London Bridge (176) - p.126*
	0 73	Battersea Pier Jcn.	
	1 23	**Battersea Park**	***Stewarts Lane - p.118***
	2 04	Pouparts Jcn.	
	2 57	**Clapham Junction**	*Waterloo/Weymouth (158) - p.110* *Waterloo/Reading (147) - p.115* *Kensington Olympia - p.118*
	4 05	**Wandsworth Common**	
	4 52	**Balham**	*Beckenham/W. Croydon (178) - p.124*
	6 14	Streatham North Jcn.	*Sutton/Epsom (178) - p.124*
	6 48	**Streatham Common**	*London Bridge (178) - p.125*
	7 36	**Norbury**	
	8 54	**Thornton Heath**	
	9 31	**Selhurst**	**0 00 Selhurst** **1 08 Norwood Junction** (p.121)
9 60	**9 60**	Gloucester Road Jcn.	**9 60** Gloucester Road Jcn. **10 50 West Croydon** *Victoria/Sutton (178) - p.124* *L. Bridge via Streatham - p.125* *Wimbledon (179) - p.126*
M.M.			
9 69	**10 01**	Windmill Bridge Jcn.	
10 28	**10 40**	**East Croydon**	*London Bridge (186) - p.121*
11 21	**11 33**	**South Croydon**	*E. Grinstead/Uckfield (184) - p.123*
12 34	**12 46**	**Purley Oaks**	
13 29	**13 41**	**Purley**	*Caterham (178) - p.123*
14 20	**14 32**	Stoats Nest Jcn.	*Brighton via Redhill - p.120*
17 24	**17 36**	Quarry Tunnel (North)	
20 62	**20 74**	Redhill Tunnel (North)	
21 50	**21 62**	**Earlswood**	
23 37	**23 49**	**Salfords**	
25 60	**25 72**	**Horley**	
26 47	**26 59**	**Gatwick Airport**	
29 21	**29 33**	**Three Bridges**	*Horsham/Bognor (186) - p.120*
31 28	**31 40**	Balcombe Tunnel Jcn.	
32 02	**32 14**	Balcombe Tunnel (North)	***Bluebell Railway - p.123***
33 64	**33 76**	**Balcombe**	
37 00	**37 12**	Copyhold Jcn.	**0 00** Copyhold Jcn. **1 34** Ardingly ARC
37 59	**37 71**	**Haywards Heath**	
40 52	**40 64**	**Wivelsfield**	
40 69	**41 01**	Keymer Jcn.	*Lewes/Eastbourne (189) - p.122*
41 39	**41 51**	**Burgess Hill**	
43 42	**43 54**	**Hassocks**	
44 44	**44 56**	Clayton Tunnel (North)	
47 65	**47 77**	Patcham Tunnel (North)	
49 21	**49 33**	**Preston Park**	**0 00 Preston Park** **1 35 Hove** *Portsmouth (186) - p.121* *Lewes (189) - p.122*
50 33	**50 45**	Montpelier Jcn.	
50 49*	**50 61***	**Brighton**	

LONDON BRIDGE & VICTORIA — BRIGHTON via Redhill (B.R. Table 186)

M. P.	M C	M C		
0 00	**0 00**		**London Bridge**	
		0 00	**Victoria**	
	9 69	**10 01**	Windmill Bridge Jcn.	
	10 28	**10 40**	**East Croydon**	
14 20	**14 20**	**14 32**	Stoats Nest Jcn.	
C.M.M.				
17 03	**15 19**	**15 31**	**Coulsdon South**	
19 09	**17 25**	**17 41**	Merstham Tunnel (North)	
20 59	**18 75**	**19 07**	**Merstham**	
22 30	**20 46**	**20 58**	Redhill 'A' (closed)	
22 40	**20 56**	**20 68**	**Redhill** ——►	*Guildford/Tonbridge (124) - p.123*
22 53	**20 69**	**21 01**	Redhill 'B' (closed)	
C.M.M.				
21 50	**21 45**	**21 57**	**Earlswood**	
50 49	**50 44***	**50 56***	**Brighton**	

***NOTE: The preceding tables show the four different distances between London and Brighton. Southern Region equalise mileages at Windmill Bridge Jcn. and Earlswood so, *officially*, it is 50 miles 49 chains by whichever route is travelled. This is actually the distance from London Bridge to Brighton via Quarry (see M.P. column - p.119).**
According to B.R. records, Windmill Bridge is 12 chains further from Victoria than from London Bridge, and the Quarry line is 5 chains longer than the Redhill route. However, these figures may have changed physically by the odd chain or so during recent track re-modelling.
To confuse matters further, mileposts between Coulsdon South, Redhill and Earlswood show distances from Charing Cross!

VICTORIA - LITTLEHAMPTON & BOGNOR REGIS via Quarry (B.R. Table 186)

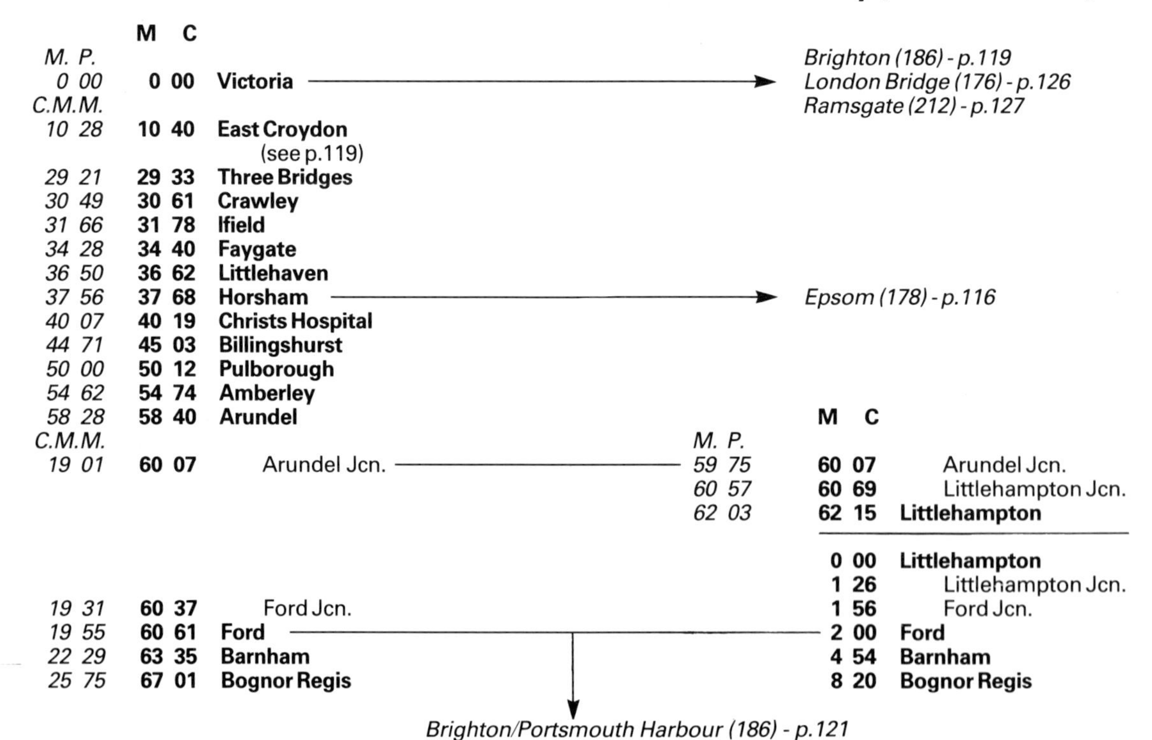

M. P.	M C		
0 00	**0 00**	**Victoria** ——►	*Brighton (186) - p.119* *London Bridge (176) - p.126* *Ramsgate (212) - p.127*
C.M.M.			
10 28	**10 40**	**East Croydon** (see p.119)	
29 21	**29 33**	**Three Bridges**	
30 49	**30 61**	**Crawley**	
31 66	**31 78**	**Ifield**	
34 28	**34 40**	**Faygate**	
36 50	**36 62**	**Littlehaven**	
37 56	**37 68**	**Horsham** ——►	*Epsom (178) - p.116*
40 07	**40 19**	**Christs Hospital**	
44 71	**45 03**	**Billingshurst**	
50 00	**50 12**	**Pulborough**	
54 62	**54 74**	**Amberley**	
58 28	**58 40**	**Arundel**	
C.M.M.			
19 01	**60 07**	Arundel Jcn. ——	
19 31	**60 37**	Ford Jcn.	
19 55	**60 61**	**Ford** ——	
22 29	**63 35**	**Barnham**	
25 75	**67 01**	**Bognor Regis**	

M. P.	M C	
59 75	**60 07**	Arundel Jcn.
60 57	**60 69**	Littlehampton Jcn.
62 03	**62 15**	**Littlehampton**

M C	
0 00	**Littlehampton**
1 26	Littlehampton Jcn.
1 56	Ford Jcn.
2 00	**Ford**
4 54	**Barnham**
8 20	**Bognor Regis**

Brighton/Portsmouth Harbour (186) - p.121

LONDON BRIDGE - EAST CROYDON (B.R. Tables 178/186)

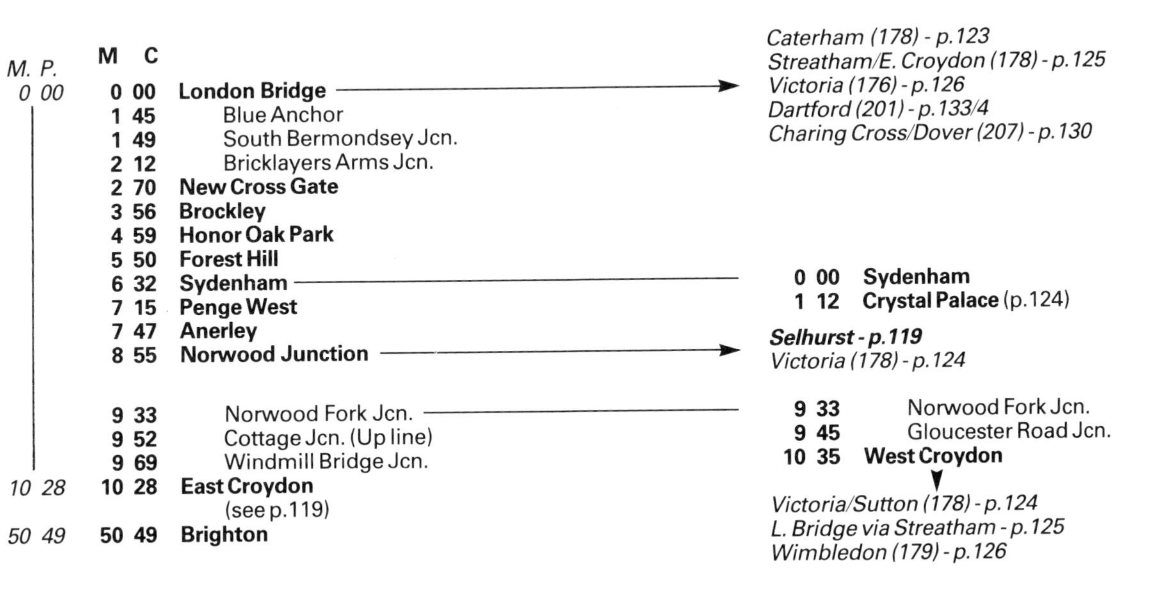

M. P.
M C
0 00
0 00 London Bridge
1 45 Blue Anchor
1 49 South Bermondsey Jcn.
2 12 Bricklayers Arms Jcn.
2 70 New Cross Gate
3 56 Brockley
4 59 Honor Oak Park
5 50 Forest Hill
6 32 Sydenham
7 15 Penge West
7 47 Anerley
8 55 Norwood Junction
9 33 Norwood Fork Jcn.
9 52 Cottage Jcn. (Up line)
9 69 Windmill Bridge Jcn.
10 28
10 28 East Croydon
(see p.119)
50 49
50 49 Brighton
Caterham (178) - p.123
Streatham/E. Croydon (178) - p.125
Victoria (176) - p.126
Dartford (201) - p.133/4
Charing Cross/Dover (207) - p.130
0 00 Sydenham
1 12 Crystal Palace (p.124)
Selhurst - p.119
Victoria (178) - p.124
9 33 Norwood Fork Jcn.
9 45 Gloucester Road Jcn.
10 35 West Croydon
Victoria/Sutton (178) - p.124
L. Bridge via Streatham - p.125
Wimbledon (179) - p.126

BRIGHTON - PORTSMOUTH HARBOUR (B.R. Table 186)

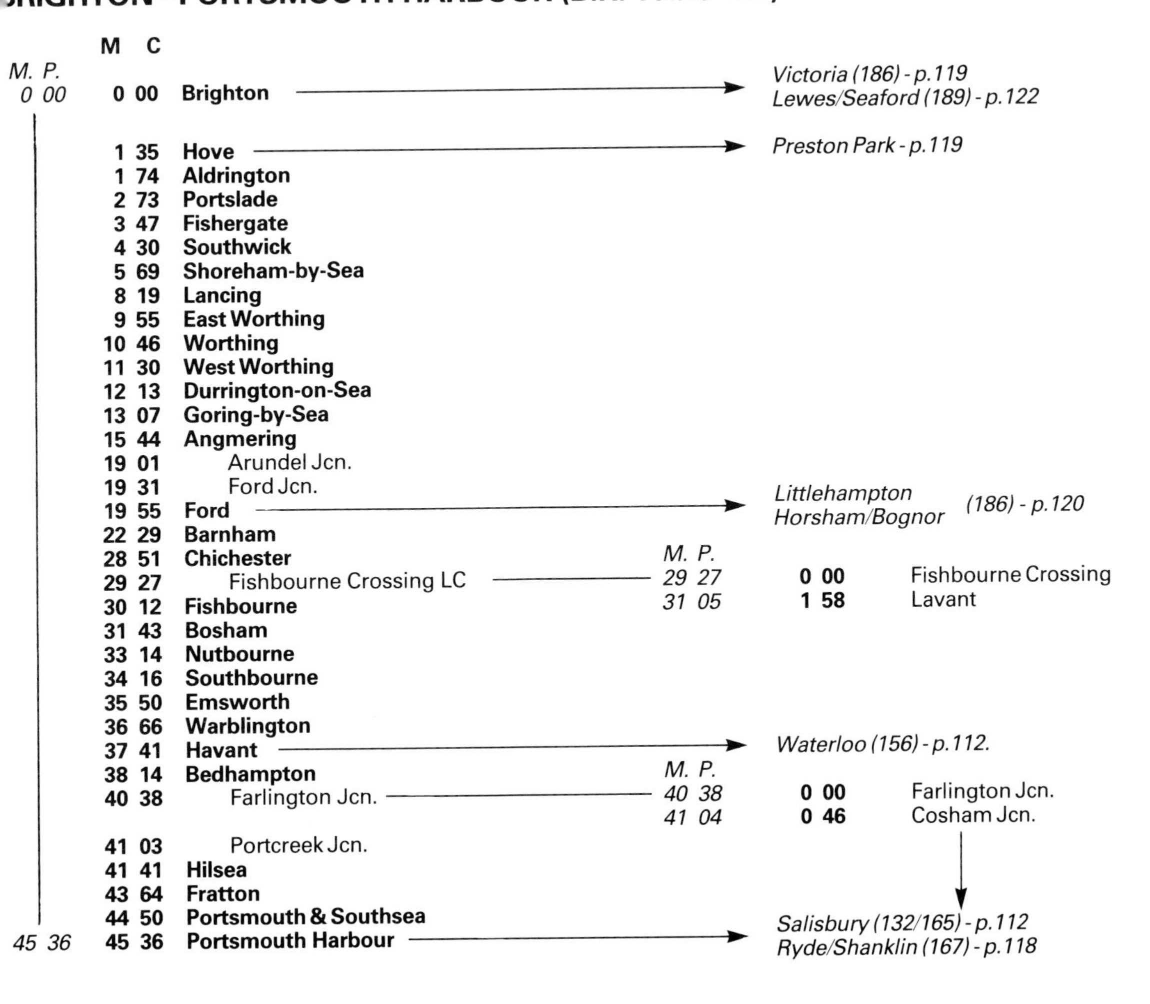

M C
M. P.
0 00
0 00 Brighton
1 35 Hove
1 74 Aldrington
2 73 Portslade
3 47 Fishergate
4 30 Southwick
5 69 Shoreham-by-Sea
8 19 Lancing
9 55 East Worthing
10 46 Worthing
11 30 West Worthing
12 13 Durrington-on-Sea
13 07 Goring-by-Sea
15 44 Angmering
19 01 Arundel Jcn.
19 31 Ford Jcn.
19 55 Ford
22 29 Barnham
28 51 Chichester
29 27 Fishbourne Crossing LC
30 12 Fishbourne
31 43 Bosham
33 14 Nutbourne
34 16 Southbourne
35 50 Emsworth
36 66 Warblington
37 41 Havant
38 14 Bedhampton
40 38 Farlington Jcn.
41 03 Portcreek Jcn.
41 41 Hilsea
43 64 Fratton
44 50 Portsmouth & Southsea
45 36
45 36 Portsmouth Harbour
Victoria (186) - p.119
Lewes/Seaford (189) - p.122
Preston Park - p.119
Littlehampton
Horsham/Bognor
(186) - p.120
M. P.
29 27
31 05
0 00 Fishbourne Crossing
1 58 Lavant
Waterloo (156) - p.112.
M. P.
40 38
41 04
0 00 Farlington Jcn.
0 46 Cosham Jcn.
Salisbury (132/165) - p.112
Ryde/Shanklin (167) - p.118

BRIGHTON - LEWES & SEAFORD (B.R. Table 189)

M. P.	M C	Station	Connection
0 00	0 00	**Brighton**	*Victoria (186) - p.119* *Portsmouth (186) - p.121*
	0 57	**London Road**	
	1 65	**Moulsecoomb**	
	3 39	**Falmer**	
7 77	7 77	**Lewes**	*Victoria/ Eastbourne (189) - See Below*
C.M.M.			
51 11	9 14	Southerham Jcn.	
53 40	11 43	**Southease**	
56 25	14 28	**Newhaven Town**	
56 51	14 54	**Newhaven Harbour**	**14 54 Newhaven Harbour** **14 76 Newhaven Marine**
58 03	16 06	**Bishopstone**	
58 77	17 00	**Seaford**	

VICTORIA - EASTBOURNE (B.R. Table 189)

M. P.	M C	Station	Connection
0 00	0 00	**Victoria**	
C.M.M.		(see p.119)	
10 28	10 40	**East Croydon**	*London Bridge (186/9) - p.121*
37 59	37 71	**Haywards Heath** (via Quarry)	
40 52	40 64	**Wivelsfield**	
40 69	41 01	Keymer Jcn.	*Brighton (186) - p.119*
44 42	44 54	**Plumpton**	
47 31	47 43	**Cooksbridge**	
49 74	50 06	**Lewes**	*Brighton /Seaford (189) - see above*
C.M.M.			
9 14	51 23	Southerham Jcn.	
11 14	53 23	**Glynde**	
15 50	57 59	**Berwick**	
19 42	61 51	**Polegate**	
21 38	63 47	Willingdon Jcn.	*Hastings (189) - See Below*
21 75	64 04	**Hampden Park**	
23 73	66 02	**Eastbourne**	

EASTBOURNE - HASTINGS (B.R. Table 189)

M. P.	M C	Station	Connection
23 73	0 00	**Eastbourne**	*Lewes/ Victoria (189) - See Above*
21 75	1 78	**Hampden Park**	
21 38	2 35	Willingdon Jcn.	
C.M.M.			
23 07	4 04	**Pevensey & Westham**	
23 68	4 65	**Pevensey Bay**	
25 77	6 74	**Normans Bay**	
27 53	8 50	**Cooden Beach**	
29 04	10 01	**Collington**	
29 69	10 66	**Bexhill**	
C.M.M.			
60 69	13 73	Bopeep Jcn.	*Tonbridge (206) - p.131*
61 55	14 59	**St. Leonards Warrior Square**	
C.M.M.			
82 34	15 37	**Hastings**	*Ashford (206) - p.132*

GUILDFORD - TONBRIDGE & GATWICK AIRPORT (B.R. Table 124)

M. P.	M C	Station	Connections
30 27	0 00	**Guildford** →	*Waterloo/Portsmouth (156) - p.112* *Effingham (152) - p.114* *Ascot (147) - p.114* *Reading (124) - p.115*
C.M.M.			
41 60	1 15	Shalford Jcn.	
41 02	1 73	**Shalford**	
39 15	3 60	**Chilworth**	
35 21	7 54	**Gomshall**	
30 42	12 43	**Dorking Town**	
29 65	13 10	**Deepdene**	
27 17	15 58	**Betchworth**	
24 27	18 48	**Reigate**	
22 40	20 35	**Redhill** (see p.120) (REV.)	
C.M.M.			
24 47	22 42	**Nutfield**	
28 13	26 08	**Godstone**	
33 03	30 78	**Edenbridge**	
38 03	35 78	**Penshurst**	
39 56	37 51	**Leigh**	
42 16	40 11	**Tonbridge** →	*Hastings (206) - p.131* *Charing X/Ashford (207) - p.130*

M. P.	M C	Station
22 40	20 35	**Redhill**
C.M.M.		
26 47	26 21	**Gatwick Airport** (p.119)

VICTORIA - EAST GRINSTEAD & UCKFIELD (B.R. Table 184)

M. P.	M C	Station	Connections
0 00	0 00	**Victoria** →	*Brighton (186) - p.119* *Eastbourne (189) - p.122*
C.M.M.	2 57	**Clapham Junction** (see p.110)	
10 28	10 40	**East Croydon** →	*London Bridge (178/186) - p.121*
11 21	11 33	**South Croydon**	
11 59	11 71	Selsdon Jcn.	
12 23	12 35	**Sanderstead**	
13 38	13 50	**Riddlesdown**	
15 33	15 45	**Upper Warlingham**	
17 15	17 27	**Woldingham**	
20 25	20 37	**Oxted**	
21 20	21 32	**Hurst Green**	
21 35	21 47	Hurst Green Jcn.	
25 47	25 59	**Edenbridge Town**	
27 27	27 39	**Hever**	
29 26	29 38	**Cowden**	
32 08	32 20	**Ashurst**	
C.M.M.			
27 75	34 68	Birchden Jcn. (see note p.131)	
26 78	35 65	**Eridge**	
23 40	39 23	**Crowborough**	
18 64	43 79	**Buxted**	
16 40	46 23	**Uckfield**	
	46 60	End of line	

M. P.	M C	Station
21 35	21 47	Hurst Green Jcn.
26 23	26 35	**Lingfield**
27 62	27 74	**Dormans**
30 04	30 16	**East Grinstead**

Bluebell Railway

M. P.	M C	Station
	0 00	Buffer stop
	0 18	**Sheffield Park**
9 49	0 00	**Sheffield Park**
		Freshfield Halt
14 07	4 38	**Horstead Keynes**
	4 55	End of line
20 35	10 66	East Grinstead **(proposed)**

LONDON BRIDGE - CATERHAM & TATTENHAM CORNER (B.R. Table 178)

M. P.	M C	Station	Connections
0 00	0 00	**London Bridge** → (see p.121)	*Streatham (178) - p.125* *Victoria (176) - p.126* *Charing X/Dover (207) - p.130*
	10 28	**East Croydon**	
	11 21	**South Croydon**	
12 34	12 34	**Purley Oaks**	
C.M.M.			
15 13	13 29	**Purley**	
16 29	14 45	**Kenley**	
17 58	15 74	**Whyteleafe**	
18 18	16 34	**Whyteleafe South**	
19 70	18 06	**Caterham**	

M. P.	M C	Station
15 13	0 00	**Purley**
15 65	0 52	**Reedham**
16 47	1 34	**Smitham**
17 40	2 27	**Woodmansterne**
18 41	3 28	**Chipstead**
20 72	5 59	**Kingswood**
22 18	7 05	**Tadworth**
23 37	8 24	**Tattenham Corner**

VICTORIA - BECKENHAM JUNCTION & WEST CROYDON, SUTTON & EPSOM DOWNS (B.R. Table 178)

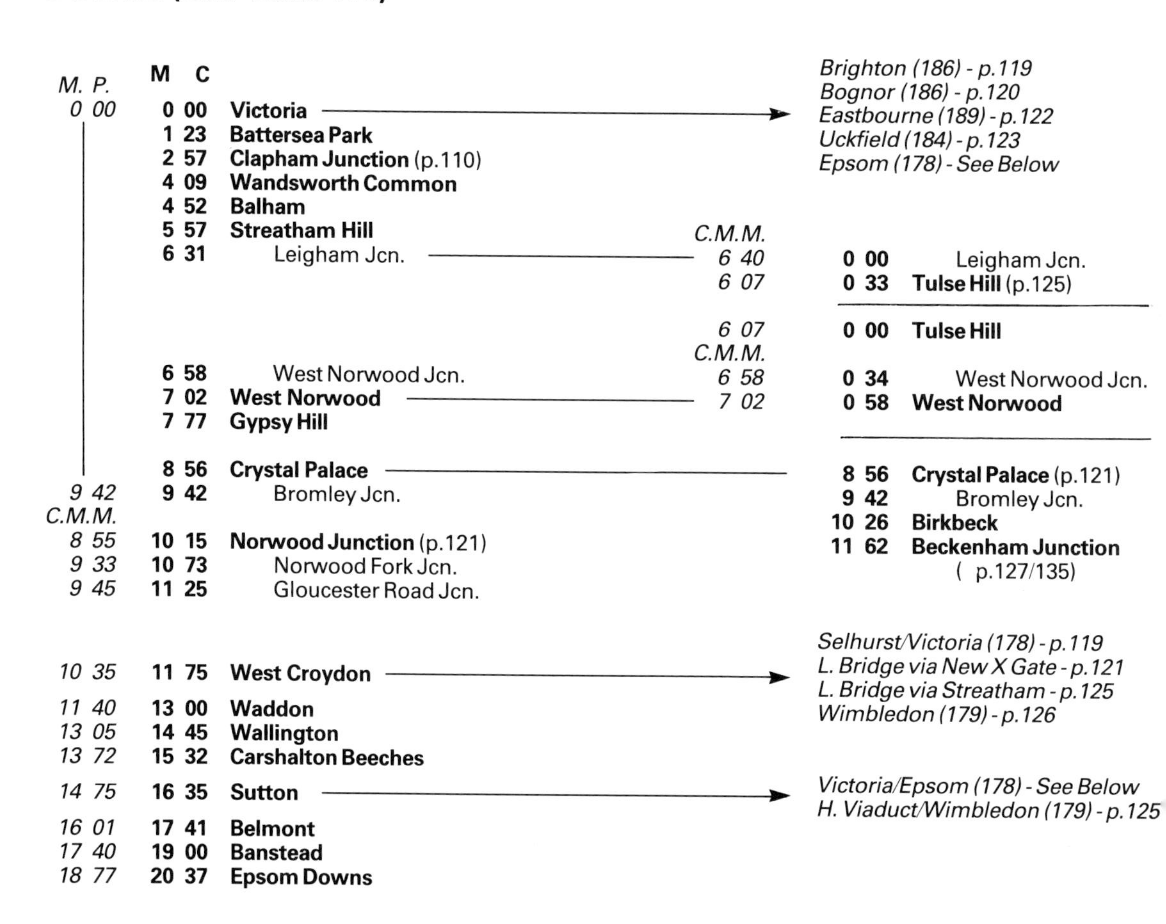

M. P.	M C	Station	C.M.M.	Connections
0 00	0 00	**Victoria** →		*Brighton (186) - p.119* *Bognor (186) - p.120* *Eastbourne (189) - p.122* *Uckfield (184) - p.123* *Epsom (178) - See Below*
	1 23	**Battersea Park**		
	2 57	**Clapham Junction** (p.110)		
	4 09	**Wandsworth Common**		
	4 52	**Balham**		
	5 57	**Streatham Hill**		
	6 31	Leigham Jcn.	*6 40* *6 07*	
	6 58	West Norwood Jcn.	*6 07* C.M.M. *6 58*	
	7 02	**West Norwood**	*7 02*	
	7 77	**Gypsy Hill**		
	8 56	**Crystal Palace** →		
9 42	9 42	Bromley Jcn.		
C.M.M.				
8 55	10 15	**Norwood Junction** (p.121)		
9 33	10 73	Norwood Fork Jcn.		
9 45	11 25	Gloucester Road Jcn.		
10 35	11 75	**West Croydon** →		*Selhurst/Victoria (178) - p.119* *L. Bridge via New X Gate - p.121* *L. Bridge via Streatham - p.125* *Wimbledon (179) - p.126*
11 40	13 00	**Waddon**		
13 05	14 45	**Wallington**		
13 72	15 32	**Carshalton Beeches**		
14 75	16 35	**Sutton** →		*Victoria/Epsom (178) - See Below* *H. Viaduct/Wimbledon (179) - p.125*
16 01	17 41	**Belmont**		
17 40	19 00	**Banstead**		
18 77	20 37	**Epsom Downs**		

M C	Station
0 00	Leigham Jcn.
0 33	**Tulse Hill** (p.125)

M C	Station
0 00	**Tulse Hill**
0 34	West Norwood Jcn.
0 58	**West Norwood**

M C	Station
8 56	**Crystal Palace** (p.121)
9 42	Bromley Jcn.
10 26	**Birkbeck**
11 62	**Beckenham Junction** (p.127/135)

VICTORIA - EPSOM (B.R. Table 178)

M. P.	M C	Station	Connections
0 00	0 00	**Victoria**	
	2 57	**Clapham Junction**	
	4 52	**Balham**	
6 14	6 14	Streatham North Jcn.	
C.M.M.			
8 11	6 43	Streatham South Jcn. →	*Wimbledon (179) - p.125*
10 30	8 62	**Mitcham Junction** →	*W. Croydon (179) - p.126*
11 41	9 73	**Hackbridge**	
12 30	10 62	**Carshalton**	
C.M.M.			
14 75	12 08	**Sutton** →	*Epsom Downs (178) - See Above* *H. Viaduct/Wimbledon (179) - p.125*
15 76	13 09	**Cheam**	
17 27	14 40	**Ewell East**	
18 73	16 06	**Epsom** →	*Waterloo/Effingham (152) - p.116* *Horsham (178) - p.116*

LONDON BRIDGE - EAST CROYDON via Streatham (B.R. Table 178)

M. P.	M C	Station	*C.M.M.*	Connections
0 00	0 00	**London Bridge** →		*Croydon via New X Gate - p.121* *Victoria (176) - p.126* *Charing X/Dover (207) - p.130*
	1 03	Spa Road		
	1 45	Blue Anchor		
	1 49	South Bermondsey Jcn.		
	1 63	**South Bermondsey**		
	2 58	**Queens Road (Peckham)**		
	3 36	**Peckham Rye**		
	4 23	**East Dulwich**		
	4 64	**North Dulwich**		
	6 07	**Tulse Hill** →		*H. Viaduct (179) - See Below* *West Norwood - p.124*
7 48	7 48	**Streatham** →		*Wimbledon (179) - See Below*
M.M.				
6 48	8 15	**Streatham Common** →		*Victoria (178/186) - p.119*
7 36	9 03	**Norbury**		
8 54	10 21	**Thornton Heath**		
9 31	10 78	**Selhurst** →		***Norwood Junction - p.119***
9 60	11 27	Gloucester Road Jcn. —	*9 45*	**11 27** Gloucester Road Jcn.
M.M.			*10 35*	**12 17** **West Croydon** (p.124)
9 69	11 48	Windmill Bridge Jcn.		
10 28	12 07	**East Croydon** →		*Brighton (186) - p.119* *Bognor (186) - p.120* *Eastbourne (189) - p.122* *Uckfield (184) - p.123* *Caterham (178) - p.123*

HOLBORN VIADUCT - WIMBLEDON & SUTTON (B.R. Table 179)

M. P.	M C	Station	Connections
0 00	0 00	**Holborn Viaduct** →	*Sevenoaks (195)* *Lewisham (201)* - *p.129*
	0 30	**Blackfriars** —	**0 00** **Blackfriars** **0 64** Metropolitan Jcn. (p.130)
	1 47	**Elephant & Castle**	
	3 37	Loughborough Jcn. →	***Canterbury Road Jcn. - p.126***
3 48	3 48	**Loughborough Junction**	
M.M.			
3 76	4 36	**Herne Hill** →	*Victoria (195) - p.127*
M.M.			
6 07	5 42	**Tulse Hill** →	*West Norwood - p.124* *L. Bridge/E. Croydon - See Above*
7 48	7 03	**Streatham**	
M.M.			
0 00	7 47	Streatham South Jcn. →	*Victoria/Sutton (178) - p.124*
0 76	8 43	**Tooting**	
2 18	9 65	**Haydons Road**	
M.M.			
7 12	10 43	Wimbledon 'A'	
7 21	10 52	**Wimbledon** →	*Waterloo/Weymouth (158) - p.110* *Guildford (152) - p.114* *Chessington/Epsom (152) - p.116* *Shepperton (152) - p.117* *W. Croydon (179) - p.126*
7 51	11 02	Wimbledon West Jcn.	
8 13	11 44	**Wimbledon Chase**	
8 61	12 12	**South Merton**	
9 32	12 63	**Morden South**	
9 69	13 20	**St. Helier**	
10 67	14 18	**Sutton Common**	
11 47	14 78	**West Sutton**	
12 50	16 01	**Sutton** →	*Victoria/Epsom* *Epsom Downs* *(178) - p.124*

WIMBLEDON - WEST CROYDON via Mitcham (B.R. Table 179)

M. P.	M C	Station	Connections
			Waterloo/Weymouth (158) - p.110
			Guildford (152) - p.114
0 00	**0 00**	**Wimbledon** →	*Chessington/Epsom (152) - p.116*
	0 51	**Merton Park**	*Shepperton (152) - p.117*
	1 08	**Morden Road**	*H. Viaduct/Sutton (179) - p.125*
	2 24	**Mitcham**	
	3 04	**Mitcham Junction** →	*Victoria/Sutton (178) - p.124*
	3 57	**Beddington Lane**	
	4 79	**Waddon Marsh**	*Selhurst/Victoria (178) - p.119*
6 12	**6 12**	**West Croydon** →	*L. Bridge via New X Gate - p.121*
			L. Bridge via Streatham - p.125
			Victoria/Sutton (178) - p.124

LONDON BRIDGE - VICTORIA (B.R. Table 176)

via Atlantic Lines

M. P.	M C	Station	Connections
			Croydon via New X Gate - p.121
0 00	**0 00**	**London Bridge** →	*Croydon via Streatham - p.125*
			Caterham (178) - p.123
			Charing X/Dover (207) - p.130
	1 03	Spa Road	
	1 45	Blue Anchor	
	1 49	South Bermondsey Jcn.	
	1 63	**South Bermondsey**	
	2 58	**Queens Road (Peckham)**	
	3 36	**Peckham Rye**	
	3 67	Crofton Road Jcn.	
	4 23	**Denmark Hill**	
	6 21	**Clapham**	
	6 33	Voltaire Road Jcn.	
	6 52	**Wandsworth Road**	
6 58	**6 58**	Factory Jcn. →	***Cambria Jcn. - See Below***
			Longhedge Jcn. - p.118
C.M.M.			
1 23	**7 27**	**Battersea Park**	
0 73	**7 57**	Battersea Pier Jcn. →	***Stewarts Lane - p.118***
			Brighton (186) - p.119
			Bognor (186) - p.120
			Eastbourne (189) - p.122
0 00	**8 50**	**Victoria** →	*Uckfield (184) - p.123*
			Beckenham/W. Croydon
			Sutton/Epsom (178) - p.124
			Ramsgate (212) - p.127

Victoria - Factory Jcn. - Cambria Jcn.

via Chatham Lines

M. P.	M C	Station	Connections
0 00	**0 00**	**Victoria**	
	0 73	Battersea Pier Jcn. →	***Stewarts Lane p.118***
	1 61	Factory Jcn.	***Longhedge Jcn.***
	2 05	Voltaire Road Jcn.	
	3 08	Brixton Jcn.	
	3 24	Canterbury Road Jcn. —	**0 00** Canterbury Road Jcn.
			0 42 Loughborough Jcn. ↓
			Holborn Viaduct (195) - p.125
			Sevenoaks (195)
3 70	**3 70**	Cambria Jcn. →	*Lewisham (201) - p.129*

SECTION IV - SOUTHERN REGION

(c) South Eastern Division

VICTORIA - RAMSGATE via Chatham (B.R. Table 212)
VICTORIA - ORPINGTON (B.R. Table 195)

M. P.	M C	Station	Connection
0 00	**0 00**	**Victoria**	*See p.126 for Table Refs.*
	0 71	Battersea Pier Jcn.	***Stewarts Lane - p.118***
	1 61	Factory Jcn.	
	2 05	Voltaire Road Jcn.	
	3 08	Brixton Jcn.	***Canterbury Road Jcn. - p.126***
	3 14	**Brixton**	
	3 76	**Herne Hill**	*H. Viaduct/Wimbledon (179) - p.125*
	5 02	**West Dulwich**	
	5 57	**Sydenham Hill**	
	7 15	**Penge East**	
	7 66	**Kent House**	
	8 53	**Beckenham Junction**	*Victoria (178) - p.124* ***New Beckenham - p.135***
	9 57	Shortlands Jcn.	
	10 03	**Shortlands**	*H. Viaduct/Sevenoaks (195) - p.129*
	10 71	**Bromley South**	
	11 76	**Bickley**	
	12 38	Bickley Jcn.	(see Orpington branch below)
	12 62	Chislehurst Jcn.	
	13 17	St. Mary Cray Jcn.	
	14 57	**St. Mary Cray**	
	17 31	**Swanley**	*Ashford (198) - p.129*
	20 41	**Farningham Road**	
	23 30	**Longfield**	
	25 76	**Meopham**	
	26 71	**Sole Street**	
	33 01	Rochester Bridge Jcn.	
	33 61	**Rochester**	*Charing Cross (201) - p.133*
	34 25	**Chatham**	
	35 75	**Gillingham**	(see Chatham Dockyard branch below)
	38 74	**Rainham**	
	41 44	**Newington**	
	43 70	Western Jcn.	*Sheerness (213) - p.128*
	44 18	Eastern Jcn.	*Sheerness (213) - p.128*
	44 59	**Sittingbourne**	*Sheerness (213) - p.128*
	47 74	**Teynham**	
	51 77	**Faversham**	*Dover (212) - p.128*
	54 77	Graveney LC	
	59 06	**Whitstable**	
	60 45	**Chestfield & Swalecliffe**	
	62 58	**Herne Bay**	
	70 56	**Birchington-on-Sea**	
	72 35	**Westgate-on-Sea**	
	73 69	**Margate**	
	77 09	**Broadstairs**	
	78 26	**Dumpton Park**	
79 21	**79 21**	**Ramsgate**	*Ashford (207) - p.128* *Dover (207) - p.131*

M. P.	M C	Station
12 38	**12 38**	Bickley Jcn.
C.M.M.		
12 25	**13 31**	Petts Wood Jcn.
12 55	**13 61**	**Petts Wood**
13 65	**14 71**	**Orpington** (see p.130)

M C	Station
0 00	**Gillingham**
0 57	Chatham Dockyard

SITTINGBOURNE - SHEERNESS-ON-SEA (B.R. Table 213)

M.P.	M C	Location		M C	Connection
44 59	0 00	**Sittingbourne**	→		*Victoria/Ramsgate (212) - p.127*
C.M.M. 0 00	0 41	Eastern Jcn.			↑
				0 00	Western Jcn.
C.M.M. 44 13	0 64	Middle Jcn.	—	0 23	Middle Jcn.
45 20	1 71	**Kemsley**	—	0 00	**Kemsley**
				1 47	Ridham Dock
47 15	3 66	**Swale**			
49 22	5 72	**Queenborough**	—	0 00	**Queenborough**
				1 77	Sheerness Steelwork
51 19	7 70	**Sheerness-on-Sea**			

Sittingbourne & Kemsley Light Railway

M C	Location
0 00	**Sittingbourne**
1 58	**Kemsley Down**

VICTORIA - DOVER WESTERN DOCKS via Faversham (B.R. Table 212)

M.P.	M C	Location		M C	Connection
0 00	0 00	**Victoria** (see p.127)			
	51 77	**Faversham**			
	53 51	Clock House LC			
	55 18	**Selling**			
	58 65	Chartham Hatch LC			
	61 65	**Canterbury East**			
	64 58	**Bekesbourne**			
	67 60	**Adisham**			
	68 66	**Aylesham**			
	69 60	**Snowdown**			
	69 73	Snowdown Colliery		2 17	Tilmanstone Colliery
	71 60	**Shepherds Well**	—	0 00	**Shepherds Well**
	73 14	Lydden Tunnel (South)			
	75 09	**Kearsney**			
	76 32	Buckland Jcn.			
	77 23	**Dover Priory**	→		*Charing X/Ramsgate (207) - p.131*
	77 72	Hawkesbury Street Jcn.			
				0 30	Archcliffe Jcn.
78 30	78 30	**Dover Western Docks**	—	0 00	**Dover Western Docks**

ASHFORD - RAMSGATE via Canterbury West (B.R. Table 207)

M.P.	M C	Location		M C	Connection
56 09	0 00	**Ashford**	→		*Victoria (198) - p.129* *Charing X/Dover (207) - p.130* *Hastings (206) - p.132*
56 34	0 25	Canterbury Jcn.			
60 32	4 23	**Wye**			
65 09	9 00	**Chilham**			
67 14	11 05	**Chartham**			
70 27	14 18	**Canterbury West**			
72 58	16 49	**Sturry**			
75 16	19 07	Chislet Colliery			
81 64	25 55	**Minster**	—	0 00	**Minster**
				0 42	Minster South Jcn.
82 17	26 08	Minster East Jcn.			↓
85 67	29 58	**Ramsgate**	→		*Dover/Charing Cross (207) - p.131* *Chatham/Victoria (212) - p.127*

'ICTORIA - MAIDSTONE EAST & ASHFORD (B.R. Table 198)

M. P.	M C	Station	Connections
0 00	0 00	**Victoria** (see p.127)	*Orpington (195)* / *Chatham/Ramsgate (212)* - *p.127*; *Central Division Refs. - p.126*
	17 31	**Swanley**	
	18 67	Eynsford Tunnel (North)	
	20 32	**Eynsford**	
	22 52	**Shoreham**	
	24 07	**Otford**	
	24 53	Otford Jcn.	*Sevenoaks (195) - See Below*
	26 79	**Kemsing**	
	29 46	**Borough Green & Wrotham**	
	34 61	**West Malling**	
	35 64	**East Malling**	
	37 43	**Barming**	
	39 76	**Maidstone East**	
	42 59	**Bearsted**	
	45 02	**Hollingbourne**	
	47 36	**Harrietsham**	
	49 11	**Lenham**	
	53 11	**Charing**	**0 00 Charing**
55 61	55 61	Hothfield Staff Halt	**3 53** Hothfield Stone Term.
.M.M.			
55 53	58 61	Maidstone Jcn.	
56 09	59 17	**Ashford**	*Ramsgate (207) - p.128*; *Charing X/Dover (207) - p.130*; *Hastings (206) - p.132*

IOLBORN VIADUCT - LEWISHAM (B.R. Table 201) & SEVENOAKS via Catford Loop (B.R. Table 195)

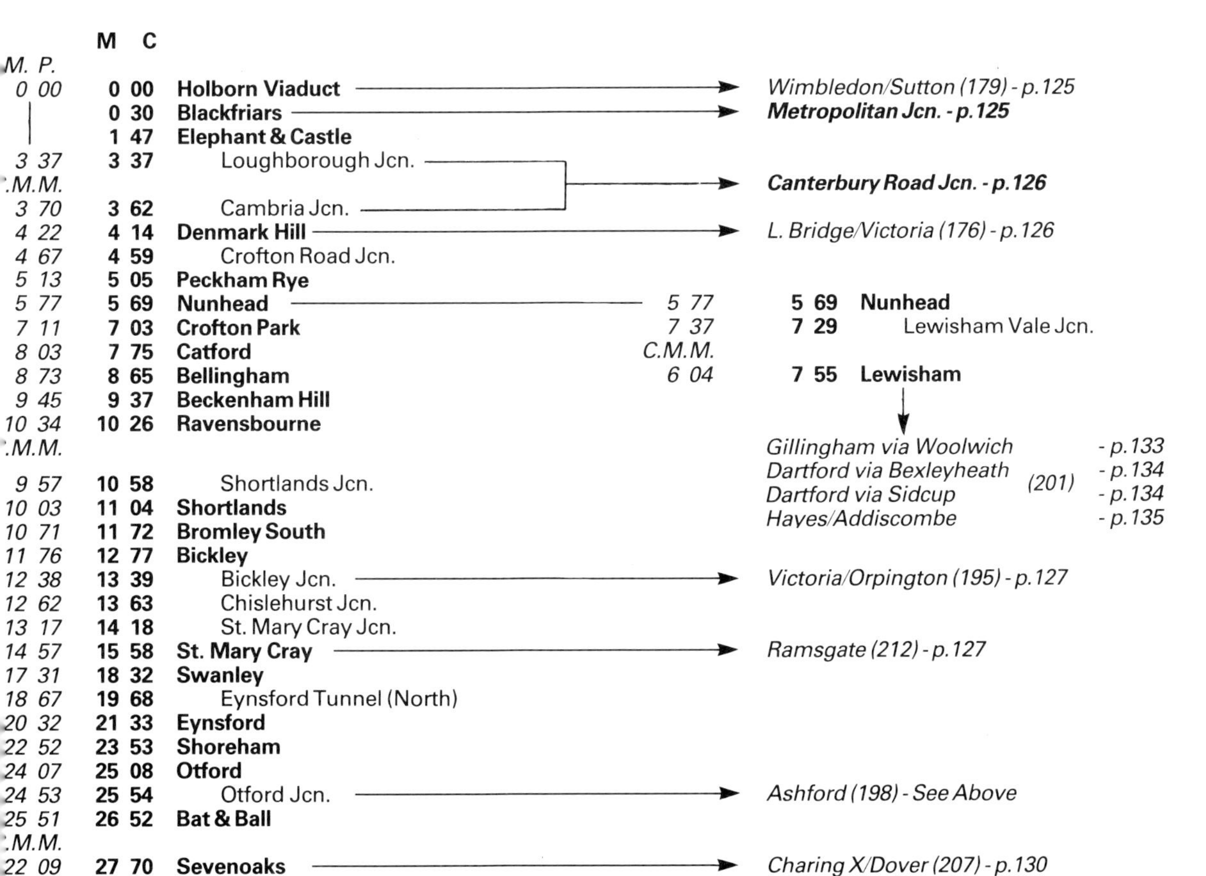

M. P.	M C	Station	Connections
0 00	0 00	**Holborn Viaduct**	*Wimbledon/Sutton (179) - p.125*
	0 30	**Blackfriars**	***Metropolitan Jcn. - p.125***
	1 47	**Elephant & Castle**	
3 37	3 37	Loughborough Jcn.	***Canterbury Road Jcn. - p.126***
.M.M.			
3 70	3 62	Cambria Jcn.	***Canterbury Road Jcn. - p.126***
4 22	4 14	**Denmark Hill**	*L. Bridge/Victoria (176) - p.126*
4 67	4 59	Crofton Road Jcn.	
5 13	5 05	**Peckham Rye**	
5 77	5 69	**Nunhead**	*5 77* — **5 69 Nunhead**
7 11	7 03	**Crofton Park**	*7 37* — **7 29** Lewisham Vale Jcn.
8 03	7 75	**Catford**	*C.M.M.*
8 73	8 65	**Bellingham**	*6 04* — **7 55 Lewisham**
9 45	9 37	**Beckenham Hill**	
10 34	10 26	**Ravensbourne**	
.M.M.			
9 57	10 58	Shortlands Jcn.	
10 03	11 04	**Shortlands**	
10 71	11 72	**Bromley South**	
11 76	12 77	**Bickley**	
12 38	13 39	Bickley Jcn.	*Victoria/Orpington (195) - p.127*
12 62	13 63	Chislehurst Jcn.	
13 17	14 18	St. Mary Cray Jcn.	
14 57	15 58	**St. Mary Cray**	*Ramsgate (212) - p.127*
17 31	18 32	**Swanley**	
18 67	19 68	Eynsford Tunnel (North)	
20 32	21 33	**Eynsford**	
22 52	23 53	**Shoreham**	
24 07	25 08	**Otford**	
24 53	25 54	Otford Jcn.	*Ashford (198) - See Above*
25 51	26 52	**Bat & Ball**	
.M.M.			
22 09	27 70	**Sevenoaks**	*Charing X/Dover (207) - p.130*

From Lewisham (201):

Gillingham via Woolwich	*(201)*	*- p.133*
Dartford via Bexleyheath	*(201)*	*- p.134*
Dartford via Sidcup	*(201)*	*- p.134*
Hayes/Addiscombe	*(201)*	*- p.135*

CHARING CROSS - DOVER & RAMSGATE via Tonbridge (B.R. Table 207)

M. P.	M C	Location	KEY PLAN
0 00	0 00	**Charing Cross**	
	0 61	**Waterloo East** →	*Waterloo/Weymouth (158) - p.110* *Waterloo/Reading (147) - p.115* *Waterloo/Bank (150) - p.117*
	1 31	Metropolitan Jcn. (p.125)	M. P. *1 31* / *1 73* — M C 0 00 Metropolitan Jcn.; 0 42 **Cannon Street**
	1 51	Borough Market Jcn.	M C 0 00 **Cannon Street**; 0 38 Borough Market Jcn.
	1 70	**London Bridge** →	*Croydon via New X Gate - p.121* *Croydon via Streatham - p.125* *Caterham (178) - p.123* *Victoria (176) - p.126*
	2 71	Spa Road	
	3 32	Blue Anchor	
	4 25	North Kent East Jcn. →	*Greenwich/Dartford (201) - p.133*
	4 68	**New Cross**	
	5 29	Tanners Hill Jcn.	
	5 47	**St. Johns** →	*Gillingham (201) - p.133* *Bexleyheath/Dartford (201) - p.134* *Sidcup/Dartford (201) - p.134* *Hayes/Addiscombe (201) - p.135*
	6 14	Parks Bridge Jcn. (p.135)	
	6 36	Courthill Loop Jcn. South (p.134)	
	7 16	**Hither Green**	
	7 44	Lee Spur Jcn. →	***Lee Jcn. - p.134***
	8 78	**Grove Park**	M. P. *8 78* — M C 0 00 **Grove Park**
	9 61	**S/L** Chislehurst Tunnels (N.)	M. P. *10 12* — M C 1 14 **Sundridge Park**
	9 63	**F/L** Chislehurst Tunnels (N.)	M. P. *10 47* — M C 1 49 **Bromley North**
	10 21	**Elmstead Woods**	
	11 19	**Chislehurst**	
	11 33	Chislehurst Jcns.	M. P. *11 33* — M C 0 00 Chislehurst Jcn.
	11 55	Chislehurst Jcns.	M. P. *12 10* — M C 0 57 St Mary Cray Jcn. (p.127)
	12 25	Petts Wood Jcn.	
	12 55	**Petts Wood**	
	13 65	**Orpington** →	*Victoria (195) - p.127*
	15 25	**Chelsfield**	
	16 44	**Knockholt**	
	20 46	**Dunton Green**	
	22 09	**Sevenoaks** →	*H. Viaduct (195) - p.129*
	24 50	Sevenoaks Tunnel (South)	
	27 02	**Hildenborough**	
	29 42	**Tonbridge** →	*Guildford (124) - p.123* *Hastings (206) - p.131*
	34 65	**Paddock Wood** →	*Strood (205) - p.132*
	39 31	**Marden**	
	41 69	**Staplehurst**	
	45 20	**Headcorn**	
	50 35	**Pluckley**	
	55 53	Maidstone Jcn.	
	56 09	**Ashford** →	*Victoria (198) - p.129* *Ramsgate (207) - p.128* *Hastings (206) - p.132*
	56 34	Canterbury Jcn.	
	64 15	**Westenhanger**	
	65 36	**Sandling**	***Romney, Hythe & Dymchurch Railway - p.132***
	66 21	Saltwood Tunnel (East)	
	68 16	Cheriton	
	69 22	**Folkestone West**	
69 73	69 73	**Folkestone Central**	

CHARING CROSS - DOVER & RAMSGATE via Tonbridge (B.R. Table 207) cont.

M.P.	M	C	Location	Connection
0 00	0	00	**Charing Cross**	
69 73	69	73	**Folkestone Central**	
	70	76	Folkestone East Staff Halt	
	70	79	Folkestone East Jcn.	→ Folkestone Harbour branch
	71	22	Martello Tunnel (West)	
	72	02	Folkestone Warren Staff Halt	
	73	23	Abbotscliffe Tunnel (West)	
	75	09	Shakespeare Staff Halt	
	75	14	Shakespeare Tunnel (West)	
76 42	76	42	Archcliffe Jcn.	→ Dover Western Docks branch
.M.M.				
77 72	76	57	Hawkesbury Street Jcn.	
77 23	77	26	**Dover Priory**	→ *Victoria (212) - p.128*
.M.M.				
99 05	78	17	Buckland Jcn.	
97 44	79	58	Guston Tunnel (South)	
95 05	82	17	**Martin Mill**	
92 27	84	75	**Walmer**	
90 56	86	46	**Deal**	
89 11	88	11	Betteshanger Colliery	
86 46	90	56	**Sandwich**	
85 24	91	78	Richborough LC	
82 70	94	32	Richborough Sidings	
.M.M.				
0 32	95	01	Minster South Jcn.	→ *Minster - p.128*
.M.M.				
82 17	95	33	Minster East Jcn.	
85 67	99	03	**Ramsgate**	→ *Ashford (207) - p.128* *Chatham/Victoria (212) - p.127*

M.P.	M	C	Location
70 79	0	00	Folkestone East Jcn.
71 29	0	30	Folly Road LC
72 02	1	03	**Folkestone Harbour**
	1	19	Pierhead

M	C	Location
76	42	Archcliffe Jcn.
76	72	**Dover Western Docks**

CHARING CROSS - HASTINGS (B.R. Table 206)

M.P.	M	C	Location	Connection
0 00	0	00	**Charing Cross** (see p.130)	
	29	42	**Tonbridge**	
	32	70	**High Brooms**	
	34	32	**Tunbridge Wells Central**	
	34	53	Grove Jcn. (see note below)	
	36	53	**Frant**	
	39	23	**Wadhurst**	
	40	40	Wadhurst Tunnel (South)	
	43	66	**Stonegate**	
	45	36	Crowhurst Bridge LC	
	47	34	**Etchingham**	
	49	47	**Robertsbridge**	
	51	78	Mountfield Sidings GF	
	55	46	**Battle**	
	57	50	**Crowhurst**	
	60	59	**West St. Leonards**	
	60	69	Bopeep Jcn.	
	61	55	**St. Leonards Warrior Square**	
62 33	62	33	**Hastings**	→ *Eastbourne (189) - p.122* *Ashford (206) - p.132*

Kent & East Sussex Railway

M	C	Location	
0	00	**Tenterden Town**	
0	40	Cranbrook Road LC	
1	33	**Rolvenden**	
4	09	**Wittersham Road**	
5	00	Hexden Bridge	
6	39	Northiam	proposed
		Dixter Halt	proposed
10	71	Bodiam	proposed

NOTE: The line from **Grove Jcn. to Birchden Jcn.** is closed and lifted at the Tunbridge Wells end. However, it is hoped to re-open all, or part, of it as a private railway. Mileages were as follows:

C.M.M.	M	C	Location
50 22	0	00	Grove Jcn.
49 47	0	55	**Tunbridge Wells West**
46 46	3	56	**Groombridge**
C.M.M.			
27 75	4	61	Birchden Jcn. (see p.123)

ASHFORD - HASTINGS (B.R. Table 206)

M. P.	M C		
56 09	**0 00**	**Ashford** →	*Ramsgate (207) - p.128* *Victoria (198) - p.129* *Charing X/Dover (207) - p.130*
61 51	**5 42**	**Ham Street**	
64 50	**8 41**	**Appledore** →	
66 47	**10 38**	Becketts LC	
69 20	**13 11**	Star LC	
71 34	**15 25**	**Rye**	
73 22	**17 13**	**Winchelsea**	
77 43	**21 34**	**Doleham**	
78 65	**22 56**	**Three Oaks**	
80 26	**24 17**	Ore Tunnel (North)	
81 42	**25 33**	**Ore**	
82 34	**26 25**	**Hastings** →	*Eastbourne (189) - p.122* *Tonbridge (206) - p.131*

M. P.		
64 50	**0 00**	**Appledore**
67 20	**2 50**	Brookland LC
71 51	**7 01**	Lydd Town LC
74 00	**9 30**	Dungeness (End of line)

STROOD - PADDOCK WOOD (B.R. Table 205)

M. P.	M C		
31 11	**0 00**	**Strood** →	*Dartford/Gillingham (201) - p.133*
32 02	**0 71**	Metal Box Siding GF	
33 36	**2 25**	**Cuxton**	
35 18	**4 07**	**Halling**	
36 59	**5 48**	**Snodland**	
38 03	**6 72**	**New Hythe**	
38 74	**7 63**	**Aylesford**	
42 00	**10 69**	**Maidstone Barracks**	
42 36	**11 25**	**Maidstone West**	
C.M.M.			
42 75	**13 11**	**East Farleigh**	
39 77	**16 09**	**Wateringbury**	
38 19	**17 67**	**Yalding**	
36 50	**19 36**	**Beltring**	
34 65	**21 21**	**Paddock Wood** →	*Charing X/Dover (207) - p.130*

Romney, Hythe & Dymchurch Railway

M C	
0 00	**Hythe**
0 71	Prince of Wales Bridge
2 25	Botolph's Bridge
2 79	Willop Bridge
4 00	Burmarsh Road
4 77	**Dymchurch**
5 61	Golden Sands (closed)
6 11	**Jefferstone Lane**
6 52	Collins Bridge
7 28	Warren Bridge
8 13	**New Romney**
9 39	Greatstone (closed)
10 14	**Romney Sands**
10 74	Lade (closed)
11 71	Kerton Road Bridge
12 37	Pilot (closed)
12 78	Britannia Points
13 34	**Dungeness**

CHARING CROSS - GILLINGHAM via North Kent Line (B.R. Table 201)

M. P.	M C	Location	Connection
0 00	0 00	**Charing Cross**	→ *Dover/Ramsgate (212) - p.130*
	0 61	**Waterloo East**	→ *Waterloo Main - p.110*
	1 31	Metropolitan Jcn.	
	1 51	Borough Market Jcn.	→ *Cannon Street - p.130*
	1 70	**London Bridge**	→ *Croydon via New X Gate - p.121* *Croydon via Streatham - p.125* *Caterham (178) - p.123* *Victoria (176) - p.126*
	2 71	Spa Road	
	3 32	Blue Anchor	
	4 25	North Kent East Jcn.	via Greenwich (see below)
	4 68	**New Cross**	
	5 29	Tanners Hill Jcn.	
	5 47	**St. Johns**	
	6 04	**Lewisham** (see p.134)	
	6 75	**Blackheath**	
7 30	7 30	Blackheath Tunnel (South)	
M.M.			
7 44	8 70	**Charlton**	(see below)
8 56	10 02	**Woolwich Dockyard**	
9 32	10 58	**Woolwich Arsenal**	
10 01	11 27	**Plumstead**	
11 43	12 69	**Abbey Wood**	
12 75	14 21	**Belvedere**	
14 18	15 44	**Erith**	
15 30	16 56	**Slade Green**	→ *Perry Street Fork Jcn. - p.134*
15 66	17 12	Crayford Creek Jcn.	→ *Lewisham (201) - p.134*
16 42	17 68	Crayford Spur 'A' Jcn.	→ ***Crayford Spur 'B' Jcn. - p.134***
17 05	18 31	Dartford Jcn.	
M.M.			
17 12	18 58	**Dartford**	→ *Dartford Loop (201) - p.134*
19 07	20 53	**Stone Crossing**	
19 69	21 35	**Greenhithe**	
20 70	22 36	Swanscombe Siding GF	
21 14	22 60	**Swanscombe**	(see below)
21 69	23 35	**Northfleet**	
23 75	25 41	**Gravesend**	
27 07	28 53	Hoo Staff Halt (Down)	
27 19	28 65	Hoo Jcn.	(see below)
27 26	28 72	Hoo Staff Halt (Up)	
28 42	30 08	**Higham**	
29 45	31 11	Higham Tunnel (South)	
30 74	32 40	Strood Tunnel (South)	
31 11	32 57	**Strood**	→ *Paddock Wood (205) - p.132*
31 34	33 00	Rochester Bridge Jcn.	
M.M.			
33 61	33 60	**Rochester**	→ *Victoria/Ramsgate (212) - p.127*
34 25	34 24	**Chatham**	
35 75	35 74	**Gillingham**	→ ***Chatham Dockyard - p.127***

via Greenwich

M C	Location
4 25	North Kent East Jcn.
4 76	**Deptford**
5 36	**Greenwich**
6 27	**Maze Hill**
6 76	**Westcombe Park**
7 44	**Charlton**

M C	Location
0 00	**Charlton**
1 02	Angerstein Wharf

M. P.	M C	Location
21 14	0 00	**Swanscombe**
21 51	0 37	Junction Points
21 70	0 56	B.R./Blue Circle Boundary
		via Northfleet Loop
21 70	2 52	B.R. Boundary
21 51	2 71	Junction Points
21 14	3 28	**Swanscombe**

M. P.	M C	Location
27 19	0 00	Hoo Jcn.
28 61	1 42	Signal D.12
32 06	4 67	Wybourne LC
36 77	9 58	Stoke LC
38 22	11 03	Grain LC

CHARING CROSS - DARTFORD via Bexleyheath (B.R. Table 201)

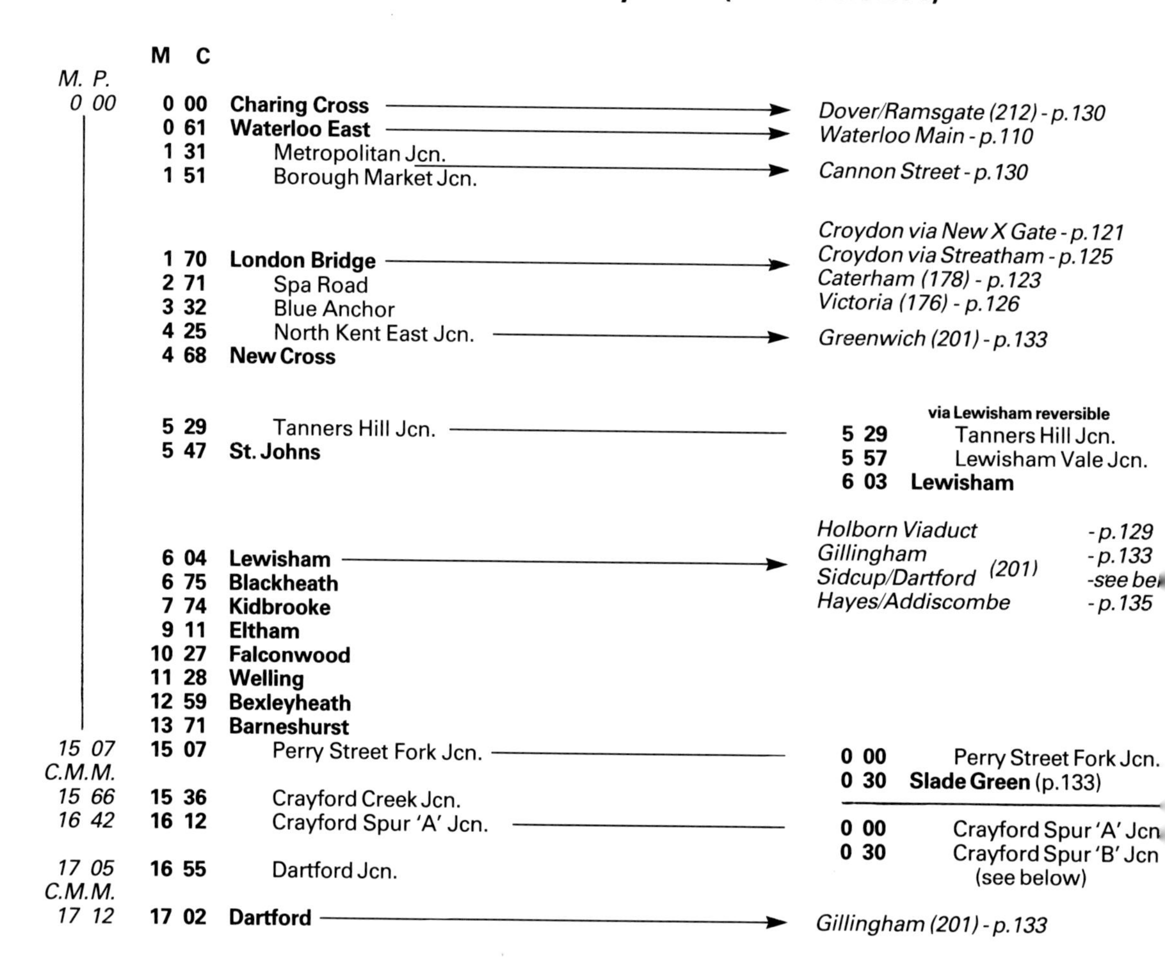

M. P.	M C		Connections
0 00	0 00	**Charing Cross**	→ *Dover/Ramsgate (212) - p.130*
	0 61	**Waterloo East**	→ *Waterloo Main - p.110*
	1 31	Metropolitan Jcn.	
	1 51	Borough Market Jcn.	→ *Cannon Street - p.130*
	1 70	**London Bridge**	→ *Croydon via New X Gate - p.121* *Croydon via Streatham - p.125* *Caterham (178) - p.123* *Victoria (176) - p.126*
	2 71	Spa Road	
	3 32	Blue Anchor	
	4 25	North Kent East Jcn.	→ *Greenwich (201) - p.133*
	4 68	**New Cross**	
	5 29	Tanners Hill Jcn.	— via Lewisham reversible
	5 47	**St. Johns**	
	6 04	**Lewisham**	→ *Holborn Viaduct - p.129* *Gillingham (201) - p.133* *Sidcup/Dartford (201) -see be* *Hayes/Addiscombe - p.135*
	6 75	**Blackheath**	
	7 74	**Kidbrooke**	
	9 11	**Eltham**	
	10 27	**Falconwood**	
	11 28	**Welling**	
	12 59	**Bexleyheath**	
	13 71	**Barneshurst**	
15 07 C.M.M.	15 07	Perry Street Fork Jcn.	—
15 66	15 36	Crayford Creek Jcn.	
16 42	16 12	Crayford Spur 'A' Jcn.	—
17 05 C.M.M.	16 55	Dartford Jcn.	
17 12	17 02	**Dartford**	→ *Gillingham (201) - p.133*

via Lewisham reversible

M C	
5 29	Tanners Hill Jcn.
5 57	Lewisham Vale Jcn.
6 03	**Lewisham**

M C	
0 00	Perry Street Fork Jcn.
0 30	**Slade Green** (p.133)

M C	
0 00	Crayford Spur 'A' Jcn.
0 30	Crayford Spur 'B' Jcn (see below)

CHARING CROSS - DARTFORD via Sidcup (B.R. Table 201) (Dartford Loop)

M. P.	M C		Connections
0 00	0 00	**Charing Cross** (see above)	
	6 04	**Lewisham**	
6 21 C.M.M.	6 21	Courthill Loop Jcn. North (p.135)	
6 36	6 43	Courthill Loop Jcn. South (p.130)	
7 16	7 23	**Hither Green**	
7 43	7 50	Lee Jcn.	—
7 66	7 73	**Lee**	
9 40	9 47	**Mottingham**	
10 32	10 39	**New Eltham**	
11 73	12 00	**Sidcup**	
12 68	12 75	**Albany Park**	
13 69	13 76	**Bexley**	
15 25	15 32	**Crayford**	
16 11	16 18	Crayford Spur 'B' Jcn.	→ ***Crayford Spur 'A' Jcn. - See Above***
16 65	16 72	Dartford Jcn.	
17 12	17 19	**Dartford**	

M C	
0 00	Lee Jcn.
0 29	Lee Spur Jcn. (p.130)

CHARING CROSS - HAYES & ADDISCOMBE (B.R. Table 201)

M. P.	M C	Station	M. P.	M C	Station
0 00	0 00	**Charing Cross** (see p.134)			*via Ladywell loop*
	5 47	**St. Johns**		5 47	**St. Johns**
	6 04	**Lewisham**		6 14	Parks Bridge Jcn. (p.130)
	6 21	Courthill Loop Jcn. North			
	6 62	**Ladywell**		6 50	**Ladywell**
	7 42	**Catford Bridge**			
	9 02	**Lower Sydenham**	*M. P.*		
	9 44	**New Beckenham**	*9 44*	0 00	**New Beckenham**
			C.M.M. *8 53*	0 52	**Beckenham Junction**
					↓ *Crystal P/Victoria (178) - p.124*
	10 23	**Clock House**			*Victoria/Ramsgate (212) - p.127*
			M. P.		
	11 07	**Elmers End**	*11 07*	0 00	**Elmers End**
	12 34	**Eden Park**			
	13 19	**West Wickham**	*12 10*	1 03	**Woodside**
4 32	14 32	**Hayes**	*12 77*	1 70	**Addiscombe**

Culvert Road Jcn. The non-electrified lines from Kensington Olympia join the so-called Ludgate Line from Clapham Junction. The loco propelling the Gatwick Express has just passed Pouparts Jcn. from where an electrified spur connects the Victoria fast lines with the Ludgate Line at Longhedge Jcn. (see p.118). *(David Maxey).*

SECTION V - SCOTRAIL

(a) East Coast

BERWICK - EDINBURGH / EDINBURGH - ABERDEEN (B.R. Tables 26 & 241)

M.P.	M C	Location	KEY PLAN
	0 00	**Kings Cross**	
M. P.			
0 00	268 56	**Newcastle**	
67 00	335 56	**Berwick-upon-Tweed**	→ *ECML (North) KEY PLAN - p.27*
C.M.M.			
54 49	338 43	***ER/ScR Boundary***	
47 14	345 78	Reston GSP	
41 14	351 78	Grantshouse	
34 40	358 52	Innerwick GSP	
31 20	361 72	Oxwellmains	
29 05	364 07	**Dunbar**	
26 28	366 64	North Belton LC	
24 42	368 50	Stenton GSP	
22 14	370 78	Markle LC	
17 79	375 13	Drem Jcn.	
17 60	375 32	**Drem**	→ North Berwick branch (below)
13 18	379 74	**Longniddry**	
11 52	381 40	St. Germains LC	
9 65	383 27	**Prestonpans**	
6 15	386 77	Monktonhall Jcn.	→ ***Millerhill - p.138***
3 39	389 53	Portobello Jcn.	→ ***Edinburgh Area - p.138***
2 16	390 76	Craigentinny Jcn.	→ ***Edinburgh Area - p.138***
0 61	392 31	Abbeyhill Jcn.	→ ***Edinburgh Area - p.138***
0 26	392 66	Carlton Tunnels (West)	
0 00	393 12	**Edinburgh Waverley**	→ *Carstairs (65) - p.140* *Glasgow Central (225) - p.140* *Glasgow Queen Street (228) - p.141* *Perth/Inverness (231) - p.142* *Bathgate (225) - p.141*
0 00	0 00	**Edinburgh Waverley**	
	0 25	Princess Street Gardens	
1 19	1 19	**Haymarket**	
* dual mile posts			
**45 73*	*1 28	Haymarket East Jcn.	
**45 35*	*1 66	Haymarket Central Jcn.	→ ***Gorgie Jcn. - p.138***
**44 73*	*2 28	Haymarket West Jcn.	
4 45	4 45	**South Gyle**	
	9 02	Dalmeny Jcn.	→ Winchurch Jcn. branch (below)
	9 35	**Dalmeny**	
	11 16	Forth Bridge (North)	
	11 22	**North Queensferry**	
	13 01	Inverkeithing South Jcn.	→ ***Rosyth Dockyard - p.139***
	13 12	**Inverkeithing**	
	13 21	Inverkeithing Central Jcn.	→ *Dunfermline (241) - p.139*
	13 49	Inverkeithing East Jcn.	→ ***Inverkeithing North Jcn. - p.139***
	17 34	**Aberdour**	
	19 41	Newbiggin	
	20 10	**Burntisland**	
	22 59	**Kinghorn**	
25 70	25 70	**Kirkcaldy**	

M.P.	M C	Location
22 29	4 49	**North Berwick**
17 79	0 19	Drem Jcn.
17 60	0 00	**Drem**

M.P.	M C	Location
34 54	4 29	Winchurch Jcn. (p.14
39 03	0 00	Dalmeny Jcn.

EDINBURGH - ABERDEEN (B.R. Tables 26 & 241)

M.P.	M C	
0 00	0 00	**Edinburgh Waverley**
25 70	25 70	**Kirkcaldy**
	26 73	Sinclairtown Up Siding GF
	28 00	Dysart
	30 24	Thornton South Jcn. → *Thornton West Jcn. - p.139*
	30 62	Thornton North Jcn.
	33 16	Markinch Down Sidings GF
	33 20	**Markinch**
	39 08	**Ladybank**
	39 10	Ladybank Jcn.
	40 46	Bow of Fife LC
	41 69	Hospital Mill LC
	42 26	**Springfield**
	44 50	**Cupar**
	50 68	**Leuchars**
	56 36	Tay Bridge (South)
58 71	58 71	Tay Bridge Central Jcn.
C.M.M.		
0 00	59 15	**Dundee**
C.M.M.		
0 21	59 73	Camperdown Jcn.
3 36	63 08	**Broughty Ferry**
5 00	64 52	**Balmossie**
5 72	65 44	**Monifieth**
8 67	68 39	**Barry Links**
9 70	69 42	**Golf Street**
10 35	70 07	**Carnoustie**
16 45	76 17	**Arbroath**
C.M.M.		
23 11	82 22	Inverkeilor
28 40	87 51	Usan
30 55	89 66	**Montrose**
C.M.M.		
205 08	94 34	Craigo
210 60	100 06	Laurencekirk
219 39	108 65	Carmont LC
224 75	114 21	**Stonehaven**
230 59	120 05	Newtonhill
232 70	122 16	**Portlethen**
240 40	129 66	Ferryhill Jcn.
241 06	130 32	**Aberdeen** (bays)
241 08	130 34	**Aberdeen** (through platforms) → *Elgin/Inverness (240) - p.143*
0 00		

M C	
0 00	Thornton North Jcn.
5 48	Methil East
6 79	Methil West

M C	
0 00	Markinch Down Sdgs GF
1 44	Auchmuty

C.M.M.	M C	
0 06	39 10	Ladybank Jcn.
7 78	47 02	Newburgh
C.M.M.		
149 17	54 58	Hilton Jcn.
150 04	55 45	Moncrieffe Tunnel (N)
151 25	56 66	**Perth**

(see p.142)

C.M.M.	M C	
20 64	0 00	**Perth**
19 69	0 75	Barnhill
15 41	5 23	Inchyra LC
12 35	8 29	Murie LC
10 39	10 25	**Errol**
8 11	12 53	Inchture LC
6 00	14 64	Temple Hall LC
3 50	17 14	**Invergowrie**
0 53	20 11	Buckingham Jcn.
0 00	20 64	Tay Bridge Central Jcn.
C.M.M.		
59 15	21 08	**Dundee**

Lochty Private Railway

M C	
0 00	**Lochty**
0 76	Knightsward

Edinburgh Area Freight Lines

1. Monktonhall Jcn. - Haymarket Jcns.

M. P.	M C	
6 15	**0 00**	Monktonhall Jcn. (p.136)
5 56	**0 39**	Wanton Walls (see below)
C.M.M.		
6 33	**2 26**	Niddrie West Jcns.
6 30	**2 29**	
1 17	**7 42**	Craiglockhart Jcn.
C.M.M.		
0 00	**8 17**	Gorgie Jcn
0 36	**8 53**	Haymarket West Jcn.

Dundee/Aberdeen (241) - p.136
Glasgow Queen Street (228) - p.141
Perth/Inverness (231) - p.142

M. P.	M C	
3 39	**0 00**	Portobello Jcn. (p.136)
C.M.M.		
6 30	**1 00**	Niddrie West Jcn.

C.M.M.	M C	
0 00	**7 42**	Craiglockhart Jcn.
0 48	**8 10**	Slateford Jcn. (p.140)

C.M.M.	M C	
0 42	**8 17**	Gorgie Jcn.
0 11	**8 48**	Haymarket Central Jcn.
C.M.M.		
1 28	**9 06**	Haymarket East Jcn.
1 19	**9 15**	**Haymarket**
0 00	**10 34**	**Edinburgh Waverley** (see p.136)

2. Monktonhall Jcn. - Millerhill/Bilston Glen - Portobello Jcn.

M. P.	M C	
6 15	**0 00**	Monktonhall Jcn. (p.136)
C.M.M.		
1 40	**0 39**	Wanton Walls (see above)
C.M.M.		
6 01	**1 48**	Millerhill South Jcn.
5 42	**2 07**	Millerhill SB
4 46	**3 03**	Niddrie South Jcn.
3 39	**4 10**	Portobello Jcn. (p.136)

M. P.	M C	
10 33	**4 32**	Bilston Glen
6 01	**0 00**	Millerhill South Jcn.

C.M.M.	M C	
7 08	**3 03**	Niddrie South Jcn.
6 33	**3 58**	Niddrie West Jcn. (see above)

3. Portobello Jcn. - Abbeyhill Jcn./Leith & Granton

M. P.	M C	
3 39	**0 00**	Portobello Jcn.
2 16	**1 23**	Craigentinny Jcn. (p.136)
C.M.M.		
1 40	**2 09**	Meadowbank
1 31	**2 18**	Lochend Jcn.
1 03	**2 46**	London Road Jcn.
0 61	**2 68**	Abbeyhill Jcn.
0 00	**3 49**	**Edinburgh Waverley** (see p.136)
1 30	**0 00**	Easter Road Jcn.
1 03	**0 27**	London Road Jcn.

C.M.M.	M C	
0 00	**0 00**	Portobello Jcn.
1 78	**1 78**	Leith South

C.M.M.	M C	
0 00	**0 00**	Lochend Jcn.
0 04	**0 04**	Easter Road Jcn.
C.M.M.		
102 42	**4 05**	Granton East
101 68	**4 59**	Granton Gas Works

EDINBURGH - CARDENDEN (B.R. Table 241) & Thornton Jcns.

M. P.	M C	Location		C.M.M. / M. P.	M C	Location
0 00	**0 00**	**Edinburgh Waverley** (see p.136)	→			*Berwick (26) - p.136* *Glasgow Central (225) - p.140* *Glasgow Queen St. (228) - p.141* *Perth/Inverness (231) - p.142* *Bathgate (225) - p.141*
	11 22	**North Queensferry**				
				C.M.M.	**M C**	
				1 21	**1 19**	Rosyth Dockyard
				1 00	**0 78**	Ferry Toll Tunnel (E)
	13 01	Inverkeithing South Jcn.	—	*0 02*	**0 00**	Inverkeithing S. Jcn.
	13 12	**Inverkeithing**				
	13 21	Inverkeithing Central Jcn.	→			*Perth/Aberdeen (241) - p.136*
					0 00	Inverkeithing E. Jcn.
	13 51	Inverkeithing North Jcn.	—		**0 33**	Inverkeithing N. Jcn.
	14 52	**Rosyth**				
	16 41	Charlestown Jcn.	→			***Longannet/Alloa - See Below***
	16 68	**Dunfermline**				
				C.M.M.	**M C**	
				12 44	**9 51**	Comrie
				16 00	**6 15**	Oakley GF
				20 48	**1 47**	Dunfermline Upper GF
	18 56	Townhill Jcn.	—	*22 15*	**0 00**	Townhill Jcn.
	19 12	Halbeath LC				
22 41	**22 41**	**Cowdenbeath**				
.M.M.						
27 67	**24 60**	**Lochgelly**				
					1 14	End of line
					0 57	Bowhill
29 37	**26 30**	Glencraig Jcn. GF	—		**0 00**	Glencraig Jcn. GF
29 77	**26 70**	**Cardenden**				
32 16	**29 09**	Clunybridge Jcn.				
				M. P.	**M C**	
				28 54	**4 73**	Westfield GF
33 04	**29 77**	Thornton Yard		*33 04*	**0 43**	Thornton Yard
33 25	**30 18**	Thornton Yard		*33 25*	**0 22**	Thornton Yard
33 47	**30 40**	Redford Jcn.	—	*33 47*	**0 00**	Redford Jcn.
34 62	**31 55**	Thornton West Jcn.	—	*34 62*	**31 55**	Thornton West Jcn.
				35 38	**32 31**	Thornton South Jcn.
.M.M.						
0 00	**32 44**	Thornton North Jcn.	→			***Methil*** *Perth/Aberdeen - p.137*

Charlestown Jcn. - Longannet - Alloa - Stirling

M.M.	M C	Location		M. P.	M C	Location
5 38	**0 00**	Charlestown Jcn. (see above)				
4 14	**1 24**	Elbowend Jcn.	—		**0 00**	Elbowend Jcn.
5 62	**9 56**	Longannet			**2 14**	Charlestown Foundry LC
3 45	**11 73**	Kincardine station (Disused)				Crombie RNAD
M.M.						
8 21	**15 34**	former Kincardine Jcn. (Disused)				
6 20	**17 35**	Alloa West LC (Disused)				
4 61	**18 74**	Alloa Yard Jcn.				
4 38	**19 17**	Cambus Jcn.	—	*0 19*	**0 00**	Cambus Jcn.
M.M.				*2 12*	**1 73**	Menstrie (BR Boundary)
8 38	**23 41**	Stirling North Jcn.				
8 24	**23 55**	**Stirling**	→			*Edinburgh/Inverness (231) - p.142*

EDINBURGH - GLASGOW CENTRAL via Shotts (B.R. Table 225)
EDINBURGH - CARSTAIRS (B.R. Table 65)

M. P.	M C	Location	Connections
0 00	**0 00**	**Edinburgh Waverley** →	*Berwick/Aberdeen (26/241) - p.136* *Glasgow Queen St. (228) - p.141* *Perth/Inverness (231) - p.142* *Bathgate (225) - p.141*
	0 25	Princes Street Gardens	
1 19	**1 19**	**Haymarket**	
C.M.M.			
100 42	**1 28**	Haymarket East Jcn.	
100 20	**1 50**	Distillery Siding GF	
99 25	**2 45**	Slateford Jcn. →	***Craiglockhart Jcn. - p.138***
98 75	**2 75**	**Slateford**	
98 05	**3 65**	**Kingsknowe**	
95 45	**6 25**	Curriehill GSP	
90 70	**11 00**	**Kirknewton**	
C.M.M.			
23 12	**11 74**	Midcalder Jcn.	

M. P.	M C	Location
89 76	**11 74**	Midcalder Jcn.
79 34	**22 36**	Auchengray LC
74 11	**27 59**	Carstairs East Jcn. (p.145)
C.M.M.		
73 43	**28 50**	Carstairs Station Jcn.
73 53	**28 60**	**Carstairs**

Carlisle/Glasgow (65) - p.145

M. P.	M C	Location	Connections
22 12	**12 74**	Contentibus Shale Siding GF	
21 06	**14 00**	**Livingstone South**	
18 28	**16 58**	**West Calder**	
16 50	**18 36**	**Addiewell**	
14 00	**21 06**	**Breich**	
11 70	**23 16**	**Fauldhouse**	
11 11	**23 75**	Benhar Jcn.	
8 30	**26 56**	**Shotts**	
6 62	**28 24**	**Hartwood**	
3 52	**31 34**	**Cleland**	
1 69	**33 17**	**Carfin**	
1 35	**33 51**	Holytown Jcn.	
1 10	**33 76**	**Holytown**	
C.M.M.			
3 63	**34 48**	Mossend East Jcn.	
3 05	**35 26**	Mossend West Jcn. (p.146)	
2 30	**36 01**	**Bellshill**	
0 53	**37 58**	Viewpark Sidings	
C.M.M.			
93 55	**38 34**	Uddingston Jcn.	
93 72	**38 51**	**Uddingston**	
95 36	**40 15**	Newton East Jcn. →	*Motherwell (226) - p.151*
95 57	**40 36**	**(Newton)** →	*Kirkhill (223) - p.150*
95 67	**40 46**	Newton West Jcns.	
95 72	**40 51**	Newton West Jcns.	
97 24	**42 03**	**Cambuslang**	
98 32	**43 11**	Rutherglen East Jcn. →	***Whifflet Jcn. - p.151***
98 77	**43 56**	Rutherglen Central Jcn. →	***London Road Depot*** *Glasgow Central (226)* - p.151
99 20	**43 79**	Rutherglen West Jcn. →	***Rutherglen North Jcn. - p.146***
100 15	**44 74**	Polmadie	
101 01	**45 60**	Larkfield Jcn. →	***Muirhouse South Jcn. - p.147*** ***Shields Jcn. - p.152***
101 39	**46 18**	Eglington Street Jcn.	
101 56	**46 35**	Bridge Street Jcn.	
102 27	**47 06**	**Glasgow Central** →	*See p.146 for Table Refs.*

M C	Location
2 42	Polkemmet Colliery
1 59	BR Boundary
0 00	Benhar Jcn.

M. P.	M C	Location
86 31	**0 00**	**Wishaw** (p.145)
86 63	**0 32**	Wishaw Central Jcn.
88 15	**1 64**	Ravenscraig No. 2
89 48	**3 17**	Holytown Jcn.
	3 42	**Holytown**

M. P.	M C	Location
0 31	**34 48**	Mossend E. Jcn. (p.146
C.M.M.		
91 08	**34 79**	Mossend S. Jcn. (p.146
89 51	**36 36**	Motherwell Jcn.
89 38	**36 49**	**Motherwell**

Carlisle (65) - p.145
Glasgow Central (226) - p.151

M. P.	M C	Location
95 67	**0 00**	Newton West Jcn.
96 23	**0 36**	Redpath GF

DINBURGH - GLASGOW QUEEN STREET (B.R. Table 228)
DINBURGH - BATHGATE (B.R. Table 225)

M. P.	M C	Location	M. P.	M C	Connection
0 00	**0 00**	**Edinburgh Waverley** →			*See p.140 for table refs.*
	0 25	Princes Street Gardens			
1 19	**1 19**	**Haymarket**			
M.M.					
45 73	**1 28**	Haymarket East Jcn.			
45 35	**1 66**	Haymarket Central Jcn. →			***Gorgie Jcn. - p.138***
44 73	**2 28**	Haymarket West Jcn.			
41 63	**5 38**	Gogar GF		**M C**	
			M. P.		
38 59	**8 42**	Newbridge Jcn. —	35 21	**8 42**	Newbridge Jcn.
			31 60	**12 03**	Cowburn Jcn.
			31 09	**12 54**	**Uphall**
			29 03	**14 60**	**Livingston North**
			28 52	**15 11**	Carmondean Jcn.
			25 16	**18 42**	Bathgate Yard
			25 05	**18 58**	**Bathgate**
35 48	**11 53**	Winchburgh Tunnel (South)			
34 54	**12 47**	Winchburgh Jcn. →			***Dalmeny Jcn. - p.136***
29 56	**17 45**	**Linlithgow**			
27 19	**20 02**	Bo'ness			
25 00	**22 21**	**Polmont**			**via Grahamston**
			C.M.M.		
24 60	**22 41**	Polmont Jcn. —	21 20	**22 41**	Polmont Jcn. (p.142)
22 35	**24 66**	Falkirk Tunnel (East)	23 71	**25 12**	Grangemouth Jcn.
21 63	**25 38**	**Falkirk High**	24 20	**25 41**	**Falkirk Grahamston**
			25 79	**27 20**	Carmuirs East Jcn. (p.142)
			C.M.M.		
			108 76	**27 60**	Carmuirs West Jcn.
			106 55	**30 01**	Greenhill Lower Jcn. (see below)
			C.M.M.		
17 29	**29 72**	Greenhill Upper Jcn. —	17 29	**30 49**	Greenhill Upper Jcn.
11 40	**35 61**	**Croy**		**47 78**	**Queen Street H.L.**
10 25	**36 76**	Gartshore			
6 20	**41 01**	**Lenzie**			
5 40	**41 61**	Cadder Yard			
4 46	**42 55**	Cadder Yard			
3 19	**44 02**	**Bishopbriggs**			
2 12	**45 09**	Cowlairs East Jcn. —		**0 00**	Cowlairs East Jcn.
				0 21	Cowlairs North Jcn.
1 67	**45 34**	Cowlairs West Jcn. →			*Springburn/Mossend (65) - p.146*
0 60	**46 41**	Queen Street H.L. Tunnel (North)			
0 00	**47 21**	**Queen Street H.L.** →			*Perth (229/231) - See Below* *Oban/Mallaig (227) - p.154* *Queen Street L.L. - p.152/3*

;LASGOW QUEEN STREET - PERTH (B.R. Tables 229 & 231)

M. P.	M C	Location	Connection
0 00	**0 00**	**Queen Street H.L.** (see above)	
17 29	**17 29**	Greenhill Upper Jcn.	
:.M.M.			*Falkirk Grahamston - See Above*
06 55	**17 77**	Greenhill Lower Jcn. →	*Mossend (65) - p.146*
08 76	**20 18**	Carmuirs West Jcn.	
09 41	**20 63**	Larbert Jcn. →	*Edinburgh (230/1) - p.142*
10 17	**21 39**	**Larbert**	
18 24	**29 46**	**Stirling** →	***Alloa - p.139***
21 10	**32 32**	**Bridge of Allan**	
23 19	**34 41**	**Dunblane**	
35 50	**46 72**	**Gleneagles**	*Edinburgh (241) - p.137*
51 25	**62 47**	**Perth** →	*Dundee/Aberdeen (229) - p.137* *Inverness (231) - p.142*

EDINBURGH - PERTH via Stirling
PERTH - INVERNESS (B.R. Tables 230 & 231)

M. P.	M C	Location	Connections
0 00	**0 00**	**Edinburgh Waverley** →	*Berwick/Aberdeen (26/241) - p.136* *Cardenden (241) - p.139* *Carstairs (65) - p.140* *Glasgow Central (225) - p.140* *Glasgow Queen St. (228) - p.141*
		(see p.141)	
C.M.M.			
25 00	**22 21**	**Polmont**	
C.M.M.			
21 20	**22 41**	Polmont Jcn.	
23 71	**25 12**	Grangemouth Jcn. →	see Grangemouth branch
24 20	**25 41**	**Falkirk Grahamston**	
25 79	**27 20**	Carmuirs East Jcn.	
C.M.M.			
109 41	**27 56**	Larbert Jcn. →	*Glasgow Queen St. (229/231) - p.141*
110 17	**28 32**	**Larbert** →	*Mossend (65) - p.146*
114 26	**32 41**	Plean Jcn.	
116 62	**34 77**	Polmaise	
118 24	**36 39**	**Stirling** →	***Alloa - p.139***
118 38	**36 53**	Stirling North Jcn.	
119 59	**37 74**	Cornton LCs	
120 10	**38 25**	Cornton LCs	
121 10	**39 25**	**Bridge of Allan**	
122 38	**40 53**	Kippenross Tunnel (South)	
123 19	**41 34**	**Dunblane**	
129 21	**47 36**	Greenloaning	
133 28	**51 43**	Blackford LC	
135 50	**53 65**	**Gleneagles**	
137 41	**55 56**	Auchterarder	
140 24	**58 39**	Whitemoss LC	
141 56	**59 71**	Dunning	
144 45	**62 60**	Forteviot LC	
149 17	**67 32**	Hilton Jcn.	
150 04	**68 19**	Moncrieffe Tunnel (North)	
151 25	**69 40**	**Perth** →	*Edinburgh (241) - p.137* *Dundee/Aberdeen (229) - p.137* *Glasgow Queen St. (229/231) - p.141*

Grangemouth branch:

M C	Location
3 70	B.P. Oil Terminal
2 43	Docks GF
1 51	Fouldubs Jcn.
0 00	Grangemouth Jcn.

M C	Location
0 27	B.A.C. Sidings
0 00	Fouldubs Jcn.

Bo'ness & Kinneil Railway

M C	Location
0 00	**Bo'ness**
0 32	Lows Crossing
0 54	Avon Place
1 38	**Kinneil Halt**
3 40	Birkhill **(proposed)**

M. P.	M C	Location	Connections
151 25	**0 00**	**Perth**	
152 32	**1 07**	Perth Yard South	
C.M.M.			
7 02	**7 13**	Stanley Jcn.	
10 15	**10 26**	Murthly LC	
12 78	**13 09**	Kingswood Tunnel (East)	
15 31	**15 42**	**Dunkeld**	
16 71	**17 02**	Inver Tunnel (North)	
20 23	**20 34**	**Dalguise Halt (proposed)**	
23 61	**23 72**	Ballinluig LC	
25 33	**25 44**	Moulinearn LC	
28 21	**28 32**	**Pitlochry**	
31 66	**31 77**	Killiecrankie Tunnel (South)	
35 09	**35 20**	**Blair Atholl**	
44 76	**45 07**	Dalnacardoch GF	
51 22	**51 33**	Dalnaspidal	
58 47	**58 58**	**Dalwhinnie**	
68 62	**68 73**	**Newtonmore**	
71 43	**71 54**	**Kingussie**	
77 23	**77 34**	Kincraig Loop	
77 55	**77 66**	Kincraig Loop	
83 42	**83 53**	**Aviemore**	***Strathspey Railway - p.143***

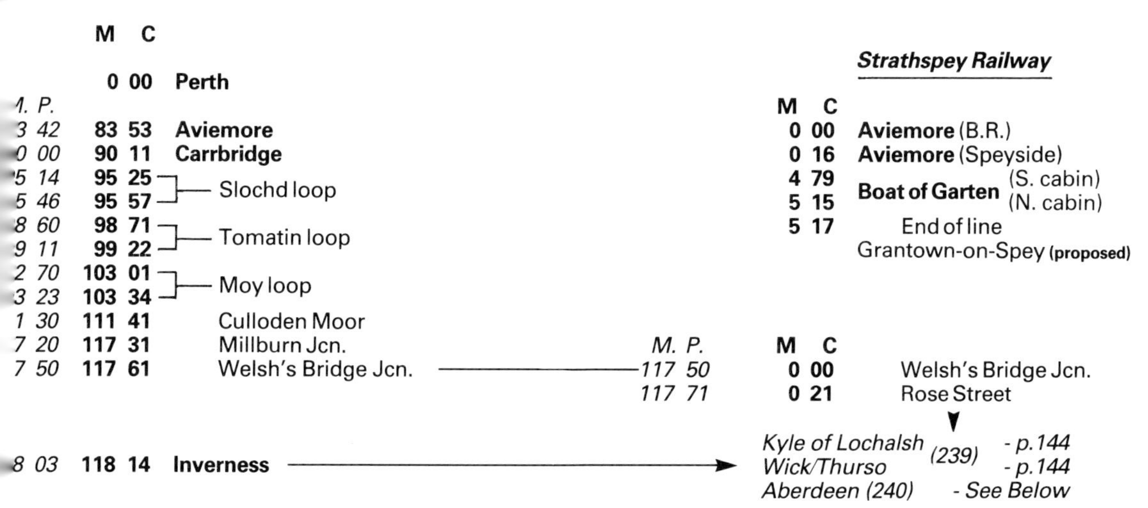

ERTH - INVERNESS (B.R. Table 231) cont.

M. P.	M C		M. P.	M C	
	0 00	**Perth**			
3 42	83 53	**Aviemore**			
0 00	90 11	**Carrbridge**			
5 14	95 25	Slochd loop			
5 46	95 57				
8 60	98 71	Tomatin loop			
9 11	99 22				
2 70	103 01	Moy loop			
3 23	103 34				
1 30	111 41	Culloden Moor			
7 20	117 31	Millburn Jcn.			
7 50	117 61	Welsh's Bridge Jcn.	117 50	0 00	Welsh's Bridge Jcn.
			117 71	0 21	Rose Street
8 03	118 14	**Inverness**			

Kyle of Lochalsh (239) - p.144
Wick/Thurso (239) - p.144
Aberdeen (240) - See Below

Strathspey Railway

M C	
0 00	**Aviemore** (B.R.)
0 16	**Aviemore** (Speyside)
4 79	**Boat of Garten** (S. cabin)
5 15	**Boat of Garten** (N. cabin)
5 17	End of line
	Grantown-on-Spey **(proposed)**

BERDEEN - ELGIN - INVERNESS (B.R. Table 240)

M. P.	M C		M. P.	M C	
0 00	0 00	**Aberdeen**			*Dundee/Edinburgh (26/241) - p.137*
	0 32	Schoolhill Tunnel (South)			
	0 67	Hutcheon Street Tunnel (North)			
				1 57	Waterloo Goods
	1 59	Kittybrewster GF		0 00	Kittybrewster GF
	6 20	**Dyce**			
	8 30	Pitmedden LC			
	12 78	Boat of Kintore LC			
	15 25	Port Elphinstone GF			
	16 79	**Inverurie**			
	24 51	Oyne LC			
	27 47	**Insch**			
	32 71	Kennethmont			
	35 77	Gartly LC			
	40 67	**Huntly**			
2 48	52 48	Keith East	64 08	11 02	End of line
M.M.			64 00	10 74	Dufftown platform
0 45	53 06	Keith Jcn.	53 06	0 00	Keith Jcn.
0 32	53 19	**Keith**			
7 20	56 31	Rosarie LC			
2 18	71 33	**Elgin**			
6 75	76 56	Alves GF		0 00	Alves GF
				1 72	Roseisle GF
				4 46	Burghead platform
				4 70	End of line
3 10	80 41	Kinloss LC			
0 21	83 30	Waterford LC			
0 00	83 51	**Forres**			
M.M.					
2 61	87 06	Brodie LC			
8 72	93 17	**Nairn**			
7 17	101 42	Dalcross LC			
0 55	105 00	Allanfearn LC			
M.M.					
7 20	107 45	Millburn Jcn.			
7 50	107 75	Welsh's Bridge Jcn.			
8 03	108 28	**Inverness**			

INVERNESS - WICK & THURSO (B.R. Table 239)

M. P.	M C	Station	
0 00	**0 00**	**Inverness**	*Perth/Edinburgh (231) - p.143* *Elgin/Aberdeen (240) - p.143*
	0 19	Rose Street	
	1 50	Clachnaharry	
	3 58	Bunchrew LC	
	5 69	Lentran	
	13 04	**Muir of Ord**	
	18 58	**Dingwall**	*Kyle of Lochalsh (239) - See Below*
	19 00	Dingwall North	
	22 76	Foulis LC	
	26 05	Teaninich LC	
	28 70	**Alness**	
	31 37	**Invergordon**	
	32 72	M.K. Shand GF	
	34 79	Delny LC	
	39 25	Nigg LC	
	40 60	**Fearn**	
	44 23	**Tain**	
	57 70	**Ardgay**	
	61 00	**Culrain**	
	61 34	**Invershin**	
	66 78	**Lairg**	
	77 01	**Rogart**	
	82 44	Kirkton LC	
	84 30	**Golspie**	
	86 15	**Dunrobin**	
	90 48	**Brora**	
	101 40	**Helmsdale**	
	111 05	**Kildonan**	
	118 20	**Kinbrace**	
	125 69	**Forsinard**	
	133 76	**Altnabreac**	
	143 02	**Scotscalder**	
	145 59	Halkirk LC	
	147 20	**Georgemas Junction**	(Thurso branch, see below)
	153 68	Watten LC	
161 36	**161 36**	**Wick**	

M.M.	M C	Station
0 00	**0 00**	**Georgemas Junction**
	0 72	Hoy LC
6 50	**6 50**	**Thurso**

INVERNESS - KYLE OF LOCHALSH (B.R. Table 239)

M. P.	M C	Station
0 00	**0 00**	**Inverness** (See Above)
18 58	**18 58**	**Dingwall**
C.M.M.		
0 19	**19 00**	Dingwall North
4 55	**23 36**	Achterneed LC
11 65	**30 46**	**Garve**
17 20	**36 01**	**Lochluichart**
21 34	**40 15**	**Achanalt**
27 72	**46 53**	**Achnasheen**
40 34	**59 15**	**Achnashellach**
42 12	**60 73**	Balnacra LC
45 64	**64 45**	**Strathcarron**
48 22	**67 03**	**Attadale**
53 15	**71 76**	**Stromeferry**
57 09	**75 70**	**Duncraig**
58 22	**77 03**	**Plockton**
59 58	**78 39**	**Duirinish**
63 64	**82 45**	**Kyle of Lochalsh**

NOTE: Cal-Mac ferry fans heading south will find the Mallaig - Fort William table on p.154.

SECTION V - SCOTRAIL

(b) West Coast

ARLISLE - GLASGOW CENTRAL (B.R. Table 65)

KEY PLAN

M. P.	M	C	Location		Connections
0 00	0	00	**Carlisle**	→	*Newcastle (48) - p.42* *WCML (North) KEY PLAN - p.69* *Skipton (36) - p.86* *Barrow (113) - p.87*
	8	00	***LMR/ScR Boundary***		
	8	57	Gretna Jcn.	→	*Kilmarnock (222) - p.147*
	10	13	Quintinshill		
	13	43	Cove LC		
	17	02	Kirtlebridge GF		
	25	66	**Lockerbie**		
	28	55	Nethercleugh LC		
	34	35	Wamphray GF		
	39	40	Beattock loop		
	40	03			
	49	64	Beattock Summit		
	51	48	Bodsbury LC		
	57	70	Abingdon		
	66	01	Symington GF		
	73	13	Carstairs South Jcn.	—	**73 13** Carstairs South Jcn. **74 11** Carstairs East Jcn.
	73	43	Carstairs Station Jcn.		
	73	53	**Carstairs**	→	*Edinburgh (65) - p.140*
	75	47	Newmill LC		
	76	08	Lanark Jcn.	—	*M. P. 2 45 C.M.M. 76 08* **M C** **0 00** **Lanark** **2 45** Lanark Jcn.
	76	24	Cleghorn LC		
	81	75	**Carluke**		
	84	09	Law Jcn.	—	**via Wishaw loop** **84 09** Law Jcn. **86 31** **Wishaw** (see p.140) **86 63** Wishaw Central Jcn.
	84	59	Garrionghill Jcn.		
	87	39	Shieldmuir Jcn.	—	**87 43** Shieldmuir Jcn.
	89	38	**Motherwell**	→	*Holytown/Edinburgh (225) - p.140* *Mossend/Larbert (65) - p.146* *Mossend/Cowlairs* *Bellshill/Hamilton (226) - p.151*
	89	50	Motherwell Jcns.		
	89	51			
	89	77	Logans Road LC		
	93	55	Uddingston Jcn.		
	93	72	**Uddingston**		
	95	36	Newton East Jcn.		
	95	57	**(Newton)**	→	*Kirkhill (223) - p.150*
	95	67	Newton West Jcns.	→	***Redpath - p.140***
	95	72			
7 24	97	24	**Cambuslang**		

CARLISLE - GLASGOW CENTRAL (B.R. Table 65) cont.

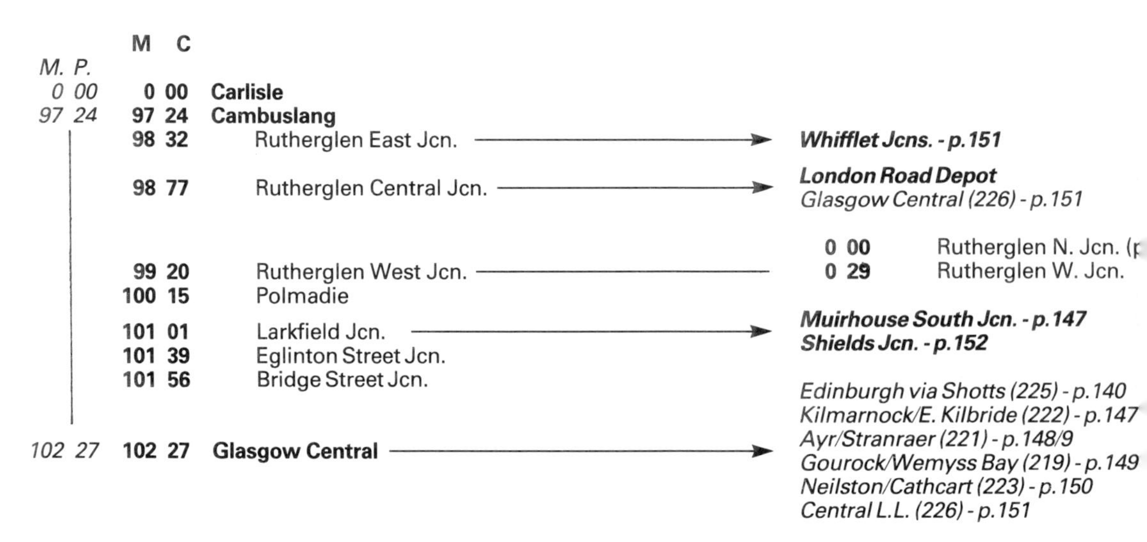

M C
M. P.
0 00 0 00 Carlisle
97 24 97 24 Cambuslang
98 32 Rutherglen East Jcn.
Whifflet Jcns. - p.151
98 77 Rutherglen Central Jcn.
London Road Depot
Glasgow Central (226) - p.151
0 00 Rutherglen N. Jcn.
0 29 Rutherglen W. Jcn.
99 20 Rutherglen West Jcn.
100 15 Polmadie
101 01 Larkfield Jcn.
101 39 Eglinton Street Jcn.
101 56 Bridge Street Jcn.
Muirhouse South Jcn. - p.147
Shields Jcn. - p.152
Edinburgh via Shotts (225) - p.140
Kilmarnock/E. Kilbride (222) - p.147
Ayr/Stranraer (221) - p.148/9
Gourock/Wemyss Bay (219) - p.149
Neilston/Cathcart (223) - p.150
Central L.L. (226) - p.151
102 27 102 27 Glasgow Central

MOTHERWELL - MOSSEND YARD
MOSSEND - LARBERT/COWLAIRS

M. P.	M C		M. P.	M C	
0 00	**0 00**	**Carlisle** (see p.145)			
89 38	**89 38**	**Motherwell**			
	89 51	Motherwell Jcn.			
	89 63 / **90 17**	Braidhurst goods loops			
			88 40	**2 35**	Ravenscraig No. 3
	90 75	Mossend South Jcn.	90 75	**0 00**	Mossend South Jcn.
	91 08	Mossend South Jcn.	91 08	**0 00**	Mossend South Jcn.
			91 49	**0 41**	Mossend West Jcn. (see p.140)
				0 35	Mossend East Jcn.
	91 42	Mossend North Jcn.		**0 00**	Mossend North Jcn.
	91 75	Mossend Yard			

M. P.	M C		M. P.	M C	
91 75	**0 00**	Mossend Yard			
92 12	**0 17**	Burnhouse			
93 66	**1 71**	Whifflet South Jcn.	9 65	**0 00**	Whifflet South Jcn.
			8 43	**1 22**	Sunnyside Jcn. (p.15
			7 75	**1 70**	Gunnie Yard
94 05	**2 10**	Whifflet North Jcn. → ***Rutherglen East Jcn. - p.151***			
94 49	**2 54**	Coatbridge Jcn.			
94 62	**2 67**	**Coatbridge Central**	M. P.		
95 64	**3 69**	Gartsherrie South Jcn.	95 64	**3 69**	Gartsherrie South Jc
97 05	**5 10**	Garnqueen North Jcn.	97 09	**5 14**	Gartcosh Jcn.
101 18	**9 23**	**Cumbernauld** (see p.152)	99 27	**7 32**	Cardowan
103 52	**11 57**	Abronhill Tunnel (South)	102 64	**10 69**	Sighthill East Jcn.
106 55	**14 60**	Greenhill Lower Jcn.	C.M.M.		
108 76	**17 01**	Carmuirs West Jcn. (p.141)	0 61	**11 46**	Sighthill Jcn.
109 41	**17 46**	Larbert Jcn.	0 42	**11 65**	**Springburn** (see p.152)
110 17	**18 22**	**Larbert**	C.M.M.		
			8 26	**12 28**	Cowlairs West Jcn.

↓ *Queen St./Perth (229/231) - p.141*
Edinburgh/Inverness (231) - p.142

↓ *Queen St./Mallaig (227) - p.154*
Falkirk/Edinburgh (228) - p.141

ARLISLE - KILMARNOCK - GLASGOW CENTRAL (B.R. Table 222)

1. P.	M	C	Location	
0 00	0	00	**Carlisle**	→ *WCML (North) KEY PLAN - p.69*
M.M.	8	00	***LMR/ScR Boundary***	
6 13	8	57	Gretna Jcn.	→ *Carstairs/Glasgow Cent. (65) - p.145*
9 75	14	75	Eastriggs GF	
7 12	17	58	**Annan**	
0 42	24	28	Ruthwell	
3 51	31	19	Brasswell LC	
1 63	33	07	**Dumfries**	— (branch below)
8 31	36	39	Holywood LC	
4 26	40	44	Auldgirth	
7 58	47	12	Thornhill	
4 32	50	38	Carronbridge	
3 05	51	65	Drumlanrig Tunnel (North)	
5 32	59	38	Sanquhar	
2 31	62	39	**Kirkconnel**	
4 75	69	75	New Cumnock	
4 06	70	64	Bank Jcn.	— (branch below)
7 40	77	30	**Auchinleck**	
6 16	78	54	Barony Jcn.	— (branch below)
3 02	81	68	Mauchline Jcn.	→ ***Annbank Jcn. - see note p.149***
1 20	83	50	Mossgiel Tunnel (North)	
5 50	89	20	Hurlford	
4 41	90	29	Kay Park Jcn.	— (branch below)
3 59	91	11	**Kilmarnock**	→ *Ayr (220) - p.148*
3 48	91	22	Kilmarnock Jcn.	
M.M.				
1 48	93	22	**Kilmaurs**	
8 20	96	50	**Stewarton**	
6 02	98	68	**Dunlop**	
3 51	101	19	Lugton	— (branch below)
6 77	107	73	**Barrhead**	
5 30	109	40	**Nitshill**	
3 70	111	00	**Kennishead**	
3 18	111	52	Busby Jcn.	— (branch below)
2 66	112	04	**Pollockshaws West**	
1 60	113	40	**Crossmyloof**	
M.M.				
0 00	113	51	Muirhouse South Jcn.	— (branch below)
0 15	113	66	Muirhouse Central Jcns.	— (branch below)
0 19	113	70		
0 32	114	03	Muirhouse North Jcn.	
M.M.				
1 39	114	41	Eglinton Street Jcn.	
1 56	114	58	Bridge Street Jcn.	
2 27	115	29	**Glasgow Central**	→ *See p.146 for Table Refs.*

M	C	Location
0	00	**Dumfries**
0	15	Maxwelltown Goods Jcn.
3	15	Maxwelltown I.C.I.

M	C	Location
0	00	Bank Jcn.
1	60	Knockshinnoch

M	C	Location
1	25	Barony Colliery
0	00	Barony Jcn.

M	C	Location
1	31	Riccarton
0	00	Kay Park Jcn.

M	C	Location
4	35	Giffen (M.O.D. Gates)
0	00	Lugton

M. P.	M	C	Location
7 65	0	00	**East Kilbride**
6 14	1	51	**Hairmyres**
4 54	3	11	**Thorntonhall**
3 54	4	11	**Busby**
2 69	4	76	**Clarkston**
1 45	6	20	**Giffnock**
0 53	7	12	**Thornliebank**
C.M.M.			
3 18	7	65	Busby Jcn.
2 66	8	17	**Pollockshaws West**
1 60	9	23	**Crossmyloof**
	11	42	**Glasgow Central**

M	C	Location
0	00	Muirhouse South Jcn.
0	54	Larkfield Jcn. (p.146)

M	C	Location
0	00	Muirhouse Central Jcn.
0	36	Terminus Jcn. (p.152)

GLASGOW CENTRAL - KILWINNING - LARGS
KILWINNING - AYR - STRANRAER (B.R. Tables 220 & 221)

M. P.	M C	Location	Connections
102 27	**0 00**	**Glasgow Central**	→ *Edinburgh via Shotts (225) - p.140*; *Carstairs/Carlisle (65) - p.146*; *Kilmarnock/Carlisle (222) - p.147*; *Gourock/Wemyss Bay (219) - p.149*; *Neilston/Cathcart (223) - p.150*; *Central L.L. (226) - p.151*
C.M.M.			
0 00	**0 51**	Bridge Street Jcn.	
0 19	**0 70**	Smithy Lye C.S.	
1 00	**1 51**	Shields Jcns.	→ ***High Street Jcn. - p.152***
1 02	**1 53**	Shields Jcns.	→ ***Terminus Jcn. - p.152***
1 05	**1 56**	Shields Jcns.	→ branch below (Shields Jcn. – Hawkhead Siding GF)
3 11	**3 62**	**Cardonald**	
3 28	**3 79**	Cardonald Jcn.	→ branch below (Cardonald Jcn. – Shieldhall)
3 62	**4 33**	**Hillington East**	
4 29	**5 00**	**Hillington West**	
6 47	**7 18**	**Paisley Gilmour Street**	→ *Gourock/Wemyss Bay (219) - p.149*
9 22	**9 73**	Elderslie	
10 09	**10 60**	**Johnstone**	
13 08	**13 59**	Howwood	
15 57	**16 28**	**Lochwinnoch**	
17 49	**18 20**	Beith North	
19 63	**20 34**	**Glengarnock**	
22 42	**23 13**	**Dalry**	
25 70	**26 41**	Kilwinning Jcn.	
26 00	**26 51**	**Kilwinning**	
26 68	**27 39**	Dubbs Jcn.	→ branch below (Dubbs Jcn. – Byrehill Jcn.)
28 25	**28 76**	**Stevenston**	
29 55	**30 26**	**Saltcoats**	
30 38	**31 09**	**Ardrossan South Beach**	→ branch below (Ardrossan Harbour)
30 48	**31 19**	Holm Jcn.	
35 10	**35 61**	**West Kilbride**	
36 52	**37 23**	Hunterston	→ branch below (Hunterston – Low Level Sidings)
39 01	**39 52**	**Fairlie**	
39 57	**40 28**	Fairlie Tunnel (North)	
42 07	**42 58**	**Largs**	

M. P.	M C	Location
1 05	**1 56**	Shields Jcn.
2 33	**3 04**	Corkerhill No. 1 SB
3 11	**3 62**	Corkerhill
5 60	**6 31**	Hawkhead Siding GF

M C	Location
0 00	Cardonald Jcn.
1 20	Shieldhall

M C	Location
0 60	Byrehill Jcn. (see belo[w])
0 00	Dubbs Jcn.

M. P.	M C	Location
30 38	**0 00**	**Ardrossan South Beach**
30 48	**0 10**	Holm Jcn.
31 51	**1 13**	**Ardrossan Harbour**

M C	Location
0 00	Hunterston
2 71	Low Level Sidings (B.S

M. P.	M C	Location	Connections
26 00	**26 51**	**Kilwinning**	
26 70	**27 41**	Byrehill Jcn. (see above)	
28 21	**28 72**	Bogside Jcn.	→ branch below (Bogside Jcn. – End of line)
29 28	**29 79**	**Irvine**	
31 17	**31 68**	Gailes LC	
33 00	**33 51**	**Barassie**	
C.M.M.			
0 01	**33 60**	Barassie Jcn.	→ branch below (Kilmarnock – Newton-on-Ayr)
1 16	**34 75**	**Troon**	
C.M.M.			
36 28	**37 17**	Prestwick B.P. Siding	
37 34	**38 23**	**Prestwick**	
38 78	**39 67**	Falkland Jcn.	→ branch below (Falkland Jcn. – Ayr Harbour Jcn.)
39 33	**40 22**	**Newton-on-Ayr**	

M C	Location
0 40	End of line
0 25	Snodgrass I.C.I.
0 00	Bogside Jcn.

M. P.	M C	Location
33 59	**0 00**	**Kilmarnock** (see p.147)
33 48	**0 11**	Kilmarnock Jcn.
C.M.M.		
0 49	**0 65**	St. Marnocks GF
2 60	**2 76**	Gatehead LC
5 70	**6 06**	Shewalton GF
7 56	**7 72**	Barassie Jcn.
	9 07	**Troon**
	12 35	**Prestwick**
	14 34	**Newton-on-Ayr**

M C	Location
0 00	Falkland Jcn.
0 45	Ayr Harbour Jcn. (p.1

GLASGOW CENTRAL - AYR - STRANRAER (B.R. Table 221) cont.

M. P.	M C	
	0 00	**Glasgow Central**
M. P.		
39 33	**40 22**	**Newton-on-Ayr**
39 40	**40 29**	Newton Jcns.
39 42	**40 31**	
40 49	**41 38**	**Ayr**
41 37	**42 26**	Belmont Jcn.
41 45	**42 34**	Belmont LC
49 46	**50 35**	**Maybole**
53 76	**54 65**	Kilkerran LC
C.M.M.		
0 15	**62 64**	**Girvan**
4 27	**66 76**	Pinmore Tunnel (South)
8 28	**70 77**	Pinwherry
12 35	**75 04**	**Barrhill**
20 70	**83 39**	Glenwhilly
C.M.M.		
47 72	**94 54**	Dunragit LC
53 19	**100 01**	Stranraer Yard GF
54 19	**101 01**	**Stranraer Harbour**

M C	
0 29	Ayr Harbour
0 17	Ayr Harbour Jcn. (p.148)
0 00	Newton Jcn.

M. P.	M C	
39 42	**0 00**	Newton Jcn.
39 62	**0 20**	Blackhouse Jcn.
43 51	**4 09**	*Annbank Jcn.
51 55	**8 04**	Killoch Colliery

M C	
0 00	Belmont Jcn.
11 17	Waterside (BR Boundary)

*** Annbank Jcn. - Mauchline Jcn. (p.147) - 6m. 57c. - is closed**

GLASGOW CENTRAL - GOUROCK & WEMYSS BAY (B.R. Table 219)

M. P.	M C	
	0 00	**Glasgow Central**
M. P.		*(see p.148)*
6 47	**7 18**	**Paisley Gilmour Street**
C.M.M.		
08 46	**8 01**	**Paisley St. James**
12 60	**12 15**	**Bishopton**
12 72	**12 27**	R.O.F. Sidings GF
14 04	**13 39**	Bishopton No. 2 Tunnel (West)
16 66	**16 21**	**Langbank**
19 45	**19 00**	**Woodhall**
20 71	**20 26**	**Port Glasgow**
21 28	**20 63**	Wemyss Bay Jcn.
21 65	**21 20**	**Bogston**
22 30	**21 65**	Ladyburn Jcn. (see below)
22 52	**22 07**	**Cartsdyke**
23 38	**22 73**	**Greenock Central**
24 10	**23 45**	**Greenock West**
24 15	**23 50**	Newton St. Tunnel (East)
25 40	**24 75**	**Fort Matilda**
26 58	**26 13**	**Gourock**

C.M.M.	M C	
0 00	**20 63**	Wemyss Bay Jcn.
1 07	**21 70**	Containerbase Jcn. (see below)
1 58	**22 41**	Cartsburn Tunnel (W.)
4 08	**24 71**	**Branchton**
5 22	**26 05**	I.B.M. Halt
6 09	**26 72**	Dunrod loop
6 31	**27 14**	Dunrod loop
7 62	**28 45**	**Inverkip**
10 03	**30 66**	**Wemyss Bay**

M C	
0 00	Ladybank Jcn.
1 02	James Watt Dock

M C	
0 00	Containerbase Jcn.
0 38	Balwhirley Tunnel (E.)
2 29	Union St. Tunnel (N.)
	Containerbase gate

GLASGOW CENTRAL - CATHCART, NEWTON & NEILSTON via Queens Park (B.R. Table 223)

M. P.	M C	
102 27	**0 00**	**Glasgow Central** → *Edinburgh via Shotts (225) - p.140; Carstairs/Carlisle (65) - p.146; Kilmarnock/E. Kilbride (222) - p.147; Ayr/Stranraer (221) - p.148/9; Gourock/Wemyss Bay (219) - p.149; Central L.L. (226) - p.151*
101 56	**0 51**	Bridge Street Jcn.
C.M.M.		
0 70	**0 68**	Eglington Street Jcn.
C.M.M.		
0 00	**1 26**	Muirhouse North Jcn.
0 10	**1 36**	**Pollokshields East**
0 43	**1 69**	**Queen's Park**
0 78	**2 24**	**Crosshill**
1 41	**2 67**	**Mount Florida**
1 63	**3 09**	Cathcart North Jcn. → (see branch below)
2 14	**3 40**	**Cathcart**
C.M.M.		
100 76	**3 51**	Cathcart West Jcn.
101 49	**4 24**	**Muirend**
102 73	**5 48**	**Williamwood**
103 61	**6 36**	**Whitecraigs**
104 58	**7 33**	**Patterton**
108 48	**11 23**	**Neilston**

M. P.	M C	
1 63	**3 09**	Cathcart North Jcn.
C.M.M.		
100 35	**3 50**	Cathcart East Jcn.
100 02	**4 03**	**King's Park**
99 45	**4 40**	**Croftfoot**
98 43	**5 42**	**Burnside**
97 15	**6 70**	**Kirkhill**
95 72	**8 13**	Newton West Jcn.
95 57	**8 28**	**Newton** (see below)

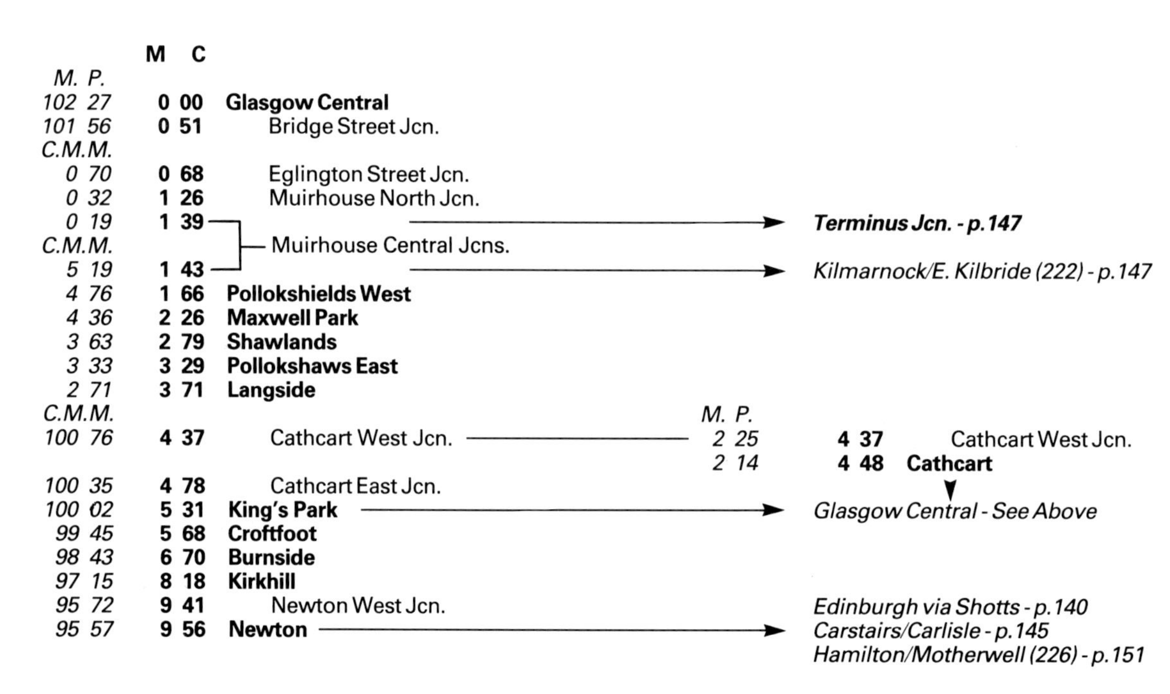

GLASGOW CENTRAL - CATHCART & NEWTON via Maxwell Park (B.R. Table 223)

M. P.	M C	
102 27	**0 00**	**Glasgow Central**
101 56	**0 51**	Bridge Street Jcn.
C.M.M.		
0 70	**0 68**	Eglington Street Jcn.
0 32	**1 26**	Muirhouse North Jcn.
0 19	**1 39**	Muirhouse Central Jcns. → ***Terminus Jcn. - p.147***
C.M.M.		
5 19	**1 43**	Muirhouse Central Jcns. → *Kilmarnock/E. Kilbride (222) - p.147*
4 76	**1 66**	**Pollokshields West**
4 36	**2 26**	**Maxwell Park**
3 63	**2 79**	**Shawlands**
3 33	**3 29**	**Pollokshaws East**
2 71	**3 71**	**Langside**
C.M.M.		
100 76	**4 37**	Cathcart West Jcn. → (see branch below)
100 35	**4 78**	Cathcart East Jcn.
100 02	**5 31**	**King's Park** → *Glasgow Central - See Above*
99 45	**5 68**	**Croftfoot**
98 43	**6 70**	**Burnside**
97 15	**8 18**	**Kirkhill**
95 72	**9 41**	Newton West Jcn.
95 57	**9 56**	**Newton** → *Edinburgh via Shotts - p.140; Carstairs/Carlisle - p.145; Hamilton/Motherwell (226) - p.151*

M. P.	M C	
2 25	**4 37**	Cathcart West Jcn.
2 14	**4 48**	**Cathcart** → *Glasgow Central - See Above*

MOTHERWELL - GLASGOW CENTRAL L.L. - PARTICK (B.R. Table 226)

	via Hamilton				via Bellshill	
M. P.	M C			M. P.	M C	
0 20	0 00	**Motherwell** —— (see pp. 140 & 145)	→	89 38	0 00	**Motherwell**
C.M.M.				89 50	0 12	
6 22	1 63	Ross Jcn.		89 51	0 13	Motherwell Jcns.
5 62	2 23	Barncluith Tunnel (West)		91 08	1 50	Mossend South Jcn. (see p.146)
5 03	3 02	**Hamilton Central**		C.M.M.		
4 12	3 73	**Hamilton West**		3 05	2 11	Mossend West Jcn.
2 29	5 56	**Blantyre**		2 30	2 66	**Bellshill** (see p.140)
				0 53	4 43	Viewpark Sidings
				C.M.M.		
				93 55	5 19	Uddingston Jcn.
C.M.M.				93 72	5 36	**Uddingston**
95 36	8 04	Newton East Jcn.		95 36	7 00	Newton East Jcn.
95 57	8 25	**Newton** —— (see p.150)	→	95 57	7 21	**Newton**

M. P.	M C	Location		Connection
95 67	8 35	Newton West Jcns.	→	***Redpath - p.140***
95 72	8 40	Newton West Jcns.	→	*Kirkhill (223) - p.150*
97 24	9 72	**Cambuslang**		
98 32	11 00	Rutherglen East Jcn.	→	***Whifflet Jcns. - See Below***
C.M.M.				
0 00	11 45	Rutherglen Central Jcn.	——	0 00 Rutherglen Central Jcn.
				1 20 London Road Depot
0 18	11 63	**Rutherglen**		
0 31	11 76	Rutherglen North Jcn.	→	***Rutherglen West Jcn. - p.146***
1 01	12 46	**Dalmarnock**		
1 41	13 06	**Bridgeton**		
1 75	13 40	Anderston Tunnel (East)		
2 60	14 25	**Argyle Street**		
3 08	14 53	**Glasgow Central L.L.**	→	*See p.150 for H.L. Refs.*

M. P.	M C	Location		M. P.	M C	Up line
3 08	0 00	**Glasgow Central L.L.**				
3 41	0 33	Anderston Tunnel (West)				
3 42	0 34	**Anderston**				
4 03	0 75	**Finnieston**	——	4 03	0 75	**Finnieston**
				4 07	0 79	Kelvinhaugh Tunnel (E)
4 41	1 33	Finnieston East Jcn.				
				4 50	1 42	Kelvinhaugh Tunnel (W)
4 74	1 66	Finnieston West Jcn.	——	4 74	1 66	Finnieston West Jcn.
C.M.M.						
2 79	2 12	**Partick**	→			*Queen Street/Dalmuir (226) - p.153*

M. P.	M C	Location		Connection
93 66	0 00	Whifflet South Jcn.	→	*Mossend Yard (65) - p.146*
94 05	0 19	Whifflet North Jcn.		

M. P.	M C	Location		M. P.	M C	Location
				8 54	1 75	Imperial Tube Works
C.M.M.				7 30	0 51	Calder Yard
6 59	0 53	Rosehall Jcn.	——	6 59	0 00	Rosehall Jcn.
				7 03	0 49	Coatbridge Jcn. (p.146)
6 34	0 78	Langloan Jcn.	——	6 34	0 00	Langloan Jcn.
1 55	5 57	Carmyle Jcn.				
0 70	6 42	Clydebridge GF				
C.M.M.						
98 32	7 36	Rutherglen East Jcn.	→			*Glasgow Central (65) - p.146*

CUMBERNAULD/SPRINGBURN - QUEEN STREET L.L. - MILNGAVIE (B.R. Table

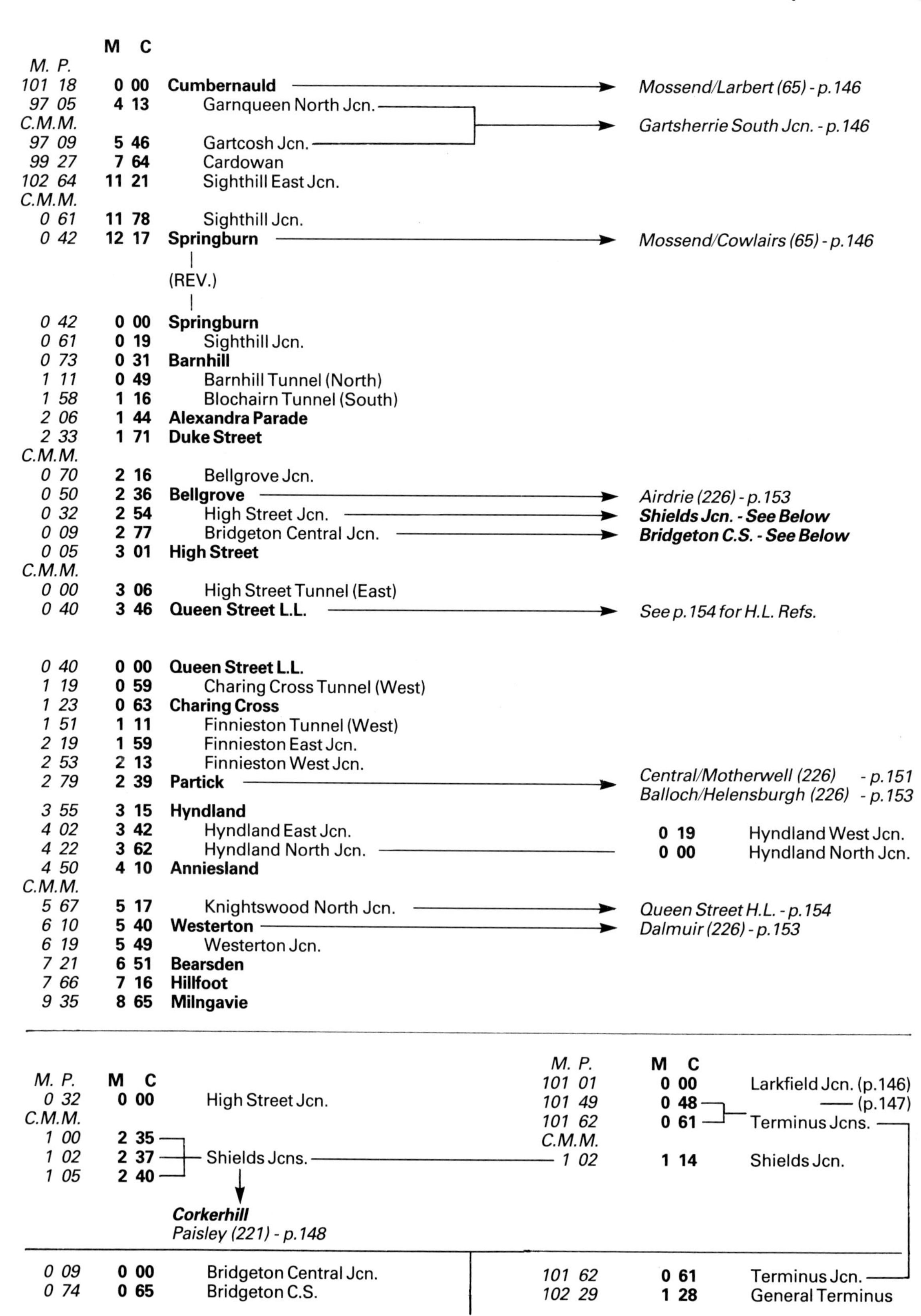

M. P.	M	C	Location	Connection
101 18	**0**	**00**	**Cumbernauld**	→ *Mossend/Larbert (65) - p.146*
97 05	**4**	**13**	Garnqueen North Jcn.	→ *Gartsherrie South Jcn. - p.146*
C.M.M.				
97 09	**5**	**46**	Gartcosh Jcn.	→ *Gartsherrie South Jcn. - p.146*
99 27	**7**	**64**	Cardowan	
102 64	**11**	**21**	Sighthill East Jcn.	
C.M.M.				
0 61	**11**	**78**	Sighthill Jcn.	
0 42	**12**	**17**	**Springburn**	→ *Mossend/Cowlairs (65) - p.146*
			(REV.)	
0 42	**0**	**00**	**Springburn**	
0 61	**0**	**19**	Sighthill Jcn.	
0 73	**0**	**31**	**Barnhill**	
1 11	**0**	**49**	Barnhill Tunnel (North)	
1 58	**1**	**16**	Blochairn Tunnel (South)	
2 06	**1**	**44**	**Alexandra Parade**	
2 33	**1**	**71**	**Duke Street**	
C.M.M.				
0 70	**2**	**16**	Bellgrove Jcn.	
0 50	**2**	**36**	**Bellgrove**	→ *Airdrie (226) - p.153*
0 32	**2**	**54**	High Street Jcn.	→ ***Shields Jcn. - See Below***
0 09	**2**	**77**	Bridgeton Central Jcn.	→ ***Bridgeton C.S. - See Below***
0 05	**3**	**01**	**High Street**	
C.M.M.				
0 00	**3**	**06**	High Street Tunnel (East)	
0 40	**3**	**46**	**Queen Street L.L.**	→ *See p.154 for H.L. Refs.*

M. P.	M	C	Location	Connection
0 40	**0**	**00**	**Queen Street L.L.**	
1 19	**0**	**59**	Charing Cross Tunnel (West)	
1 23	**0**	**63**	**Charing Cross**	
1 51	**1**	**11**	Finnieston Tunnel (West)	
2 19	**1**	**59**	Finnieston East Jcn.	
2 53	**2**	**13**	Finnieston West Jcn.	
2 79	**2**	**39**	**Partick**	→ *Central/Motherwell (226) - p.151*; *Balloch/Helensburgh (226) - p.153*
3 55	**3**	**15**	**Hyndland**	
4 02	**3**	**42**	Hyndland East Jcn.	
4 22	**3**	**62**	Hyndland North Jcn.	— **0 19** Hyndland West Jcn.; **0 00** Hyndland North Jcn.
4 50	**4**	**10**	**Anniesland**	
C.M.M.				
5 67	**5**	**17**	Knightswood North Jcn.	→ *Queen Street H.L. - p.154*
6 10	**5**	**40**	**Westerton**	→ *Dalmuir (226) - p.153*
6 19	**5**	**49**	Westerton Jcn.	
7 21	**6**	**51**	**Bearsden**	
7 66	**7**	**16**	**Hillfoot**	
9 35	**8**	**65**	**Milngavie**	

M. P.	M	C	Location
0 32	**0**	**00**	High Street Jcn.
C.M.M.			
1 00	**2**	**35**	Shields Jcns.
1 02	**2**	**37**	Shields Jcns.
1 05	**2**	**40**	Shields Jcns.

↓ ***Corkerhill***
Paisley (221) - p.148

M. P.	M	C	Location
101 01	**0**	**00**	Larkfield Jcn. (p.146)
101 49	**0**	**48**	(p.147) Terminus Jcns.
101 62	**0**	**61**	Terminus Jcns.
C.M.M.			
1 02	**1**	**14**	Shields Jcn.

M. P.	M	C	Location
0 09	**0**	**00**	Bridgeton Central Jcn.
0 74	**0**	**65**	Bridgeton C.S.

M. P.	M	C	Location
101 62	**0**	**61**	Terminus Jcn.
102 29	**1**	**28**	General Terminus

IRDRIE - QUEEN STREET L.L. - BALLOCH/HELENSBURGH (B.R. Table 226)

M C	Location
2 12	B.R. Boundary
1 72	Inverhouse GF
0 00	**Airdrie**

M. P.	M C	Location	Connection
10 38	0 00	**Airdrie**	**Airdrie**
9 48	0 70	**Coatdyke**	
8 51	1 67	**Coatbridge Sunnyside**	
8 43	1 75	Sunnyside Jcn.	***Gunnie Yard*** ***Whifflet S. Jcn.*** *- p.146*
7 75	2 43	**Blairhill**	
5 30	5 08	**Easterhouse**	
4 30	6 08	**Garrowhill**	
3 20	7 18	**Shettleston**	
2 36	8 02	**Carntyne**	
1 62	8 56	Parkhead North Jcn.	
0 70	9 48	Bellgrove Jcn.	
0 50	9 68	**Bellgrove**	*Springburn (226) - p.152*
0 32	10 06	High Street Jcn.	***Shields Jcn. - p.152***
0 09	10 29	Bridgeton Central Jcn.	***Bridgeton C.S. - p.152***
0 05	10 33	**High Street**	
.M.M.			
0 00	10 38	High Street Tunnel (East)	
0 40	10 78	**Queen Street L.L.**	*See p.154 for H.L. Refs.*

M. P.	M C	Location	Connection
0 40	0 00	**Queen Street L.L.**	
1 19	0 59	Charing Cross Tunnel (West)	
1 23	0 63	**Charing Cross**	
1 51	1 11	Finnieston Tunnel (West)	
2 19	1 59	Finnieston East Jcn.	
2 53	2 13	Finnieston West Jcn.	
2 79	2 39	**Partick**	*Central/Motherwell (226) - p.151*
3 55	3 15	**Hyndland**	
:.M.M.			
0 00	3 42	Hyndland East Jcn.	
0 12	3 54	**Jordanhill**	
0 22	3 64	Hyndland West Jcn. (p.152)	
1 20	4 62	**Scotstounhill**	
1 58	5 20	**Garscadden**	
2 04	5 46	Clydebank Dock Jcn.	
2 56	6 18	**Yoker**	
3 43	7 05	**Clydebank**	
3 60	7 22	Clydebank Central Jcn. *(see below)*	
:.M.M.			
9 75	8 24	**Dalmuir**	
10 03	8 32	Dalmuir Jcn.	
11 17	9 46	**Kilpatrick**	
12 76	11 25	**Bowling**	
15 43	13 72	**Dumbarton East**	
16 08	14 37	**Dumbarton Central**	
16 38	14 67	**Dalreoch**	
16 40	14 69	Dalreoch Jcn.	
17 04	15 33	Dalreoch Tunnels (West)	
19 50	17 79	**Cardross**	
21 19	19 48	Ardmore East LC	
23 00	21 29	Craigendoran Jcn. (p.154)	
23 18	21 47	**Craigendoran**	
24 31	22 60	**Helensburgh Central**	

via Westerton

M. P.	M C	Location
4 02	3 42	Hyndland East Jcn.
4 22	3 62	Hyndland North Jcn.
4 50	4 10	**Anniesland**
C.M.M.		(Knightswood South Jcn.)
5 67	5 17	Knightswood North Jcn.
6 10	5 40	**Westerton** (see p.152)
6 19	5 49	Westerton Jcn.
7 20	6 50	**Drumchapel**
8 10	7 40	**Drumry**
9 05	8 35	**Singer**
9 75	9 25	**Dalmuir**
10 03	9 33	Dalmuir Jcn.
11 17	10 47	**Kilpatrick**
12 76	12 26	**Bowling**
15 43	14 73	**Dumbarton East**
16 08	15 38	**Dumbarton Central**
16 38	15 68	**Dalreoch**
16 40	15 70	Dalreoch Jcn.
18 11	17 41	**Renton**
19 20	18 50	**Alexandria**
20 45	19 75	**Balloch Central**
21 04	20 34	**Balloch Pier** (closed)

M C	Location
0 00	Clydebank Central Jcn.
2 25	Old Kilpatrick

OTE: The former goods line from Knightswood South Jcn. to Maryhill Central Jcn. was re-opened briefly to passenger services because of engineering work. ileages as follows:

M. P.	M C	Location
8 26	0 00	Cowlairs West Jcn. (see p.154)
8 08	0 18	Cowlairs North Jcn.
5 51	2 55	Maryhill Central Jcn.
4 63	3 43	Knightswood South Jcn.
4 50	3 56	**Anniesland**
4 22	4 04	Hyndland North Jcn.
C.M.M.		
0 22	4 23	Hyndland West Jcn. (see above)

GLASGOW QUEEN STREET - OBAN & MALLAIG (B.R. Table 227)

M. P.	M C	Location	Connection
0 00	**0 00**	**Queen Street H.L.**	→ *Edinburgh (228) - p. 141* *Perth (229/231) - p.141* *Queen St. L.L. (226) - p.152/3*
0 60	**0 60**	Queen Street H.L. Tunnel (North)	
C.M.M.			
8 26	**1 67**	Cowlairs West Jcn.	→ *Springburn/Mossend (65) - p.146*
8 08	**2 05**	Cowlairs North Jcn.	→ ***Cowlairs East Jcn. - p.141***
C.M.M.		(Maryhill Central Jcn. - see note p.153)	
5 67	**5 53**	Knightswood North Jcn.	→ *Hyndland (226) - p.153*
6 10	**5 76**	**Westerton**	
6 19	**6 05**	Westerton Jcn.	→ *Milngavie (226) - p.152*
7 20	**7 06**	**Drumchapel**	
8 10	**7 76**	**Drumry**	
9 05	**8 71**	**Singer**	
9 75	**9 61**	**Dalmuir**	→ *Partick (226) - p.153*
10 03	**9 69**	Dalmuir Jcn.	
11 17	**11 03**	**Kilpatrick**	
12 76	**12 62**	**Bowling**	
15 43	**15 29**	**Dumbarton East**	
16 08	**15 74**	**Dumbarton Central**	
16 38	**16 24**	**Dalreoch**	
16 40	**16 26**	Dalreoch Jcn.	→ *Balloch (226) - p.153*
17 04	**16 70**	Dalreoch Tunnels (West)	
19 50	**19 36**	**Cardross**	
21 19	**21 05**	Ardmore East LC	
C.M.M.			
0 00	**22 66**	Craigendoran Jcn.	→ *Helensburgh Central (226) - p.153*
2 08	**24 74**	**Helensburgh Upper**	
8 76	**31 62**	**Garelochhead**	
15 21	**38 07**	Glen Douglas	
19 45	**42 31**	**Arrochar & Tarbet**	
27 48	**50 34**	**Ardlui**	
36 25	**59 11**	**Crianlarich**	→ Oban line (below)
41 21	**64 07**	**Tyndrum Upper**	
48 68	**71 54**	**Bridge of Orchy**	
64 36	**87 22**	**Rannoch**	
66 01	**88 67**	Cruach Snow Shed (North)	
71 54	**94 40**	**Corrour**	
78 75	**101 61**	Fersit Tunnel (South)	
81 59	**104 45**	**Tulloch**	
87 35	**110 21**	**Roy Bridge**	
90 56	**113 42**	**Spean Bridge**	
98 65	**121 51**	Mallaig Jcn.	
99 37	**122 23**	**Fort William**	
		(REV.)	
99 37	**0 00**	**Fort William**	
C.M.M.			
0 05	**0 52**	Mallaig Jcn.	
C.M.M.			
0 25	**2 19**	**Banavie**	
1 30	**3 24**	**Corpach**	
2 15	**4 09**	Annat	
4 20	**6 14**	**Loch Eil Outward Bound**	
7 79	**9 73**	**Locheilside**	
14 53	**16 47**	**Glenfinnan**	
23 67	**25 61**	**Lochailort**	
28 49	**30 43**	**Beasdale**	
29 32	**31 26**	Borrodale Tunnel (West)	
32 02	**33 76**	**Arisaig**	
36 59	**38 53**	**Morar**	
39 45	**41 39**	**Mallaig**	→ NOTE (below)

C.M.M.	M C	Location
0 00	**59 11**	**Crianlarich**
C.M.M.		
30 23	**59 55**	Crianlarich GF
34 70	**64 22**	**Tyndrum Lower**
46 76	**76 28**	**Dalmally**
49 48	**79 00**	**Loch Awe**
58 55	**88 07**	**Taynuilt**
65 30	**94 62**	**Connel Ferry**
71 44	**100 76**	**Oban**

NOTE: Cal-Mac ferry fans heading north will find the Kyle - Inverness table on p.144.

SECTION VI
METROPOLITAN SYSTEMS

(a) Glasgow Underground

E the 1977/80 modernisation, the Glasgow Under-
ıd has been fully metric and all operating data is quoted
etres. Intermediate distances from station to station
between the Outer and Inner Circles, and there are also
: differences in platform lengths. These are apparent from the cumulative metric distances in the left and right-hand columns, though barely noticeable when converted to miles and chains. All figures quoted refer to platform exit headwalls in the direction of travel.

Outer Circle					*Inner Circle*			
K.	M.	M	C		M	C	K.	M.
	0	**0**	**00**	**Buchanan Street**	**6**	**44**	10	547
	550	**0**	**27**	**St. Enoch**	**6**	**17**	9	995
1	222	**0**	**61**	**Bridge Street**	**5**	**63**	9	312
1	741	**1**	**07**	**West Street**	**5**	**38**	8	799
2	342	**1**	**36**	**Shields Road**	**5**	**08**	8	197
3	158	**1**	**77**	**Kinning Park**	**4**	**47**	7	381
3	652	**2**	**22**	**Cessnock**	**4**	**23**	6	891
4	318	**2**	**55**	**Ibrox**	**3**	**70**	6	226
4	836	**3**	**00½**	South turn-out	**3**	**41½**	5	663
4	950	**3**	**06**	North turn-out	**3**	**36**	5	548
5	237	**3**	**20**	**Govan**	**3**	**24**	5	308
6	198	**3**	**68**	**Partick**	**2**	**56**	4	349
6	757	**4**	**16**	**Kelvinhall**	**2**	**29**	3	796
7	360	**4**	**46**	**Hillhead**	**1**	**79**	3	195
8	263	**5**	**11**	**Kelvinbridge**	**1**	**34**	2	285
9	055	**5**	**50**	**St. Georges Circus**	**0**	**75**	1	502
9	763	**6**	**05**	**Cowcaddens**	**0**	**40**		802
10	565	**6**	**45**	**Buchanan Street**	**0**	**00**		0

STATIONS		**BRITISH RAIL TABLE REFERENCE**	
erground	**British Rail**		
		Edinburgh (228)	*-p.141*
ıanan Street	***Glasgow Queen Street*** →	*Perth (229/231)*	*-p.141*
		Low Level (226)	*-p.152/3*
		Edinburgh via Shotts (225)	*-p.140*
		Carstairs/Carlisle (65)	*-p.146*
		Kilmarnock/E. Kilbride (222)	*-p.147*
:noch	***Glasgow Central*** →	*Ayr/Stranraer (221)*	*-p.148/9*
		Gourock/Wemyss Bay (219)	*-p.149*
		Low Level (226)	*-p.151*
		Central/Motherwell	*-p.151*
tick	***Partick*** →	*Cumbernauld/Milngavie (226)*	*-p.152*
		Airdrie/Helensburgh	*-p.153*

(b) Tyne & Wear Metro

FORGET everything you know about British Rail track—The Tyne Metro is quite different, though it's hoped the following notes and tables will help with your conversion to the metric system.

1. Metro lines are not referred to as 'up' and 'down'; instead there is an "IN" direction and an "OUT" direction.
   The "IN" line is from St. James via the **in**side of the coastal loop (and from Bank Foot) **to** South Shields.
   The "OUT" line is **from** South Shields via the **out**side of the coastal loop to St. James (and to Bank Foot).
2. Metro "chainages" are measured in metres, east/west and south of a single Datum Point which is 28 metres north of Gosforth South Junction (the site of an old B.R. ¼-milepost).
   This Datum represents zero to the Metro in the same way as the Kings Cross buffer stops represent zero to the East Coast Main Line.
3. The distances between stations (and their distances from Datum) are measured from the top of the platform ramps or the front of a stationary train if this is significantly different. It is obvious, therefore, that there will be some discrepancy between measurements for the "IN" and "OUT" directions, so both are included in the Tables.
4. The Metro's equivalent of mileposts are the identification plates fixed to each overhead line support structure; these plates are lettered white on a blue background and presented thus:

GB	————	(a)
01	————	(b)
227	————	(c)

a) The letters indicate the electrical section in whic mast is located - in the example, between Gosfort Benton on the "OUT" line. On the "IN" line, the l will be reversed to read BG.
The letters refer to traction sub-stations or ter stations, namely:-

B - Benton Square, and also Byker   C - Chiches
G - Gosforth   H - Hebburn   K - Kenton (Bank
M - Monument   O - Gateshead Stadium (Old F
P - Percy Main   S - St. James, and also South Sh
W - Whitley Bay

b) The middle two figures show the whole numb kilometres from the Datum Point.
c) The lower three figures give the number of m from the whole kilometre shown.
The "Chainage" columns of the Tables which shov information are included only as a guide. Althoug give exact references for platform ends and othe tures, they will only approximate, within a few m to the nearest lineside mast plate.
Similarly, traction sub-stations do not always t with the passenger stations of the same name, so t too, will appear a little "out" in places.

5. The centre columns of the Tables give cumulativ tances in kilometres and metres, and refer to plat ends in the direction of travel.
6. For traditionalists, the third columns give the sam formation in miles and chains.

Table A - BANK FOOT - SOUTH GOSFORTH

"IN" Direction / ***"OUT" Direction***

"Chainage" ("IN")	K.	M.	**M**	**C**		**M**	**C**	K.	M.	*"Chainage"* ("OUT")
GK 04 901					Buffer stop					*GK 04 901*
*GK 04 788**		0	**0**	**00**	**Bank Foot**	**3**	**06**	4	953	*GK 04 863**
GK 04 713		75	**0**	**04**	Bank Foot Jcn.	**2**	**79**	4	803	*GK 04 713*
GK 04 313		475	**0**	**24**	Brunton Lane Jcn.	**2**	**59**	4	403	*GK 04 313*
KG 04 140		648	**0**	**32**	**Kingston Park**	**2**	**46**	4	133	*GK 04 043*
KG 02 701	2	087	**1**	**24**	**Fawdon**	**1**	**55**	2	710	*GK 02 620*
KG 02 109	2	679	**1**	**53**	**Wansbeck Road**	**1**	**31**	2	232	*GK 02 142*
KG 01 154	3	634	**2**	**21**	**Regent Centre**	**0**	**65**	1	309	*GK 01 219*
KG 01 046	3	742	**2**	**26**	Gosforth West Jcn.	**0**	**56½**	1	136	*GK 01 046*
KG 00 000	4	788	**2**	**78**	***DATUM POINT***	**0**	**04½**		90	*GK 00 000*
KG 00 028	4	816	**2**	**79½**	Gosforth South Jcn.	**0**	**03**		62	*GK 00 028*
*GM 00 159**	4	947	**3**	**06**	**South Gosforth**	**0**	**00**		0	*GB 00 090**

*** heads of platforms**

NOTE: British Rail refer to Gosforth West Jcn. as Regent Centre East Jcn. **(see p.43)**

ABLE B - ST. JAMES - THE COAST - SOUTH SHIELDS

"IN" Direction / ***"OUT" Direction***

"Chainage" (IN)	K.	M.	M	C		M	C	K.	M.	"Chainage" (OUT)	M	C
28 699		0	**0**	**00**	**St. James**	**31**	**41**	50	703	*MS 28 764*	**7**	**46**
28 257		442	**0**	**22**	**Monument**	**31**	**19**	50	263	*MS 28 324*	**7**	**24**
27 684	1	015	**0**	**50½**	Manors Jcn.							
27 614	1	085	**0**	**54**	**Manors**	**30**	**67**	49	621	*BM 27 682*	**6**	**72**
27 390	1	309	**0**	**65**	Manors Scissors	**30**	**53**	49	329	*BM 27 390*	**6**	**58**
27 336	1	363	**0**	**68**		**30**	**50**	49	275	*BM 27 336*	**6**	**55**
27 247	1	452	**0**	**72**	Stoddart St. Jcn.							
25 964	2	735	**1**	**56**	**Byker**	**29**	**67**	47	998	*BM 26 059*	**5**	**72**
24 861	3	838	**2**	**31**	**Chillingham Road**	**29**	**11**	46	870	*PB 24 931*	**5**	**16**
24 025	4	674	**2**	**72**	**Walkergate**	**28**	**49**	46	030	*PB 24 091*	**4**	**54**
22 243	6	456	**4**	**01**	**Wallsend**	**27**	**40**	44	248	*PB 22 309*	**3**	**45**
21 125	7	574	**4**	**57**	**Hadrian Road**	**26**	**65**	43	129	*BP 21 190*	**2**	**70**
19 745	8	954	**5**	**45**	**Howdon**	**25**	**69**	41	611	*PB 19 672*	**1**	**74**
18 374	10	325	**6**	**33**	**Percy Main**	**25**	**07**	40	358	*WP 18 419*	**1**	**12**
17 759	10	940	**6**	**64**	**Smith's Park**	**24**	**57**	39	764	*WP 17 825*	**0**	**62**
16 843	11	856	**7**	**30**	Preston Ref. Sdg.							
16 522	12	177	**7**	**46**	**North Shields (Bay)**					*WP 16 583*	**0**	**00**
16 428	12	271	**7**	**50**	**North Shields**	**23**	**71**	38	429	*WP 16 490*		
14 692	14	007	**8**	**60**	**Tynemouth**	**22**	**65**	36	709	*WP 14 770*		
12 665	16	034	**9**	**77**	**Cullercoats**	**21**	**44**	34	670	*WP 12 731*		
11 930	16	769	**10**	**34**	**Whitley Bay**	**21**	**07**	33	928	*WP 11 989*		
10 881	17	818	**11**	**06**	**Monkseaton**	**20**	**36**	32	895	*BW 10 956*		
09 623	19	076	**11**	**69**	**West Monkseaton**	**19**	**53**	31	631	*BW 09 692*		
07 706	20	993	**13**	**04**	**Shiremoor**	**18**	**36**	29	675	*BW 07 736*		
04 896	23	803	**14**	**64**	**Palmersville**	**16**	**58**	26	900	*BW 04 961*		
03 054	25	645	**15**	**75**	Benton Station Jcns.	**15**	**43**	24	993	*GB 03 054*		
03 005	25	694	**15**	**78**								
02 844	25	855	**16**	**06**	**Benton**	**15**	**35**	24	834	*GB 02 895*		
02 059	26	640	**16**	**45**	**Four Lane Ends**	**14**	**77**	24	064	*GB 02 125*		
01 190	27	509	**17**	**08**	**Longbenton**	**14**	**33**	23	195	*GB 01 256*		
00 610	28	089	**17**	**37**	Gosforth East Jcn.	**14**	**01**	22	549	*GB 00 610*		
00 000	28	699	**17**	**67**	***DATUM POINT***	**13**	**51**	21	939	*GB 00 000*		
00 028	28	727	**17**	**68½**	Gosforth South Jcn.	**13**	**49½**	21	911	*GB 00 028*		
00 159	28	858	**17**	**75**	**South Gosforth**	**13**	**46**	21	849	*MG 00 090*		
00 822	29	521	**18**	**28**	**Ilford Road**	**13**	**13**	21	182	*MG 00 757*		
01 586	30	285	**18**	**66**	**West Jesmond**	**12**	**56**	20	424	*MG 01 515*		
02 586	31	285	**19**	**36**	Jesmond Jcn.							
02 795	31	494	**19**	**46**	**Jesmond**	**11**	**75**	19	214	*MG 02 725*		
03 581	32	280	**20**	**05**	**Haymarket**	**11**	**36**	18	424	*MG 03 515*		
04 101	32	800	**20**	**31**	**Monument**	**11**	**11**	17	921	*MG 04 018*		
04 618	33	317	**20**	**57**	**Central**	**10**	**65**	17	403	*OM 04 536*		
05 020	33	719	**20**	**77**	QEII Bridge	**10**	**41**	16	919	*OM 05 020*		
05 370	34	069	**21**	**14**		**10**	**24**	16	569	*OM 05 370*		
05 967	34	666	**21**	**44**	**Gateshead**	**9**	**77**	16	032	*OM 05 907*		
07 125	35	824	**22**	**21**	**Gateshead Stadium**	**9**	**20**	14	878	*HO 07 061*		
08 279	36	978	**22**	**79**	**Felling**	**8**	**43**	13	728	*HO 08 211*		
09 314	38	013	**23**	**50**	**Heworth**	**7**	**71**	12	687	*HO 09 252*		
10 212	39	911	**24**	**15**	**Pelaw**	**7**	**26**	11	794	*HO 10 145*		
13 325	42	014	**26**	**09**	**Hebburn**	**5**	**23**	8	512	*HO 13 427*		
15 431	44	130	**27**	**34**	**Jarrow**	**4**	**07**	6	569	*CH 15 370*		
17 279	45	978	**28**	**46**	**Bede**	**2**	**70**	4	617	*CH 17 322*		
19 330	48	029	**29**	**68**	**Tyne Dock**	**1**	**53**	2	674	*CH 10 265*		
20 685	49	384	**30**	**56**	**Chichester**	**0**	**66**	1	319	*SC 20 620*		
22 004	50	703	**31**	**41**	**South Shields**	**0**	**00**		0	*SC 21 939*		

Table C - NON-PASSENGER LINES

(i) Depot Avoiding Line

"Chainage"	K.	M.	M	C		M	C	K.	M.	"Chainage"
*KG 01 154**		0	**0**	**00**	**Regent Centre**	**1**	**19**	1	998	*GK 01 219**
KG 01 046		108	**0**	**05**	Gosforth West Jcn.	**1**	**11**	1	825	*GK 01 046**
GB 00 610	1	353	**0**	**67**	Gosforth East Jcn.	**0**	**29**		580	*BG 00 610*
*GB 01 256**	1	999	**1**	**19**	**Longbenton**	**0**	**00**		0	*BG 01 190**

*** heads of platforms**

NOTE: Trains travelling from Regent Centre via the avo- ing line to Longbenton change from the "IN" to the "OUT" Direction, and *vice versa*. Mast identification plates *within* Gosforth Depot are numbered in sequence (i.e. not related to any measured distance) from 01 (Gosforth East Jcn) to 63 (West Jcn). They also carry the prefix E, to denote those at the East end of the Depot, or W for those at the West end. Structures specific to the Avoiding Line are likewise numbered in sequence (East to West) from 64 to 78, and carry the prefix AL.

(ii) Bank Foot Siding

"Chainage"	K.	M.	M	C	
GK 04 713		0	**0**	**00**	Bank Foot Jcn. (Table A)
GK 04 785		72	**0**	**03½**	Callerton Branch Jcn.
GK 04 914		201	**0**	**10**	Buffer stop

(iii) Regent Centre Siding

"IN"						"OUT"				
"Chainage"	K.	M.	M	C		M	C	K.	M.	"Chainage"
KG 01 437		0	**0**	**00**	Buffer stop	**0**	**11**		218	*KG 01 437*
*KG 01 154**		283	**0**	**14**	**Regent Centre**	**0**	**00**		0	*GK 01 219**

*** heads of platforms**

(iv) Manors Link - Stoddart Street Carriage Sidings

"Chaina ge"	K.	M.	M	C		
*GM 01 586**		0	**0**	**00**	**West Jesmond** (Table A)	
GM 02 586	1	000	**0**	**50**	Jesmond Jcn.	
GM 03 418	1	832	**1**	**11**	New Bridge Street	(Sig. 449)
GM 03 821 / *MB 27 684*	2	235	**1**	**31**	Manors Jcn.	
						"IN" Direction only
*MB 27 614**	2	305	**1**	**35**	**Manors**	
MB 27 390	2	529	**1**	**46**	Manors Scissors	
MB 27 336	2	583	**1**	**49**	Manors Scissors	
MB 27 247	2	672	**1**	**53**	Stoddart Street Jcn.	
MB 26 998	2	921	**1**	**65**	C.S. buffer stops	*** heads of platforms**

(v) Benton Carriage Sidings

"Chainage"	K.	M.	M	C	
GB 03 324		0	**0**	**00**	No. 1 Siding buffer stop
BG/ GB 03 054		270	**0**	**13½**	Benton Station Jcn. - ***"IN" & "OUT" lines*** (Table B)
GB 03 415		0	**0**	**00**	No. 2 Siding buffer stop
GB 03 334		81	**0**	**04**	Electrified limit
BG/ GB 03 054		361	**0**	**18**	Benton Station Jcn. - ***"IN" & "OUT" lines*** (Table B)

NOTE: The BG 03 005 chainage shown for Benton Station Jcn. in Table B refers to the "IN" Direction link with the B.R. line from Benton North Jcn. (see p.43)

(vi) South Shields Carriage Sidings

"Chainage"	K.	M.	M	C	
CS 22 004		0	**0**	**00**	**South Shields** (Table B)
SC 22 041		37	**0**	**02**	Junction points
SC 22 066		62	**0**	**03**	Junction points
SC 22 204		200	**0**	**10**	Electrified limit
SC 22 282		278	**0**	**14**	Buffer stop (west siding)

Signal over-run siding (from Junction points)

"Chainage"	M.	M	C	
22 066	62	**0**	**03**	
22 224	220	**0**	**11**	Buffer st[op]

(vii) Preston Refuge Siding is approximately 237 metres (12 chains) in length from the buffer stop to the junction with th[e] "IN" line at PW 16 843 (Table B).

(c) Docklands Light Railway

ocklands Light Railway is, as its name implies, a light- t Rapid Transit System which, like the Tyne & Wear , has been constructed partly on the trackbeds of r B.R. lines. It is due to open in July, 1987, and will be ı's first automatic light railway, with computer- olled driverless trains.

To begin with, the pattern of services will be Island Gardens - Tower Gateway and Island Garden - Stratford. Passengers wishing to travel from the City to Stratford will change trains at West India Quay. Proposed additions to the system are the Bank extension (construction now approved) and Poplar to Beckton and the City Stolport.

D.L.R. operating data is entirely metric; the Tables show cumulative distances in kilometres and metres with a conversion to cumulative miles and chains alongside. Figures quoted for stations refer to platform centres. Cross-references are given to nearby B.R. stations (with timetable numbers) and London Underground services.

M.	M.	C.	
0	0	00	End of line
28	0	01½	**Island Gardens**

M.	M.	C.		
0	0	00	**Island Gardens**	
47	0	02½	Island Gardens Jcn.	
330	0	16½	single to double	
441	0	22	**Mudchute**	
775	0	38½	emergency crossover	
804	0	40		
090	0	54	**Crossharbour**	
889	1	14	**South Quay**	
152	1	27	Docks Crossing South	
329	1	36	**Heron Quays**	
539	1	46	**Canary Wharf**	
727	1	56	Docks Crossing North	
747	1	57	**West India Quay**	
766	1	58	North Quay Jcn. South	
840	1	61	North Quay Jcn. West	
195	1	79	emergency crossover	
218	2	00		
307	2	04	**Westferry**	
275	2	53	**Limehouse** — (Stepney East)	*B.R. (1) - p.13*
251	3	21	emergency crossover	
336	3	25		
400	3	29	**Shadwell**	*L.T. (Metropolitan) - p.165*
452	4	01	emergency crossover	
601	4	08		
668	4	11½	**Tower Gateway** — (Tower Hill) / (Fenchurch Street)	*L.T. (Circle/District) - p.162* / *B.R. (1) - p.13*
669	4	13	End of Line	

M.	M	C	
0	0	00	North Quay Jcn. East
80	0	04	North Quay Jcn. West

M.	M	C	M	C		
0	0	00			**Island Gardens**	
747	1	57	0	00	**West India Quay**	
766	1	58	0	01	North Quay Jcn. South	
832	1	61	0	04	North Quay Jcn. East	
999	1	69	0	12	**Poplar**	
176	1	78	0	21	crossover	
278	2	03	0	26		
601	2	19	0	42	Depot Jcn. (down line)	
739	2	26	0	49	**All Saints**	
					Carmen Street (proposed)	
087	3	13	1	36	**Devons Road**	
443	3	31	1	54	Holyhead Close Tunnel	
618	3	39	3	39		
655	3	41	1	64	emergency crossover	
678	3	42	1	65		
712	3	44	1	67	**Bow Church** — (Bow Road)	*L.T. (District) - p.162*
863	3	51½	1	74½	double to single	
					Pudding Mill Lane (proposed)	
749	4	65	3	08	**Stratford**	*L.T. (Central) - p.161* / *B.R. (11/58) - p.4/12)*
781	4	67	3	10	End of Line	

(d) London Underground

LONDON Underground Working Timetables quote between-station distances, and cumulative distances between sections, in decimal miles. The between-station figures are shown in the left-hand columns, with a conversion to cumulative miles and chains alongside. Lines are listed in alphabetical order.

Rather than give interchanges between one line and another (which are well-known to regular traveller prominently displayed in L.R.T. publications), cross-ences are given to British Rail stations which have direct access or are located nearby. The main tim numbers for these stations are also shown together wi page numbers of the route tables.

Bakerloo Line

M.	M	C	Station	
	0	00	Harrow & Wealdstone	B.R. (58/59) - p.53
1.08	1	05	Kenton	
.87	1	75	South Kenton	
.56	2	40	North Wembley	
.79	3	24	Wembley Central	
1.06	4	29	Stonebridge Park	
.95	5	25	Harlesden	
.65	5	77	Willesden Junction	
.93	6	71	Kensal Green	
.82	7	57	Queen's Park	B.R. (58/59) - p.53
.49	8	16	Kilburn Park	
.55	8	60	Maida Vale	
.49	9	19	Warwick Avenue	
.55	9	63	Paddington	B.R. (127/135) - p.88
.45	10	19	Edgware Road	
.28	10	41	Marylebone	B.R. (114/115) - p.50/51
.31	10	66	Baker Street	
.55	11	30	Regents Park	
.54	11	74	Oxford Circus	
.60	12	42	Piccadilly Circus	
.34	12	69	Charing Cross	B.R. (207) - p.130
.23	13	08	Embankment	
.44	13	43	Waterloo	B.R. (158) - p.110 B.R. (147) - p.115 B.R. (150) - p.117
.39	13	74	Lambeth North	
.51	14	35	Elephant & Castle	B.R. (179) - p.125 B.R. (201) - p.129

Docklands Light Railway

Map reproduced by kind permissio of the Docklands Light Railwa

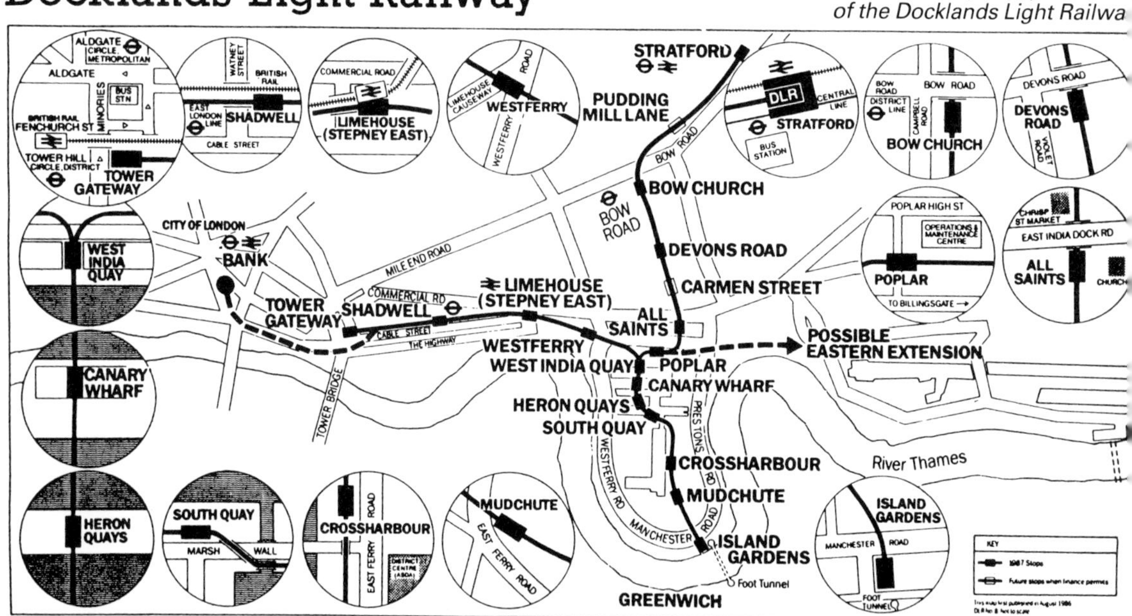

Central Line

M.	M	C	Station	Connection
	0	00	Ongar	
.52				
	3	42	North Weald	
.58				
	6	08	Epping	
	0	00	Epping	
.58				
	1	46	Theydon Bois	
.08				
	3	52	Debden	
.26				
	4	73	Loughton	
.14				
	6	04	Buckhurst Hill	
.44				
	7	40	Woodford	Woodford (Hainault loop)
.12				
	8	50	South Woodford	
.80				
	9	34	Snaresbrook	
.98				
	10	32	Leytonstone	Leytonstone (Hainault branch)
.01				
	11	33	Leyton	
.30				
	12	57	Stratford	*B.R. (11) - p.4*
.76				
	14	38	Mile End	
.02				
	15	39	Bethnal Green	
.41				
	16	72	Liverpool Street	*B.R. (11) - p.4*
.46				
	17	29	Bank	*B.R. (150) - p.117*
.46				
	17	66	St. Pauls (Holborn Viaduct)	*B.R. (179) - p.125* *B.R. (201) - p.129*
.64				
	18	37	Chancery Lane	
.25				
	18	57	Holborn	
.55				
	19	21	Tottenham Court Road	
.36				
	19	50	Oxford Circus	
.41				
	20	03	Bond Street	
.34				
	20	30	Marble Arch	
.75				
	21	10	Lancaster Gate	
.56				
	21	55	Queensway	
.43				
	22	09	Notting Hill Gate	
.38				
	22	39	Holland Park	
.54				
	23	02	Shepherds Bush	
.72				
	23	60	White City	
1.28				
	25	03	East Acton	
.69				
	25	58	North Acton	North Acton (Ealing branch)
			North Acton Jcn.	
1.55				
	27	22	Hanger Lane	
1.31				
	28	47	Perivale	
1.05				
	29	51	Greenford	*B.R. (118) - p.92*
1.11				
	30	59	Northolt	
1.42				
	32	13	South Ruislip	*B.R. (115) - p.50*
.54				
	32	56	Ruislip Gardens	
1.27				
	33	78	West Ruislip	*B.R. (115) - p.50*

M.	M	C	Station	Connection
	0	00	Hainault	
.70				
	0	56	Grange Hill	
.82				
	1	42	Chigwell	
1.42				
	2	76	Roding Valley	
.83				
	3	62	Woodford	

M.	M	C	Station	Connection
	0	00	Hainault	
.58				
	0	46	Fairlop	
.63				
	1	17	Barkingside	
.69				
	1	72	Newbury Park	
1.47				
	3	30	Gants Hill	
.79				
	4	13	Redbridge	
.76				
	4	74	Wanstead	
1.07				
	5	79	Leytonstone	*B.R. (2) - p.12*

M.	M	C	Station	Connection
	0	00	North Acton	
1.10			North Acton Jcn.	
	1	08	West Acton	
.95				
	2	04	Ealing Broadway	*B.R. (127/135) - p.88*

Circle Line

M.	M	C	Station	Via	Connection
	0	00	Liverpool Street		B.R. (11) - p.4
.32	0	26	Moorgate		B.R. (24) - p.15
.39	0	57	Barbican		B.R. (52) - p.44
.32	1	02	Farringdon		
1.15	2	14	Kings Cross		B.R. (26) - p.14
.53	2	56	Euston Square	(Euston)	B.R. (65) - p.55
.38	3	06	Great Portland Street		
.57	3	53	Baker Street	(Marylebone)	B.R. (115) - p.50
.45	4	09	Edgware Road		
.51	4	50	Paddington		B.R. (127/135) - p.88
.61	5	19	Bayswater		
.49	5	58	Notting Hill Gate		
.58	6	24	High Street Kensington		see branch below
.58	6	70	Gloucester Road		
.46	7	27	South Kensington		
.76	8	08	Sloane Square		
.65	8	60	Victoria		B.R. (186) - p.119 B.R. (212) - p.127
.45	9	16	St. James's Park		
.47	9	54	Westminster		
.43	10	08	Embankment	(Charing Cross)	B.R. (207) - p.130
.44	10	43	Temple		
.47	11	01	Blackfriars		B.R. (179) - p.125 B.R. (201) - p.129
.38	11	31	Mansion House		
.19	11	46	Cannon Street		B.R. (207) - p.130
.21	11	63	Monument		
.42	12	17	Tower Hill	(Fenchurch Street)	B.R. (1) - p.13
.31	12	42	Aldgate		
.38	12	72	Liverpool Street		

M.	M	C	Station
	0	00	High Street Kensington
.78	0	62	Earl's Court

(District Line - p.163)

District Line

M.	M	C	Station	Via	Connection
	0	00	Upminster		B.R. (4) - p.5 B.R. (1) - p.13
.77	0	62	Upminster Bridge		
.78	1	44	Hornchurch		
.93	2	38	Elm Park		
1.47	3	76	Dagenham East		
.84	4	63	Dagenham Heathway		
.85	5	51	Becontree		
1.16	6	64	Upney		
.86	7	53	Barking		B.R. (2) - p.12 B.R. (1) - p.13
1.42	9	07	East Ham		
.87	9	77	Upton Park		
.80	10	61	Plaistow		
.47	11	19	West Ham		B.R. (58) - p.12
.85	12	07	Bromley-by-Bow		
.63	12	57	Bow Road		
.34	13	04	Mile End		
.65	13	56	Stepney Green		
.62	14	25	Whitechapel		
.51	14	66	Aldgate East		
.50	15	26	Tower Hill	(Fenchurch Street)	B.R. (1) - p.13
.42	15	59	Monument		
.21	15	76	Cannon Street		B.R. (207) - p.130
.19	16	11	Mansion House		
.38	16	41	Blackfriars		B.R. (179) - p.125 B.R. (201) - p.129
.47	16	79	Temple		
.44	17	34	Embankment	(Charing Cross)	B.R. (207) - p.130

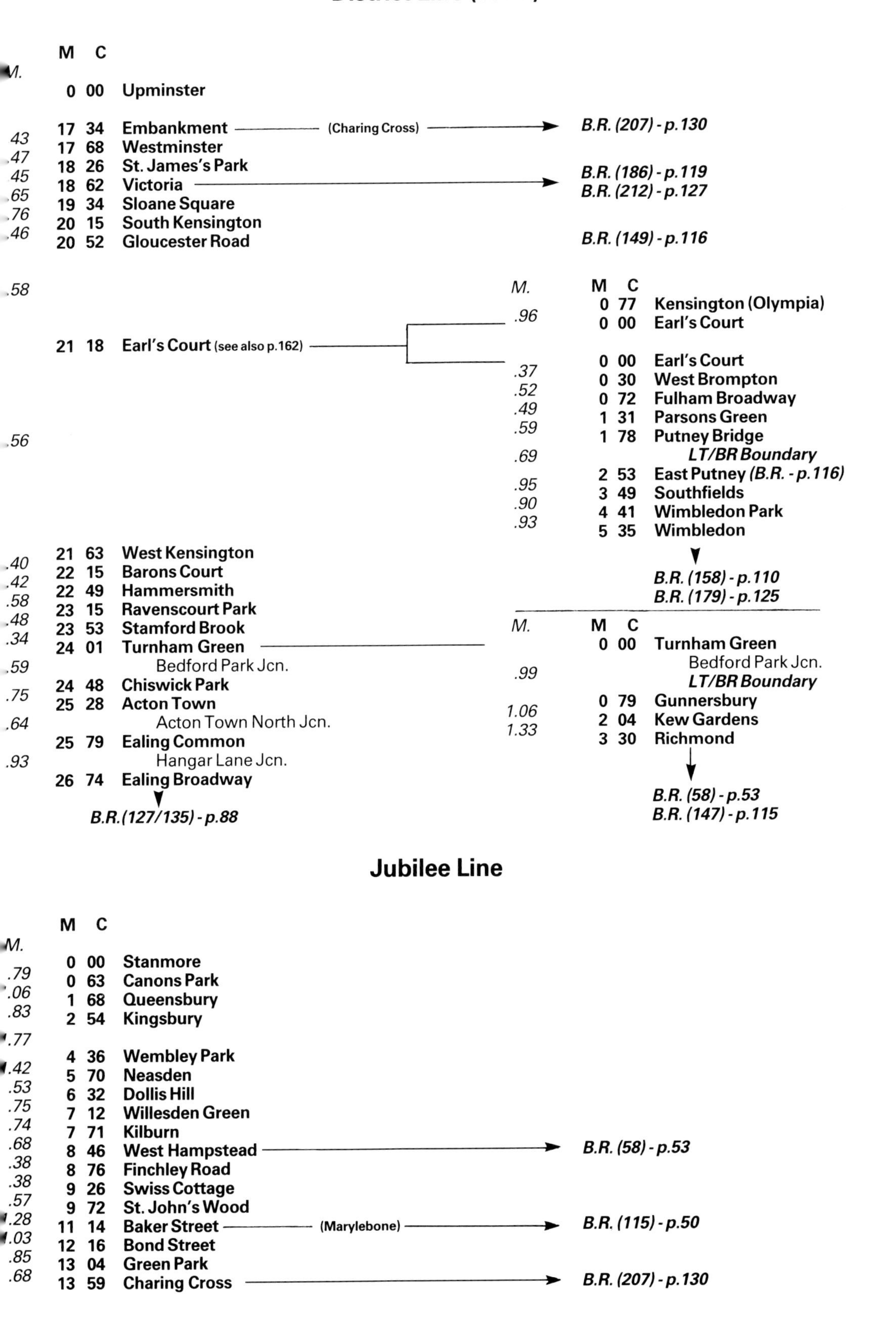

M.	M	C	Station	Connection
	0	00	Upminster	
	17	34	Embankment	(Charing Cross) → *B.R. (207) - p.130*
43	17	68	Westminster	
.47	18	26	St. James's Park	
45	18	62	Victoria	→ *B.R. (186) - p.119*, *B.R. (212) - p.127*
.65	19	34	Sloane Square	
.76	20	15	South Kensington	
.46	20	52	Gloucester Road	*B.R. (149) - p.116*
.58	21	18	Earl's Court (see also p.162)	
.56	21	63	West Kensington	
.40	22	15	Barons Court	
.42	22	49	Hammersmith	
.58	23	15	Ravenscourt Park	
.48	23	53	Stamford Brook	
.34	24	01	Turnham Green	
			Bedford Park Jcn.	
.59	24	48	Chiswick Park	
.75	25	28	Acton Town	
			Acton Town North Jcn.	
.64	25	79	Ealing Common	
			Hangar Lane Jcn.	
.93	26	74	Ealing Broadway	

B.R.(127/135) - p.88

M.	M	C	Station
	0	77	Kensington (Olympia)
.96	0	00	Earl's Court

M.	M	C	Station
	0	00	Earl's Court
.37	0	30	West Brompton
.52	0	72	Fulham Broadway
.49	1	31	Parsons Green
.59	1	78	Putney Bridge
			LT/BR Boundary
.69	2	53	East Putney *(B.R. - p.116)*
.95	3	49	Southfields
.90	4	41	Wimbledon Park
.93	5	35	Wimbledon

B.R. (158) - p.110
B.R. (179) - p.125

M.	M	C	Station
	0	00	Turnham Green
			Bedford Park Jcn.
			LT/BR Boundary
.99	0	79	Gunnersbury
1.06	2	04	Kew Gardens
1.33	3	30	Richmond

B.R. (58) - p.53
B.R. (147) - p.115

Jubilee Line

M.	M	C	Station	Connection
	0	00	Stanmore	
.79	0	63	Canons Park	
.06	1	68	Queensbury	
.83	2	54	Kingsbury	
.77	4	36	Wembley Park	
.42	5	70	Neasden	
.53	6	32	Dollis Hill	
.75	7	12	Willesden Green	
.74	7	71	Kilburn	
.68	8	46	West Hampstead	→ *B.R. (58) - p.53*
.38	8	76	Finchley Road	
.38	9	26	Swiss Cottage	
.57	9	72	St. John's Wood	
.28	11	14	Baker Street	(Marylebone) → *B.R. (115) - p.50*
.03	12	16	Bond Street	
.85	13	04	Green Park	
.68	13	59	Charing Cross	→ *B.R. (207) - p.130*

Metropolitan Line

M.	M	C	Station	Connection
	0	00	Barking	B.R. (2) - p.12; B.R. (1) - p. 13
1.42	1	34	East Ham	
.87	2	24	Upton Park	
.80	3	08	Plaistow	
.47	3	46	West Ham	B.R. (58) - p.12
.85	4	34	Bromley-by-Bow	
.63	5	04	Bow Road	
.34	5	31	Mile End	
.65	6	03	Stepney Green	
.62	6	52	Whitechapel	
.51	7	13	Aldgate East	
.57	7	58	Liverpool Street	B.R. (11) - p.4
.32	8	04	Moorgate	B.R. (24) - p.15
.39	8	35	Barbican	B.R. (52) - p.44
.32	8	61	Farringdon	
1.15	9	73	Kings Cross	B.R. (26) - p.14
.53	10	35	Euston Square	(Euston) B.R. (65) - p.55
.38	10	65	Great Portland Street	
.60	11	33	Baker Street (Main)	

M.	M	C	Station
	10	65	Great Portland Street
.57	11	31	Baker Street
.45	11	67	Edgware Road
.58	12	33	Paddington (Suburban)
.40	12	65	Royal Oak
.61	13	34	Westbourne Park
.49	13	73	Ladbroke Grove
.41	14	26	Latimer Road
.63	14	76	Shepherd's Bush
.32	15	22	Goldhawk Road
.51	15	63	Hammersmith

M.	M	C	Station
	0	00	Baker Street (Main)
2.10	2	08	Finchley Road (Jubilee Line - p.163)
4.50	6	48	Wembley Park
.91	7	41	Preston Road
1.02	8	42	Northwick Park
.80	9	26	Harrow-on-the-Hill
			Harrow North Jcn.
1.24	10	45	North Harrow
.92	11	39	Pinner
1.29	12	62	Northwood Hills
1.00	13	62	Northwood
1.38	15	13	Moor Park
2.17	17	26	Rickmansworth
2.10	19	34	Chorley Wood
2.13	21	45	Chalfont & Latimer
2.03	23	47	Amersham
			B.R. (114) - p.51

M.	M	C	Station
	9	26	Harrow-on-the-Hill
			Harrow North Jcn.
.78	10	08	West Harrow
.86	10	77	Rayners Lane
1.07	12	03	Eastcote
.71	12	60	Ruislip Manor
.45	13	16	Ruislip
1.15	14	28	Ickenham
.63	14	78	Hillingdon
1.30	16	22	Uxbridge

M.	M	C	Station
	0	00	Moor Park
1.83	1	66	Croxley - *B.R. (62) - p.52*
1.19	3	01	Watford - *B.R. (58) - p.53*

M.	M	C	Station
	2	68	Watford
1.19	1	53	Croxley
1.66	0	00	Rickmansworth

M	C	Station
0	00	Chalfont & Latimer
2	02	Chesham

Metropolitan Line (East London Branch)

B.R. (207/201) - pp.130/131 ↑

M.	M	C	Station
	0	00	**New Cross**
.41			Surrey Canal Jcn.
.54	1	33	**Surrey Docks**
.32	1	76	**Rotherhithe**
.48	2	22	**Wapping**
.61	2	60	**Shadwell**
.45	3	29	**Whitechapel**
	3	65	**Shoreditch**

B.R. (178/186) - p.121 ↑

M.	M	C	Station
	0	00	**New Cross Gate**
1.27			Surrey Canal Jcn.
	1	22	**Surrey Docks**
1.03	2	60	**Shadwell**
	3	62	**Aldgate East**

(see p.164)

Northern Line

Edgware Branch

M.	M	C	Station
	0	00	**Edgware**
.92	0	74	**Burnt Oak**
.82	1	60	**Colindale**
1.31	3	05	**Hendon Central**
.69	3	60	**Brent Cross**
.97	4	57	**Golders Green**
1.46	6	14	**Hampstead**
.75	6	74	**Belsize Park**
.69	7	49	**Chalk Farm**
.53	8	11	**Camden Town**

M	C	Station
0	00	**Mill Hill East**
0	76	**Finchley Central**

Barnet Branch

M.	M	C	Station
	0	00	**High Barnet**
1.54	1	43	**Totteridge**
.94	2	38	**Woodside Park**
.61	3	07	**West Finchley**
.71	3	64	**Finchley Central**
1.51	5	25	**East Finchley**
1.02	6	26	**Highgate**
1.06	7	31	**Archway**
.55	7	75	**Tufnell Park**
.50	8	35	**Kentish Town *(B.R.)***
.72	9	13	**Camden Town**

Charing Cross Branch

M.	M	C	Station
	0	00	**Camden Town**
.40	0	32	**Mornington Crescent**
.51	0	73	**Euston *(B.R.)***
.36	1	22	**Warren Street**
.29	1	45	**Goodge Street**
.39	1	76	**Tottenham Court Road**
.25	2	16	**Leicester Square**
.29	2	39	**Charing Cross *(B.R.)***
.17	2	53	**Embankment**
.44	3	08	**Waterloo *(B.R.)***
1.18	4	22	**Kennington***

City Branch

M.	M	C	Station
	0	00	**Camden Town**
1.07	1	06	**Euston *(B.R.)***
.38	1	36	**Kings Cross *(B.R.)***
.86	2	25	**Angel**
.90	3	17	**Old Street**
.43	3	51	**Moorgate *(B.R.)***
.51	4	12	**Bank *(B.R.)***
.43	4	46	**London Bridge *(B.R.)***
.42	5	00	**Borough**
.53	5	42	**Elephant & Castle**
.56	6	07	**Kennington***

M.	M	C	Station
	0	00	**Kennington**
.51	0	41	**Oval**
.85	1	29	**Stockwell**
.51	1	70	**Clapham North**
.39	2	21	**Clapham Common**
.78	3	03	**Clapham South**
.72	3	61	**Balham *(B.R.)***
.61	4	30	**Tooting Bec**
.69	5	05	**Tooting Broadway**
.75	5	65	**Colliers Wood**
.71	6	42	**South Wimbledon**
.91	7	34	**Morden**

*** Kennington Loop**
49 chains from centre of southbound platform to centre of northbound platform.

B.R. Refs.

Balham	*(178/186) - p.119*
Bank	*(150) - p.117*
Charing X	*(207) - p.130*
Elephant	*(179) - p.125*; *(201) - p.129*
Euston	*(58) - p.53*; *(65) - p.55*
Kentish Town	*(52) - p.44*
Kings Cross	*(26) - p.14*
L. Bridge	*(178/186) - p.121*
Moorgate	*(24) - p.15*; *(52) - p.44*
Waterloo	*(158) - p.110*; *(147) - p.115*; *(150) - p.117*

Piccadilly Line

M.	M	C	Station	Connection
	0	00	**Cockfosters**	
.79				
	0	63	**Oakwood**	
1.16				
	1	76	**Southgate**	
1.21				
	3	13	**Arnos Grove**	
.78				
	3	75	**Bounds Green**	
.95				
	4	71	**Wood Green**	
.61				
	5	40	**Turnpike Lane**	
1.44				
	6	75	**Manor House**	
.65				
	7	47	**Finsbury Park**	➤ ***B.R. (24) - pp.14/15***
.43				
	8	01	**Arsenal**	
.46				
	8	38	**Holloway Road**	
.37				
	8	68	**Caledonian Road**	
1.22				
	10	06	**Kings Cross**	➤ ***B.R. (26) - p.14***
.57				
	10	52	**Russell Square**	
.45				
	11	07	**Holborn**	→ Aldwych branch
.37				
	11	37	**Covent Garden**	
.16				
	11	50	**Leicester Square**	
.31				
	11	75	**Piccadilly Circus**	
.35				
	12	23	**Green Park**	
.66				
	12	75	**Hyde Park Corner**	
.32				
	13	20	**Knightsbridge**	
.76				
	14	01	**South Kensington**	
.44				
	14	36	**Gloucester Road**	
.49				
	14	76	**Earl's Court**	
1.01				
	15	77	**Barons Court**	
.42				
	16	30	**Hammersmith**	
.58				
	16	77	**Ravenscourt Park**	
.48				
	17	35	**Stamford Brook**	
.34				
	17	63	**Turnham Green**	
.59			Bedford Park Jcn.	
	18	30	**Chiswick Park**	
.75				
	19	10	**Acton Town**	→ Heathrow branch
.64			Acton Town North Jcn.	
	19	61	**Ealing Common**	
.59			Hanger Lane Jcn.	
	20	28	**North Ealing**	
.66				
	21	01	**Park Royal**	
1.23				
	22	19	**Alperton**	
.98				
	23	17	**Sudbury Town**	
1.03				
	24	20	**Sudbury Hill**	
.85				
	25	08	**South Harrow**	
1.18				
	26	22	**Rayners Lane**	
1.07				
	27	28	**Eastcote**	
.71				
	28	05	**Ruislip Manor**	
.45				
	28	41	**Ruislip**	
1.15				
	29	53	**Ickenham**	
.63				
	30	23	**Hillingdon**	
1.30				
	31	47	**Uxbridge**	

M	C	Station
0	00	**Holborn**
0	30	**Aldwych**

M.	M	C	Station
	19	10	**Acton Town**
1.37			Acton Town North Jcn.
	20	40	**South Ealing**
.24			
	20	59	**Northfields**
.62			
	21	29	**Boston Manor**
1.51			
	22	70	**Osterley**
.60			
	23	38	**Hounslow East**
.46			
	23	75	**Hounslow Central**
.91			
	24	68	**Hounslow West**
1.81			
	26	52	**Hatton Cross**
1.14			
	27	63	**Heathrow Terminal 4**
2.68			
	30	37	**Heathrow Terminals 1,2,3**

M.	M	C	Station
	0	00	**Heathrow Terminals 1,2,3**
1.34			
	1	27	**Hatton Cross**

Rail-Air Coach Links

B.R. Reading (127/135) - p.88
B.R. Woking (156/158) - p.110
B.R. Feltham (147) - p.115

Victoria Line

M	C	Station	
0	00	**Walthamstow Central**	
0	75	**Blackhorse Road**	*B.R. (2) - p.12*
1	63	**Tottenham Hale**	*B.R. (22) - p.10*
2	35	**Seven Sisters**	*B.R. (20) - p.11*
4	32	**Finsbury Park**	*B.R. (24) - pp.14/15*
5	48	**Highbury & Islington**	*B.R. (58) - p.12*
7	10	**Kings Cross**	*B.R. (26) - p.14*
7	47	**Euston**	*B.R. (65) - p.55*
8	04	**Warren Street**	
8	49	**Oxford Circus**	
9	26	**Green Park**	
10	00	**Victoria**	*B.R. (178/186) - p.119* *B.R. (195/212) - p.127*
10	59	**Pimlico**	*B.R. (158) - p.110*
11	19	**Vauxhall**	*B.R. (147) - p.115*
12	27	**Stockwell**	
13	24	**Brixton**	*B.R. (195/212) - p.127*

Branch from Seven Sisters:

M	C	
1	48	Northumberland Park Depot
1	39	Staff Platform
1	02	52/53 Reception Roads
0	00	**Seven Sisters**

Harrow North Jcn. A Metropolitan Line train, formed of L.T. A60 stock, heads for Baker Street past the divergence of the Met. lines to Rayners Lane and Uxbridge. *Extreme left,* are the Met. down lines to Watford and Amersham, and the B.R. Marylebone-Aylesbury lines (see p.51/164). *(Brian Morrison)*

SECTION VI - IRELAND

(a) Northern Ireland Railways

UNLIKE British Rail and the Metropolitan systems, official records of both N.I.R. and C.I.E. nowadays quote distances c
to the nearest quarter-mile. Research into old records has provided exact miles and chains measurements for virtu
all the locations shown in the Tables and, in the majority of cases, these appear to agree with the railways' own opera
data. Where doubt exists, the official distance to the nearest 1/4-mile is quoted in both milepost and miles and chains
umns.

There is very little new rail development in prospect; the only approved addition to the N.I.R. system is the link line fr
Belfast Central to York Road. However, the question of finance remains and the line is not likely to be built in the fores
able future.

We are indebted to David Parks of the Great Southern Railway Preservation Society for checking the manuscript of
Irish section.

BELFAST, YORK ROAD - LARNE HARBOUR (N.I.R. Table 5)

M. P.	M	C	
0 00	**0**	**00**	**Belfast, York Road**
	1	**60**	Fortwilliam
	4	**24**	**Whiteabbey**
	4	**56**	Bleach Green Jcn.
	5	**28**	**Jordanstown**
	6	**56**	**Greenisland**
	7	**72**	**Trooperslane**
	9	**20**	**Clipperstown**
	9	**45**	**Carrickfergus**
	10	**38**	**Downshire**
	14	**00**	Whitehead Tunnel (down line only)
	14	**55**	**Whitehead**
	16	**40**	**Ballycarry**
	19	**39**	Magheramorne Loop
	19	**60**	**Magheramorne**
	21	**48**	**Glynn**
	23	**20**	**Larne Town**
24 17	**24**	**17**	**Larne Harbour**

Branch from Bleach Green Jcn.:

M. P.	M	C	
4 56	**4**	**56**	Bleach Green Jcn.
6 05	**6**	**05**	Monkstown
C.M.M.			
9 41	**7**	**00**	Mossley
11 15	**8**	**55**	Ballyclare Jcn. LCs
11 30	**8**	**70**	Ballyclare Jcn. LCs
14 67	**12**	**27**	Ballymartin LC
16 26	**13**	**66**	Templepatrick
17 38	**15**	**00**	Kilmakee LC
19 68	**17**	**28**	Muckamore
21 60	**19**	**20**	**Antrim** (see p.169)

BELFAST CENTRAL - LONDONDERRY (N.I.R. Table 3)

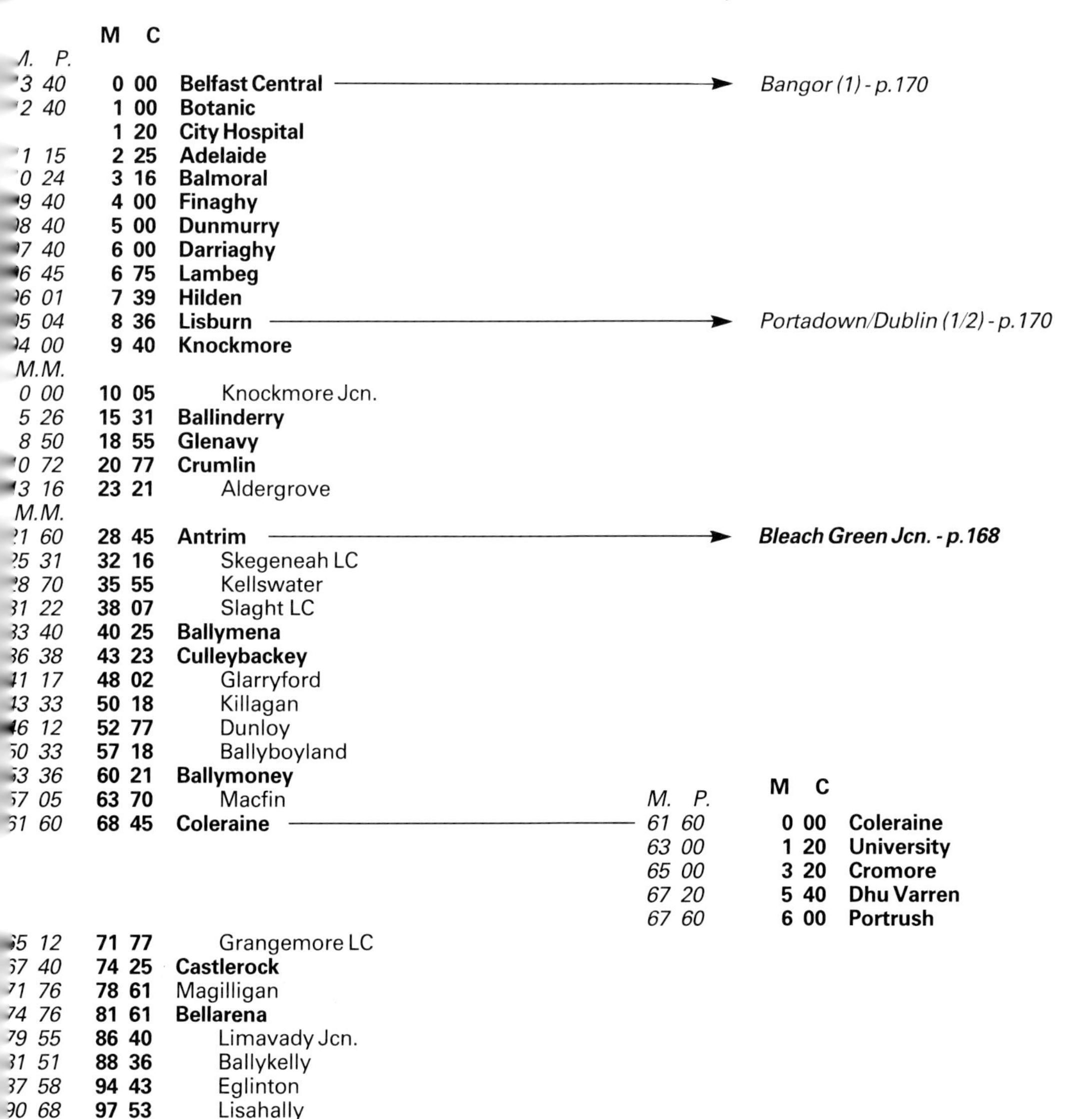

M. P.	M C	Station	
3 40	0 00	**Belfast Central**	→ *Bangor (1) - p.170*
2 40	1 00	**Botanic**	
	1 20	**City Hospital**	
1 15	2 25	**Adelaide**	
0 24	3 16	**Balmoral**	
9 40	4 00	**Finaghy**	
8 40	5 00	**Dunmurry**	
7 40	6 00	**Darriaghy**	
6 45	6 75	**Lambeg**	
6 01	7 39	**Hilden**	
5 04	8 36	**Lisburn**	→ *Portadown/Dublin (1/2) - p.170*
4 00	9 40	**Knockmore**	
M.M.			
0 00	10 05	Knockmore Jcn.	
5 26	15 31	**Ballinderry**	
8 50	18 55	**Glenavy**	
0 72	20 77	**Crumlin**	
3 16	23 21	Aldergrove	
M.M.			
1 60	28 45	**Antrim**	→ ***Bleach Green Jcn. - p.168***
5 31	32 16	Skegeneah LC	
8 70	35 55	Kellswater	
1 22	38 07	Slaght LC	
3 40	40 25	**Ballymena**	
6 38	43 23	**Culleybackey**	
1 17	48 02	Glarryford	
3 33	50 18	Killagan	
6 12	52 77	Dunloy	
0 33	57 18	Ballyboyland	
3 36	60 21	**Ballymoney**	
7 05	63 70	Macfin	
1 60	68 45	**Coleraine**	→ Portrush branch (below)
5 12	71 77	Grangemore LC	
7 40	74 25	**Castlerock**	
1 76	78 61	Magilligan	
4 76	81 61	**Bellarena**	
9 55	86 40	Limavady Jcn.	
1 51	88 36	Ballykelly	
7 58	94 43	Eglinton	
0 68	97 53	Lisahally	
5 20	102 05	**Londonderry** (Waterside)	

M. P.	M C	Station
61 60	0 00	**Coleraine**
63 00	1 20	**University**
65 00	3 20	**Cromore**
67 20	5 40	**Dhu Varren**
67 60	6 00	**Portrush**

BANGOR - BELFAST CENTRAL - PORTADOWN
BELFAST CENTRAL - DUBLIN (N.I.R. Tables 1 & 2)

M. P.	M C	M C	Station	
125 76		**0 00**	**Bangor**	
124 76		**1 00**	**Bangor West**	
124 16		**1 60**	**Carnalea**	
123 39		**2 37**	**Crawfordsburn**	
122 56		**3 20**	**Helen's Bay**	
121 33		**4 43**	**Seahill**	
120 21		**5 55**	Craigavad	
119 59		**6 17**	**Cultra**	
119 03		**6 73**	**Marino**	
118 33		**7 43**	**Holywood**	
115 46		**10 30**	**Sydenham**	
115 00		**10 76**	**Victoria Park**	
114 20		**11 56**	**Bridge End**	
113 40	**0 00**	**12 36**	**Belfast Central**	*[York Road/Larne (5) - p.168]*
112 40	**1 00**	**13 36**	**Botanic**	
	1 20	**13 56**	**City Hospital**	
111 15	**2 25**	**14 61**	**Adelaide**	
110 24	**3 16**	**15 52**	**Balmoral**	
109 40	**4 00**	**16 36**	**Finaghy**	
108 40	**5 00**	**17 36**	**Dunmurry**	
107 40	**6 00**	**18 36**	**Derriaghy**	
106 45	**6 75**	**19 31**	**Lambeg**	
106 01	**7 39**	**19 75**	**Hilden**	
105 04	**8 36**	**20 72**	**Lisburn** ——→	*Londonderry (3) - p.169*
104 00	**9 40**	**21 76**	**Knockmore**	
103 35	**10 05**	**22 41**	Knockmore Jcn.	
100 00	**13 40**	**25 76**	Damhead	
98 03	**15 37**	**27 73**	**Moira**	
94 67	**18 53**	**31 09**	Kilmore	
92 43	**20 77**	**33 33**	**Lurgan**	
90 51	**22 69**	**35 25**	Boilie	
87 16	**26 24**	**38 60**	**Portadown**	
84 50	**28 70**		Adams LC	
79 47	**33 73**		**Scarva**	
78 05	**35 35**		Acton LC	
76 73	**36 47**		**Poyntzpass**	
73 41	**39 79**		Knockarney LC	
69 20	**44 20**		**Newry**	
63 09	**50 31**		Meigh	
59 48	**53 72**		Border Post ***(NIR/CIE Boundary)***	
54 30	**59 10**		**Dundalk**	See p.171 for intermediates
31 60	**81 60**		**Drogheda**	
25 63	**87 57**		Mosney	
21 60	**91 60**		**Balbriggan**	
17 77	**95 43**		**Skerries**	
9 00	**104 40**		**Malahide**	
0 00	**113 40**		**Dublin Connolly** ——→	*See p.171 for Table Refs.*

(b) Córas Iompair Éireann

e the Northern system, C.I.E. records have mainly quoted measurements to the nearest quarter-mile, although some ıtes are shown in exact miles and chains. Once again, reference has been made to old records to confirm distances and lepost changes. The C.I.E. is currently in the process of conversion to the metric system and public timetables now ote distances exclusively in kilometres. However, the original Imperial measures are still in place at the trackside as own in the following tables.

ɔUBLIN CONNOLLY - DUNDALK - BELFAST (C.I.E. Table 1)

M. P.	M C		Connections
0 00	0 00	**Dublin Connolly**	*Wexford/Rosslare (7) - p.172* *Mullingar/Sligo (12) - p.172* *Athlone/Galway (10) - p.173*
	0 57	East Wall Jcn.	East Wall Jcn. branch (below)
	2 31	**Killester**	
	3 00	**Harmonstown**	
	3 57	**Raheny**	
	4 40	**Kilbarrack**	
	4 64	**Howth Junction**	Howth branch (below)
	6 56	**Portmarnock**	
	9 00	**Malahide**	
	11 35	**Donabate**	
	13 74	**Rush and Lusk**	
	17 77	**Skerries**	
	21 60	**Balbriggan**	
	24 00	**Gormanstown**	
	25 63	Mosney	
	27 13	**Laytown**	
	31 60	**Drogheda**	Navan/Kingscourt branch (below)
	32 48	Cement Branch Jcn.	Cement branch (below)
	37 24	Kellystown	
	41 56	**Dunleer**	
	43 51	Dromin Jcn.	
	47 16	Castlebellingham	
	53 40	Dundalk South Jcn.	Barrack St. branch (below)
	54 30	**Dundalk**	
	59 48	Border Post ***(CIE/NIR Boundary)***	
	69 20	**Newry**	See p.170 for intermediates and Table Refs,
	87 16	**Portadown**	
	92 43	**Lurgan**	
	105 04	**Lisburn**	
113 40	113 40	**Belfast Central**	

M C	
0 00	Church Road Jcn. (p.173)
0 40	East Wall Jcn.

M. P.	M C	
0 00	0 00	**Howth Junction**
	1 00	**Bayside**
	1 60	**Sutton**
3 34	3 34	**Howth**

M. P.	M C	
0 00	0 00	**Drogheda**
	8 40	Lougher
16 75	16 75	Navan
C.M.M.		
30 42	17 20	Tara Mines Jcn.
39 70	26 48	Castletown
50 45	37 23	Kingscourt

M C	
0 00	Tara Mines Jcn.
0 20	Tara Mines

M C	
0 00	Cement Branch Jcn.
0 60	End of Branch

M C	
0 00	Dundalk South Jcn.
1 40	Barrack St. Goods

DUBLIN CONNOLLY - WEXFORD - ROSSLARE (C.I.E. Table 7)

M. P.	M C		
1 00	**0 00**	**Dublin Connolly** →	*Dundalk/Belfast (1) - p.171* *Mullingar/Sligo (12) - See Below* *Athlone/Galway (10) - p.173*
0 20	**0 60**	**Tara Street**	
C.M.M.			
0 00	**1 00**	**Dublin Pearse**	
1 07	**2 07**	**Lansdowne Road**	
1 52	**2 52**	**Sandymount**	
2 20	**3 20**	**Sydney Parade**	
3 20	**4 20**	**Booterstown**	
4 07	**5 07**	**Blackrock**	
4 60	**5 60**	**Monkstown & Seapoint**	
5 26	**6 26**	**Salthill**	
6 00	**7 00**	**Dun Laoghaire**	
6 58	**7 58**	**Sandycove**	
7 20	**8 20**	**Glenageary**	
8 05	**9 05**	**Dalkey**	
9 74	**10 74**	**Killiney**	
11 00	**12 00**	**Shankill**	
C.M.M.			
10 42	**12 77**	Shanganagh Jcn.	
12 20	**14 55**	**Bray**	
17 05	**19 40**	**Greystones**	
19 66	**22 21**	**Kilcoole**	
22 38	**24 73**	Newcastle	
28 20	**30 55**	**Wicklow**	
32 54	**35 09**	Ballymanus LC	
37 24	**39 59**	**Rathdrum**	
42 66	**45 21**	Avoca	
46 68	**49 23**	Shelton Abbey	
49 00	**51 35**	**Arklow**	
53 38	**55 73**	Inch	
59 33	**61 68**	**Gorey**	
69 71	**72 26**	Ferns	
77 40	**79 75**	**Enniscorthy**	
86 16	**88 51**	Killurin	
C.M.M.			
6 20	**95 35**	**Wexford**	
5 25	**96 30**	Wexford South	
C.M.M.			
110 66	**101 55**	**Rosslare Strand** →	*Waterford/Limerick (6) - p.175*
113 60	**104 49**	**Rosslare Harbour** (Mainland)	
114 20	**105 09**	**Rosslare Harbour Pier**	

DUBLIN CONNOLLY - MULLINGAR - SLIGO (C.I.E. Table 12)

M. P.	M C	
1 00	**0 00**	**Dublin Connolly**
1 24	**0 24**	West Road
C.M.M.		
4 18	**0 44**	North Strand Jcn. (see p.173)
C.M.M.		
0 58	**1 77**	Glasnevin Jcn.
C.M.M.		
1 33	**2 55**	Liffey Jcn.
3 08	**4 30**	**Ashtown**
7 08	**8 30**	**Clonsilla**
11 20	**12 42**	**Leixlip**
14 72	**16 14**	**Maynooth**
19 12	**20 34**	Kilcock
26 40	**27 62**	Enfield
35 55	**36 77**	Hill of Down
41 60	**43 02**	Killucan
50 17	**51 39**	**Mullingar**

M. P.	M C	
2 46	**0 00**	**Dublin Connolly**
2 24	**0 22**	Newcomen Jcn.
0 58	**1 68**	Glasnevin Jcn.

M C	
0 00	North Wall Cont'ner Terminal
0 56	Newcomen Jcn.

DUBLIN CONNOLLY - MULLINGAR - SLIGO (C.I.E. Table 12) cont.
MULLINGAR - ATHLONE - GALWAY (C.I.E. Table 10)

M. P.	M C	Station
	0 00	**Dublin Connolly**
50 17	51 39	**Mullingar**
57 63	59 05	Multyfarnham
67 42	68 64	**Mostrim**
76 22	77 44	**Longford**
87 22	88 44	**Dromod**
97 62	99 04	**Carrick-on-Shannon**
06 28	107 50	**Boyle**
20 06	121 28	**Ballymote**
27 56	128 78	**Collooney**
28 03	129 25	Collooney Jcn.
34 16	135 38	**Sligo** MacDiarmada
	135 58	Sligo Quay

M. P.	M C	Station
50 17	51 39	**Mullinger**
58 22	59 44	Castletown
68 33	69 55	**Moate**
78 05	79 27	**Athlone**

Dublin Heuston/Westport (11) - See Below

M. P.	M C	Station
78 05	0 00	**Athlone**
78 24	0 19	Athlone West Jcn.
84 71	6 66	Carrowduff
91 53	13 48	**Ballinasloe**
101 40	23 35	**Woodlawn**
107 15	29 10	**Attymon Junction**
113 36	35 31	**Athenry** (see p.176)
121 32	43 27	Oranmore Siding
126 53	48 48	**Galway** Ceannt

DUBLIN HEUSTON - WESTPORT & BALLINA (C.I.E. Table 11)

M. P.	M C	Station
0 00	0 00	**Dublin Heuston**
	0 53	Islandbridge Jcn.
	1 60	Inchicore
	6 33	Lucan South
	10 00	Hazelhatch
	17 75	Sallins
	20 73	Caragh
	25 40	**Droichead Nua** (Newbridge)
	27 40	Curragh
	30 00	**Kildare** → *Kilkenny (5) - p.174*
	32 36	Cherryville Jcn.
	36 34	Monasterevan
	41 58	**Portarlington** → *Limerick/Cork (2) - p.174*
	45 50	Bord Na Mona Bridge
	50 24	Geashill
	57 71	**Tullamore**
	65 00	**Clara Halt**
	73 00	Clonydonnin
80 40	80 40	Athlone (Southern)
M.M.		
78 05	81 00	**Athlone** → *Galway (10) - See Above*
78 24	81 19	Athlone West Jcn.
88 20	91 15	Lecarrow
90 00	92 75	Knockcroghery
96 20	99 15	**Roscommon**
07 55	110 50	Ballymoe
12 60	115 55	**Castlerea**
18 60	121 55	Ballinlough
24 12	127 07	**Ballyhaunis**
35 00	137 75	**Claremorris** → ***Athenry - p.176***
42 35	145 30	Balla
45 71	148 66	Manulla Jcn.
50 10	153 05	**Castlebar**
55 39	158 34	Islandeady
61 11	164 06	**Westport**

M. P.	M C	Station
5 28	0 00	North Wall Goods
4 51	0 57	Church Rd. Jcn. (p.171)
4 18	1 10	North Strand Jcn.
2 55	2 53	Glasnevin Jcn. (p.172)
1 68	3 40	Cabra
0 00	5 28	Islandbridge Jcn.

M. P.	M C	Station
145 71	148 66	Manulla Jcn.
150 30	153 25	Ballyvary
157 14	160 09	Foxford
166 44	169 39	**Ballina**

DUBLIN HEUSTON - CORK - COBH (C.I.E Table 2)
DUBLIN HEUSTON - KILKENNY (C.I.E. Table 5)
DUBLIN HEUSTON - LIMERICK (C.I.E. Table 4)

M. P.	M C	Station
0 00	**0 00**	**Dublin Heuston**
	0 53	Islandbridge Jcn. → *North Wall Branch - p.173*
		(see p.173)
	30 00	**Kildare**
	32 36	Cherryville Jcn.
	36 34	Monasterevan
	41 58	**Portarlington** (see p.173)
	47 75	Straboe
	50 72	**Portlaoise**
	53 37	Clonkeen LC
	61 50	Cuddagh LC
	66 59	**Ballybrophy** (see p.175)
	72 34	Lisduff
	78 67	**Templemore**
	86 40	**Thurles**
	87 20	Thurles Sugar Factory
	95 09	Goold's Cross
	99 39	Dundrum
	106 23	Kyle Crossing
	107 00	**Limerick Junction** (see p.175)
	117 04	Knocklong
	124 09	Kilmallock
	129 16	**Rathluirc** (Charleville)
	137 16	Buttevant
	144 37	**Mallow**
	145 18	Killarney Jcn.
	148 18	Mourne Abbey
	154 24	Rathduff
	159 28	Blarney
	161 31	Rathpeacon Siding
	163 16	Kilbarry
	165 40	**Cork** (Kent)
	166 60	Tivoli Sidings
	169 70	**Little Island**
	171 17	**Cobh Junction**
	172 41	**Fota**
	174 25	**Carrigaloe**
	175 60	**Rushbrooke**
176 60	**176 60**	**Cobh**

Kildare – Kilkenny branch:

M. P.	M C	Station
30 00	**30 00**	**Kildare**
	32 36	Cherryville Jcn.
	40 70	Kilberry
	44 64	**Athy**
	51 00	Mageney
	55 68	**Carlow**
	60 09	Milford
	65 78	**Muine Bheag**
	70 35	Jordanstown
	78 40	Lavistown Jcn.
80 66	**80 66**	**Kilkenny**

Waterford (5) - p.175

Kyle Crossing – Limerick branch:

M. P.	M C	Station
106 23	**106 23**	Kyle Crossing
C.M.M.		
21 33	**106 70**	Milltown Crossing
15 41	**112 62**	Cross LC
11 46	**116 57**	Dromkeen
7 50	**120 53**	Boher
4 20	**124 03**	Killonan Jcn.
0 70	**127 33**	Ennis Jcn.
0 45	**127 58**	Limerick Check (p.176
0 00	**128 23**	**Limerick** (Colbert)

Ballybrophy (4) - p.175
Waterford (6) - p.175

Mallow – Tralee branch:

M. P.	M C	Station
144 37	**0 00**	**Mallow**
C.M.M.		
0 00	**0 61**	Killarney Jcn.
1 24	**2 05**	Beet Factory Sidings
5 40	**6 21**	Lombardstown
10 60	**11 41**	**Banteer**
19 00	**19 61**	**Millstreet**
24 28	**25 09**	Fry-Cadbury Sidings
25 37	**26 18**	**Rathmore**
39 67	**40 48**	**Killarney**
50 44	**51 25**	**Farranfore**
54 28	**55 09**	Gortatlea
61 35	**62 16**	**Tralee** (Casement) (see p.176)

Cobh Junction – Youghal branch:

M. P.	M C	Station
0 00	**0 00**	**Cobh Junction**
	6 18	Midleton
	11 38	Mogeely
	14 15	Killeagh
20 63	**20 63**	Youghal

MERICK - WATERFORD - ROSSLARE (C.I.E. Table 6)
MERICK - BALLYBROPHY (C.I.E. Table 4)
LKENNY - WATERFORD (C.I.E. Table 5)

M. P.	M C	Station	
0 00	0 00	**Limerick** (Colbert)	→ *Dublin Heuston (4) - p.174*
	0 45	Limerick Check	→ ***Foynes - p.176***
	0 70	Ennis Jcn.	— ***Athenry/Tralee - p.176***
	4 20	Killonan Jcn.	— *C.M.M. 52 48*
	7 50	Boher	
	11 46	Dromkeen	
	15 41	Cross LC	
	21 33	Milltown Crossing	
	21 56	Keane's Points	— *M. P. 21 56*
	24 63	**Tipperary**	
	33 03	Cappagh LC	
	38 26	**Cahir**	
	43 19	Nicholastown LC	
	49 20	**Clonmel**	
	55 33	Kilsheelan	
	63 06	**Carrick-on-Suir**	
	67 28	Fiddown	
	70 03	Grange	
	75 44	Dunkitt	
7 20	77 20	**Waterford**	— *M. P. 58 36*
M.M.			
6 20	77 40	Abbey Jcn.	— *C.M.M. 115 40*
1 40	82 60	Barrow Bridge (West)	
4 48	85 68	**Campile**	
9 25	90 45	**Ballycullane**	
3 27	94 47	**Wellington Bridge**	
8 02	99 22	Duncormick	
3 72	105 12	**Bridgetown**	
7 54	108 74	Killinick	
0 66	112 06	**Rosslare Strand**	→ *Wexford/Dublin (7) - p.172*
3 60	115 00	**Rosslare Harbour** (Mainland)	
4 20	115 40	**Rosslare Harbour Pier**	

C.M.M.	M C	Station
52 48	4 20	Killonan Jcn.
47 03	9 65	Castleconnell
42 36	14 32	**Birdhill**
35 19	21 49	Silvermines Jcn.
29 33	27 35	**Nenagh**
20 00	36 68	**Cloughjordan**
10 04	46 64	**Roscrea**
0 00	56 68	**Ballybrophy**

↓ *Dublin/Cork (2) - p.174*

	M C	Station
M. P.		
21 56	21 56	Keane's Points
C.M.M.		
107 00	21 78	**Limerick Junction**

↑ *Dublin Heuston (5) - p.174*

M. P.	M C	Station
28 35	0 00	**Kilkenny**
30 61	2 26	Lavistown Jcn.
34 15	5 70	Bennetsbridge
39 04	10 59	**Thomastown**
43 23	14 78	Ballyhale
51 45	23 20	Mullinavat
54 45	26 20	Kilmacow
56 60	28 35	Dunkitt
58 36	30 11	**Waterford**

C.M.M.	M C	Station
115 40	0 00	Abbey Jcn.
108 00	7 40	Glenmore
102 00	13 40	New Ross

Claremorris - Athenry - Limerick - Foynes

M. P.	M C	Station	
17 00	**0 00**	**Claremorris** →	*Westport/Ballina (11) - p.173*
12 44	**4 36**	Ballindine	
8 49	**8 31**	Milltown	
4 37	**12 43**	Castlegrove	
1 50	**15 30**	Tuam Sugar Factory	
C.M.M.			
76 15	**17 00**	Tuam	
69 76	**23 19**	Ballyglunin	
59 69	**33 26**	**Athenry** →	*Galway/Athlone (10) - p.173*
55 13	**38 02**	Craughwell	
49 06	**44 09**	Ardrahan	
42 25	**50 70**	Gort	
32 37	**60 58**	Crusheen	
24 60	**68 35**	Ennis	
23 00	**70 15**	Clarecastle Siding	
16 58	**76 37**	Ballycar	
9 60	**83 35**	Cratloe	
6 32	**86 63**	Meelick LC	
3 49	**89 46**	Shannon Bridge	
0 70	**92 25**	Ennis Jcn.	
0 45	**92 50**	Limerick Check	*Dublin Heuston (4) - p.174* *Ballybrophy (4) - p.175* *Waterford (6) - p.175*

C.M.M.	M C	Station
0 45	**0 00**	Limerick Check
1 00	**0 35**	Foynes Jcn.
7 26	**6 61**	Patrickswell
11 04	**10 39**	Adare LC
17 27	**16 62**	Ballingrane Jcn.
20 70	**20 25**	Askeaton LC
26 65	**26 20**	Foynes

M C	Station
0 00	Limerick Check
4 45	Castlemungret Cemer Factory

The following lines are closed but still *in situ*, and may re-open if required:

Dromin Jcn. *(p.171)*	- **Ardee**	**4m. 66c.**
Curragh *(p.173)*	- **Racecourse Platform**	**0m. 40c.**
Claremorris *(p.173)*	- **Collooney Jcn.** *(p.173)*	**46m. 20c.**
Gortatlea *(p.174)*	- **Castleisland**	**4m. 34c.**
Waterford *(p.175)*	- **Ballynacourty**	**27m. 00c.**
Ballingrane Jcn. *(see above)*	- **Newcastle West**	**9m. 71c.**
Newcastle West	- **Rock Street** *(see below)*	**42m. 65c.**

The line from Tralee (p.174) to Fenit is being restored by the Great Southern Railway Preservation Society. Ori mileages as follows:

M. P.	M C	Station
0 00	**0 00**	**Tralee** (Casement)
	0 29	Rock Street LC
	1 52	Limerick Line Divergence
	4 24	Spa
	6 20	Kilfenora
7 77	**7 77**	Fenit